Music Theory and Natural Order from the Renaissance to the Early Twentieth Century

Music theory of almost all ages has relied on nature in its attempts to explain music. The understanding of what nature is, however, is subject to cultural and historical differences. In exploring ways in which music theory has represented and employed natural order since the scientific revolution, this volume asks some fundamental questions not only about nature *in* music theory, but also about the nature *of* music theory. In an array of different approaches, ranging from physical acoustics to theology and Lacanian psychoanalysis, these essays examine how the multifarious conceptions of nature, located variously between scientific reason and divine power, are brought to bear on music theory. They probe the changing representations and functions of nature in the service of music theory and highlight the ever-changing configurations of nature and music, as mediated by the music-theoretical discourse.

Suzannah Clark is a Research Fellow at Merton College, Oxford and Alexander Rehding is a Research Fellow at Emmanuel College, Cambridge.

Music Theory and Natural Order from the Renaissance to the Early Twentieth Century

EDITED BY

SUZANNAH CLARK AND
ALEXANDER REHDING

CAMBRIDGE
UNIVERSITY PRESS

CAMBRIDGE UNIVERSITY PRESS
Cambridge, New York, Melbourne, Madrid, Cape Town, Singapore, São Paulo

Cambridge University Press
The Edinburgh Building, Cambridge CB2 2RU, UK

Published in the United States of America by Cambridge University Press, New York

www.cambridge.org
Information on this title: www.cambridge.org/9780521771917

© Cambridge University Press 2001

First published 2001
This digitally printed first paperback version 2005

A catalogue record for this publication is available from the British Library

Library of Congress Cataloguing in Publication data

Music theory and natural order from the Renaissance to the early twentieth century /
edited by Suzannah Clark and Alexander Rehding.
p.   cm.
Includes bibliographical references (p. ****) and index.
ISBN 0 521 77191 9 (hardback)
1. Nature and music theory.   2. Music–Theory–History.   3. Music–Philosophy and
aesthetics.   I. Clark, Suzannah, 1969–   II. Rehding, Alexander.
ML3800.M885   2001
781'.09–dc21   00-027904

ISBN-13 978-0-521-77191-7 hardback
ISBN-10 0-521-77191-9 hardback

ISBN-13 978-0-521-02392-4 paperback
ISBN-10 0-521-02392-0 paperback

Contents

v

Contents

Illustrations

Contributors

Linda Phyllis Austern is Associate Professor of Musicology at Northwestern University in Evanston, Illinois. She has published extensively on relationships between music and other fields of intellectual enquiry in sixteenth- and seventeenth-century Europe, particularly England. Her work has been funded by the American Council of Learned Societies, the British Academy and the National Endowment for the Humanities, as well as a variety of private agencies. She is presently finishing a book on music in Elizabethan and early Stuart life and thought.

Ian Biddle graduated from Nottingham University in 1988 and completed his Ph.D. at Newcastle University in 1995. He has also studied composition with Roman Haubenstock-Romati at the Hochschule für Musik in Vienna. Since then he has taught at the University of East Anglia in Norwich and now teaches at Newcastle University. He has recently published articles on contemporary British music, on music theory and aesthetics in the nineteenth century, music historiography and music and gender. He is currently working on a book, *Musics and Masculinities in European Culture, 1800–1900*.

Leslie David Blasius, Assistant Professor of Music Theory at the University of Wisconsin-Madison, received his Ph.D. in theory and composition from Princeton University. His first book, *Schenker's Argument and the Claims of Music Theory*, published by Cambridge University Press in 1996, was the recipient of the 1997 Young Scholar Award from the Society for Music Theory. His second book, *The Music Theory of Godfrey Winham*, appeared in 1997. He is currently working on a study of music and the notions of 'truth' and 'authenticity'.

Scott Burnham, Associate Professor of Music at Princeton University, is the author of *Beethoven Hero* (Princeton University Press, 1995) and editor/translator of A. B. Marx, *Musical Form in the Age of Beethoven* (Cambridge University Press, 1997). He and Michael P. Steinberg are co-editing a volume of essays entitled *Beethoven and His World*, to be released on the occasion of the Bard Festival 2000.

Daniel K. L. Chua has taught at St John's College, Cambridge, and King's College London. He is the author of *The 'Galitzin' Quartets of Beethoven*. His study *Absolute Music* *and the Construction of Meaning* has recently been published by Cambridge University Press.

Suzannah Clark recently completed a Junior Research Fellowship at Merton College, Oxford and is now a British Academy Postdoctoral Fellow there. She holds a Ph.D. from Princeton University. Her interests include analysis, the history of theory and Schubert reception, as well as aspects of the thirteenth-century motet.

David E. Cohen received his Ph.D. in music theory from Brandeis University. He has taught at the State University of New York at Stony Brook, Brandeis University and Tufts University, and is currently Assistant Professor of Music at Harvard University. His research focuses on the history of music theory with particular attention to the influence of philosophical and scientific ideas on the development of music-theoretical concepts.

Peter A. Hoyt, Assistant Professor at Wesleyan University, studied at the University of Pennsylvania, where he received his Ph.D. in music theory. Much of his research examines eighteenth- and nineteenth-century accounts of musical form in light of concurrent intellectual influences, such as rhetoric and neoclassical dramatic criticism.

Alexander Rehding is a Research Fellow at Emmanuel College, Cambridge. He received his Ph.D. from Cambridge University. His main research interests are in the field of nineteenth- and twentieth-century music and the history of music theory.

Acknowledgements

The idea for this book was suggested by nature itself. On 16 August 1996, Scott Burnham took us both to a baseball game in the Philadelphia Veterans Stadium (Phillies v. San Francisco Giants). Play had to be stopped when, during sudden torrential rain, lightning struck the stadium, making it impossible for the players to continue. In the face of this powerful display of the force of nature, the idea of hosting a forum for an in-depth discussion of the use of nature in music-theoretical discourse came into our minds. This book, then, grew out of a conference, *Music Theory's Nature*, which was held at Merton College, Oxford, on 28–29 March 1998. We would like to thank all those who made the conference possible: Jeannette Hudson-Pudwell and the Staff of Merton College, the Music Faculty of Oxford University and the Society for Music Analysis. We are also grateful to John Deathridge, William Drabkin, Jonathan Dunsby and Alan Street, who chaired the sessions at the conference. Sam Thompson provided us with valuable assistance in setting the music examples for this book. We are especially indebted to Penny Souster for her advice and support, which she kindly offered throughout all stages of this project.

S. C. and A. R.

Introduction

SUZANNAH CLARK AND ALEXANDER REHDING

At the outset of his short treatise on music, the *Compendium musicae* of 1618, Descartes recounts that if two drums are struck at the same time, one made with sheep's skin and the other with wolf's skin, the drum with sheep's skin will not sound. Descartes suggests that, owing to the natural order of the animal kingdom, the sheep is as frightened of the wolf in death as in life.[1] This transcendent hierarchy seems to manifest itself even when the animals are made into musical instruments. For Descartes, this natural order ultimately controls the production (or smothering) of sound.

From someone whom we have come to appreciate as a key player in the scientific revolution, this seems a surprising and absurd tale. However, the very absurdity of the tale points us to a different epistemology, a fundamentally different understanding of what constitutes nature. In fact, comparable arguments were commonly found in music treatises of the decades preceding the *Compendium musicae*.[2] In that sense, Descartes's sheep is mutton dressed as lamb: he seems to be reflecting upon an older notion of nature that comprises irrational and magical elements.[3] The idea underlying the sheep-and-wolf story is related to the Great Chain of Being, positing a transcendental hierarchy that all things and living beings obey.[4]

The question for Descartes, as for the majority of music theorists, was not so much *whether* music was connected with nature but *how* it was connected with it. A

We are grateful to Daniel K. L. Chua and Peter Tregear for their comments on this introduction.

[1] René Descartes, *Compendium of Music*, trans. Walter Robert, notes by Charles Kent (n.p.: American Institute of Musicology, 1961).

[2] The editor of the German translation of Descartes's treatise, Johannes Brockt, mentions that the anecdote of the sheep and wolf surfaces in other treatises of the time, such as Ambroise Paré's work on animals of 1575 and Marin Mersenne's *Questiones celeberrime in Genesin* of 1623. See Descartes, *Leitfaden der Musik*, trans. and ed. Johannes Brockt, 2nd edn (Darmstadt: Wissenschaftliche Buchgesellschaft, 1992), p. 71.

[3] A corresponding epistemology has been explored in Gary Tomlinson, *Music in Renaissance Magic: Toward a Historiography of Others* (London and Chicago: University of Chicago Press, 1993), based on Michel Foucault's 'archaeological' method expounded, above all, in *The Order of Things: An Archaeology of the Human Sciences* (London: Tavistock/Routledge, 1974).

[4] See Arthur O. Lovejoy's classic exploration of this concept in *The Great Chain of Being* (Cambridge, Mass.: Harvard University Press, 1936).

1

conception of nature – in the broadest sense – was deemed necessary for music theorists if they did not want to expose themselves to the criticism that the rules of their systems were arbitrary and unfounded. Nature in music theory thus imposes order: it may function as a source of legitimation for the rules it proposes, as an authority from which to generate supposedly incontestable laws, and as a resource of knowledge and values apparently impervious to cultural and historical changes.

This use of nature has its problems. Is the totalising tendency underlying the definition of nature not undermined by the fact that our understanding of what constitutes nature changes? While it is part and parcel of any idea of nature to rely on the assumption of an essence independent from historical or cultural context, the images invoked in support of this idea will necessarily reflect the culture and historical age in which they arose.[5] It is on the basis of this circumstance that Descartes's point above appears absurd to us. However, the impression of absurdity is not endemic to his argument; rather, it arises from our fundamentally different understanding of nature, which on the one hand embraces empiricism and on the other offers no place for the Great Chain of Being. The purpose of this book is ultimately not to assess the validity of competing concepts of nature but rather to examine their impact on musical knowledge: in the case of Descartes, the anecdote allows us to see most clearly a clash between one totalising argument of a familiar nature and that of an unfamiliar one.

Music theories employ a concept of nature in the search for an external reference point with which to anchor the stuff we call music and to confer meaning on it. The problem is Archimedean in the very assumption that there *must* be an external reference point, and that pinning down meaning will not itself be arbitrary. While in modern society nature is figured as separated from the human sphere, in fact, as the Marxist scholar Raymond Williams has observed, 'the idea of nature is the idea of man; and this not only generally, or in ultimate ways, but the idea of man in society, indeed the ideas of kinds of societies'.[6] Thus, in bestowing natural order on music, music theorists assign it a place in their world.

THE ANIMAL KINGDOM

Although Descartes's use of the animal kingdom emphasised natural hierarchy, more commonly it was the sounds of animals in their natural habitat that captured the imagination of music theorists. These sounds are generally proposed as the source of music, and an obvious starting point was birdsong.[7] Most theorists who drew on bird-

---

[5] It is debatable whether modern scientific understanding forms an exception to this. The understanding of nature, as the object of scientific investigation, is forever provisional, and liable to change in light of new discoveries. Not least since Karl Popper, scientific knowledge is conceived as reliable rather than certain knowledge. To be sure, scientific practice aims for context-free observation. Whether it fulfils those tasks is a hotly disputed matter, as seen for example in the repercussions of the recent Sokal affair. On the contextuality of scientific thinking see Thomas S. Kuhn, *The Structure of Scientific Revolutions* (Chicago: University of Chicago Press, 1970).

[6] Raymond Williams, 'Ideas of Nature', in *Problems in Materialism and Culture* (London and New York: Verso, 1980), p. 71.

[7] See Matthew Head, 'Birdsong and the Origins of Music', *Journal of the Royal Musical Association* 122 (1997), 1–23.

Lib.I. Anatomicus de Natura soni & vocis. **27**

Musica Haut siue Pigritię Animalis Americani.

Ha ha ha ha ha ha ha ha ha ha ha.

Figura Animalis Haut.

Mirum tamen, nullam huiusmodi animalis anatomiam vnquàm ab vllo confectam esse: ex interiori enim constitutione facilè de eiusdem naturalibus facultatibus conijcere poterant: Si enim os & dentes, si stomachum habeat, non video cur natura membra cibi reconditoria sine vsu ipsis assignauerit: Sed non dubito, quin mea instructione informati Patres nostri Americani exactiorem in posterum omnium experientiam sint sumpturi.

Voces ceterorum quadrupedum cùm notae sint passim, ijs non inhærebimus, sed ad

Illus. I.1 The American sloth singing the hexachord, from Athanasius Kircher, *Musurgia Universalis*, vol. I (Rome: Francesco Corbelletti, 1650), p. 27

song would comment on how birds would perform different melodic or rhythmic fragments of music. The question for them was always to assess the degree to which such chirping and clucking constituted music.

Other animals, most notably mammals, also drew attention by their song. It should not come as a surprise, for example, that Charles Darwin, in a comprehensive survey of music in the animal world, attached particular significance to monkeys in his explanation of the origin of music. He observed that while song is commonly used for sexual selection in lower animal classes, mammals make comparatively little use of their vocal organs to attract the opposite sex.[8] However, there are two notable exceptions, both apes: the American *Mycetes caraya* and a closer relative of man, a gibbon of the species *Hylobates agilis*. Darwin quoted an observer's description of their song:

It appeared to me that in ascending and descending the scale; the intervals were always exactly half-tones; and I am sure that the highest note was the exact octave to the lowest. The quality of the notes is very musical; and I do not doubt that a good violinist would be able to give a correct idea of the gibbon's composition, excepting as regards its loudness.[9]

[8] Charles Darwin, *The Descent of Man and Selection in Relation to Sex*, intro. John Tyler Bonner and Robert M. May, 2 vols. in 1 (Princeton: Princeton University Press, 1981). [9] *Ibid.*, vol. II, p. 332.

Two centuries previously, the scholar and Renaissance man Athanasius Kircher had made a similar point using a sloth (Illus. I.1). Kircher, otherwise an unlikely bedfellow of Darwin, made the observation that

the voice is not emitted by this animal [the sloth] except at night, and that it is truly wonderful. When its voice is interrupted by a duration of a single breath or semipause, by ascending and descending through the usual known intervals of six steps, it perfectly intones the first elements of music, *Ut, re, mi, fa, sol, la; la, sol, fa, mi, re, ut* in such a way that the Spanish, from the moment they first possessed those shores and heard by night the distinct calling of this kind, thought that they were hearing human beings trained in the rules of our art of music. It was called a 'Haut' by the inhabitants for no other reason than that it repeats this voice, *ha, ha, ha, ha, ha etc.*, through the six individual steps. In order that you understand better the appearance of the animal as well as its voice, it has seemed a good idea to put everything together with a synopsis before your eyes.[10]

What the two observers hear is of supreme theoretical import: Kircher's seventeenth-century listener heard the hexachord, whereas Darwin's nineteenth-century ear-witness heard the chromatic scale. It is surely no coincidence that in both cases, what the observers heard in nature – and what the theorists chose to report as significant – corresponds to the structural basis of the music of their respective eras.

It would seem that for their respective ages both Kircher and Darwin had solved what Guido Adler in 1924 called one of the most difficult problems of music theory: how to show the derivation of the scalic material.[11] In this sense, Kircher's sloth and Darwin's apes represent both pure nature and pure theory. Unlike birds, which sing rudimentary music (see Illus. I.2), the sloth and the ape each sing a musical rudiment.

This said, however, it would be wrong to assume that Darwin simply reiterated an argument that had been commonplace for centuries. The difference between the two is that for Darwin the proximity of apes to humans, as their progenitors, was all-important, while for Kircher it was precisely the remoteness of the sloth that made it attractive. Not only did the distance that separated the New World from Kircher's readership in Europe guarantee that few readers would be in a position to challenge his statement, but, what is more, the connotations of America itself were such that in 1650, the year in which Kircher's *Musurgia universalis* was published, the continent was still largely *terra incognita*. As such, America came to signify savage, raw nature itself, the Other to Europe's culture and civilisation.[12] Peter Hoyt, who assesses in this volume the implications of this 'savage' concept of America for eighteenth-century

10 Athanasius Kircher, *Musurgia universalis*, 2 vols. (Rome: Francesco Corbelletti (vol. I) and Ludovico Grignani (vol. II), 1650), vol. I, p. 37. Translation by Raymond J. Clark.
11 Guido Adler (ed.), *Handbuch der Musikgeschichte* (Frankfurt am Main: Frankfurter Verlagsanstalt, 1924), p. 8.
12 See, for instance, Antonello Gerbi, *Nature in the New World: From Christopher Columbus to Gonzalo Fernandez de Oviedo*, trans. Jeremy Moyle (Pittsburgh: University of Pittsburgh Press, 1985), and Joseph M. Powell, *Mirrors of the New World: Images and Image-makers in the Settlement Process* (Folkestone: Dawson, 1977).

Illus. I.2 Birds and their songs, from Athanasius Kircher, *Musurgia Universalis*, vol. I
(Rome: Francesco Corbelletti, 1650), p. 30

European music theory, explores in greater detail European projections of the fabulous and exotic on this supposedly untouched continent.

Kircher contrasts the exotic sloth with a selection of domestic birds in his *Musurgia universalis*. While the sloth is presented as an unquestionable theoretical authority, the effects of human contact are represented by the parrot in Illus. I.2: it says 'hello' – in Greek, no less. Clearly trained in domestic circumstances, the parrot represents a reverse mimesis, imitating as it does human speech. These various animals support very different theoretical claims: some, such as birds, draw a mimetic link between music and the animal kingdom; others, such as the sloth and Darwin's apes, are more aligned with the 'sound of nature' itself. In other words, those theorists using birds would argue that birdsong can tell us where music came from, whereas the ape and the sloth tell us how music ought to go. This latter, prescriptive domain is more commonly associated with acoustics, the 'hard' sciences, and the laws of nature.

MUSIC THEORY AS HARD SCIENCE

Descartes begins his *Compendium musicae*, mentioned initially, with a terse program-matic statement: 'Its object is sound.'[13] With only slight exaggeration one could claim that these four words sum up the impact of the scientific revolution on music – the change from music as a divine force to music as a material phenomenon. As the latter, it could be subjected to scientific scrutiny; music theory turned particularly towards the mathematical and physical sciences as well as physiology. Indeed, Descartes's age witnessed the encroachment of acoustical science on music or, to put it conversely from the perspective of music, the reduction of music to quantifiable sound.[14] For the feminist historian of science Carolyn Merchant, the scientific revolution brought on the death of the female figure of *Natura*. In her influential study on this subject, Merchant describes the changing understanding of nature, from the medieval nurtur-ing womb of which the material world was born, to a corpse on whose body scientific experiments are carried out.[15] This condition is, as Daniel K. L. Chua argues in this volume, the principal trait of modernity, of which music theory forms an integral part.

Why would the music theorists discussed in this volume have taken it as under-stood that the laws of nature should also be the laws of music? On one level, the 'scientific turn' of music theory seemed a self-evident consequence of its medieval legacy, where music – notably in its significance of the 'harmony of the spheres' – had been firmly associated with the discipline of astronomy, as part of the quadrivium. As the study of astronomy became a modern science with figures such as Kepler and Galilei, so did the study of music. That which began as simple experiments with musical tuning turned out to be of enormous consequences to the history of tonality in the Western world, as Chua argues. Schiller's *bon mot* of the 'disenchantment of the world' (*Entzauberung der Welt*), which was adopted by Max Weber and the Frankfurt School to signify the process of increasing rationalisation in the modern age, can indeed be applied to large parts of music theory since the Renaissance. What the *cognoscenti* of the Florentine Camerata and elsewhere did in their studies of tuning was simply to 'correct' what they conceived of as flaws in nature. By taking such measures as eliminating the Pythagorean or syntonic commas, which invariably hamper the full enharmonic potential of the diatonic system, they forcibly closed the gap in the 'spiral of fifths' and created the 'cycle of fifths' on which the modern conception of the nature of tonal music has rested ever since.

These changes made to music at the turn of the seventeenth century could be likened to the establishment of 'nature reserve areas' in more recent times: an area of landscape is fenced off with the purpose of perennial preservation in exactly the same

[13] Descartes, *Compendium of Music*, p. 1. Translation modified.

[14] See H. F. Cohen, *Quantifying Music: The Science of Music at the First Stage of the Scientific Revolution, 1580–1650* (Dordrecht, Boston and Lancaster: D. Reidel Publishing Company, 1984).

[15] Carolyn Merchant, *The Death of Nature: Women, Ecology, and the Scientific Revolution* (San Francisco: Harper and Row, 1980).

state. However, the illusion of untouched nature in areas from which change is emphatically banished is in fact predicated upon an intrusive coercion of the processes of nature. Continual labour and maintenance – as well as their repression – are necessary to maintain this semblance of nature.[16] Likewise, tonal structure first had to be closed off before its nature could be seen to flourish.

In order to prove the natural derivation of triadic material, music theorists of the tonal era commonly resorted to explanations that either drew on the division of the monochord or the harmonic series. While nature readily provided the elements for the consonance of the major triad, its bounteousness was more generous than the theorists had hoped: the harmonic series had to be cut off after the sixth harmonic at the latest, while the string could not be divided more than five times. For music theorists between Zarlino and Schenker, arguments why part of the 'sound of nature' had to be truncated were evidently difficult to find, let alone justify.

Furthermore, owing to the resistance of the natural material, music theorists often had great difficulty relating all aspects of harmony, namely the generation of scales, triads and the relations between chords, to one and the same natural principle. As Suzannah Clark suggests in this volume, the physicist Arthur von Oettingen's dualistic view of harmony came closest to bringing them into alignment. In the second half of the nineteenth century it seemed that 'naturalistic' music theory, above all in the writings of the harmonic dualists Oettingen and Hugo Riemann, had completed the rationalisation of the musical material; the scientific rigour of the 'naturalistic' approach to music theory appeared to have reached the bottom of certain knowledge about music.

The re-creation of nature in the service of music theory appeared to give theorists full authority over music: the structure of tonal music seemed to comply with the givens of nature; music theorists deemed themselves to possess full knowledge of the nature of music. This power has often been understood to imply the authority of music theory to *prescribe* how music ought to go. Hugo Riemann, for instance, used Strauss's *Salome* as a pretext to hurl the condemnation of 'degeneration' against the condition of modern music, a verdict which implies that such creations are monstrous, unliveable creatures of music – in short, that they are unnatural.[17] While this

[16] On the dilemma of 'untouched' nature reserve areas and labour see Joachim Radkau, 'The Wordy Worship of Nature and the Tacit Feeling for Nature in the History of German Forestry', in *Nature and Society in Historical Context*, ed. Mikulas Teich, Roy Porter and Bo Gustafsson (Cambridge: Cambridge University Press, 1997), pp. 228–39; David M. Grabner, 'Resolute Biocentrism: The Dilemma of Wilderness in National Parks', in *Reinventing Nature? Responses to Postmodern Deconstruction*, ed. Michael E. Soulé and Gary Lease (Washington DC and Covelo, Calif.: Island Press, 1995), pp. 123–35; and Raymond Williams, 'Ideas of Nature', p. 78.

[17] Hugo Riemann, 'Degeneration und Regeneration in der Musik', *Max Hesses deutscher Musiker-Kalender* 23 (1908), 136–41. The article, which appeared in the context of a debate led by the composer Felix Draeseke, is reprinted in *'Die Konfusion in der Musik': Felix Draesekes Kampfschrift von 1906 und ihre Folgen*, ed. Susanne Shigihara (Bonn: G. Schröder, 1990). On the issue of 'degeneration' as a cultural trope around 1900, see particularly Max Nordau's classic study *Degeneration* (London: Heinemann, 1913), and for an up-to-date discussion of the manifestations of 'degeneration' see Daniel Pick, *Faces of Degeneration: A European Disorder, c.1848–c.1918* (Cambridge: Cambridge University Press, 1989).

conclusion is all too easily drawn, and was shared by a great many other theorists, it in fact overtaxes the normative power in which nature is used in this music-theoretical context. The tension between music theory and musical works, and the struggle for authority behind this tension – which can be understood in terms of Michel Foucault's nexus of Power/Knowledge[18] – are issues that are almost invariably connected with the employment of the category of nature and that form an underlying theme in various chapters of this book.

Carl Dahlhaus has noted that the theoretical power to tell how music ought to go, to know right from wrong in music, is independent of what actually happens in musical structures.[19] In fact, in the later nineteenth century it was left to a natural scientist to warn music theorists not to exaggerate their authoritative claims about the normative power of the nature of music. In an oft-quoted statement (which was, however, widely ignored by music theorists at the time), the eminent physicist and physiologist Hermann von Helmholtz protested

that the construction of scales and harmonic tissues is a product of artistic invention and by no means furnished by the natural formation or natural function of our ear, as has been hitherto most generally asserted.[20]

Helmholtz was well aware of the authoritative power of science. As natural science counted – and continues to count – as an epistemologically privileged discourse, many music theorists of his time sought to partake of its prestige, and its apparently pure access to knowledge, but were less rigorous as far as its methods were concerned. Although Helmholtz himself was on occasion prone to making high-handed judgements about music from the perspective of its purported nature, his warning points towards another central theme of this book, the inherently cultural dimension of music-theoretical claims based on nature.

The limitations of the scientific view made themselves felt ubiquitously. As Leslie David Blasius observes in this volume, at the very moment that music theory believed to have discovered the truth about music, music itself began to lie. Scientific truth and moral values seemed to be poles apart. Throughout the history of music theory in the modern age runs an undercurrent of discontent, a feeling that the principles of scientific analysis, which informed the basis of much music theory, left something to be desired. Chua's essay proposes that no sooner did the disenchantment of music begin than there were attempts to re-enchant music, to re-endow it with a pre-modern (super)natural force, as a futile effort to counter the effects of rationalisation.

[18] Michel Foucault's talk 'The Order of Discourse' first introduces this trope and the notion of 'genealogy'. The main books in which he explores these ideas are *Discipline and Punish*, trans. Alan Sheridan (Harmondsworth: Penguin, 1979), and *The History of Sexuality*, vol. I, trans. Robert Hurley (Harmondsworth: Penguin, 1978). One of the most widely read studies on Foucault's writings remains Hubert L. Dreyfus and Paul Rabinow, *Michel Foucault: Beyond Structuralism and Hermeneutics* (Brighton: Harvester, 1982).

[19] Carl Dahlhaus, *Die Musiktheorie im 18. und 19. Jahrhundert: Zweiter Teil Deutschland*, ed. Ruth E. Müller (Darmstadt: Wissenschaftliche Buchgesellschaft, 1989), pp. 252–60.

[20] Hermann von Helmholtz, *On the Sensations of Tone*, trans. Alexander J. Ellis, rpt (New York: Dover, 1954), p. 365.

The discontent with the scientific method, the sense that something was missing from the dissected body of music and the ensuing desire to achieve again the blissful state of enchanted music, however, form a reverse strand to Merchant's dead (or dying) *Natura*, to the process of the increasing rationalisation of music. Linda Phyllis Austern's contribution examines the representation and iconography of music and nature in English natural philosophy in the seventeenth century and traces the transformations of the marvellous figure of *Natura* and the ensuing changes in the understanding of music in the age of Purcell. David E. Cohen's contribution discusses a related figure in Rameau's theorising, the *mère bien faisante*, who is the source of the 'Gift of Nature' to humans. In Rameau's view, it is she who offers us both the *corps sonore* and the instinct to grasp it, an instinct which, as Clark demonstrates in her chapter, Oettingen attempts to put into question.

Nowhere is the attempt to re-establish a connection between nature and elements that transcend nature made clearer than within Rameau's *corps sonore*, which, on the one hand, formed the theoretical basis of music in nature, but was, on the other hand, employed in Rameau's stage works exclusively to signify supernatural events.[21] The *corps sonore*, the pinnacle of Rameau's rational theorisation – which also meant the amputation of the upper harmonics of the sonorous 'corpse' of nature – harks back to its magical legacy in the harmony of the spheres. If *Natura* was indeed a casualty of the scientific revolution, who had ended up on the slab of the laboratory scientist, it seems that her musical relative was not quite dead – and music theorists seemed anxious to keep her alive.

BREATHING LIFE INTO MUSIC

Perhaps the most influential line of thought that sought to evade post-Newtonian science was the doctrine of organicism, rooted above all in the work of such thinkers as Coleridge, Schelling and Goethe.[22] While physics is the epitome of the Newtonian sciences – or, in Friedrich Schlegel's classification, the 'mechanical' sciences, which in his usage was tantamount to pronouncing them 'dead' – the organic model centred on biology, the life sciences. Indeed, the stuff of life, which itself seemed to resist scientific explanation, was at the core of the organicist approach. As Goethe wrote at the outset of his short essay *On Laokoon*, a veritable compendium of organicism,

---

[21] Two examples, from *Pygmalion* and *Castor et Pollux*, are discussed in Thomas Christensen, *Rameau and Musical Thought in the Enlightenment* (Cambridge: Cambridge University Press, 1993), pp. 218–31, and Brian Hyer, '"Sighing Branches": Prosopopoeia in Rameau's *Pygmalion*', *Music Analysis* 13 (1984), 7–50, and 'Before Rameau and After', *Music Analysis* 15 (1996), 93–7.

[22] The classic introduction to theories of organicism in art remains Meyer H. Abrams, *The Mirror and the Lamp: Romantic Theory and the Critical Tradition* (Oxford: Oxford University Press, 1971), pp. 156–225. See also Severine Neff, 'Schoenberg and Goethe: Organicism and Analysis', in *Music Theory and the Exploration of the Past*, ed. Christopher Hatch and David W. Bernstein (Chicago: University of Chicago Press, 1993), pp. 409–33; William Pastille, 'Music and Morphology: Goethe's Influence on Schenker's Thought', in *Schenker Studies*, ed. Hedi Siegel (Cambridge: Cambridge University Press, 1990), pp. 29–44; and Lotte Thaler, *Organische Form in der Musiktheorie des 19. und beginnenden 20. Jahrhunderts*, Berliner musikwissenschaftliche Arbeiten, vol. XXV, ed. Carl Dahlhaus and Rudolf Stephan (Munich and Salzburg: Katzbichler, 1984).

A genuine work of art remains, like a work of nature, forever unending to our intellect: it is beheld, it acts on us, but it cannot actually be known, much less even can its essence, its merit be expressed in words.[23]

The organic work of art is in this conception fundamentally anti-theoretical; it resists intellectual scrutiny. Like a vivisection, the dissection of music – a metaphor which Johann Mattheson had happily embraced in 1754[24] – for analytical purposes would amount to an act of cruelty in the organicist view. In Chapter 8 Ian Biddle investigates the change in attitude to the musical work during the early Romantic period and shows how critical writing on music responded to the organicist challenge.

If the musical work resists the scalpel of the analyst, how can the music theorist proceed? The way out required a shift of emphasis from a consideration of the part-to-whole construction to the reverse. Most commonly, this image was supported by an analogy between nature and art which was drawn via the morphology of the plant: the whole work 'grows' out of a 'germ cell'.

The emphasis on the supremacy of the whole over the individual parts gave rise to *Formenlehre*, the theory of forms. Theorists such as Adolf Bernhard Marx attempted to approach the spiritual content of the musical work by understanding its form. In both defining form as a generic category, and at the same time recognising that there could be as many forms as there are works of art, Marx highlighted a tension between the universal and the particular.[25] This tension has been the cause of numerous mis-representations of *Formenlehre*, as a dry, schematic 'textbook' approach, in direct opposition to the organicist idealism from which it stemmed. Recognising the risk of losing sight of the intention behind the organicist viewpoint by becoming mechanical, Ernst Kurth had to remind music theorists at the beginning of the twentieth century that *Formenlehre* should be a theory of *Erformung*, that is it should concentrate on the 'process of forming'.[26] Kurth's contemporary and mentor, August Halm, attached particular significance to this continual 'process of forming' that underlies the musical work. His analysis of Beethoven's *Tempest* Sonata, discussed in this volume by Alexander Rehding, highlights the process by which the thematic material finally 'finds itself', as Halm expressed it, by rupturing the form.

If music 'grows' organically, it has a spirit and takes on a life of its own. Music theorists endeavoured to capture the spiritual essence of the musical work, referring to it

[23] Johann Wolfgang von Goethe, 'Über Laokoon', in *Werke (Hamburger Ausgabe)*, vol. XII: *Schriften zur Kunst und Literatur, Maximen und Reflexionen*, 12th edn (Munich: C. H. Beck, 1994), p. 56. Translation by Alexander Rehding. See also Thaler, *Organische Form*, pp. 56–66.

[24] See Ian Bent (ed.), *Music Analysis in the Nineteenth Century*, 2 vols. (Cambridge: Cambridge University Press, 1994), vol. I, p. 7. On Mattheson, see also Peter Schleuning, *Die Sprache der Natur: Natur in der Musik des 18. Jahrhunderts* (Stuttgart: Metzler, 1998), pp. 59–80.

[25] See Thaler, *Organische Form*, and Scott Burnham, 'Criticism, Faith, and the *Idee*: A. B. Marx's Early Reception of Beethoven', *19th-Century Music* 13 (1990), 183–92. On the work-concept, see Lydia Goehr, *The Imaginary Museum of Musical Works: An Essay in the Philosophy of Music* (Oxford: Oxford University Press, 1992). See also Mark Evan Bonds, *Wordless Rhetoric: Musical Form and the Metaphor of the Oration* (Cambridge, Mass. and London: Harvard University Press, 1991).

[26] Ernst Kurth, *Bruckner*, 2 vols. (Berlin, 1925; rpt Hildesheim: Georg Olms, 1971), vol. I, p. 239.

in anthropomorphic terms. Scott Burnham explores the anthropological dimension of sonata form by probing the meaning of its essential element, the return. The sonata becomes an archetypal journey home. For an organicist like Heinrich Schenker, likewise, a work seems to resemble the journey through life. The work has its own biographical drama:

In the art of music, as in life, motion toward the goal encounters obstacles, reverses, disappointments, and involves great distances, detours, expansions, interpolations, and, in short, retardations of all kinds. Therein lies the source of all artistic delaying, from which the creative mind can derive content that is ever new. Thus, we hear in the middleground and foreground an almost dramatic course of events.[27]

For Schenker, the task of the theorist consisted in tracing back these 'retardations' to their common source, in the *Ursatz* whence they came.

The demonstration of musical organicism at work was soon tied to both the amount and the degree of integration of the musical material.[28] This was translated in subsequent critical traditions into 'economical' qualities that such organic compositions displayed.[29] Given that the ideal of organicism is to follow the growth of a small germ cell into a large-scale work this might seem a natural conclusion.[30] However, the assumptions encapsulated in the 'economy' of the musical work reveal a fundamentally different concept of nature from the organicists. Marked not by unknowable qualities but rather by a quasi-capitalist notion of material resources offering the prospect of maximal exploitation, the organic musical work was in effect returned to the rational realm from which it sought to escape.

For the organicists, nature revealed itself to the composer, and to him only: this was the birth of the genius, who was instinctively and unconsciously in touch with nature. In Kant's famous definition, 'genius is the aptitude (*ingenium*) through which nature gives the rule to art'.[31] Two implications of this concept particularly affected music theory. First, the genius was considered unaware of what he was doing, being often referred to as a 'sleepwalker'.[32] The genius-artist was sometimes even believed to be creating against his will, nature thus not so much being a source of inspiration as

---

[27] Heinrich Schenker, *New Musical Theories and Fantasies*, vol. III: *Free Composition*, trans. and ed. Ernst Oster (New York: Longman, 1979), p. 5.

[28] See Ruth A. Solie, 'The Living Work: Organicism and Music Analysis', *19th-Century Music* 3 (1980), 148.

[29] August Halm was one of the first to introduce this economic metaphor to modern music criticism. He used it in *Von zwei Kulturen der Musik*, ed. Gustav Wyncken, 3rd edn (Stuttgart: Ernst Klett, 1947). See also pp. 152–3 in this volume.

[30] See Janet Levy, 'Covert and Casual Values in Recent Writings About Music', *Journal of Musicology* 5 (1987), 7–11.

[31] Immanuel Kant, *Kritik der Urteilskraft*, ed. Wilhelm Weischedel (Frankfurt am Main: Suhrkamp, 1968), para. 46, p. 241.

[32] See Solie, 'The Living Work', 155. Schenker, for one, uses the term 'sleepwalker' in *Neue musikalische Theorien und Phantasien*, vol. I: *Harmonielehre* (Vienna: Universal Edition, 1906) and *Die letzten fünf Sonaten Beethovens*, 4 vols. (Vienna: Universal Edition, 1913, 1914, 1915, 1920), as discussed by Robert Snarrenberg in *Schenker's Interpretive Practice* (Cambridge: Cambridge University Press, 1997), pp. 84–6.

a *force* of inspiration.[33] In this sense, the unconscious knowledge of nature's rule necessarily withholds a theoretical capacity from the genius. Second, as 'nature is at work within the genius', as Ruth Solie puts it, these special abilities separate the genius from ordinary humans. As a result, it is solely given to the genius figure to be original. In this framework the ambitions of the theorist are easily considered presumptuous.

It is these two points that are at the centre of the troubled relationship between art and theory. Where the 'mechanical' theorists were at liberty to mediate directly between nature and sound, this task of mediating between nature and art was taken on by the genius.[34] The theorist in the system of organic thought finds it much more difficult to locate himself beside the genius. More often than not, the composer and the theorist are in a state of tension: the theorist has the power to demystify part of what makes the genius special, without, however, himself possessing the creativity and originality of the genius.

For Schoenberg, this was a matter of greatest importance, and one where the position of the theorist was non-negotiable: first, artists had to pursue a path, then theorists had to follow suit, describing this path.[35] Under no circumstances was theory to step out of the queue to instruct composers: 'To hell with all these theories, if they always serve only to block the evolution of art and if their positive achievement consists in nothing more than helping those who will compose badly anyway to learn it quickly.'[36] Notwithstanding the strong tone of his opinion, however, Schoenberg did recognise the necessity of theory, notably when he wrote at the end of his *Harmonielehre* in a much more conciliatory tone:

Laws apparently prevail here. What they are, I do not know. Perhaps I shall know in a few years. Perhaps someone after me will find them.[37]

The idea that, on the one hand, the rules which the work of art obeys are generated from within the work, and that, on the other hand, they form the basis of universal values results in a dilemma for the composer, and Schoenberg voices both sides of the argument here. The postulate of originality demanded that the rules were hitherto unknown. Theorists, who were commonly condemned for draining the life out of art, therefore posed a genuine threat to genius-composers. At the same time, however, the existence of these unconscious rules had to be confirmed for a genius to be recognised as one – and this, again, was the task of the theorist. It is not without irony that the common reproach against theory – that its explanations are only delivered after

---

[33] See Solie, 'The Living Work', 155.

[34] The exception may be seen to prove the rule: Schenker pointedly sided with the 'artist', and considered himself to be one, publishing his treatise on harmony anonymously as 'von einem Künstler' ('by an artist').

[35] Arnold Schoenberg, *Theory of Harmony*, trans. Roy E. Carter (London: Faber and Faber, 1978), p. 345. See also Hans Heinrich Eggebrecht, 'Musikalisches and Musiktheoretisches Denken', in *Geschichte der Musiktheorie*, vol. I, ed. Frieder Zaminer (Darmstadt: Wissenschaftliche Buchgesellschaft, 1985), pp. 40–58.   [36] Schoenberg, *Theory of Harmony*, p. 9.

[37] *Ibid.*, p. 421. See also Carl Dahlhaus, *Die Musiktheorie im 18. und 19. Jahrhundert: Erster Teil, Grundzüge einer Systematik* (Darmstadt: Wissenschaftliche Buchgesellschaft, 1984), p. 28.

the phenomenon it seeks to describe is past – is exactly a consequence of this double-bind.

As seen in these expository reflections, the beauty – and the difficulty – accompanying the incorporation of nature in music theory is that any embodiment of nature is at once both vague and specific. Any attempt to give a hard and fast definition will be thwarted instantly by mutually contradictory images, for nature can variously stand for a benevolent or dangerous force, eternal stasis or constant flux, a power that humans subjugate or are subjugated to, raw simplicity or perfect refinement, a knowable or unknowable entity.[38] All the above images are correct, or rather have been correct within certain contexts.

As we have seen, music theory absorbs these ideas of nature, persuaded that natural order is nature's command. The assumption that nature should have such a command is an illusion, however. Insofar as natural order reflects the position of the human in society, as Raymond Williams indicated, nature's seemingly objective command is in the first place our projection onto it. In this sense, the study of nature through the eyes of the music theorist is the study of the nature of music theory itself. Ultimately, probing into music theory's nature converges with the fundamental questions: How did music come to exist? Why does it exist?

Although at the time of the scientific revolution, our starting point in this book, music theory ceased once and for all to be a central discipline, the subsequent history of ideas reveals that in many ways it did not stop being the nexus of investigation into the natural world and human nature. There was a sense in which music, as one of the deepest mysteries of mankind, demanded this kind of thorough exploration. Behind the desire to know the secrets of music in the quadrivium was the conviction that such investigation would reveal the secrets of the universe. In a sense, music theory has never lost sight of this task.

---

[38] See Kate Soper, *What is Nature?* (Oxford: Blackwell, 1995).

Part I

The disenchantment and re-enchantment of music

Chapter One

■

Vincenzo Galilei, modernity and the division of nature

DANIEL K. L. CHUA

What is the nature of nature?[1] Music theory for about the last 400 years has tried to ground itself in 'nature', in distinction to the supernatural and unnatural, believing that nature can somehow validate its truths; nature is the origin or ground that legitimises the theory. But what legitimises nature? What has been invested in nature that enables it to underwrite the enterprise of music theory?

In this essay I explore the idea that the grounding of music in the 'natural' is a symptom of modernity. This symptom does not occur tangentially, as if it were a side-effect of the attempt of modernity to cure itself of its failures, but centrally as the very dis-ease that divides the ancient from the modern world. To adopt the more catastrophic tones of the discourse of modernity itself, the alliance of music and nature lies at the epicentre of an epistemological earthquake.[2] Unfortunately, this is not the place to tell this epic tale of apocalyptic proportions, which, in any case, has been recounted on numerous occasions by men as eminent and miserable as Rousseau and Adorno.[3] I merely plan to give a glimpse of this epistemological shift in the music theory of Vincenzo Galilei, by presenting two contrasting scenes of the

---

[1] The material for this chapter is closely related to a study the author was concurrently preparing for publication, *Absolute Music and the Construction of Meaning* (Cambridge: Cambridge University Press, 1999).

[2] The words 'epistemological earthquake' may trigger images of Foucauldian archaeology. Indeed, this chapter, in terms of its method, is not so much a normal 'music history' as an archaeology of music. As such it carries with it the risks of 'generalising' involved in digging out huge epistemological layers in which the details are symbolic forms embedded within a stratum of knowledge. There is a necessary tension between the general narrative, which in this paper will concern the disenchanting effect of modernity upon magical forms of knowledge, and the particular detail, in this case Vincenzo Galilei, who functions as a symbolic representation of the narrative rather than an agent of historical change that divides one episteme (ground of knowledge) from another.

[3] See, for example, Theodor W. Adorno and Max Horkheimer, *Dialectic of Enlightenment*, trans. John Cumming (London: Verso, 1979), and Jean-Jacques Rousseau, *Essai sur l'origine des langues* (1764); translations of Rousseau's essay can be found in *The Origin of Language*, trans. John H. Moran and Alexander Gode (New York: Frederick Ungar, 1966), and in *The First and Second Discourses together with the replies to Critics and Essay on the Origin of Languages*, ed. and trans. Victor Gourevitch (New York: Harper and Row, 1986).

Ancient Cosmos

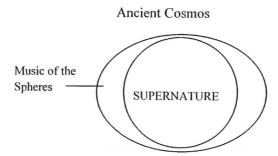

Figure 1.1   The Supernatural Cosmos

natures of music theory. But to make sense of the scenes, I need, at least, to give a synopsis of the tragic tale that modernity never ceases to tell itself as both its definition and its consolation.

In the beginning, when the world was ancient, the universe was indeed a *uni*verse; the ancient world was a unified totality and humanity was at one with the cosmos. But unlike the modern world, this universe was not natural, or at least, what was called natural was in fact *super*natural. Nature was not a ground of knowledge, but was embedded within a supernature, an enchanted cosmos of divine, immutable essences (Figure 1.1).

It is precisely the question of enchantment that is pivotal to modernity's identity, for according to the German sociologist Max Weber, modernity is marked by 'the disenchantment of the world'.[4] Once desacralised, the world becomes *natural* matter amenable to the interrogation and technological control of human rationality.

The problem with this process of disenchantment, claims Weber, is that it divides a formerly integrated world into a fractured universe where the human subject, in its pursuit of knowledge, is alienated from the objects it disenchants, creating a rift between fact and value, knowledge and meaning, the self and the cosmos. The price of progress, so the story goes, is the loss of meaning.

Central to this narrative of progress and loss is the 'naturalisation' of music. If disenchantment divides, then to ground music theory in nature is to divide the nature of music. This essay focuses on one telling symptom of this fissure: the attempt towards the end of the sixteenth century to transfer music from the medieval quadrivium of music, geometry, astronomy and arithmetic to the rhetorical arts of the trivium; the shift split the nature of music (Figure 1.2). First, the music that remained in the quadrivium was modernised in the name of *natural* science; music was objectified as an acoustic fact; it became natural matter for the control of empirical experimentation and the verification of the ear. Second, the transfer of music from the quadrivium to the trivium collapsed the music of the spheres into the rhetorical will of the human ego, shifting the magic of the cosmos to the voice of human nature.

[4]   Max Weber, 'Science as Vocation' (1917), translated in *From Max Weber*, ed. H. H. Mills and C. Wright Mills (New York: Oxford University Press, 1946), p. 155.

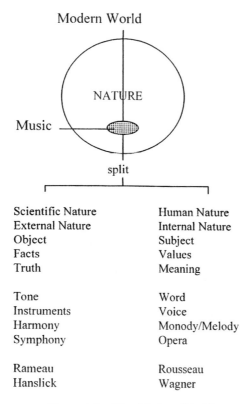

Figure 1.2 The Modern World

Music as a scientific fact of external nature is therefore pitted against music as the interior, moral power of human nature. This division is important because it has bedevilled the history of the changing natures of music theory, as the somewhat simplistic diagram in Figure 1.2 shows. Music is set in opposition to itself as subject and object; human values are set against scientific facts, vocal melody against instrumental harmony, opera against the symphony. It is this division that defines the quarrel between Rousseau and Rameau in the eighteenth century and the debate between Wagner and Hanslick in the nineteenth.

These divisions, however, are merely two sides of the same coin, and in Vincenzo Galilei's case, two sides of the same brain. The quadrivium and trivium ride in tandem. Admittedly, Galilei's writings are neither systematic nor consistent, and it is not my aim to tidy up his works by simplifying them into my two contrasting scenes.[5] What I want to suggest is that these contradictions are not simply personal aberrations but a condition of a modern world whose relationship to the past is ambivalent. On the one hand, modernity defines itself by contrasting its scientific progress with the superstitious dead end of the ancient world, yet on the other hand, it laments its

[5] See Daniel P. Walker, *Studies in Musical Science in the Late Renaissance* (London: The Warburg Institute, 1978; Leiden: E. J. Brill, 1978), pp. 14–19.

19

loss of meaning by idealising the magic of an ancient world as its Utopian future. Modernity simultaneously wants to disenchant and re-enchant the world. Similarly, the scientific interrogation of music by Galilei runs parallel with his attempt to re-invent a modern 'magic' through monody and its operatic aftermath.

MUSIC THEORY AND SCIENTIFIC NATURE

What does Max Weber mean when he speaks of the 'disenchantment of the world'? Disenchantment is literally a process of 'de-magification', 'Ent-zauberung', whereby Western society exorcises itself of its fear of demons, ghosts and goblins. Modern humanity no longer submits itself to the spell of superstition and the sacred rituals of power, but has demystified its existence through the calculations of science and the bureaucratic apparatus of state. What was supernatural has been rationalised as merely the natural; the authority of religion has been replaced by the politics of state. The modernisation of society is therefore its secularisation.

But for Weber secularisation is a fateful process that replays the narrative of Eden in modern terms: 'The fate of an epoch which has eaten of the tree of knowledge', he writes, 'is that it must know that [it] cannot learn the *meaning* of the world from the result of its *analysis*.'[6] Modern knowledge is staged by Weber as a Fall that expels man from paradise, for humanity gains knowledge only by losing its meaning; it organises itself through the endless analysis of *facts*, but these facts have no binding *values*.[7] Disenchantment, then, is a form of knowledge, and Weber defines this knowledge as *instrumental reason*. It is instrumental precisely because reason is used as a *tool* that dissects the world as an object of investigation, distancing the human subject in the process as an outside observer. Instrumental reason is therefore knowledge as a *means* of control, a *technique* that is both ruthlessly direct and relationally remote. On the one hand, through these tools of knowledge, humanity can grasp the divine power of the cosmos as its own, transforming a formerly immutable world of essences into a malleable one that can be endlessly modernised in the name of material progress. But on the other hand, this new sovereignty, with all its instrumental prowess, turns out to be the Midas touch of reason. Everything the sovereign touches turns into facts; and these facts can only be used as a means without meaning; they are truths drained of their sacred and moral substance. Enlightenment therefore alienates humanity from Eden and ultimately leaves it empty-handed.

Music, too, according to Weber, is subject to disenchantment.[8] The melodies that had once enchanted the world have now been modernised to become an efficient

---

[6] Max Weber, *Methodology of the Social Sciences*, ed. E. A. Shils and H. A. Finch (New York: The Free Press, 1949), p. 57.

[7] See Weber, 'Science as Vocation', pp. 141–56; Michael Polanyi, *Personal Knowledge: Towards a Post-Critical Philosophy* (Chicago: University of Chicago Press, 1958), pp. 3–17; Alasdair MacIntyre, *After Virtue* (London: Duckworth, 1981), pp. 35–59; and Lesslie Newbigin, *Foolishness to the Greeks: The Gospel and Western Culture* (London: SPCK, 1986), pp. 21–41 and 65–94.

[8] See Max Weber, *The Rational and Social Foundations of Music*, trans. Don Martindale, Johannes Riedel and Gertrude Neuwirth (Carbondale and Edwardsville: Southern Illinois University Press, 1958).

means of harmonic production, he claims. By explaining the rationalisation of music as a shift from melodic incantation to harmonic calculation, Weber rehearses a trope that has haunted modernity since the end of the sixteenth century, namely, the disenchantment of song through instrumental harmony. Weber explains the disenchantment by isolating equal temperament as the most modern mode of musical rationalisation. Music, by bowing to the regulations demanded by the technology of fretted instruments, forfeits its power to enchant.[9] Modern music is therefore instrumental reason as instrumental music, for it is the mechanisation of sound that rationalises the scale with the kind of efficiency that Weber associates with modern societies. This is why Weber claims that modern tuning has desensitised modern ears with a 'dulling effect' and has shackled music in 'dragging chains'.[10]

Weber therefore implies that the history of Western music is a process of incarceration – a narrative that Theodor W. Adorno would complete in his account of modern music. For Adorno, the twelve-tone technique, as the product of equal temperament, completes the disenchantment of music.[11] If the ordering of sound reduces 'the magic essence of music to human logic' then the 'total organisation of serialism' is the ultimate alienation of music under the domination of human control.[12] The 'twelve-tone technique is truly the fate of music', he adds, echoing the catastrophic tones of Weber, and 'fate is disaster'.[13]

If Weber and Adorno are correct, then tuning turns out to be the apocalypse of modernity. The slightest adjustment between intervals, it seems, can cause catastrophe. But why should we believe this disaster of semitonal proportions announced by Adorno? Why should Weber's 'fatal comma' be so fateful?[14] After all what is a mere diesis between an ancient and modern world? Surely Weber has blown a tiny ratio out of all proportion; he is mistaken to hear so much in so small an interval. Or is he?

The very fact that tuning seems such a marginal if not an irrelevant explanation of the meaning of music today testifies to a disenchanted world. Tuning, for the ancients, was a magical formula; its numbers ordered the cosmos. The ancient world was not an irrational sphere of magic. If anything, the ancient world was far more rational than the modern world in its organisation of the cosmos, for its music was *ratio*-nality itself; this is why music was not classified as an art but belonged with geometry, astronomy and arithmetic in the sciences of the quadrivium. In Plato's

---

[9] Weber is mistaken in assigning the development of equal temperament to keyboard instruments, although by the time the piano was established equal temperament was almost invariably used. However, several theorists, including Galilei, suggest that equal temperament is required by fretted instruments such as the lute and viol. See, for example, Vincenzo Galilei, 'A Special Discourse Concerning the Unison', in *The Florentine Camerata: Documentary Studies and Translations*, ed. Claude V. Palisca (New Haven: Yale University Press, 1989). Galilei maintains that meantone tuning is more suitable for keyboard instruments because of their harshness of tone.

[10] Weber, *The Rational and Social Foundations of Music*, pp. 102–3.

[11] See Theodor W. Adorno, *Philosophie der neuen Musik* (1949), p. 126, trans. Anne G. Mitchell and Wesley V. Blomster as *Philosophy of Modern Music* (London: Sheed and Ward, 1987), p. 61.

[12] Adorno, *Philosophy of Modern Music*, pp. 65 and 69.   [13] *Ibid.*, p. 67.

[14] See Weber, *The Rational and Social Foundations of Music*, p. 99.

account of creation,[15] music tunes the cosmos according to the Pythagorean ratios, and scales the human soul to the same proportions. This enabled the inaudible sounds of the heavens to vibrate within the earthly soul, and conversely, for the audible tones of human music to reflect the celestial spheres, so that heaven and earth could be harmonised within the unity of a well-tuned scale. This scale came to be pictured as a monochord that connected the stars to the earth like a long piece of string that vibrated the structure of the universe. As the invisible and inaudible harmony of the spheres, music imposed a unity over creation, linking everything along the entire chain of being. When music moves, the earth moves with it. Thus music was not simply an object in a magical world, *but the rational agent of enchantment itself*. As the cosmic monochord, it animated the universe and tuned its very being. To disenchant music is therefore to untune the entire world. This is why tuning has apocalyptic overtones. The slightest change in global temperament can cause a collapse of the cosmic order.

Exactly when the world went out of tune is difficult to gauge; the cosmic intonation probably slipped unevenly if not imperceptibly. But perhaps the last significant stage of this magical epistemology can be heard at the end of the fifteenth century. According to Gary Tomlinson, the Neo-Platonic structure of the Renaissance world still functioned within a 'magical episteme' or ground of knowledge.[16] For writers such as Marsilio Ficino, Ramos de Pareia and Cornelius Agrippa music remained magical, commingling with astronomy, geometry and arithmetic within the quadrivium that interpreted the cosmos. Its nature was seemingly diffuse, for the entire cosmos was its notation. As the 'score' of the world, ancient music was an all-inclusive, syncretistic form of knowledge that mixed the most eclectic elements together through what Michel Foucault calls a system of resemblances. These resemblances, he notes, 'organised the play of symbols [and] made possible the knowledge of things visible and invisible' within the Renaissance world.[17] That human phlegm, the moon and the hypodorian mode could inhabit the same site of logic in the writings of Ramos de Pareia was therefore due not to an aberration of reason but to a musical logic that spun a web of similitude around the world. Enclosed within this system, Ramos could tap into the absolute music of the cosmos to influence the sublunar and celestial realms, binding the modes (*musica instrumentalis*) to the planetary spheres (*musica mundana*) to affect the bodily humours (*musica humana*) along the length of the monochord.[18]

To disenchant the world, modernity had to sever the umbilical link of the mono-

---

[15] See Plato, *Timaeus*, 34b–47c.

[16] Gary Tomlinson, *Music in Renaissance Magic: Toward a Historiography of Others* (London and Chicago: University of Chicago Press, 1993).

[17] Michel Foucault, *The Order of Things: An Archaeology of the Human Sciences* (London: Tavistock/Routledge, 1974), p. 17.

[18] See Bartolomeo Ramos de Pareia, *Musica Practica* (1482), ed. Johannes Wolf (Leipzig, s.n., 1901), and Tomlinson, *Music in Renaissance Magic*, pp. 77–84. On *musica instrumentalis*, *musica mundana* and *musica humana*, see Anicius Manlius Severinus Boethius, *De institutione musica*, trans. Calvin M. Bower as *Fundamentals of Music* (New Haven: Yale University Press, 1989), pp. 9–10.

chord, disconnecting itself from the celestial realms in order to remove music as an explanation of the world. Significantly it was Vincenzo Galilei, father of Galileo, the astronomer who disenchanted the universe,[19] that was among the first to cut the ancient monochord in a series of experiments conducted in the 1580s,[20] by subjecting instrumental sound to the instrumental reason of empirical science. Indeed, Stillman Drake suggests that Galilei's experiments with sound may have 'led to the origin of experimental physics', inspiring his son to interrogate the world to verify the laws of *nature* as empirical fact.[21] Galilei wanted to 'demonstrate real things' he said, in the spirit of Aristotle and not the numerological abstractions of Pythagorean mysticism. He collapsed music into 'reality' as an audible *fact* divorced from celestial *values*.

Galilei in these experiments exercised an instrumental rationality in two ways. First, he objectified music as a neutralised matter for experimentation. Numbers were not sonorous in themselves, he claimed, but had to be 'applied to some sonorous body'.[22] Music does not exist as some perfect numerological system out there in the celestial realms as Pythagoras and indeed Galilei's teacher, Zarlino, believed; rather sounds are emitted from bodies whose differing components colour the aural perception of their harmonic ratios. Why believe in the ancient ratio of 2:1, for example, if, as Galilei demonstrates, the diapason can be variously obtained between strings whose length is in duple proportion, or weights in quadruple proportion, or pipes in octuple proportion.[23] Empirical reality simply did not match up with the ancient ratios that were supposed to organise the universe. Music is therefore *particular* for Galilei, rather than cosmic. And what makes it particular are its imperfections. Galilei counters Pythagoras by showing how musical ratios are contingent upon the particular dimensions and material structure of the instruments that are variable in their construction and so yield *inexact* ratios. In such cases, there are no perfect, immutable sounding numbers that stabilise music, only the variability of lines, surfaces, solids, gut, steel, copper. Even the unison, from which the unity of the ancient world emanates, fails to persuade Galilei's ear of its perfect equation: sounds, he writes, 'are unisonant only insofar as the diversity of material of which they are made allows'. There are disparities among unisons 'depending', he says, 'on the quantity of sound . . . the diversity of agents that strike [the instruments], the thickness, height and length of the body on which they are stretched, and the force with which they are struck'.[24] For Galilei, empirical reality was simply out of tune with the ancient world.

Second, having demythologised music with an empirical rationality, he subjected it with an instrumental efficiency that re-tunes music for modern ears. If, as his

[19] See Alexandre Koyré, 'Galileo and Plato', in *Metaphysics and Measurement: Essays in Scientific Revolution* (London: Chapman and Hall, 1968), pp. 16–43.

[20] Indeed, Galileo may have taken part in his father's experiments. See Stillman Drake, *Galileo at Work: His Scientific Biography* (Chicago: University of Chicago Press, 1970), pp. 15–17, and 'Renaissance Music and Experimental Science', *Journal of the History of Ideas* 31 (1970), 497–8; Palisca, *The Florentine Camerata*, p. 163.   [21] Drake, 'Renaissance Music and Experimental Science', 488.

[22] Galilei, 'A Special Discourse Concerning the Diversity of the Ratios of the Diapason', in *The Florentine Camerata*, pp. 183–5.   [23] See *ibid*.

[24] Galilei, 'A Special Discourse Concerning the Unison', in *ibid*., p. 201.

Example 1.1   Demonstration of the need for equal temperament from Vincenzo Galilei,
Discorso particolare intorno all'unisono

experiments proved, sounds were necessarily imperfect and unrelated to simple numbers, then there was no reason why the irrational tuning of Aristoxenus, that is equal temperament, should not be imposed upon music played on or accompanied by instruments.[25] Indeed, the chromatic and enharmonic nature of modern music demanded it, and just to underline the point, Galilei composed 'a song' which if sung with perfect intonation would be out of tune with reality: the chromatic and enharmonic clashes of modern harmony can only be eradicated if played on instruments tuned to equal temperament (see Example 1.1). 'Voices, being naturally perfect', wrote Galilei, 'cannot sing well a song that is not composed according to their perfect usage, but an instrument tempered according to the imperfect usage [of Aristoxenus] in which this song is imperfectly composed, on the other hand, can play it.'[26] In other words, imperfect music requires the imperfect tuning of an imperfect reality.

Galilei therefore modernised music by writing a piece that is instrumental in both mode and method. In fact, the song is not a composition, but an experiment, a demonstration of instrumental rationality itself. The system of equal temperament that the piece advocates means nothing other than its rationalisation. It is a method,

[25] Galilei, 'Discourse Concerning the Various Opinions that the Three Most Famous Sects of Ancient Musicians had Concerning the Matter of Sound and Tunings', in *ibid.*, p. 175.
[26] *Ibid.*, p. 207.

whereas Pythagorean tuning is an ethos; the first is the product of an instrumental knowledge, the second an emanation of substantive reason; equal temperament reduces music to a quantitative sameness, Pythagorean tuning structures the world with a qualitative difference. Equal temperament and Pythagorean tuning therefore stand against each other as opposing structures of rationality. One is grounded in supernature, the other is the pragmatic result of empirical nature.

By conducting these experiments, Galilei instigated a line of reasoning that grounds music theory in the acoustical nature of the external world, with calculations based on physical reality. In doing so, Galilei was following the advice of his mentor, Girolamo Mei, who told him that the 'science of music' (that is the quadrivium) provides 'truths' for the 'arts' (the trivium) to 'exploit . . . for its own end'.[27] In other words, the quadrivium furnishes music theory with scientific facts for the modern subject to manipulate and control within the trivium.

MUSIC THEORY AND HUMAN NATURE

This brings us to the second scene – the trivium – where the rhetorical will of human nature tries to ground the meaning of music in a disenchanted world. Human nature attempts to re-enchant music through the power of its own voice. After all, to dis-*enchant* the world is literally to leave it un-*sung*. The revelation of this unsung condition occurred in the final decades of the sixteenth century, which witnessed an obsession with song as an Edenic mode of expression. The vocal turn in music, from which opera is born, is a symptom of disenchantment. Opera sings in an unsung world as nostalgia for an ancient age enchanted by music. This is why the earliest operas were all Arcadian pastorals,[28] filled with singing nymphs and demigods mingling among the shepherds and lovers. The pastoral is nature as a garden, a secular Eden conjured by the desires of the urban imagination. And the figure who dramatises the Arcadian landscape is Orpheus, the son of Apollo, the god of music. He is the one who undulates the landscape with the drones of his lyre; his song is the eco-system of the enchanted world. Music is the magic that makes the pastoral.

What distinguishes early opera from other forms of pastorals is that the subject of enchantment, music, is also the *medium* of enchantment; the content is the form. Opera is music about music, and, just to make it clear, the music tells you. In the prologue of Monteverdi's *Orfeo*, 'Musica' is personified on stage. She defines herself: 'I am music', she sings, after which she proceeds to elaborate the theory of her own powers; she moves, she allures, she enchants. The magic on stage is the magic you experience, presented and demonstrated before your very ears; she is both the content and intent of opera, as though she brings the reality of an ancient magic into

[27] Girolamo Mei, 'Letter [to Vincenzo Galilei] of 8 May 1575', in *ibid.*, p. 65.
[28] See Nino Pirrotta, 'Early Opera and Aria', in *New Looks at Italian Opera: Essays in Honor of Donald J. Grout*, ed. W. W. Austin (Ithaca: Cornell University Press, 1968), pp. 72–89; Ellen Harris, *Handel and the Pastoral Tradition* (London: Oxford University Press, 1980), p. 25; and Ruth Katz, *The Powers of Music: Aesthetic Theory and the Invention of Opera* (New Brunswick: Transaction Publishers, 1994), pp. 142–8.

a modern practice. By the time of Monteverdi's *Orfeo*, the question of enchantment had become the question of music itself.

So why does music reflect upon itself in the guise of opera in the early years of the seventeenth century? Why does it need to define its identity – 'I am music' – and explain its own practice? Why does it have to demonstrate in reality the magic it recounts as ancient history? Perhaps it was because modernity finally realised that its disenchantment of the world was the unsinging of music. After all, the group who allegedly created opera, the so-called 'Florentine Camerata' of Giovanni Bardi, which included Vincenzo Galilei, were driven by a sense of loss and the need to regain an ancient magic. Although it would be simplistic to claim that the Camerata invented opera,[29] the theories they espoused in the 1580s register the disenchantment of music that is the *anxiety* behind opera. They wanted to revive the bardic magic of monodic song, for modern music, they claimed, had come into a crisis of identity: music had lost its power. If it were still magical, argued Galilei, then where are the 'miracles' today that are described in the ancient texts?[30] 'Pythagoras cured alcoholics, and Empedocles the mad, and Xenocrates someone possessed of a devil', said Bardi, but modern music is merely a polyphonic confusion of affections that cannot work its magic on the soul.[31]

A hundred years earlier, magic was a musical practice for a musician like Ficino;[32] by the time of the Camerata, it could only be proposed as a *theory* for the re-enchantment of empirical reality. Their discussions testify to a disenchanted world disenchanted with itself, and so mark a critical moment of self-realisation in the progress of modernity. From now on, the future of music becomes a matter of recovery; its drive towards the new is haunted by an idealised past. In his *Dialogue On Ancient and Modern Music* (1581), Galilei stated that 'ancient music', like Arcadia itself, is 'lost . . . and its light has so dimmed that many consider its wonderful excellence a dream and a fable'.[33] Thus the Camerata forged a new strategy for modernity: they denounced the present as a pale imitation of music's 'first and happy state',[34] to quote Galilei, in order to propel the ancient strains back to the future as a paradise regained. With the disenchantment of the world, music becomes a site of both nostalgia and anticipation, where Arcadia and Utopia, fixed at either end of history, yearn for harmonisation.

To put it another way, the Camerata inaugurated the pastoralisation of music theory. Their ideas, as the impulse behind opera, created an Edenic dream evident in

[29] See, for example, Claude V. Palisca, 'The Alterati of Florence, Pioneers in the Theory of Dramatic Music', in *New Looks at Italian Opera*, pp. 9–11. The theories of the Camerata were not unique; however, I shall use the Florentine Camerata as a focus for the new theories of music discussed within the humanist circles of sixteenth-century Italy.
[30] Vincenzo Galilei, *Dialogo della musica antica e della moderna* (1581), in Oliver Strunk, *Source Readings in Music History* (New York: Norton, 1950), p. 305. Much of Galilei's argument here is taken from a letter he received in 1572 from Girolamo Mei; see Palisca, *The Florentine Camerata*, pp. 45–77.
[31] Giovanni Bardi, 'Discourse Addressed to Giulio Caccini, Called the Roman, on Ancient Music and Good Singing', in *The Florentine Camerata*, p. 111. Again, the material is adapted from Mei's letter to Galilei; see above. [32] See Tomlinson, *Music in Renaissance Magic*, p. 144.
[33] Galilei, *Dialogo*, p. 310. [34] *Ibid.*

the flurry of pastorals by Peri, Caccini and Cavalieri that purport to be the 'birth of opera' around the dawn of the seventeenth century.[35] It is a controversial matter whether these Florentine pastorals really constitute the 'birth of opera',[36] but they certainly produced, as their afterbirth, the modernity of instrumental music.

The logic is simple: what happens to music when the world is unsung? It becomes instrumental. In opposition to the pastoral, instrumental music is an empty sign, lacking the magical presence that only the voice can re-present. 'After the loss of [ancient music]', said Galilei, 'men began to derive from . . . instruments . . . rules . . . for composing and singing several airs together.'[37] A music without speech is therefore made to explain the disenchantment of music. This is why Galilei, following Zarlino,[38] called instrumental music 'artificial'; its music is a simulation of nature. But whereas Zarlino idealised nature as a metaphysics of numbers that could still be reproduced vocally, for Galilei it was an Edenic state of pure expressivity which has been lost. Thus Galilei does not only undermine instrumental music but *all* modern music. The vocal polyphony manufactured by the abstract contrapuntal laws of Zarlino is equally artificial for him. This is because the origin of polyphony, claimed Galilei, is instrumental. It was invented by ignorant musicians who started to play 'several airs in consonance' on the cithara, he said, solely 'to tickle the ear' with their clever intervallic calculations. Instrumental music is therefore the original sin of modern music. The 'modern contrapuntists' may write for voices, but their music is already unsung, because humanity has eaten from the tree of instrumental knowledge, which excludes modernity from the garden of Arcadia.[39]

The only way back to the magic of music was to break through the contrapuntal clutter with a monodic concentration, claimed Galilei. But Galilei was blind to the effects of his own theories, because far from inaugurating the return of an ancient magic, the revival of monodic song actually disenchanted music with the instrumentality that modernity fears. What monody cannot tolerate is precisely the impure mixture that characterises the ancient world of resemblances. Galilei lamented the 'composite and different natures' of modern contrapuntal music, echoing the complaints of his mentor, Mei.[40] Today's music, said Mei, 'does not work any of the miracles [known to the ancients], since it conveys to the soul of the listener at one time diverse and contrary signs of affections as it mixes indistinctly together airs and tonoi that are completely dissimilar and of natures contrary to each other'.[41] Clearly,

[35] See, for example, Claude V. Palisca, *Baroque Music* (Englewood Cliffs, NJ: Prentice Hall, 1981), pp. 29–38.

[36] See Lorenzo Bianconi, *Music in the Seventeenth Century*, trans. David Bryant (Cambridge: Cambridge University Press, 1987), pp. 161–89.   [37] Galilei, *Dialogo*, p. 119.

[38] See Michael Fend, 'The Changing Function of *Senso* and *Ragione* in Italian Music Theory of the Late Sixteenth Century', in *The Second Sense: Studies in Hearing and Musical Judgement from Antiquity to the Seventeenth Century*, ed. Charles Burnett, Michael Fend and Penelope Gouk (London: Warburg Institute, University of London, 1991), p. 211.

[39] Galilei, *Dialogo*, pp. 308, 310, 312 and 315; translation slightly modified.   [40] *Ibid.*, p. 118.

[41] Mei, 'Letter [to Vincenzo Galilei] of 8 May 1572', in Palisca, *The Florentine Camerata*, p. 61.

music for Galilei was no longer that composite mixture of the ancient world, where speech and tone could co-exist without being identical. The seemingly haphazard underlay of words beneath the melismas of ancient music is discarded by the Camerata for a music that follows the inflections of speech, as if identity constituted the unity of the word–tone divide. Monody is the rationalisation of song; it is a form of 'musical Puritanism', says D. P. Walker, for there is no waste.[42] The melody determines the meaning by fixing the emotions to denote, define and communicate a message.

But what kind of unity is this? The unity only works if there is a division of tones and words which are then forced together by the will of the monodic self. The unity is not a condition of the universe but the coercion of the ego; it is not cosmic but particular, located in the individual who controls the world by the force of rhetoric.[43] Monody is therefore an instrumental totality, for the voice is used as a *tool* that no longer requires the vertical validation of the celestial spheres but moves horizontally 'to induce in another the passion that one feels', said Galilei.[44] The magic that the Camerata wanted was ironically the very magic of instrumental reason that disenchanted the world. Giulio del Bene said as much in 1586 when he gave a speech to another Camerata in Florence, the Accademia degli Alterati, proposing that music should be transferred from the quadrivium to the trivium, that is, from the immutable structure of the medieval cosmos to the linguistic relativity of rhetoric, grammar and dialectics.[45] In the trivium, music becomes *human* and can be made infinitely malleable by the power of rhetorical persuasion. This shift allows man to bend music according to his linguistic will, twisting and distorting its intervals to vocalise his passional self, breaking the harmonic laws of the cosmos to legitimise humanity as the new sovereign who creates his own laws out of his own being. This is the second nature of the second practice.

By collapsing the harmony of the spheres into the song of the self, the moral value of music is grounded in an Arcadian human nature. As a consequence, the metaphysics of being is no longer embedded within a cosmology but an anthropology in which song becomes the natural origin of humanity, lost in some Arcadian past that modernity must recover to regain the plenitude of being that instrumental music lacks. This eventually gave rise to the speculative histories of language in the eighteenth century, most famously articulated by Rousseau, who claimed that the first intelligible utterances of humanity were sung. Singing becomes being; or to borrow Derrida's term, singing brings out from the recesses of the ego the 'metaphysics of presence' in an unsung world, bereft of divine presence.[46] The effect of opera was to divide nature

---

[42] See Walker, *Studies in Musical Science in the Late Renaissance*, pp. 63–5, and Max Weber, *The Protestant Ethic and the Spirit of Capitalism*, trans. T. Parsons (London: George Allen and Unwin, 1976), p. 181.

[43] See Katz, *The Powers of Music*, pp. 62–75 and 130–4.   [44] Galilei, *Dialogo*, p. 317.

[45] See Palisca, 'The Alterati of Florence', pp. 14–15.

[46] See Jacques Derrida's discussion of Jean-Jacques Rousseau's *Essai sur l'origine des langues*, in *Of Grammatology*, trans. Gayatri C. Spivak, corrected edn (Baltimore and London: Johns Hopkins University Press, 1998), pp. 165–255.

into subjective and objective states, with an interior realm of sung speech alienated from the cold exterior of a disenchanted world.[47]

CONCLUSION

What is clear about Vincenzo Galilei's thought is that it is confused. As a musician he advocated a modern practice, with a pragmatic, instrumental rationality that champions equal temperament as a necessary fact of modern hearing, yet as a theorist he lamented the very practice he advocated by denouncing modern music as impotent both in its polyphonic and instrumental forms. This contradiction can even be seen within a single work; Galilei's late treatise on counterpoint, which Claude Palisca describes as 'a code for the *seconda prattica*', explains the practice of modern music, yet, in the preface, Galilei, anxious to maintain his earlier position, denigrates the polyphony of his time in order to elevate the moral and intellectual power of ancient music. Palisca suggests that Galilei had come to some kind of a 'compromise' with monody in the work.[48] But perhaps it is better to see this 'compromise' as a contradiction symptomatic of an ambivalent modernity which, in its attempt to overcome *and* emulate the past, ends up splitting the nature of music theory in two: first, as a desacralised object that can be scientifically interrogated and instrumentally rationalised in the name of empirical reality, and second, as a moral subject searching for meaning, even to the point of aestheticising instrumental reason as monodic power. Modern humanity, having disenchanted the world by draining out the musical substance of the cosmos, posits itself as the new music that will re-enchant the world with an instrumental 'magic' that, by definition, can never regain the ancient unity it yearns for. Perhaps it was the need to resolve this dissonance that forced Galilei to contradict himself. And perhaps it is this same desire for reconciliation that is the dialectical force behind the history of music theory, to bring fact and value, analysis and meaning, truth and morality back together. The Utopian yet impossible hope of music theory is to harmonise the two natures, and so reverse the Edenic expulsion pronounced by Max Weber, by manufacturing a secular Eden with the fruit of human knowledge.

---

[47] See Downing A. Thomas, *Music and the Origins of Language* (Cambridge: Cambridge University Press, 1995), and Rousseau, *Essai sur l'origine des langues* (1764).

[48] Claude V. Palisca, 'Vincenzo Galilei's Counterpoint Treatise: A Code for the *Seconda Prattica*', *Journal of the American Musicological Society* 9 (1956), 95.

Chapter Two

■

''Tis Nature's Voice': music, natural philosophy and the hidden world in seventeenth-century England

LINDA PHYLLIS AUSTERN

Musica, de qua in praesenti oratione instituo, deum patre|m|, matre|m| natura|m| habet; quippe in ea quidda|m| divinum inest, quo me|n|s, imago dei, mirifice delectatur. Est etia|m| physicu|m| & naturale quidda|m|, quo non solum aures hominum, sed etiam rerum omniu|m| veluti sensus, suprà quàm dici aut cogitari potest, demulcentur.

(Music, about which I give instruction in the present speech, has God for a father, Nature for a mother; it has a divine quality whereby the mind, the image of God, is wondrously delighted. It is a physical and natural thing, by which not only the ears of men, but the senses of all beings, as it were, are comforted in a way which is beyond speech or thought.)

John Case, *Apologia musices* (1588)

At the dawn of the modern era, enquiries into the nature and properties of music were the equal province of the philosopher, the musician, the divine and the physician. As the broadly trained Oxford scholar and practising musician John Case reminds us, music was considered a God-given comfort to the rational mind and to all sensible creatures. The source of its power extended, he claimed, beyond the reaches of rational thought or language. Music moved every entity from the heavenly spheres to ghosts in sepulchres, from birds and fish to the very elements of which all things were made. For this reason, it had a definite place in the occult philosophies of his era, in the church and in the private and public lives of human beings.[1] At the same time, music was a physical force of nature with evident influence on visible and invisible bodies. Its causes and effects could therefore be described and measured by music theory or by the burgeoning disciplines of natural science. Case's seamless blend of

[1] John Case, *Apologia musices tam vocalis quam instrumentalis et mixtae* (Oxford: Joseph Barnes, 1588), pp. 1–4.

ideas later divided between rival epistemologies was typical of Northern European musical thought on the eve of the scientific revolution.

Even as new cosmologies began to silence the music of the spheres, and Baconian science and Cartesian rationalism transformed the world from a network of mysterious signs into a comprehensive storehouse of matter, musical thinkers of all descriptions continued to locate their subject between the vibrant world of nature and the celestial choir. Along with the other mathematical sciences of the ancient quadrivium, music still remained a branch of natural philosophy, the broad enquiry into the phenomena of the created world. At the same time, all of nature, and the nature of all things musical and otherwise, were ultimately the handiwork of the unseen Creator; as Thomas Robinson remarks in the introductory pages to his practical manual for would-be lute-players of 1603, the musician must first be a divine 'and above all things serve God'. Only then could he be an effective performer, composer or theorist, or otherwise participate in the discipline.[2] However, as the seventeenth century progressed, music was increasingly considered a practical art linked to rhetorical persuasion and to physical display. It thus became an emblem of social status as well as of mastery over unruly material and communion with the divine. Nowhere was the often uneasy co-existence of these ideas more evident than in England, where more music theory manuals were published during the seventeenth century than anywhere else in Europe,[3] and where such contrasting minds as Francis Bacon and Robert Fludd found music within their natural philosophies. Over a century after Case anthropomorphised his subject into the daughter of God and Nature, 'born without any incest or sin' in a seemingly blasphemous blend of myth and Christianity, Nicholas Brady and Henry Purcell still found Nature's voice working through St Cecilia, the patroness of music.[4] Throughout the era it was increasingly up to human ingenuity to work with natural materials to reveal the art in its full divine glory.

Music enjoyed a far richer and more complicated relationship with the studies of nature in early modern England than has generally been presumed. Just as historians of music theory have tended to limit their investigations to works by and for practising musicians, historians of science and philosophy have too often neglected music altogether, or overlooked important material written for would-be composers and

---

[2] Thomas Robinson, *The Schoole of Musicke: Wherin is Taught the Perfect Method of True Fingering of the Lute, Pandora, Orpharion, and Viol da Gamba* (London: Tho[mas] Este for Simon Waterson, 1603), sig. B. The second and third fields of use to the would-be musician are, according to Robinson, physic (medicine) and arithmetic, particularly the latter; *ibid.*

[3] This programme of publication was clearly linked to a great amount of private amateur music-making, which presumably dominated musical culture during a century of religious turmoil and shifting attitudes toward public performance; see W. T. Atcherson, 'Symposium on Seventeenth-Century Music Theory – England', *Journal of Music Theory* 16 (1972), 9 and 13–15, and Lillian M. Ruff, 'The Social Significance of the Seventeenth-Century English Music Theory Treatises', *The Consort* 26 (1970), 412, in which the author also points out that pictorial art indicates that the Low Countries also excelled at amateur music-making, but evidently lacked the avid amateur interest in theory and composition of the English.

[4] John Case, *Apologia musices*, p. 1: 'ipsam musicam Dei & naturae filiam sine omni incestu & labe genitam...'

performers.[5] During the seventeenth century, what we would today define as science belonged to the same branch of philosophy as did music. The increasing use of speculative music theory in the service of sound during the early years of the scientific revolution followed a course parallel to the development of a 'new' or experimental philosophy with a mathematical basis.[6] Thomas Blount's English dictionary of 1656, clearly building on the earliest exemplar to include the term, defines 'Philosophie' as

The study of wisedome: a deepe knowledge in the nature of things. There are three different kindes hereof. 1. *Rationall* Philosophy, including grammar, Logick, and Rhetorick. 2. *Naturall* Philosophy teaching the nature of all things, and conteining besides Arithmetick, Musick, Geometry and Astronomy. 2. *Morall* Philosophy, which consisteth in the knowledge and practise of civilitie and good behaviour.[7]

This positioning of music within natural philosophy had come to inform musical thought long before Blount's era. The Renaissance had inherited from Classical antiquity and from its Medieval filters several notions that the ordered harmony of music

---

[5] For work that begins to restore music to its place in early modern English science and philosophy, see Peter J. Ammann, 'The Musical Theory and Philosophy of Robert Fludd', *Journal of the Warburg and Courtauld Institutes* 30 (1967), 198–227; Penelope M. Gouk, 'Music in Francis Bacon's Natural Philosophy', in *Francis Bacon: Terminologia e fortuna nel XVII secolo*, ed. Marta Fattori (Rome: Edizioni dell'Ateneo, 1984), pp. 139–54, 'The Role of Acoustics and Music Theory in the Scientific Work of Robert Hook', *Annals of Science* 37 (1980), 573–605, and 'Speculative and Practical Music in Seventeenth-Century England: Oxford University as a Case Study', in *Atti del XIV congresso della società internazionale di musicologia: trasmissione e recezione delle forme di cultura, 1987*, ed. Angelo Pompilio, Lorenzo Bianconi and F. Alberto Gallo (Turin: E. D. T. edizioni di Torino, 1990), vol. III, pp. 199–205; J. C. Kassler and D. R. Oldroyd, 'Robert Hook's Trinity College "Musick Scripts", His Music Theory and the Role of Music in His Cosmology', *Annals of Science* 40 (1983), 559–95; and Jamie C. Kassler, *Inner Music: Hobbes, Hooke, and North on Internal Character* (Madison and Teaneck: Farleigh Dickinson University Press, 1995).

[6] See H. F. Cohen, *Quantifying Music: The Science of Music at the First Stage of the Scientific Revolution, 1580–1650* (Dordrecht, Boston and Lancaster: D. Reidel Publishing Company, 1984), pp. 13–230 and 243–59; Gary B. Deason, 'Reformation Theology and the Mechanistic Conception of Nature', in *God and Nature: Essays on the Encounters Between Christianity and Science*, ed. David C. Lindberg and Ronald L. Numbers (Berkeley and Los Angeles: University of California Press, 1986), pp. 167–75; Penelope M. Gouk, 'Some English Theories of Hearing in the Seventeenth Century: Before and After Descartes', in *The Second Sense: Studies in Hearing and Musical Judgment from Antiquity to the Seventeenth Century*, ed. Charles Burnett, Michael Fend and Penelope Gouk (London: Warburg Institute, 1991), pp. 95–114, 'Performance Practice: Music, Medicine and Natural Philosophy in Interregnum Oxford', *British Journal of the History of Science* 29 (1996), 285–7, 'Horological, Mathematical and Musical Instruments. Science and Music at the Court of Charles I', in *The Late King's Goods: Collections, Possessions and Patronage of Charles I in the Light of Commonwealth Sale Inventories*, ed. Arthur MacGregor (London and Oxford: Alistair McAlpine in Association with Oxford University Press, 1989), pp. 389–92, and 'Speculative and Practical Music', pp. 199–205; and Michael Hunter, *Science and Society in Restoration England* (Cambridge: Cambridge University Press, 1981), pp. 16–21.

[7] T[homas] B[lount], *Glossographia: Or a Dictionary Interpreting All Such Hard Words . . . As Are Now Used in Our Refined English Tongue* (London: Tho[mas] Newcomb for Humphrey Moseley, 1656), sig. Gg5. See also John Bullokar, *An English Expositor: Teaching the Interpretation of the Hardest Words Used in Our Language* (London: John Leggatt, 1616), sig. M2; Harold J. Cook, 'The New Philosophy and Medicine in Seventeenth-Century England', in *Reappraisals of the Scientific Revolution*, ed. David C. Lindberg and Robert S. Westman (Cambridge: Cambridge University Press, 1990), pp. 398–408; and Hunter, *Science and Society*, pp. 8–21.

not only stood in opposition to the primal cries of nature, but would subsume them through elevation into art. The growing body of iconographic and emblematic imagery, full of symbols drawn from natural philosophical tracts and mythographical narratives, helped to reinforce the close ties between music and the realm of nature across media and national boundaries. Filippino Lippi's fifteenth-century Florentine *Allegory of Music* (Illus. 2.1) brings together several venerable symbols of untamed music in the process of metamorphosis into human art, with a typical mixture of grace and cruelty. By the seventeenth century, these same symbols, particularly the swan and stag, had become central to international emblematic currency.[8] The earliest extant English vernacular theory treatise, the anonymous *Praise of Musicke* of 1586, emphasises that Nature wrought the world with music, as evident in the unheard harmonies of the spheres, the elements, and the soul and body of man. Yet Nature is no mere silent speculator in this treatise. She does not simply tune the world with arcane numerical ratios, or wrest music from the bodies of plants and animals, before withdrawing her presence. Here, the natural philosopher as music theorist is more interested in issues of musical sound and praxis than in ontology. His deep knowledge of the nature of things seeks to locate the boundaries between untamed and artificial sounds, to help develop his understanding of music as heard and practised. 'And who can blame nature in any reason for using her owne invention? Doth the nightingale record by Art or by nature?', asks the author of the melodious sounds of the wild world. 'But to leave nature and come to Art', he quickly continues, '. . . who can be ignorant that nature hath given her the groundworke, whereon shee a long time hath flourished?'[9]

In order to understand the interplay between music and the other fields of natural philosophy against an increasingly pragmatic background, it is necessary to examine the place of nature in the early modern English intellectual landscape. From antiquity until the age of Enlightenment, nature had a number of interrelated meanings as the opposite of all artificially created things, and as the primeval force that most directly inhabited tangible objects. The course of nature and the laws of nature were the actualisation of this force. The state of nature was the state of humankind prior to the state of grace, and to social organisation.[10] To a series of cultures given to

---

[8] See my 'Nature, Culture, Myth and the Musician in Early Modern England', *Journal of the American Musicological Society* 51 (1998), 3–7; Giovanni Battista Della Porta [John Baptista Porta], *Natural Magick in Twenty Books* (London: Thomas Young and Samuel Speed, 1658), p. 403; Nicoletta Guidobaldi, 'Images of Music in Cesare Ripa's *Iconologia*', *Imago Musicae* 7 (1990), 45–6; Richard Leppert, 'Music, Representation, and Social Order in Early-Modern Europe', *Cultural Critique* 4 (1989), 53–4; and Emanuel Winternitz, *Musical Instruments and Their Symbolism in Western Art* (London: Faber and Faber, 1967), pp. 40 and 222.

[9] Anon., *The Praise of Musicke* (Oxenford: Joseph Barnes, 1586), pp. 2–3. See also Case, *Apologia musices*, in which music is defined at once as the daughter of nature, teacher of morals and governess of mind, linking together the branches of philosophy through the nature of music.

[10] See Michel de Certeau, *The Writing of History*, trans. Tom Conley (New York: Columbia University Press, 1988), pp. 219–20; Thomas DaCosta Kauffman, *The Mastery of Nature: Aspects of Art, Science and Humanism in the Renaissance* (Princeton: Princeton University Press, 1993), p. 97; Carolyn Merchant, *The Death of Nature: Women, Ecology, and the Scientific Revolution* (San Francisco: Harper and Row, 1980), pp. xix and 10–13; and Stephen Toulmin, *The Return to Cosmology: Postmodern Science and the Theology of Nature* (Berkeley and Los Angeles: University of California Press, 1982), pp. 1–8.

Illus. 2.1   Natural music in process of becoming human art, with typical mixture of grace
and cruelty. Filippino Lippi, *Allegory of Music*, fifteenth century

emblematic modes of thought and for whom the distinction between the literal and the metaphorical remained unimportant, nature came to be personified as a female being. 'Nature', said Pliny in a work that remained current for over a millennium, '[is] the worke-mistresse and mother of all.'[11] As such, she generated the phenomenal world through deep, pre-rational knowledge, eternally pregnant with the dark secrets of growth, change, movement and decay. From the beginning to the end of the early modern era, Natura was imagined as a comely lactating woman, fully exposed to the rapacious gaze, holding a vulture on her hand to signify the unity of passive and active principles, and the concomitant nurturance and corruption of created things (Illus. 2.2a and 2b). Hers was passive matter, waiting to give life with the masculine principle of Idea, her fruitful body responsive to the knowing touch. Alternately ferocious and nurturing according to co-existing traditions, she offered true wisdom and the secrets of creativity to men of skill and erudition, through processes increasingly analogised in boastful male sexual terms.[12] This construct of Nature as nubile woman, deeply rooted in the Western psyche for so long, held out even as the scientific method came to overshadow mystical philology and analogical epistemes in the investigation of natural phenomena. As late as the 1660s, the poet Abraham Cowley could still praise the impressive achievements of the Royal Society in natural philosophy and the growing fields of experimental science in terms of voyeurism and blatant erotic conquest.[13] The parallels to the fecund Lady Music of such tracts as *The Praise of Musicke* –

---

[11] Pliny [C. Plinius, Secundus], *The Historie of the World. Commonly called, The Natural Historie* (London: Adam Islip, 1601), p. 1. See William B. Ashworth, 'Natural History and the Emblematic World View', in *Reappraisals of the Scientific Revolution*, ed. David C. Lindberg and Robert S. Westman (Cambridge: Cambridge University Press, 1990), pp. 312–13; Susan Bordo, 'The Cartesian Masculinization of Thought', in *Sex and Scientific Inquiry*, ed. Sandra Harding and Jean F. O'Barr (Chicago and London: University of Chicago Press, 1987), p. 260; Donna J. Haraway, *Primate Visions: Gender, Race, and Nature in the World of Modern Science* (New York: Routledge, 1989), pp. 3–4; and Merchant, *The Death of Nature*, pp. 2–6 and 143–4.

[12] See Denise Albanese, *New Science, New World* (Durham, NC, and London: Duke University Press, 1996), p. 37; Albert Borgmann, 'The Nature of Reality and the Reality of Nature', in *Reinventing Nature? Responses to Postmodern Deconstruction*, ed. Michael E. Soulé and Gary Lease (Washington, DC and Covelo, Calif.: Island Press, 1995), pp. 32–3; Genevieve Lloyd, 'Reason, Science, and the Domination of Matter', in *Feminism in Science*, ed. Evelyn Fox Keller and Helen Longino (Oxford and New York: Oxford University Press, 1996), p. 47; Cesare Ripa, *Della Novissima Iconologia* [(Padua: Tozzi, 1624)], pp. 457–8; Ripa, *Iconologia: Or, Moral Emblems* (London: Benj[amin] Motte, 1709), fol. 56; and Londa Schiebinger, *Nature's Body: Gender and the Making of Modern Science* (Boston: Beacon Press, 1993), pp. 56–9. Susan Bordo points out that the period between 1550 and 1650 was particularly gynophobic, and witnessed an obsession within the burgeoning empirical sciences to assault and tame all of nature and the potentially disordered female universe, 'The Cartesian Masculinization of Thought', pp. 261–3; see also Merchant, *The Death of Nature*, pp. 164–91. As early as Pliny, she had been at once 'a kind of mother, or a hard and cruell step-dame', *The Historie of the World*, p. 152.

[13] A[braham] Cowley, Dedication 'To the Royal Society', in Tho[mas] Spratt, *The History of the Royal-Society of London, for the Improving of Natural Knowledge* (London: T. R. for J. Martyn, 1667), sig. B3. For further information on the gradual paradigm shift between Renaissance occult mentalities and early modern scientific thought with particular reference to the treatment of nature, see Scott Atran, *Cognitive Foundations of Natural History: Toward an Anthropology of Science* (Cambridge: Cambridge

Illus. 2.2a   Nature embodied as beautiful, lactating virgin, from Cesare Ripa, *Della Novissima Iconologia* [Padua: Tozzi, 1624]

Illus. 2.2b   Nature embodied as beautiful, lactating virgin, from Cesare Ripa, *Iconologia: Or,*
Moral Emblems (London: Benj[amin] Motte, 1709)

described as exquisite, marriageable and 'as pregnant as Libia alwaies breeding some new thing' – become all the more explicable by the filial relationship of her discipline to Dame Nature's.[14]

The modern scholar Donna Haraway recognises in her classic study of gender, race and nature in modern science that standard Western accounts of the human place in the natural world are built on a discursive blend of fact and fiction, customarily accepted as truth. They also rely on a self-conscious disconnection of the investigator from the category of 'nature', necessary to his species's self-realisation and transcendence.[15] During the Jacobean era, Francis Bacon had likewise written that 'Doctrine and Discourse maketh *Nature* lesse Importune: But Custome onely doth alter & subdue Nature.'[16] Tudor and Stuart England had inherited the notion that all natural things had been made for man's sake according to divine plan. Recent scholarship has re-emphasised the mutual interplay between theology and the development of the natural sciences during the seventeenth century, particularly in Protestant countries such as England.[17] According to Lutheran and Calvinist thought, the Creator was the only active principle in existence; he merely spoke, and the world was. He did not depend on nature, which, according to Luther, was incapable of such achievement. The Reformation thus conceived of nature as entirely passive. God retained complete sovereignty over this non-resisting force, and could command natural things to behave in any way, for they had no powers which he did not bestow upon them.[18] These precepts supported both religious and scientific investigations

footnote 13 (*cont.*)
University Press, 1990), pp. 22 and 212–13; I. Bernard Cohen, *Revolution in Science* (Cambridge, Mass.: Harvard University Press, 1985), pp. 146–9; Page Dubois, 'Subjected Bodies, Science and the State: Francis Bacon, Torturer', in *Body Politics: Disease, Desire and the Family*, ed. Michael Ryan and Avery Gordon (Boulder, San Francisco and Oxford: Westview Press, 1994), p. 180; William Eamon, *Science and the Secrets of Nature: Books of Secrets in Medieval and Early Modern Culture* (Princeton: Princeton University Press, 1994), pp. 310–19; Michel Foucault, *The Order of Things: An Archaeology of the Human Sciences* (New York: Random House, 1973), pp. 32–6; William L. Hine, 'Marin Mersenne: Renaissance Naturalism and Renaissance Magic', in *Occult and Scientific Mentalities in the Renaissance*, ed. Brian Vickers (Cambridge: Cambridge University Press, 1984), pp. 165–70; Eilean Hooper-Greenhill, *Museums and the Shaping of Knowledge* (London and New York: Routledge, 1992; rpt edn 1995), pp. 89–90; Philip Kuberski, *The Persistence of Memory: Organism, Myth, Text* (Berkeley and Los Angeles: University of California Press, 1992), pp. 95–6; Barbara J. Shapiro, *Probability and Certainty in Seventeenth-Century England: A Study of the Relationships Between Natural Science, Religion, History, Law, and Literature* (Princeton: Princeton University Press, 1983), pp. 15–73; and Brian Vickers, 'Analogy Versus Identity: The Rejection of Occult Symbolism, 1580–1680', in *Occult and Scientific Mentalities*, pp. 102–26.
[14] *The Praise of Musicke*, pp. 3–4. See also my '"My Mother Musicke": Music and Early Modern Fantasies of Embodiment', in *Mothers and Others: Caregiver Figures in Early Modern Europe*, ed. Naomi Miller and Naomi Yavneh (Aldershot: Ashgate, 2000) pp. 248–59.
[15] See Haraway, *Primate Visions*, pp. 4 and 282. See also Bordo, 'The Cartesian Masculinization of Thought', pp. 245–59, and Kuberski, *The Persistence of Memory*, p. 95.
[16] Francis Bacon, *The Essays, Newly Enlarged* (London: John Haviland, 1632), p. 227.
[17] See Bordo, 'The Cartesian Masculinization of Thought', pp. 260–1; Deason, 'Reformation Theology and the Mechanistic Conception of Nature', pp. 185–7; Shapiro, *Probability and Certainty*, pp. 74–118; and Keith Thomas, *Man and the Natural World: Changing Attitudes in England 1500–1800* (London: Allen Lane, 1983), p. 29.
[18] Deason, 'Reformation Theology and the Mechanistic Conception of Nature', pp. 175–85.

into the nature of things, and the development of mutually influential theories of knowledge across related branches of philosophy. 'Religion, however mistaken or misrepresented by some', says Henry Purcell's librettist and Anglican preacher Nicholas Brady in a sermon in defence of music, 'is the most entertaining thing in Nature.'[19] By the Restoration, the quest for a natural theology, whose reliance on mathematical demonstration and sense data linked it closely with natural philosophy, had become a dominant element of English religious thought. This intellectual strain is especially evident in Thomas Mace's music theory, in which not only are the rules of music rooted in nature, but its 'mystical and contemplative part' comes from a blend of nature and divinity largely founded on number.[20]

Throughout the sixteenth and seventeenth centuries, as justified by close readings of Aristotle, the Stoics, the Bible and numerous exegetes, every creature and every tangible object served some human purpose. To the natural philosopher or scientist, the whole purpose of study was to know, master and manage nature for human benefit, for 'man hath the use of all creatures, or for his *profit*, or for his pleasure'.[21] As Adam had given names to all lower life-forms, it was up to his descendants to read their hidden marks to discover their uses. If natural things served no clear utilitarian purpose, then they had been designed by a hidden hand for moral edification, for aesthetic value, or for the increasingly important mental exercise of wonder. Human dominion over nature was hard won, God-given, and often brutal; on these points, occult and early scientific thought found common ground.[22] Increasingly in an era on the edge of a scientific world-view and global expansion, human civilisation was

---

[19] Nicholas Brady, *Church-Musick Vindicated* (London: Joseph Wilde, 1697), p. 6. The same sermon also labels music the 'obsequious and useful Handmaid' of religion within this context of nature, pp. 6–7.

[20] Tho[mas] Mace, *Musicks Monument: Or, a Remembrancer Of the Best Practical Musick* (London: T. Ratcliffe and N. Thompson for Thomas Mace and John Carr, 1976), pp. 264–72. See also Charles Butler, *The Principles of Musik*, in *Singing and Setting* (London: John Haviland, 1636), sigs. Qq' and Qq3, and John Playford, *An Introduction to the Skill of Musick* (London: W. Godbid for J. Playford, 1674), sigs. A4'–A5'. For a classic if limited overview of seventeenth-century English music theory as utterly rational and often linked to mathematics, see Barry Cooper, 'Englische Musiktheorie im 17. und 18. Jahrhundert', in *Entstehung nationaler Traditionen: Frankreich [und] England*, ed. Barry Cooper and Wilhelm Seidel, in *Geschichte der Musiktheorie*, vol. IX, ed. Frieder Zaminer (Darmstadt: Wissenschaftliche Buchgesellschaft, 1986), pp. 158–73. For information about the deep intellectual connections between changing notions of nature, divinity and mathematics (of which music was often considered part) in seventeenth-century England, see William B. Ashworth, 'Catholicism and Early Modern Science', in *God and Nature*, ed. Lindberg and Numbers, pp. 136–48; Deason, 'Reformation Theology and the Mechanistic Conception of Nature', pp. 167–75; Eamon, *Science and the Secrets of Nature*, pp. 319–21; Hunter, *Science and Society*, pp. 16–21; and Shapiro, *Probability and Certainty in Seventeenth-Century England*, pp. 82–94 and 117. Even beyond the realm of theology, the influence of the mathematical sciences on ideas about nature and widespread cultural habits of thought in seventeenth-century England can scarcely be estimated; see Cohen, *Revolution in Science*, pp. 160–75.

[21] John Day, *Day's Descant on Davids Psalmes* (Oxford: John Lichfield and James Short, 1610), p. 213.

[22] See James J. Bono, *The Word of God and the Languages of Man: Interpreting Nature in Early Modern Science and Medicine*, vol. I: *Ficino to Descartes* (Madison: University of Wisconsin Press, 1995), pp. 48–84; Foucault, *The Order of Things*, p. 38; Donna J. Haraway, *Simians, Cyborgs, and Women: The Reinvention of Nature* (New York: Routledge, 1991), p. 81; Kuberski, *The Persistence of Memory*, pp. 97–100; and Thomas, *Man and the Natural World*, pp. 17–30.

based on conquering, subduing and often transforming natural things into artificial marvels as a hedge against disorder. Hugh Platt likens the calculated elevation of nature into art to the ensoulment of an unruly body. 'Art doth perfect nature', Platt explains,

... for although Nature appears a most fair and fruitful Body, and as admirable in her variety as abundance; yet the Art here mentioned is as a Soul to inform that Body, to examine and refine her actions, and to teach her to understand those abilities of her own, which before lay undiscovered to her.[23]

Here we see the natural philosopher as missionary, or as Pygmalion to an exotic Galatea, bringing the gifts of grace and civilisation to some half-formed being. Indeed, a renewed interest in the conflation of nature's secrets, the exotic and the marvellous was part of a new sensibility that emerged in polite society during the seventeenth century. It was closely allied with active participation in natural philosophy and its sub-disciplines.[24]

The musical implications of this emphasis on intellectual virtuosity, on this clever transformation of nature into novelty, were remarkably varied. Naturalist-music theorists like the English country parson Charles Butler could elevate the summery sound of bees at work into witty art-songs.[25] John Playford goes beyond the older Renaissance convention of simply citing Classical references to the powers of music over wild creatures when he adds his own witness of the use of bagpipe and violin to herd stags from Yorkshire to Hampton Court. For Playford, these swift and elegant beasts are no longer mere symbols of the velocity of sound. The animals represented are not ancient dolphins from some distant sea come to the aid of some long-dead musician. Instead, owing to the increasingly important authority of personal observation, they have become manageable modern resources under clever musical control.[26] The talented animal husbandman could go even further and form a musical consort of the dogs that assisted him in the favoured blood-sport against undomesticated Nature. In building a company of hunting-hounds, Gervase Markham suggests that

[23] Hugh Platt, *The Jewel House of Art and Nature* (London: Elizabeth Alsop, 1653), sig. A2ᵛ. With particular reference to music, theorist-composer Thomas Ravenscroft considers that nature plus reason constitute 'the soule of all *Arts*', *A Briefe Discourse*, sig. A2ᵛ. See also Dubois, 'Subjected Bodies', pp. 175–81; Merchant, *The Death of Nature*, pp. 192–3; and Thomas, *Man and the Natural World*, p. 25.

[24] See Certeau, *The Writing of History*, pp. 219–20; Eamon, *Science and the Secrets of Nature*, p. 301; and Hooper-Greenhill, *Museums and the Shaping of Knowledge*, pp. 89–90.

[25] See my 'Nature, Culture, Myth and the Musician', pp. 9–18; Charles Butler, *The Feminine Monarchie or the History of Bees* (London: John Haviland for Roger Jackson, 1623), sigs. K4ᵛ–K6; Nan Cooke Carpenter, 'Charles Butler and the Bees' Madrigal', *Notes and Queries* n.s. 2 (1955), 103–6; Gerald R. Hayes, 'Charles Butler and the Music of the Bees', *The Musical Times* 66 (1 June 1925), 512–15; and James Pruett, 'Charles Butler – Musician, Grammarian, Apiarist', *The Musical Quarterly* 49 (1963), 499–500.

[26] Playford, *An Introduction to the Skill of Musick*, sig. A5ᵛ. For more traditional music-theoretical approaches to the powers of music over the animal kingdom, see Case, *Apologia musices*, pp. 2–3 and 24–5, and Anon., *The Praise of Musicke*, pp. 46–7. For information about the symbolic use of the stag in musical imagery, see Leppert, 'Music, Representation, and Social Order in Early-Modern Europe', 53–4, and Winternitz, *Musical Instruments and Their Symbolism in Western Art*, p. 40.

the country gentleman should select them to form a three-part chorus of bass, countertenor and mean. 'If you would have your Kennel for sweetness of cry', he says, 'then you must compound it of some large dogs, that have deep solemn Mouths, and are swift in spending, which must as it were bear the base in the consort.'[27] He goes on to explain that

your Kennel thus composed of the swiftest Hounds, you shall nigh as you can, sort their mouths into three equal parts of Musick, that is to say, Base, Counter-tenor, and Mean . . . [O]f these three sorts of mouths, if your Kennel be (as near as you can) equally compounded, you shall find it most perfect and delectable: for though they have not the thunder and loundness of the great dogs, which may be compared to the high wind-Instruments, yet they have the tunable sweetness of the best compounded consorts; and sure a man may find as much Art and delight in a Lute, as in an Organ.[28]

As waning symbological epistemologies encountered the burgeoning machine metaphor, musical instruments, carefully crafted of natural materials and often rendered into precious artefacts, acquired renewed significance. The era of Mersenne and Praetorius and the rise of instrumental virtuosity was also the age of emblematics, and of collecting extraordinary specimens of every sort, natural and artificial. Early modern poetry, occult philosophy and emblematic traditions are full of images of plants and animals transfigured through great force and cunning into musical instruments of extraordinary power. Uniting several ancient traditions, this sublimation of once-living creatures into artefacts of passionate persuasion represented an ultimate triumph of human ingenuity over Nature. Only expert craftsmanship could realise and preserve the occult capabilities of the original materials, otherwise doomed to wither. Like later mythical cyborgs, organic materials were blended with mechanical art and cunning until the final product was superior to both, a tribute to its maker and its master. Any instrument with such artificially amplified natural capacities granted almost Orphic power to its performer.[29] The awakening of the dormant potentiality of natural objects in musical instruments was also sometimes cast in erotic terms, the feminine body ensouled by the manly touch, as in this riddle of a lute:

> A certain dead creature in mine armes I take,
> With her back to my bosome, great glee doth shee make.
> As thus I doe hold her she greatly doth cheere mee,

[27] G[ervase] Markham, *Country Contentments. Or, the Husbandmans Recreations*, 11th edn (London: George Sawbridge, 1675), p. 6.

[28] *Ibid.*, pp. 8–9. Live animals continued to be used for musical entertainment well into the eighteenth century, sometimes with what would today be considered great cruelty; see Thomas L. Hankins and Robert J. Silverman, *Instruments and Imagination* (Princeton: Princeton University Press, 1995), pp. 77–8.

[29] See my 'The Siren, the Muse and the God of Love: Music in Seventeenth-Century English Emblem Books', *Journal of Musicological Research* 18 (1999), 110–12; Robert Heath, *Clarastella* (London: Humph[rey] Moseley, 1650), pp. 19–20; John Hollander, *The Untuning of the Sky: Ideas of Music in English Poetry 1500–1700* (Princeton: Princeton University Press, 1961), pp. 167, 301 and 311–13; Merchant, *The Death of Nature*, p. 193; and della Porta, *Natural Magick*, p. 403.

And wel are they pleasèd, that see me and heare me.
While erst it remaynèd in forest and field,
It silent remayning, no speech forth did yeeld.
But since she of life, by death was deprived,
With language she speaketh mens sprites are revived.[30]

The domesticated fruits, flowers, exotic birds and idealised pastoral scenes on the sound-boards and lids of keyboard instruments may suggest a similar transference of the metaphysical power, as well as the healing capacities and encoded moral lessons, of the objects represented. The careful craftsmanship of such exquisite instruments as the London maker Thomas White's 1642 virginals (Illus. 2.3) may therefore reinforce not only the owner-performer's social status, but the re-channelling of hidden power and control of the natural world through music.[31]

Such ideas did not belong exclusively to poetic wit or an increasingly outmoded science of linked networks and never-ending mutual reflection of symbol and symbolised. The continuity between natural magic and natural science in the early modern era has been considered most evident in the treatment of instruments. Nowhere is this more true than with musical instruments at the flexible boundary between natural philosophy, musical performance and music theory.[32] Thomas Mace's comprehensive musical treatise of 1676, *Musicks Monument*, refers repeatedly to 'revealing the *Occult and Hidden Secrets* of the *Lute*' to would-be performers of the instrument.[33] Mace links the discourses of nature and human words to the mysteries of divine language in a hierarchical chain rising through 'the language of LUTE's Mysterie'.[34] In spite of such locutions, this is no mystical tract or even a book of practical Renaissance magic, but 'A Remembrancer Of the Best Practical Musick', full of the most pragmatic lessons for composer and performer. Following a natural philosophical trend away from the older methods of natural magic, the work is

[30] Humfrey Gifford, *A Posie of Gillowflowers* (London: John Perin, 1580), 'Riddles ensuing, translated out of Italian verse', fol. 76ᵛ. As late as the nineteenth century poetic images of making musical instruments drew on such ancient allegories of the mastery of nature and sadistic male triumph over gentle femininity to bend, gut, re-shape and render passive living natural objects for musical purposes; see John Fletcher, 'Poetry, Gender, and Primal Fantasy', in *Formations of Fantasy*, ed. Victor Burgin, James Donald and Cora Kaplan (London and New York: Routledge, 1986), pp. 126–9.

[31] This particular instrument, whose form of decoration is not uncommon, is described in Howard Schott, *Catalogue of Musical Instruments in the Victoria and Albert Museum, Part I: Keyboard Instruments* (London), pp. 59–61. For further information about decorated keyboard instruments against the background of early modern ideas about music, see my 'Musical Treatments for Lovesickness: The Early Modern Heritage', in *A History of Music Therapies from Antiquity*, ed. Peregrine Horden (Aldershot: Ashgate Publishing, 2000), pp. 232–7; Thomas McGeary, 'Harpsichord Decoration – A Reflection of Renaissance Ideas About Music', *Explorations in Renaissance Culture* 6 (1980), 5–6; and Grant O'Brien, *Ruckers: A Harpsichord and Virginal Building Tradition* (Cambridge: Cambridge University Press, 1990), pp. 145–6.

[32] See Gouk, 'Some English Theories of Hearing', p. 95, 'Performance Practice', p. 258, 'Speculative and Practical Music', pp. 199–205; and Hankins and Silverman, *Instruments and the Imagination*, pp. 4–5. One of the fundamental qualities of seventeenth-century thought of all sorts was a non-visibility of meaning; see Certeau, *The Writing of History*, pp. 134–5.

[33] Mace, *Musicks Monument*, sig. A2ᵛ, pp. 37, 40 and 231. [34] *Ibid.*, pp. 37–8.

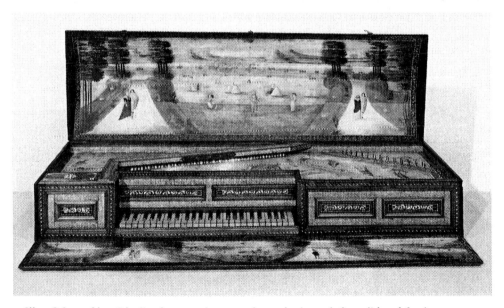

Illus. 2.3a and b   Idealised pastoral scene of couples in park from lid and further nature-inspired decorations from soundboard of 1642 virginals made by Thomas White of London, Victoria and Albert Museum keyboard catalogue no. W11-1933

founded on hands-on processes of demystification through the meticulous separation of signifier and signified, and the use of instruments.[35] In this case, its goals and its instruments are musical. The book's title page proclaims, in the best fusion of the era's shifting occult and scientific languages, that 'the Second PART treats of the *Noble Lute*, (the *Best* of *Instruments*) now made *Easie* and all Its Occult-Lock'd-up-secrets Plainly laid Open, never before Discovered'. To buy Mace's book and learn his music and his method was to embark on a bold voyage to an infinitely persuasive music, founded on the mastery of an artificial object and a hidden language, resonant with traces of the natural and the divine disclosed.

The increasing fascination with musical instruments and their technical capacities throughout the seventeenth century clearly belongs to a more general admiration for artificial means to extend human physical abilities and thus improve on nature.[36] From the early modern era onward, the relationship of Westerners to nature has become progressively alienated through escalating technological domination.[37] Cesare Ripa, whose internationally circulating compendium of symbolic imagery offers unparalleled insight into the era's ways of conceptualising, personifies Art as a green-gowned woman who holds the simple tools by which nature can be imitated and improved.[38] In the same well-informed vision, Artifice becomes a machine-using man in a richly embroidered garment, on the grounds that the engines contrived by industry have performed such incredible things as perpetual motion. Yet this conception remains incomplete without the beehive beside the clever gentleman. It serves as a reminder of the diligence and great achievement of nature's inconsequential little engineers, next to those of God's favoured sons.[39]

Early modern culture continually placed art and nature in similar oscillation, either in competition or in partnership.[40] The two were brought together repeatedly in music, as we have already seen in references to the general debt which music owed to nature. Because the discipline was both an art and a science the relationship was particularly complex. Music lacked the empirical foundation of the other natural sciences, and its primary effect on the listening body was to delight the senses and hence move the passions.[41] The nature of music, like the music of nature, thus remained nebulously powerful in an era increasingly obsessed with delimitation and control. Charles Butler, champion of church music and of the human capacity to improve on apian musical industriousness, is quick to emphasise that 'the Voice, which is the woork of Nature, dooth far exceede all these woorks of Art [which are musical instruments]'.[42] However, he addresses the king of England by explaining that

[35] See Eamon, *Science and the Secrets of Nature*, pp. 316–18; Hankins and Silverman, *Instruments and the Imagination*, pp. 8–9, and Vickers, 'Analogy Versus Identity', pp. 106–10.
[36] See Eamon, *Science and the Secrets of Nature*, p. 310; Gouk, 'Performance Practice', p. 258; Gouk, 'Horological, Mathematical and Musical Instruments', pp. 389–92; and Hankins and Silverman, *Instruments and the Imagination*, pp. 4–6.
[37] See Haraway, *Simians, Cyborgs, and Women*, p. 22, and Merchant, *The Death of Nature*, p. 193.
[38] Ripa, *Della Novissima Iconologia*, pp. 50–2, and Ripa, *Iconologia*, fol. 7.
[39] Ripa, *Della Novissima Iconologia*, p. 52, and Ripa, *Iconologia*, fol. 7.
[40] Hooper-Greenhill, *Museums and the Shaping of Knowledge*, p. 90.
[41] See Cohen, *Quantifying Music*, p. 253, and Gouk, 'Performance Practice', pp. 285–6.
[42] Butler, *The Principles of Musik*, p. 95.

meerly to Speak and to Sing, ar of Nature . . . but to speak well, and to sing well ar of art: so that among the best Wits of the moste civilised people, none may attain unto perfection in either facultie, without the Rules and Precepts of Art, confirmed by the practice of approoved Authors.[43]

Thus, for Butler, it is rules, precepts and prior authority that enable the improvement of nature through musical art. Mere nature, uncontrolled and unperfected, is common, barbarous, witless and implicitly un-English in an era marked by rising xenophobia. Thomas Ravenscroft likewise remarks that sounds made by voices are natural, whereas those produced by instruments are artificial. Yet both are ordered in music by time and by pitch.[44] Thomas Mace, perhaps seventeenth-century England's greatest defender and de-mystifier of instrumental technique, reminds his readers that such inventions as musical instruments were ultimately signs of divine wisdom, becoming, by implication, God's creatures in the natural order, meant for man's wise use.[45]

The quintessential seventeenth-century English image of the relationship between music, artifice and nature in a world wrought by the divine remains Robert Fludd's. Although the occult philosopher and physician Fludd is usually positioned outside the intellectual mainstreams of natural philosophy, early science and music theory, his contributions to each make use of widely circulating material. His massive history of the cosmos is deeply informed by the triplicate Boethian division of music into its universal, human and practical components. For him, the art largely remains within the realm of mysticism, tied closely to divinity and to the waning occult sciences of alchemy and numerology. Music is considered as much symbol as sound. All forms, audible as well as arcane, ultimately arose from the primordial unison of creation that gave rise to all sorts of harmony.[46]

The first and most comprehensive of the graphic schemes that dominate the treatise includes music and some familiar images as part of 'The Mirror of All Nature and the Image of Art' (Illus. 2.4). Here, we see the entire sublunary world laid out beneath the shining presence of God, signified by an anthropomorphic hand extending from a cloud-blocked radiance labelled with the Hebrew letters JHWH. The divine Creator is thus omnipresent and all-powerful, but inscrutable to mortal lines of sight. Following Fludd's accompanying Latin description, the eye is brought most directly to the figure of Nature, the very embodiment of the 'most fair and fruitful body' of Platt's later description. Visually, she is the most prominent object in the representation of occult and evident properties. This exquisite naked virgin, with the true sun on her breast and the moon on her belly is, Fludd explains, no goddess, but the proximate minister of God over the subcelestial world.[47] Like Ripa's Nature, her full

[43] *Ibid.*, sigs. Q2–Q2ᵛ. John Playford later paraphrases this sentence in *An Introduction to the Skill of Musick*, sig. A3. [44] Ravenscroft, *A Briefe Discourse*, sigs. B–Bᵛ. [45] Mace, *Musicks Monument*, p. 231.

[46] See Ammann, 'The Musical Theory and Philosophy of Robert Fludd', 202–9; Robert Fludd [Robertus Fluctibus], *Utriusque Cosmi Majoris scilicet et Minoris Metaphysica, Physica atque Technica Historia* (Oppenheim: Johann-Theodore de Bry, 1617), tractatus 1, pp. 79–106 and tractatus 2, pp. 160–243; and Joscelyn Godwin, 'Robert Fludd on the Lute and Pandora', *Lute Society Journal* 15 (1973), 11–12.

[47] Fludd, *Utriusque Cosmi . . . Historia*, tractatus 1, pp. 7–8.

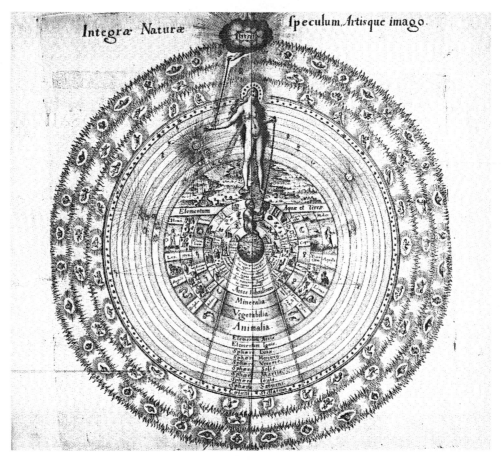

Illus. 2.4   Nature as proximate minister of God over the sub-celestial world, further assisted by the Ape of Nature who is called Art, who imitates her and produces things resembling hers, including music. 'Integrae Naturae speculum Artisque imago' or the 'Mirror of All Nature and Image of Art' from Robert Fludd, *Utriusque Cosmi Majoris scilicet et Minoris Metaphysica, Physica atque Technica Historia* (Oppenheim: Johann-Theodore de Bry, 1617)

breasts lactate as she nourishes all lower creatures, and she is rooted to the firm and watery earth. In this case, her milk lights the stars and planets from her heart, and she stands on contrasting elements in a graphic alchemical image.[48] Fludd's beauteous Nature needs no vulture of corruption, for she is tied to God and to art as an embodiment of creativity and nurturance. Just as a chain about her right wrist links her to the deity who so obviously animates her limbs, she has, says the author, an assistant who imitates her and produces things resembling hers. It is the Ape of Nature whom we call Art. This simian mimic has arisen from human ingenuity, and ultimately works through the divine with earthly materials. The industrious creature, who measures

[48] *Ibid.*

46

with a compass a tiny simulacrum of the terrestrial globe on which she crouches, holds dominion over four realms of improvement on nature: the liberal arts, including music, engineering and mathematics; art supplanting Nature in the animal realm; art assisting Nature in the vegetable realm, and art correcting Nature in the mineral realm.[49] Thus is Nature controlled from above and perfected from below in a linked hierarchy.

The music-theoretical treatise included within the second tract of the philosopher's cosmic history is ultimately rather pedestrian, part of a natural philosophy that found a place for the discipline. The author uses his own words and conceptual schemata to outline an old-fashioned history and terminological etymology of music, and the basic considerations of sound, intervals, scales, notation, rhythm, instruments and composition. None of Fludd's information would be particularly useful to the scholar or performer who did not already have some passing acquaintance with the art and science of music. Indeed, the seven 'books' on music as liberal art, dedicated to Fludd's student of music theory, the Marquis de Orizon, Visconte de Cadenet, serve more as novel *aides-mémoire* for the informed practitioner than anything else;[50] even the authorities cited are the most common: Plato, Aristotle, Boethius, Guido of Arezzo and Marsilio Ficino. Perhaps most interestingly, however, the author devotes space to mechanical and automatic instruments, some fantasies of his own invention in an age increasingly concerned with engines to simplify tasks and alter natural forces.[51]

Over half a century later, Thomas Salmon's highly controversial *Essay to the Advancement of Musick* begins with a remarkably similar frontispiece, itself subject to the derogatory accusation of lurid advertising by John Playford (Illus. 2.5).[52] Here, the occultised hand of the Creator freely proffers an image of concord in form of Salmon's proposed universal system of musical notation, and discord as a set of

---

[49] *Ibid.*, p. 8.

[50] Ammann, 'The Musical Theory and Philosophy of Robert Fludd', 205–6, and Fludd, *Utriusque Cosmi . . . Historia*, tractatus 2, part II, pp. 160–243. See also Joscelyn Godwin, 'Instruments in Robert Fludd's *Utriusque Cosmi . . . Historia*', *Galpin Society Journal* 26 (1973), 2 and 12, and 'Robert Fludd on the Lute and Pandora', 12.

[51] Fludd, *Utriusque Cosmi . . . Historia*, tractatus 2 pars II, pp. 160–243. See also Ammann, 'The Musical Theory and Philosophy of Robert Fludd', 206; Godwin, 'Instruments in Robert Fludd's *Utriusque Cosmi . . . Historia*', 2–14; and 'Robert Fludd on the Lute and Pandora', 13–19.

[52] John Playford, 'To Thomas Salmon, M.A. of Trinity College, Oxon. Author of the *Essay to the Advancement of Musick*', in Matthew Locke, *The Present Practice of Musick Vindicated Against the Exceptions and New Way of Attaining Musick* (London: N. Brooke and J. Playford, 1673), pp. 77–8, and Thomas Salmon, *An Essay To the Advancement of Musick* (London: J. Macock, 1672). Salmon's highly derided proposal to modify musical notation for universal use is best understood against the background of a more general attempt in late seventeenth-century England to develop a universal 'rational' language for intellectual and philosophical discourse; see Hooper-Greenhill, *Museums and the Shaping of Knowledge*, pp. 145–57; Kassler and Oldroyd, 'Hook's "Musick Scripts"', pp. 579–81; Robert E. Lawrence, 'Science, Lute Tablature, and Universal Languages: Thomas Salmon's *Essay to the Advancement of Musick* (1672)', *Journal of the Lute Society of America* 26–7 (1993–4), 60–7; Ruff, 'The Social Significance of the Seventeenth-Century English Music Treatises', 418; and Salmon, *An Essay to the Advancement of Musick*, pp. 11–70.

Illus. 2.5   Frontispiece from Thomas Salmon, M. A., *An Essay To the Advancement of Musick* (London: J. Macock, 1672), presenting the theorist's innovations in notation as the ultimate concord, and borrowing from stock images of divinely conceived music and its earthly realisation through Dame Nature

conventional notes and clefs. Closest to the extended wrist lies a tidy image of nature controlled, in form of a fountain and orderly tree-lined garden in geometric rows. Gone are zodiacal radiances beyond the bounds of Earth. Gone are traces of arcane studies. Gone are cruel chains and lively simian. Yet opposite the deity and his divine harmony sits the evident recipient and facilitator of his concord, Dame Nature metamorphosed into a decorous Lady Music with her most ordered instruments. The wild wood behind her, full of dark shadows and the raw materials for her collection of bowed and plucked strings, could scarcely contrast more with the bright, husbanded plot of land and orderly mansion on the side of God. This is no mystical alchemical map, no exposé, of the progress of artifice. Yet the message remains much the same. Under divine command and the primordial sound of order from which the creative world issued, the embodied liberal art still brings order to an unruly natural world. Implicitly, the consumer of the book, converted to Salmon's theories, will possess similar power and know the true notated language of music.

Francis Bacon, the other English natural philosopher of the era who deals significantly with music in a general work, could hardly contrast more. Stereotypically considered the father of English scientific methodology, he was far more concerned with experience, probability and degrees of certitude than with the intellectual inheritance of an emblematic world-view. His philosophy of nature embraced direct involvement with the physical world in place of irreproducible metaphysics. Understanding was largely based on empirical data gathered directly from sources evident in a passive and rather effeminate Nature.[53] 'Another Error hath proceeded from too great a reverence, and a kind of adoration of the minde and understanding of man', he says in a diatribe against blind acceptance of received textual wisdom, 'by meanes whereof, men have withdrawne themselves too much from contemplation of Nature, and the observations of experience: and have tumbled up and downe in their owne reason and conceits.'[54] Although he remained indebted to the aspects of natural magic that emphasised discovery of nature's secrets through induction and manipulation, he was famously opposed to the arcane concerns and methodologies that infuse virtually everything that Fludd and many others wrote. Philosophical speculation was anathema to Francis Bacon. The natural world had not been encoded in a divine language for human decryption, and symbolic networks of correspondence were worthless human fancies. 'But as in the inquirie of the divine truth', he says with particular reference to those who clung to Scholastic methodologies,

their pride enclined to leave the Oracle of Gods word, and to vanish in the mixture of their owne inventions: so in the inquisition of Nature, they ever left the Oracle of Gods works, and

[53] See Ashworth, 'Natural History and the Emblematic World View', pp. 323–5; John O. Leary, *Francis Bacon and the Politics of Science* (Ames: Iowa State University Press, 1994), pp. 151–2; Merchant, *The Death of Nature*, pp. 164–91; Shapiro, *Probability and Certainty*, pp. 15–73; and Michael R. G. Spiller, *'Concerning Natural Experimental Philosophie': Meric Casaubon and the Royal Society* (The Hague, Boston and London: Martinus Nijhoff, 1980), pp. 39–44.

[54] Bacon, *The Twoo Bookes of the Proficiencie and Advancement of Learning* (London: Henrie Tomes, 1605), fol. 25.

49

adored the deceiving and deformed Images, which the unequall mirrour of their owne minds, or a few received Authors or principles, did represent unto them.[55]

For Bacon, intellectual curiosity was vital, and Nature's deepest secrets could be unlocked by keen observation and a consequent understanding of its fundamental principles. This was as true for music as for any other field of natural philosophy.

Bacon was the first English natural philosopher of his era to outline a proposal for the study of sound and its properties, with emphasis on music. In the second and third centuries of his *Sylva Sylvarum*, a heterogeneous work intended to demonstrate the method of compiling natural histories, he is uninterested in the mythic origins, notational schemes, general rules of composition, or civil uses of music which concerned many other theorists of the era. These music-theoretical sections of his template for further study are dominated by a sense of physical experimentation that is closer to acoustical science than to performance practice. They are also infused with the same ramshackle exuberance and indiscriminate collecting of information that pervades much of his more famous work. 'Musick in the *Practice*, hath bin well persued; and in good Variety', he explains at the beginning of the second century,

But in the *Theory*, and especially in the *Yeelding* of the *Causes* of the *Practique*, very weakly; Being reduced into certain Mysticall Subtilties, of no use, and not much Truth. We shall therefore, after our manner, joyne the Contemplative and Active Part together.[56]

Bacon proceeds to present an almost indiscriminate mass of information with great enthusiasm, featuring demonstrable observations and experimental approaches to music and more general acoustics; all are designed to be logically deductible and reproducible by a curious and musically literate reader. He also offers the modern scholar, if not the seventeenth-century gentleman practitioner of music, insight into what sorts of sounds were considered pleasing and which most moving to the passions, and explains the aesthetics of various consonances, dissonances, cadential formulae and combinations of instruments in consort. He is equally concerned with judgement, physical effect and the nature of sound, instrumental and vocal; human, animal and machine. Like others of his era, his general fascination with instruments which extend human capacities and which mediate between the objective external world and the subjective mind extends to musical ones. Much of his approach is synaesthetic and requires extrapolation between the senses of vision, touch and hearing. This is not a manual for the would-be composer or performer, but a sourcebook for the curious investigator of physical phenomena who also happens to be a musician

[55] Bacon, *Advancement of Learning*, fol. 21. See Ashworth, 'Natural History and the Emblematic World View', pp. 322–3; Eamon, *Science and the Secrets of Nature*, pp. 310–16; Leary, *Bacon and the Politics of Science*, p. 151; Paolo Rossi, *Bacon: From Magic to Science*, trans. Sacha Rabinovitch (Chicago: University of Chicago Press, 1968), pp. 9 and 12–14; and Charles Whitney, *Francis Bacon and Modernity* (New Haven and London: Yale University Press, 1986), pp. 86–7.

[56] Francis Bacon, *Sylva Sylvarum or a Naturall History*, 2nd edn (London: W. Lee, 1629), p. 35; Gouk, 'Music in Francis Bacon's Natural Philosophy', p. 139, and 'Some English Theories of Hearing', pp. 96–9 and 112; Hunter, *Science and Society*, pp. 17–18; and Lawrence, 'Salmon's *Essay to the Advancement of Musick* (1672)', 61–3.

50

with access to a variety of instruments.[57] Like Fludd and other natural philosophers who incorporate music theory, he presumes membership in a class of amateur instrumental performers and previous acquaintance with the intellectual precepts of the discipline. But beneath Bacon's concerns lies the fundamental principle that man operates on nature to create something new and artificial, evident in much of his work as it is among even his most methodologically distant contemporaries.[58]

Such contrasting considerations of the flexible linkage between art and nature in music intersected yet another early modern intellectual impulse. The concern with exemplariness and with categorical division between ordinary and extraordinary that marks such a range of natural philosophical and musical treatises belonged to a wider set of trends that ultimately contributed to the birth of the museum, the rise of anthropology and the foundation of scientific collecting of fact and artefact.[59] From the mid-sixteenth century and throughout the seventeenth, the concepts of both natural wonders and artistic wondrousness became powerful cultural forces. On the border between occult and scientific worldviews, when the greatest rarities of nature were endowed with contrasting signification and man-made marvels helped to guarantee several forms of communication between the visible and invisible worlds, wonder was considered the first passion of the soul.[60] The Aristotelian discourse of wonder became if anything more influential within a set of intellectual systems based on a taste for the metamorphic and on fluid boundaries between various worlds of experience and their elements.[61] As ancient evidence of miracles was disenchanted and carried from the church in the aftermath of the Reformation, and as exotic materials began to reach Europe in greater quantity from distant parts of the globe, there developed a climate in which specific collections for wonder and further investigation could flourish. Even as Bacon called for assembling the irregularities of nature and early scientific societies sought practical information from similar things, antiquarians and transcendentalists contemplated other rarities for their own purposes. In the brief historical moment between the iron rule of the church and the

[57] Bacon, *Sylva Sylvarum*, pp. 35–75; Gouk, 'Music in Francis Bacon's Natural Philosophy', pp. 140–5; and Hankins and Silverman, *Instruments and the Imagination*, pp. 10–11.

[58] See Merchant, *The Death of Nature*, p. 171.

[59] See Tony Bennett, *The Birth of the Museum: History, Theory, Politics* (London and New York: Routledge, 1995), pp. 94–7, and Margaret T. Hodgen, *Early Anthropology in the Sixteenth and Seventeenth Centuries* (Philadelphia: University of Pennsylvania Press, 1964), pp. 129–54.

[60] See Bennett, *The Birth of the Museum*, pp. 95–6; Jean Céard, *La Nature et les prodiges: l'insolite au XVIe siècle, en France* (Geneva: Librairie Droz, 1977), pp. x–xii; and James V. Mirollo, 'The Aesthetics of the Marvelous: The Wondrous Work of Art in a Wondrous World', in *The Age of the Marvelous*, ed. Joy Kenseth (Hanover, NH: Hood Museum of Art, Dartmouth College, 1991), p. 69.

[61] See Bennett, *The Birth of the Museum*, pp. 40–1; Céard, *La Nature et les prodiges*, pp. 115–18 and 220–1; Lorraine Daston and Katharine Park, *Wonders and the Order of Nature 1150–1750* (New York: Zone Books, 1998), pp. 276–301; Eamon, *Science and the Secrets of Nature*, pp. 301–2 and 315; Hooper-Greenhill, *Museums and the Shaping of Knowledge*, pp. 120–2; Mirollo, 'The Aesthetics of the Marvelous', pp. 63–9, and *The Poet of the Marvelous: Giambattista Marino* (New York and London: Columbia University Press, 1963), pp. 117–18; Krzystof Pomian, *Collectors and Curiosities: Paris and Venice, 1500–1800*, trans. Elizabeth Wiles-Portier (Cambridge: Polity Press, 1990), pp. 20–5; and Roland Schaer, *L'Invention des musées* (Paris: Gallimard, 1993), pp. 21–7.

dominion of modern science, unbridled curiosity in all of its contradictory forms could hold sway.[62]

Many thinkers were especially fascinated by improbable commerce between the traditionally opposite shores of art and nature. This had long been possible through the tools of language, as in fables of musical instruments which expressed their arcane natural power only after craftsmanship. But for the later Renaissance and Baroque, an age of physical and metaphysical exploration of uncharted territory, tangible objects from somewhere between the commonplace and the miraculous took on new significance. Even now, such items become increasingly desired and ultimately fetishised as they are distanced from ordinary use and placed into collections.[63] It was a short step from picturing the world in diagrams, as does Fludd, to seeing the same correspondences between meaningful things, or from re-thinking the use of objects to possessing and categorising them. The gleaming shell from a distant sea became a goblet, the tusks of giant beasts transformed to filigree, and other metamorphic unities of art and nature were particularly prized.[64] These things spoke to many forms of experience, and whispered of unseen marvels just beyond phenomenological understanding. 'Within the development of culture under an exchange economy, the search for authentic experience and, correlatively, the search for the authentic object become critical', says Susan Stewart in her study of the collecting impulse,

As experience is increasingly mediated and abstracted, the lived relation of the body to the phenomenological world is replaced by a nostalgic myth of contact and presence. 'Authentic' experience becomes both elusive and allusive as it is placed beyond the horizon of present lived experience, the beyond in which the antique, the pastoral, the exotic, and other figurative domains are articulated. In this process of distance, the memory of the body is replaced by the memory of the object, a memory standing outside the self and thus representing both a surplus and lack of significance. The experience of the object lies outside the body's experience – it is saturated with meanings that will never be fully revealed to us.[65]

Nowhere has this been more true than in the West as the Renaissance dissolved into modernity through extraordinary experience and signs upon signs.

[62] See Daston and Park, *Wonders and the Order of Nature*, pp. 159–60; Eamon, *Science and the Secrets of Nature*, p. 314; Hodgen, *Early Anthropology*, pp. 111–15; Joy Kenseth, 'A World of Wonders in One Closet Shut', in *The Age of the Marvelous*, pp. 83–8; Arthur MacGregor, 'Collectors and Collections of Rarities in the Sixteenth and Seventeenth Centuries', in *Tradescant's Rarities: Essays on the Foundation of the Ashmolean Museum 1683*, ed. MacGregor (Oxford: Clarendon Press, 1983), pp. 70–1; Steven Mullaney, *The Place of the Stage: License, Play and Power in Renaissance England* (Chicago and London: University of Chicago Press, 1988), pp. 61–2; Pomian, *Collectors and Curiosities*, pp. 37–40 and 64; and Francis Henry Taylor, *The Taste of Angels: A History of Art Collecting from Rameses to Napoleon* (Boston: Little, Brown and Company, 1948), pp. 410–17.
[63] Susan Stewart, *On Longing: Narratives of the Miniature, the Gigantic, the Souvenir, the Collection* (Baltimore and London: Johns Hopkins University Press, 1984), pp. 163–4.
[64] See Daston and Park, *Wonders and the Order of Nature*, pp. 260–1 and 276–7; Eamon, *Science and the Secrets of Nature*, pp. 314–15; Hooper-Greenhill, *Museums and the Shaping of Knowledge*, pp. 101–4, 109–10 and 145; and Pomian, *Collectors and Curiosities*, pp. 26–8.
[65] Stewart, *On Longing*, p. 133. See also pp. 132–6 and 139–45.

Perhaps the dominant manifestation of this early modern culture of collecting was the *Kunst-* or *Wunderkammer*, a private place of marvels, of contemplation, of meditation. A hotchpotch of artefacts that often spoke of its owner's social or political position as well as his ways of conceiving the world, the cabinet of curiosities was meant to represent and reflect all forms of amazing workmanship in a universe comprised of art and nature but still governed by an almighty God.[66] The arrangement and content of these private places of retreat was as variable as their collectors from one end of Europe to the other. Sometimes naturalia and artificialia were separately categorised, sometimes painting and sculpture were set apart from other things. Instruments, including musical ones, were at times mixed in and at others given their own classification. For they were at once rare marvels and mere tools to produce earthly works, things with which to extend the imagination or to replicate and study sensory phenomena.[67] In fact, it is in the significant representation of such collections, visually and in text, that the place of music within this cultural discourse of wonder becomes most evident.

The excesses of the genre and of the habit of assembling significant objects are particularly well expressed in Jan Brueghel's *Allegory of Hearing* (Illus. 2.6). The image at once invites the viewer into a private chamber to ogle the collector's opulent possessions, and to consider the allegorical significance of each object and the sum total. Thrown together indiscriminately are glorious objects of art and nature, from exotic tropical birds to expansive paintings of ancient fables, from hunting horns discarded on the floor to clocks shelved with pride of place. In spite of evidently random arrangement, all are categorised tidily for the eye to scan, and each group

[66] For further information on this massive topic, see Bennett, *The Birth of the Museum*, pp. 92–3; Daston and Park, *Wonders and the Order of Nature*, pp. 149–59 and 260–301; Hodgen, *Early Anthropology*, pp. 116–31; Hooper-Greenhill, *Museums and the Shaping of Knowledge*, pp. 64 and 78–132; Kauffman, *The Mastery of Nature*, pp. 174–84; Kenseth, 'A World of Wonders in One Closet Shut', pp. 84–6; Mullaney, *The Place of the Stage*, pp. 61–4; Pomian, *Collectors and Curiosities*, pp. 77–8; Schaer, *L'Invention des musées*, pp. 21–7; Stewart, *On Longing*, pp. 148 and 161; and Taylor, *The Taste of Angels*, pp. 185–270.

[67] See Franz Adrian Dreier, 'The *Kunstkammer* of Hessian Landgraves in Kassel', in *The Origins of Museums: The Cabinet of Curiosities in Sixteenth- and Seventeenth-Century Europe*, ed. Oliver Impey and Arthur MacGregor (Oxford: Clarendon Press, 1985), p. 106; Hooper-Greenhill, *Museums and the Shaping of Knowledge*, pp. 123–5; Gouk, 'Horological, Mathematical and Musical Instruments', pp. 387 and 399; Hankins, *Instruments and the Imagination*, p. 6; Kenseth, 'A World of Wonders in One Closet Shut', pp. 81–2 and 93; MacGregor, 'Collectors and Collections of Rarities', pp. 71–3 and 78–9; Joachim Menzhausen, 'Elector Augustus's *Kunstkammer*: An Analysis of the Inventory of 1587', in *The Origins of Museums*, p. 74; Mirollo, 'The Aesthetics of the Marvelous', pp. 61–2; and Lorenz Seelig, 'The Munich *Kunstkammer*', in *The Origins of Museums*, p. 83. For particular reference to musical instruments and the myriad classification schemes for including or excluding them, see Gouk, 'Horological, Mathematical, and Musical Instruments', pp. 387 and 397–8; Impey and MacGregor (eds.), *The Origins of Museums*, pp. 14, 26, 34, 49, 63, 65, 93 and 107; Pomian, *Collectors and Curiosities*, pp. 45–49; and Gottfried von Bülow (ed. and trans.), 'Diary of the Journey of Philip Julius, Duke of Stettin-Pomerania, Through England in the Year 1602', *Transactions of the Royal Historical Society* n.s. 6 (1892), 26–7. Several collectors included non-Western musical instruments as part of ethnographical or geographical collections; see Impey and MacGregor (eds.), *The Origins of Museums*, pp. 118, 131, 148, 234, 246 and 248.

Illus. 2.6 Jan Brueghel, *Allegory of Hearing*, presenting grouped assemblages of significant musical and related natural objects with stock allegorical figures (Museo del Prado, Madrid)

evokes particular combinations of sound and sensory delight from art or nature. Slightly out of place is a tableau at the centre, a nude woman playing a lute to an entranced stag, a wingless *putto* and a crested cockatoo. Here, allegory and wonder merge seamlessly, resonant with many of the culture's ideas about music at the cusp of artifice and mundane marvel. The stag, ancient emblem and attribute of Musica, stands entranced by a performer who appears at once Musica and Natura, though she is often identified as Venus or Euterpe.[68] Like a fantastical combination of Nature and her Ape in an earthly sphere, this beautiful woman, so provocatively posed, draws together and renders useful to man all sorts of auditory wonder in objects to be collected, possessed and treasured. An actual seventeenth-century collection owned by the Paston family of Yarmouth is similarly displayed to impress the viewer and challenge the mind (Illus. 2.7). Painted by an unknown Dutch artist around 1665, the image was almost certainly commissioned by Sir Robert Paston, later Viscount Yarmouth and Earl of Yarmouth, to record some family treasures.[69] Here indeed are the curious, the rare and the wondrous, the blend of nature and artifice, of the familiar and the exotic. The musical instruments of the seventeenth-century English nobleman and patron of the arts are all present, jumbled randomly among scientific instruments and natural specimens, unplayed and unsounding. Little distance separates the whorls of a nautilus goblet from the rounded belly of a lute. Both become expensive consumer goods of polished natural materials, turned to functional artefacts for lordly delight.

Against this background, it becomes clear that the collector's impulse and the desire to display the wondrous and the unique are evident in music theory treatises. In an era still in transition between the primacy of auditory and visual media, these more specialised cultural texts have been overlooked as treasure-houses of the curious, the novel, the perfect, the miniaturised and the deliberately managed. In this tacit domain of liberal arts improving on nature, the emphasis is on demystifying the composer's and performer's arts for the lay student. As with other forms of cultural expression, virtuosity was possible only through display and mastery of the greatest marvels. In an age of collecting and categorising, of exposing hidden truths for human understanding, the theoretical tract came to intersect the anthology for middle-class consumers. As early as the turn of the century, theorists not only began to feature

---

[68] See Leppert, 'Music, Representation and Social Order in Early-Modern Europe', 53–4, and Winternitz, *Musical Instruments and Their Symbolism in Western Art*, p. 40. The embodiment of Armonia, too, was a female musician with Orphic power over the natural realm, so this image is especially complex through its lack of particular signifiers; see Ripa, *Della Novissima Iconologia*, p. 48. For information on the use of natural objects in conjunction with musical ones in visual contexts of eroticism (Venus), see Albert Pomme de Mirimonde, 'La Musique dans les allégories de l'Amour II – Eros', *Gazette des beaux-arts* 69 (1967), 327–8.

[69] See John Harris, 'Oh Happy Oxnead', *Country Life* 88 (5 June 1986), 1630–1; Andrew W. Moore, *Dutch and Flemish Painting in Norfolk: A History of Taste and Influence, Fashion and Collecting* (London: Her Majesty's Stationery Office, 1988), pp. 90–1; John Adey Repton, 'Inventory of Ornamental Plate, &c. Formerly at Oxnead Hall', *The Gentleman's Magazine* (1844), 23–4 and 150–3; and Robert Wenley, 'Robert Paston and *The Yarmouth Collection*', *Norfolk Archaeology* 41 (1991), 118–21.

Illus. 2.7   Unknown Dutch artist (c. 1665), *The Yarmouth Collection*, elevating an actual collection of the rare and the marvellous to allegorical status

outstanding full-length examples of styles and genres for the apt pupil to learn and emulate. They also incorporated ingenious wonders of the composer's art. Thomas Morley, for instance, not only includes numerous examples of the rules he outlines and pieces explicitly meant for practice in his *Plaine and Easie Introduction to Practicall Musicke* of 1597, he also features novelties to challenge and delight his reader.[70] We also see in these English treatises a particular fascination with order, control and the increasingly fluid boundary between art and nature. Elway Bevin especially unites these realms with a certain amount of allegory as he exemplifies the composition of canons with one particular marvel. 'This Canon hath a resemblance to the frame of this world', he explains as he introduces one of his models in a manner that would please any later impresario,

for as this world doth consist of the foure Elements, viz. Fire, Ayre, Water, and the Earth, and in either of them sundry living and moveable creatures: So likewise this Canon consisteth and is devided into four severall Canons, and to every one belongeth fifteene parts, a certaine number for an uncertaintie. The whole sixty parts are contained in these seven.[71]

Like the auditory equivalent of a diagram or collection designed to reflect the workmanship of the world, this piece recreates the universe in miniature, for proprietorship and delight. In contrast to a princely wonder-cabinet, the extraordinary position it reinforces for its possessor is one of intellectual, not social or political, dominance.

Thomas Ravenscroft's *Briefe Discourse Of the true (but neglected) use of Charact'ring the Degrees* of 1614 is the first theory treatise to devote fully half of its length to an assemblage of '*Harmonicall Examples*' which explicitly enable the reader 'to search for Richer and riper discoveries in this *Musicall Continent*', as if collecting rare treasures from an imaginary landscape.[72] These examples are neatly organised into five 'common *Recreations* that men take', with the explicit goal of disclosing the passions discovered in each, one by one in the manner of a scientific investigation. The first two, hunting and hawking, are concerned with human governance of the natural world for pleasure and profit. They involve imitation of natural sound and of the professional calls of hunters and hawkers. The final three, dancing, drinking and enamouring, are set up as miniature musical ethnographies, complete with dialect and evocations of distant and wondrous customs.[73] To buy such books was not only to learn the elements of

---

[70] Thomas Morley, *A Plaine and Easie Introduction to Practicall Musicke* (London: Peter Short, 1597), pp. 36–53 and 173–4.

[71] Elway Bevin, *A Briefe and Short Instruction of the Art of Musicke* (London: R. Young, 1631), p. 45. See also Christopher Simpson, *A Compendium of Practical Music Reprinted from the Second Edition of 1667*, ed. Phillip Lord (Oxford: Blackwell, 1970), p. 80. [72] Ravenscroft, *A Briefe Discourse*, sig. Q3.

[73] *Ibid.*, sigs. A2ᵛ–A3 and [Part II], pp. 1–20. Thomas Hobbes later emphasises that the effects on the passions by the senses, Ravenscroft's stated goal, are measurable by natural philosophy, *Humane Nature: or, the Fundamental Elements of Policie* (London: T. Newcomb for Fra[ncis] Bowman, 1650), pp. 6–19, and *Elements of Philosophy* (London: R. and W. Leybourn for Andrew Crooke, 1656), pp. 290–305. The same sort of impulse is used to a very different musical end in such pieces as Thomas Weelkes's 'Thule, the Period of Cosmography' and 'The Andalusian Merchant' from *Madrigals of 5. and 6. Parts* (London: Thomas Este for Thomas Morley, 1600), nos. 7 and 8.

composition and enhanced performance, but to possess ingenious wonders of the masters' art in a flat little cabinet of pages.

In the manner of some forms of collecting and of linking art to nature, there are also evocations of related fields and the indiscriminate jumble of objects of enquiry. The epistle of 'The Stationer to the Ingenious Reader' at the beginning of the English translation of Descartes's *Compendium musicae* emphasises that the complete musician must make his own all of the arts and sciences represented by the objects in Paston's collection, or in Fludd's diagrams. These are listed as for the reader's intellectual possession and personal mastery, if not display.[74] The gossamer shadow of Vanity or the impermanence of earthly creativity also overlays some of these works. Butler, for instance, explicitly mentions in his *Principles of Musik* that music, though 'alloued by God, [and] agreeable to Nature', like fine houses and gardens like golden treasures and worldly wisdom, is but a vanity.[75] Like all earthly things, it decays. But that stops him no more from outlining the rules of music for composers and performers than it does Fludd, or the artist who captured the Paston family treasures with an embedded lesson in transcendence.

Vis-à-vis the material aspects of theory treatises, Nature's voice is even stronger, and more strongly guided. Harmony, discord and the scales and keys of music are generally considered things of nature, which the competent musician may tidy up. Music theory, as part of natural philosophy or on its own, has always been concerned with grounds and rules for ordering material, giving proper names to sensory phenomena and harnessing a natural force for human delight. This became particularly meaningful to an era that witnessed increasing cultural obsession with these same points. 'Harmony', says William Holder in the English work that perhaps most carefully balances natural philosophy, music theory and the reflection of divinity, 'results from Practick Musick, and is made by the Natural and Artificial Agreement of different sounds . . . by which the Sense of Hearing is delighted.'[76] Earlier in the century, the naturalist-divine Butler had called upon the language of earthly and heavenly marvel to refer to harmony as 'a delightful congruiti of all the Partes of a Song among themselvs, throogh the Concordanc[e] of certain Intervalls, which God in Nature (not without a woonder) hath made to agree together'.[77] Butler further explains that the octave is an aspect of nature expressed through the simplest element of musical artifice, 'becaus there are in Nature but 7 distinct sounds, exprest in Musik, by 7 distinct Notes, in the 7 several Cliefs of the Scale'.[78] Bacon adds that the very intervals of that scale, with its particular sequences of tones and semitones, is received from nature and thus not a true intellectual computation. By examining data gathered from voice and lute he concludes 'that after every three whole *Notes* [tones]

[74] René Descartes, *Compendium of Musick* (London: Thomas Harper for Humphrey Moseley, 1653), sigs. A4–B^v. For two contrasting views, see Locke, *Musicke Vindicated*, pp. 14–15, and Salmon, *An Essay to the Advancement of Musick*, pp. 91–2. [75] Butler, *Principles of Musik*, p. 129.
[76] William Holder, *A Treatise of the Natural Grounds, and Principles of Harmony* (London: J. Heptinstall for J. Carr, B. Aylmer and L. Meredith, 1694), sig. B^v. [77] Butler, *Principles of Musik*, p. 46.
[78] *Ibid.*, p. 10.

Nature requireth, for all Harmonicall use, one *halfe Note* [semitone] to be interposed'.[79] Further along the same continuum, Morley explicates modulation to related tonal areas as a deep natural marvel. '[T]hough the ayre of everie key be different one from the other, yet some love (by a wonder of nature) to be joined to others', he concludes. Likewise, he compares 'going out of key' to an unnatural act: 'as much as to wrest a thing out of his nature, making the asse leape upon his maister and the Spaniel bear the load'.[80]

No large-scale work brings together more musical and cultural concerns with the shifting relationships between art, nature and the unseen in early modern England than Nicholas Brady and Henry Purcell's celebrated *Ode to St. Cecilia* of 1692. Written for a saint's festival for a people who had officially rejected the trappings of Catholicism some century and a half earlier, the piece and its occasion hover in the liminal spaces between the holy and the mundane. Its text likewise combines contemporary imagery with defunct epistemes subsumed by literary conceits. With the same blithe syncretism that had dominated English thought for close to two centuries, even the title saint seems to morph into shapes from distant narratives. The entirety is a typically representative product of a culture that delighted in interpretative mind play, in the multiplexity of signs and significances.

The definite association of St Cecilia with music was evidently a product of the high Renaissance. Before that time, she had been one of many virgin martyrs, and the sacred embodiments of music were a varied group of male saints and Old Testament figures. However, with the rise of the cult of the Virgin and coincidental growth of craft guilds, Cecilia filled a distinct need and took over the position of 'Musica' in the iconography of the liberal arts. By the late sixteenth century, her feast was celebrated throughout Catholic parts of Europe.[81] Restoration England, too, desired an embodied representation of music after a Puritan government had silenced the public over a generation. Cecilia was an obvious choice for a musical culture that admired all things foreign. Where there is Cecilia, Continental iconography had established there is Musica, and, as many English realised, where there is Musica there is Nature:

> *Nature*, which is the vast Creation's Soul,
> That steady curious Agent in the whole,
> The Art of Heaven, the Order of this Frame,
> Is only *Musick* in another name.

explains Katherine Phillips in praise of Henry Lawes, in a passage quoted by John Playford in Purcell's youth.[82] From 1683 until well into the next century, a group of musical amateurs and professionals incorporated as The Musical Society sponsored an

---

[79] Bacon, *Sylva Sylvarum*, p. 36.   [80] Morley, *A Plaine and Easie Introduction to Practicall Musicke*, p. 147.

[81] For further information on the history of St Cecilia and her celebrations, see Thomas Connolly, *Mourning into Joy: Music, Raphael, and St. Cecilia* (New Haven and London: Yale University Press, 1994), pp. 23–59; Hollander, *The Untuning of the Sky*, pp. 390–1; William Henry Husk, *An Account of the Musical Celebrations on St. Cecilia's Day* (London: Bell and Daldy, 1857), pp. 8–9; and Richard Luckett, 'St. Cecilia and Music', *Proceedings of the Royal Musical Association* 99 (1972–3), 18–29.

[82] Playford, *An Introduction to The Skill of Musick*, sig. A5.

annual celebration of the saint's day in London each 22 November. These public occasions included a formal ode in praise of music written and set by the most outstanding poets and composers of the day, a feast, and sometimes a sermon in defence of church music or a specially composed anthem for a musical service. The odes were not of religious character, but were intended to demonstrate the affective and persuasive powers of music through the finest union of harmony, melody and the musical art of poetry.[83]

Nicholas Brady, Minister of St Catherine Cree church, chaplain to the King and Queen and collaborator on the latest English version of the metrical psalms, provided the text for the 1692 ode, 'Hail, Bright Cecilia', which was set by Henry Purcell. The work is, of course, a famously exquisite display of Purcell's mature artistry, full of careful craftsmanship and innovative devices. It is the composer's largest and grandest choral work, and, to judge from the number of surviving sources, also his most popular.[84] What has gone previously unremarked is its extraordinary homage to the era's shifting attitudes towards natural philosophy. Somewhere between its first and final choruses of 'Hail! Bright Cecilia', the saint undergoes a series of metamorphoses into trees that speak when transmuted into instruments, the voice of nature, the world-soul, the mechanised recipient of sacred notes from the Divine, and a series of musical instruments displayed one by one with all the marvel of a musical wonder-cabinet. A complete analysis of the work in this light is beyond the scope of the current study, but some brief examples are most revealing.

The second stanza of Brady's interlocking set of poems is set as a spectacularly florid countertenor solo, whose initial performance has been legendarily, if dubiously, ascribed to the composer.[85] This declamatory air is a miniaturised show-piece of the passions moved by hearing music, and for its singer. It follows the passage of music from nature's voice, as activated by the saint, through the woodland full of life and into the interior faculties of heart and mind through sense and ear. Hobbes reminds us in his natural philosophy that this is exactly what sound does in the natural world:

Sound is *Sense generated by the action of the Medium, when its motion reacheth the Eare and the rest of the Organs of Sense.* Now the motion of the Medium is not the Sound it self, but the cause of it. For the Phantasme which is made in us, that is to say, the Reaction of the Organ is properly that which we call *Sound.*[86]

---

[83] See Ernest Brennecke, Jr., 'Dryden's Odes and Draghi's Music', *Proceedings of the Modern Language Association* 49 (1934), 2–9; Hollander, *The Untuning of the Sky*, pp. 390–401; Husk, *An Account of the Musical Celebrations on St. Cecilia's Day*, pp. 10–82; Luckett, 'St. Cecilia and Music', 29; Brewster Rogerson, 'The Art of Painting the Passions', *Journal of the History of Ideas* 14 (1953), 90–2; and Ian Spink, 'Purcell's Odes: Propaganda and Panegyric', in *Purcell Studies*, ed. Curtis Price (Cambridge: Cambridge University Press, 1995), pp. 161–2.

[84] See Brennecke, 'Dryden's Odes and Draghi's Music', 31–3; Peter Holman, *Henry Purcell* (Oxford: Oxford University Press, 1995), pp. 181–4; Husk, *An Account of the Musical Celebrations on St. Cecilia's Day*, p. 29; Spink, 'Purcell's Odes: Propaganda and Panegyric', pp. 165–6; and Bruce Wood, 'Purcell's Odes: A Reappraisal', in *The Purcell Companion*, ed. Michael Burden (Portland: Amadeus Press, 1995), p. 243.

[85] Brennecke, 'Dryden's Odes and Draghi's Music', 32; Holman, *Henry Purcell*, p. 182; and Spink, 'Purcell's Odes', p. 165.   [86] Hobbes, *Elements of Philosophy*, p. 361.

In keeping with its textual myth of origin, the air's orchestral colour is close to mono-chrome; only the continuo accompanies the countertenor. Melodically, it is full of fantastical twists and turns, with unexpected stops and starts. Harmonically, it is quite dull. But the entirety is filled with symbols of the very 'Nature's voice' it describes. Thomas Campion reminds readers of his theory treatise, reprinted by John Playford in Purcell's youth, that the four voices have been likened to the four natural elements of which all things are made. The mean (alto or countertenor), he tells us, is the air, the very stuff of which sound and spirit, voice and soul, were thought to be com-prised. The bass 'is the foundation of the other three . . . [which] must preceed from the lowest', since 'every part in nature doth affect his proper and natural place, as the Elements do'.[87] Thus, we have Nature's own airy voice rising from its very foundation 'thro' all the moving Wood' to 'court the Ear and strike the Heart' of the listening audience as it does in the elemental world presented (Example 2.1). The voice only begins on a weak beat after the continuo has established a strong F major tonic. Not only does it literally rise from the most fundamental element in nature, but, according to Thomas Mace, 'the *Good Quality* in *Nature*' known as a concord plainly shows itself as 'the very *Single Unity* (or *Unison*) alone'.[88] This is quite evident in the sustained drone of the accompaniment in the opening bars. As the singer enters, he outlines the tonic triad twice, in two different inversions. Mace waxes ecstatic by explaining that the aspect of nature

is more wonderfully apparent in the *Connexion*, or *Uniting* together of the *3 Parts* [of the triad] . . . and will significantly *Explain*, That forementioned 2[d.] *Great Mystery*, which is a kind of *Trinity* in *Unity*, and *Unity* in *Trinity*, (with *Reverence* be It spoken) . . . And there is such an *Amplitude*, or *Fullness* of *Satisfaction*, in *Those 3 Conchords*, that no *Expression* of *Words* is sufficient to declare them the *Height* of *Pleasure*, and *Satisfaction* received from Them. Much less unfold the *Secret*, or *Occult Mystery* which lies in Them.[89]

Thus, we hear the mysteriously creative process taking place just as Nature's voice begins to act on the world. The countertenor unfolds stability experimentally from its component parts. The three need to unite into full pleasing chords, which they proceed to do in time for the same occult voice to move and be understood with a mighty madrigalism (Example 2.1). We become satisfied, pleased and moved just as the heart and passions are struck in the narrative of origin.

The bass solo 'Wond'rous machine' (Example 2.2) not only evokes the passion of wonder in its text, but also the vast power of artifice and the conquest of Nature by Machine through its music. The insistent, relentless two-bar ground bass which anchors the entirety here serves as the auditory equivalent of the emblematic per-petual motion generator of Ripa's embodied Artifice. Again, the voice outlines the

[87] Thomas Campion, *The Art of Descant: Or, Composing of Musick in Parts*, annotated by Chr[istopher] Simpson (London: John Playford, 1674), pp. 1–2. On the physical composition of airy entities, and their resemblance to music, see Henry Cornelius Agrippa von Nettesheim, *Three Books of Occult Philosophy*, trans. J. F. (London: R. W. for Gregory Moule, 1657), pp. 257–8, and T[homas] W[alking-ton], *The Opticke Glasse of Humors* ([London:] J. D. for L. B., 1639), pp. 98–9.
[88] Mace, *Musicks Monument*, p. 266.   [89] *Ibid.*, pp. 266–7.

Example 2.1   Henry Purcell, ''Tis Nature's Voice', from *Ode to St. Cecilia* (beginning)

tonic triad, here in root position, as it emphasises the wondrousness of the title machine, the organ. Beyond the implication of good qualities in nature, the same triad is linked to high artifice and the wonder of the world's machine by Christopher Simpson, again quoted by Playford:

and which's most wonderful, the whole Mystery of this Art is comprized in the compass of three Notes or Sounds, which is most ingeniously observed by Mr. *Christopher Simpson*, in his *Division Violist*, pag. 18, in these words, *All Sounds that can possibly be joyned at once together in Musical Concordance, are still but the reiterated Harmony in* Three; *A significant Emblem of that Supreme and Incomprehensible Trinity,* Three in One, *Governing and Disposing the whole Machine of the World, with all its included Parts in a perfect harmony; for in the Harmony of Sounds, there is some great and hidden Mystery above what hath been yet discovered.*[90]

[90] Playford, *An Introduction to the Skill of Musick*, sig. A4ᵛ.

Example 2.2   Henry Purcell, 'Wondrous Machine', from *Ode to St. Cecilia* (beginning)

Machine emblem, human voice, and the divine mystery of creation are joined together, the more so from the preceding trio, 'With That Sublime Celestial Lay', whose text outlined the creation or mystic ensoulment of the organ from angel-breath. Like Mace's bridge from natural to human to divine language, the musical instrument here is key. The use of paired oboes in this aria may also reinforce the idea of higher power and authority in addition to evoking the breathy sound of the organ, for Western thought has long associated such wind instruments with purity and transcendence.[91] Even as Brady's poem refers to the organ's victorious combat with the lute, Purcell contrasts the latter's periodic and uneven warbles with the former's steady ground (Example 2.3). 'To thee the Warbling LUTE, Though us'd to Conquest, must be forc'd to yield', states Brady, reminding the well-read listener of the widespread seventeenth-century English literary topos of the lute causing the death of any natural creature who challenges it for musical dominance.[92] At the same time,

[91] See Robin Maconie, *The Concept of Music* (Oxford: Clarendon Press, 1990), p. 64.
[92] See my 'Nature, Culture, Myth and the Musician', 24–6, and Hollander, *The Untuning of the Sky*, pp. 220–38.

Example 2.3 Henry Purcell, 'Wondrous Machine' (continued)

Example 2.3 (*cont.*)

Example 2.3 (*cont.*)

Purcell has completely silenced the instrument, for only the singer imitates it. There is no plucked string to be heard. The inferior mechanics of the lute have indeed been conquered by the greater organ, closer to the angels than to mere wood and gut.

However, we still hear the voice, the most natural instrument of all, giving precise textual meaning to the sounds. '[T]he replacement of the older, "natural" ways of thinking by a new and "unnatural" form of life [the machine] – seeing, thinking, and behaving – did not occur without a struggle', says the historian of science Carolyn Merchant of Brady and Purcell's era, 'The submergence of the organism by the machine engaged the best minds of the times during a period fraught with anxiety, confusion, and instability in both the intellectual and social spheres.'[93] After the seventeenth century, as scientific thought came to dominate the West, music and magical epistemologies parted company from studies of the natural world. The world of wonder has been retained in the composer's and performer's art, even as understanding of the material world has been disenchanted. But for one brief historical moment, these things coexisted in ever-shifting ways.

. . . ars & natura canunt, natura enim vocem, ars instrumentum dedit, at mirabilis est artis & naturae in voce ac instrumentis consensus & harmonia

(. . . art & nature sing, for nature supplied the voice, art the instrument; and wondrous is the consent & harmony of art & nature in voice and instrument.)[94]

[93] Merchant, *The Death of Nature*, p. 193.
[94] Case, *Apologia musices*, p. 45.

Chapter Three

▬

The 'gift of nature': musical 'instinct' and musical cognition in Rameau

DAVID E. COHEN

Rameau is widely, and rightly, acknowledged as the inaugurator of modern harmonic theory. Indeed, it has recently been suggested that his contribution was even more fundamental, that Rameau may be regarded as the founder of the 'discursive practice' of modern music theory in general, in that, as Brian Hyer has put it, 'From Rameau onwards, [and due to his influence], theories of music became first and foremost matters of belief, about musical *structure* on the one hand, [and about] the *cognition* of music on the other.'[1] Similarly, in a substantial study entitled 'Valeur épistémologique de la théorie de la basse fondamentale', Marie-Elisabeth Duchez points out that the fundamental bass, since it 'shows [us] that which makes it possible for one chord to follow another', must be recognised as having 'a cognitive function', in that it explains and represents music's 'intelligibility'.[2]

The idea that Rameau's historical importance is related to his discovery of the problem of musical cognition is one that I find appealing. At the same time, however, at least for those interested in a historically informed interpretation of Rameau's thought, this view of it raises a number of questions, the most basic of which is what Rameau's own understanding of his theoretical project might have been.

This chapter grew out my wish to see whether Rameau himself might have understood his own project in terms that we would recognise as 'cognitive', which I take in a broad sense as meaning simply 'having to do with knowledge and the mind'. The question, then, is: is Rameau's theory 'cognitive', in this broad sense, from his own point of view? And if not, how did *he* understand what he was doing?

RAMEAU'S 'SOUS-ENTENDU': HARMONIC 'GRAMMAR' AND MUSICAL 'COMPETENCE'

Rameau's theory is, at the most basic level, an attempt to ground music in a 'natural principle'. At first, in the *Traité de l'harmonie* (1722), this natural principle was the undivided string. But Rameau's discovery of Joseph Sauveur's work on the harmonic

---

[1] Brian Hyer, 'Before Rameau and After', *Music Analysis* 15 (1996), 81. Emphasis added.
[2] Marie-Elisabeth Duchez, 'Valeur épistémologique de la théorie de la basse fondamentale de Jean-Philippe Rameau: connaissance scientifique et représentation de la musique', *Studies on Voltaire and the Eighteenth Century* 254 (1986), 122. Emphasis added.

series, published two decades earlier,[3] provided him with a new principle, the 'sounding body' or *corps sonore*, which was far more satisfactory, since it included within itself, in the purely natural acoustical phenomenon of harmonic partials, the consonant tones and intervals of the major triad, which in the earlier method of string division could be actualised only by human intervention. From the publication of his *Nouveau système* in 1726 until the end of his life, and with ever-increasing conviction and emphasis in his later years, Rameau insisted on the unique role of the *corps sonore* as the 'source' of proportional relations of all kinds, given to man by a benevolent Nature – an idea to which we shall return.

Rameau's mature theory, from at least *Génération harmonique* (1737) on, is an attempt to derive deductively from this 'natural principle' all of the essential aspects of harmonic organisation of the music of his time – the basic structures and mutual relations of the fundamental chords, their transmutations via inversion and other alterations, the rules governing their use in musical utterances and much else besides, by means of a complicated combination of acoustical, mathematical and psychological arguments. His main conceptual instrument in all this is, of course, the fundamental bass.

As is now widely recognised, the fundamental bass does not simply announce the acoustical generator of each chord; it also represents the harmonic logic by which chords relate to and succeed one another. It thus constitutes an *interpretation* of the musical surface in terms of Rameau's theoretical principles. Now among these principles is the stipulation that the fundamental bass progresses properly by harmonic intervals, that is, thirds and fifths (or their inversions). Progression by step is therefore somewhat problematical for Rameau. His typical solution, at least for progressions by ascending step, is to regard them as being, in effect, elliptical expressions of a more correct progression, consisting of a descending third followed by an ascending perfect fourth, which is 'understood' (*sous-entendu*) by the listener.[4] In a fundamental-

---

[3] Sauveur's first two and most important acoustical studies appeared in the *Mémoires* of the French Royal Academy of Sciences in 1701 and 1702, in *Joseph Sauveur: Collected Writings on Musical Acoustics (Paris 1700–1713)*, ed. Rudolf Rasch (Utrecht: Diapason Press, 1984). For a concise account, see Thomas Christensen, *Rameau and Musical Thought in the Enlightenment* (Cambridge: Cambridge University Press, 1993), pp. 137–9; for more detailed discussion, see Burdette L. Green, 'The Harmonic Series from Mersenne to Rameau: An Historical Study of Circumstances Leading to Its Recognition and Application to Music', (Ph.D. thesis, Ohio State University, 1969), esp. pp. 395, 403–26.

[4] Jean-Philippe Rameau, *Traité de l'harmonie réduite à ses principes naturels* (1722), in *Jean-Philippe Rameau: Complete Theoretical Writings*, ed. Erwin Jacobi (Rome: American Institute of Musicology, 1967–72), p. 214 (hereafter cited as *Traité*, and the complete edition as *CTW*); trans. Philip Gossett, *Treatise on Harmony* (New York: Dover, 1971), p. 234 (hereafter cited as Gossett): 's'il est permis de faire monter la Basse-fondamentale d'un Ton ou d'un semi-Ton, la progression d'une Tierce & d'une Quarte y est *toujours sous-entenduë*'. See also pp. 50–1 (Gossett, pp. 60–1). An alternative explanation, by which Rameau accounts for certain specific instances of fundamental-bass progression by ascending step, is the 'deceptive cadence' (*cadence rompuë*); see e.g. Rameau, *Génération harmonique ou traité de musique théorique et pratique* (1737), in *CTW*, vol. III; trans. Deborah Hayes, 'Rameau's Theory of Harmonic Generation: An Annotated Translation and Commentary of *Génération harmonique* by Jean-Philippe Rameau' (Ph.D. thesis, Stanford University, 1968), Chapter 15 (hereafter cited as Hayes). See also Rameau's very different explanation in *Traité*, Book II, Chapter 6.

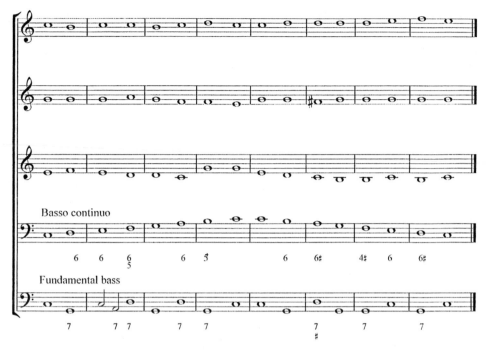

Example 3.1   Jean-Philippe Rameau, *Traité de l'harmonie*, Book III, Chapter 11, p. 212

bass analysis, the result is the so-called 'interpolated bass' to which Marpurg so vehemently objected.[5] An example of such an interpolated fundamental-bass note is seen in bar 2 of Example 3.1, where Rameau's fundamental-bass analysis shows *three* fundamental-bass notes as opposed to the two notes of the *basso continuo*. The interpolated fundamental bass note – here the low A – analyses the step progression as an elliptical expression of the more 'correct' progression by descending third and ascending fourth. It thus represents an element (a chord) of a more basic, paradigmatic sequence of harmonic events that, in Rameau's view, underlies and thereby *explains* the coherence and aural intelligibility of a musical passage in which that element does not actually occur.[6]

As Allan Keiler has pointed out, the fundamental bass in such cases is thus functioning as a metalinguistic, analytical paraphrase which represents the way in which

[5] In Anglophone scholarship, these points were first clarified in Cecil Powell Grant, 'The Real Relationship Between Kirnberger's and Rameau's Concept of the Fundamental Bass', *Journal of Music Theory* 21 (1977), 324–38.

[6] Allan R. Keiler, 'Music as Metalanguage: Rameau's Fundamental Bass', in *Music Theory: Special Topics*, ed. Richmond Browne (New York: Academic Press, 1981), pp. 88–9, 94 (n. 14), 99, discussing such cases of 'interpolated' fundamental-bass notes and the closely related matter of the *double emploi*, points out that Rameau had no 'absolute stricture' against fundamental-bass progression by step (and that such progressions occur at times in the fundamental-bass analyses of his post-*Traité* writings), and argues that the real purpose of interpolated notes in the fundamental bass is to represent a 'structural ambiguity' in the 'harmonic function' of the affected chord – an interpretation that is at least open to a cognitive reading.

the musical surface, although apparently deviant from Rameau's harmonic principles, is to be understood as actually conforming to and embodying them.[7] Rameau believes these harmonic principles to have been (unknowingly) derived by human beings as logical consequences of the 'natural principle' of music (the 'undivided string'; the *corps sonore*), so that music which behaves in accord with those principles is behaving in accord with its 'source' in nature and thus in accord with nature itself. He further assumes that our perception of music as orderly, expressive and (above all) comprehensible is due to our intuitive perception of these naturally derived principles. Thus for Rameau to show how a passage that is intuitively perceived as harmonically coherent actually conforms to these principles, even when it does not seem to do so, is indeed to provide, as Duchez puts it, an explanation of how that passage is 'intelligible'.

The concept that permits Rameau to have the fundamental bass include notes that are not actually present in the written bass part – and thus to make the fundamental bass analytical in a deeper, cognitive sense – is the concept of *le sous-entendu*. When Rameau wants to make the sort of claim just discussed he typically says that the listener 'understands' (*sous-entend*) the fundamental-bass note in question, or that the note itself is 'understood' (*sous-entendu*).[8] The verb *sous-entendre*, a compound of *sous* ('below', 'under') and *entendre* ('to intend, understand, hear') which is attested in French texts since *c.* 1650, is defined as meaning 'to have [something] in the mind without explicitly saying [it], to let [it] be understood', 'to suggest'.[9] This sense is evidently based on the meaning of *entendre* in the sense of 'intend', so that *sous-entendre* is an act performed by the *speaker*. The opposite sense, however, is suggested by the cognate late-Latin words *subaudire* and *subintellegere* (*sub*, 'under' or 'below', plus *audire*, 'to hear' or *intellegere*, 'to understand'), both of which denote an act performed by the *hearer* (or reader) and mean 'to understand *or* supply in thought (a word implied but not expressed)'.[10] It is in this latter sense that Rameau uses and indeed defines *sous-entendre* as denoting an act performed by the hearer – more precisely, by the 'ear' of the musical listener – at the same time interpreting the word in a more literal way as referring directly to hearing (*entendre*), and indeed to the 'hearing' of the fundamental bass 'below' (*dessous*) the actual bass:

By the word *sous-entendre* one must be made aware that the sounds to which it is applied can be heard in chords in which they are not in fact present; and with regard to the fundamental

---

[7] Keiler, 'Music as Metalanguage', esp. p. 93.

[8] See, for example, above, n. 4. Jairo Moreno, 'The Complicity of the Imaginary: Rameau's Implied Dissonances', paper delivered at 21st Meeting of the Society of Music Theory, Chapel Hill, NC (December 1998), also addresses Rameau's concept of *sous-entendre*, but in a different context and from a very different perspective.

[9] See *Le Nouveau Petit Robert, Dictionnaire de la langue française* (Paris: Dictionnaires Le Robert, 1993), p. 2126.

[10] See A. Souter, *A Glossary of Later Latin to 600 A.D.* (Oxford: Clarendon Press, 1949), pp. 390, 393; also P. G. W. Glare, *Oxford Latin Dictionary* (Oxford: Clarendon Press, 1996), p. 1836. The words are commonly used in Latin writings down to the present day, especially in interpretative commentaries, to indicate a verbal element that is to be 'supplied' or 'understood' by the reader.

sound, it is even necessary to imagine that [this sound] must be heard below the other sounds, when one says that it is *sous-entendu*.[11]

Sous-entendre thus expresses the idea, crucial to the deeper analytical function of the fundamental bass and to a 'cognitive' interpretation thereof, that a structurally necessary element can be elided in particular cases because the very fact of its necessity allows it to be 'understood' or 'assumed' to be there, unmistakably 'implied' by its context. Rameau thus believes that human subjects routinely refer actual musical events to a set of tacitly held expectations about how music is 'supposed' to work, a set of rules defining paradigms of musical structure by reference to which deviations from those paradigmatic structures can be intuitively recognised as such and rendered intelligible by the act of *sous-entendre*, for it is only in this way that they could be capable of 'supplying' elements of musical structure that are not explicitly present. The whole idea of *sous-entendre* thus suggests, and indeed suggested at the time, an analogy with the use of elliptical utterances in language, that is, utterances in which elements that are grammatically necessary are omitted, and *can* be omitted precisely *because* they are necessary, and therefore are mentally supplied by the listener. There is a clear parallel between such cases of omission and implication of essential elements in linguistic utterances and cases of harmonic *sous-entendu* such as the 'interpolated bass'.[12] The analogy was noted almost immediately by Castel, in his review of the *Traité de l'harmonie*. Indeed, he attributes it to Rameau himself who, Castel writes,

has remarked that in Music as in Language, one sometimes expresses oneself incompletely, and that the ear has the property of often supplying what it does not hear. He points out that musicians are continually saying that 'such and such a sound or chord is implied', in such a way, [Rameau] says, that this expression is often used by him who least knows its force.[13]

---

[11] *Traité*, 'Table des Termes', p. xxi: 'Par le mot de *Sous-entendre* on doit être prévenue que les Sons ausquels on l'applique, peuvent être entendus dans les Accords où ils ne se trouvent point; & même, à l'égard du Son-Fondamental, il faut s'imaginer qu'il devroit être pour lors *entendu au dessous* des autres Sons, lorsqu'on dit qu'il est *Sous-entendu*.' Emphasis in the original. (See Gossett, p. xlv, s.v. 'Imply'.) A full translation of *sous-entendre* in Rameau's sense would thus be something like: 'to supply mentally in the act of hearing an element that is not actually present in the acoustical stimulus'. This, clearly, is too unwieldy for regular use. For lack of any clearly superior solution I have chosen to keep to the familiar English renderings ('imply', 'understand', etc.).

[12] For example, when we reply 'Fine' to the question 'How are you?', we omit two grammatically necessary elements: the subject noun phrase ('I') and the verb ('am'). Keiler, 'Music as Metalanguage', pp. 89–96, provides a more detailed discussion of the relationship between such transformations in linguistic grammar and Rameau's fundamental bass.

[13] Castel, review of *Traité*, *Journal de Trévoux* (October 1722), p. 1732, in *CTW*, vol. I, p. xxxiv. Louis-Bertrand Castel, one of Rameau's early supporters and advisors, may be recalling remarks made by Rameau in private communication, for I have been unable to find them in his published writings. Castel returned to the linguistic analogy in his review of the *Nouveau système* six years later. Explaining the 'irregular' cadence, he writes that it 'seems to lack an intermediary sound and chord . . . [which] is suppressed and assumed [*on sous-entend*]. This pleases the ear, as when in ordinary discourse something is left out, to be divined by the mind' (*Journal de Trévoux* (March 1728), 477–8, in *CTW*, vol. II, p. xix); see Glenn Chandler, 'Rameau's "Nouveau système de musique théorique": An Annotated Translation with Commentary' (Ph.D. thesis, Indiana University, 1975), p. 121 (hereafter cited as Chandler). Here too Castel may be reporting remarks made by Rameau to him personally. A few pages later Castel

The 'force' of this notion of implication, which, according to Castel, Rameau finds musicians commonly using 'without giving it much thought', is that of tacitly held principles or rules that control our linguistic, and also our musical, behaviour, including our interpretation of the linguistic and musical input we receive from others. In other words, Rameau's use of the notion of *sous-entendre* implies a belief in the existence and functioning in musical subjects of something analogous to a 'grammar', as this is understood in certain influential strains of modern linguistics: the system of principles and rules that must be posited in order to account for the linguistic abilities of native speakers.[14] In both cases, the explanatory notions of omission and implication entail a system of rules, literally 'grammatical' in the case of language, metaphorically so in the case of music, which is applied and therefore in some sense 'known' by the relevant parties.

In linguistics, of course, such grammatical knowledge is understood to be largely if not entirely inaccessible to direct conscious introspection; it is held and operates unconsciously. Similarly, for Rameau, neither the subjective act of *sous-entendre* itself nor the element it supplies as 'understood' need be objects of the subject's conscious awareness. Rameau is not claiming that the interpolated chords are *consciously* present to the minds of listeners and musicians, at least ordinarily. He is claiming, rather, that the principles by which music is orderly and intelligible demand that those chords be 'understood' to be there, and he is implying, at least, that he believes that if such a passage does make harmonic sense to musical subjects, they must be presumed to have mentally supplied them – *even though they are not aware of having done so.* That this is so is shown by the fact that, in all cases in which chordal inversion has occurred, Rameau considers the fundamental bass to be *sous-entendu.*[15] For musicians had been using inverted chords for years, and, according to Rameau's firmly held belief, understanding them *as* inverted chords *without knowing it*, as he explicitly says in a famous passage from the *Préface* to *Génération harmonique*, in which he refers to 'that

writes: 'With this author [Rameau], music has become a regular and coherent entity, which one can treat (*manier*) as one treats a speech or discourse, by analysing it, tracing its design, following it through, etc.' (p. 480; *CTW*, vol. II, p. xx; trans. in Christensen, *Rameau and Musical Thought*, p. 110, and in Chandler, p. 123).

[14] Primary among these is the ability to create and understand an infinite number of grammatical utterances. More properly, a 'grammar' in the standard linguistic sense is a highly formalised set of rules designed to model this knowledge in an explicit way. Grammars, in this sense, are primarily concerned with representing the structures which speaker-hearers (unconsciously) assign to verbal utterances. This concept of grammar, introduced by Noam Chomsky, is widely accepted in contemporary linguistics. It is closely linked with such Chomskyan concepts as 'competence' (to be discussed shortly), 'generative grammar' and 'universal grammar'. For further discussion, see Noam Chomsky, *Knowledge of Language: Its Nature, Origin, and Use* (New York: Praeger, 1986), pp. 1–56; also Vivian J. Cook and Mark Newson, *Chomsky's Universal Grammar: An Introduction*, 2nd edn (Cambridge, Mass.: Blackwell, 1996), pp. 1–3, 21–3. See also Fred Lehrdahl and Ray Jackendoff, *A Generative Theory of Tonal Music* (Cambridge, Mass.: MIT Press, 1983), pp. 1–6.

[15] *Traité*, Book II, Chapter 1, p. 57: 'If the fundamental bass is removed and one of the other parts is put in its place, all the resulting chords will be inversions of the original chords. The harmony will remain good, for even when the fundamental bass is removed, it is always understood (*sous-entendue*)'; trans. Gossett, p. 67; for 'sous-entendu' I have replaced Gossett's 'implied' with 'understood'.

fundamental bass, the musician's invisible guide, *which has always directed him in all his musical works without his having yet noticed it . . .*[16] Thus when, in the *Traité*, Rameau says that the fundamental bass of each chord is *sous-entendu*, we can reasonably assume that for him the process or act of *sous-entendre* is one that can and typically does occur without the conscious awareness of the musical subject.

Rameau's theories can thus be understood in terms of the modern linguistic concept of 'competence', which denotes the 'tacit knowledge' that native speakers have of the grammar of their language.[17] The qualification 'tacit' is essential: the grammatical knowledge in question is *unconscious*, just as is the quasi-grammatical musical knowledge that is the object of Rameau's theories. Rameau's project can thus be seen as an attempt (or rather, a series of attempts) to formulate an account of human musical competence, specifically one whose system of principles and rules is deductively derived, in good Cartesian fashion, from a single 'natural principle' – the undivided string or, later, the acoustical phenomenon of the *corps sonore*. From this point of view Rameau's theory appears as a theory of the quasi-grammatical knowledge of music possessed by all human subjects, albeit without their conscious awareness of the fact. As such, it would be a theory concerned with issues of human musical cognition.

THE QUESTION OF 'AGENCY': THE SUBJECT AND THE MUSICAL 'EAR'

The difficulties with interpreting Rameau in the light of our modern understanding of 'cognition' become apparent as soon as one considers the following question: What mechanism, process or faculty within the human subject is responsible for the supposed transmutation of the physical 'principle' provided by 'nature', the *corps sonore*, into *knowledge* of musical grammar? The *corps sonore*, after all, is not itself an ideal, mental entity, but an acoustical, that is a *physical* phenomenon. Even when it occurs within the body – as in the case of the human voice – it remains a physical, material (that is a non-mental) event. As such, the acoustical data it provides must undergo a series of perceptual and cognitive processes before they can appear in the mind as knowledge. Rameau believes indeed that human subjects 'sense' the data provided by the *corps sonore*, but that they do so without knowing it, which is to say that they perceive these data unconsciously. As we shall shortly see, this alone raises very serious problems. But Rameau goes much further than this. He maintains that human subjects routinely 'derive', that is, deduce, from this raw acoustical data all of the manifold 'consequences' that his theory is meant to exhibit and render explicit. But,

---

[16] *Génération harmonique, Préface*, fol. iii. For the French text, see below, n. 29.

[17] Andrew Radford, *Syntax: A Minimalist Introduction* (Cambridge: Cambridge University Press, 1997), p. 2. The distinction between 'competence' (defined as 'the speaker-hearer's knowledge of his language') and 'performance' ('the actual use of language in concrete situations') was introduced in Chomsky, *Aspects of the Theory of Syntax* (Cambridge, Mass.: MIT Press, 1965), p. 4. See Chomsky, *Rules and Representations* (Cambridge, Mass.: Blackwell, 1980), 59. For a discussion of 'musical competence' see Keiler, 'Bernstein's *The Unanswered Question* and the Problem of Musical Competence', *The Musical Quarterly* 64 (1978), 195–222.

Rameau believes, this deduction also occurs without any awareness of the process on the part of those in whom it occurs. Yet, exactly how does all this take place? What is the nature of the process itself, and what is the organ or faculty that accomplishes it? These questions are important for two reasons. First, because without an answer Rameau cannot be said to have made a complete and convincing case for the efficacy of the *corps sonore* as the actual cause of *any* of the effects he attributes to it, since a crucial connecting link remains absent: the means or agency by which the raw acoustical data of a physical event that is not even consciously perceived can have the kind of influence on human behaviour that Rameau attributes to it. And second, because in attempting to provide the answer (one that Rameau himself does not provide), we come to a fuller and, I think, historically more revealing understanding of his thought. Despite the apparent urgency (at least within the 'cognitive' interpretation of Rameau's theory) of this question of 'agency', Rameau not only never explicitly addresses it as such, but seems not even to recognise the extent to which it *is* a problem. This alone suggests that Rameau understood the entire matter in a way that was somehow quite different from that implied by the cognitive interpretation. Indeed, as we shall see, he explicitly states that, until he himself discovered the role of the *corps sonore* and its 'consequences', the 'knowledge' of them that musicians and composers possessed, which 'guided' them in all their musical actions, was in fact not 'knowledge' at all.

This is not to say, however, that every aspect of the cognitive interpretation as outlined above must simply be wrong. In fact there are several ways in which it is at least arguably right. In particular, it seems right to understand Rameau as attempting to give an account of something like a musical 'grammar' that is somehow possessed by human subjects – a point which, at least for the present, I shall take to have been sufficiently argued above, on the basis of Rameau's concept of *sous-entendu*. And that concept – the idea that grammatically essential musical elements can be omitted because they are nonetheless 'understood' or 'implied' – itself logically implies, as a correlative, the activity of a subject who is doing this 'understanding', a person by whom the implicit element is understood and to whom it is implied. Thus, while it is true that much of the time Rameau deduces and explains the various elements and relationships of tonal harmony as if they were purely objective realities, independent of the 'mental' processes of musicians and listeners, his use of the concept of *sous-entendu* always includes at least an implicit reference to the activity of a human subject. In this light, his theory seems in fact to be concerned with a system of quasi-grammatical musical principles and rules somehow possessed, albeit unconsciously, by human subjects. The crucial differences between this reading of Rameau and one that is properly 'cognitive', then, have to do with Rameau's own conception of the *nature* of the posited musical 'grammar' and the 'agency' or faculty by which it is produced: as long as it remains unconscious and inexplicit, this 'grammar' is not 'knowledge', and the faculty which produces and possesses it is not the mind.

That faculty is, instead, something that Rameau calls the 'ear' (*l'oreille*), 'sensation' or 'feeling' (*sentiment*) and in later writings 'instinct' (*instinct*). The most important of these terms, and the first to appear in his writings, is the 'ear'. Duchez, in the article cited earlier, has pointed out the importance of the 'ear' in Rameau's thought, calling attention to his 'presentiment' that

[a]long with sonic phenomena that are . . . dependent on the objective properties of sounds studied by physics, music utilises psycho-physiological phenomena that are subjective . . . Along with the elaboration of his theory of the fundamental bass, Rameau insists on the psycho-physiological factors of its reception. In particular, he insists on the ear as active psychic receptor: the selective ear that privileges the fundamental bass, with which it is 'constantly occupied' . . . For the idea of the fundamental bass is tied to and accompanied by 'the sensitivity of the ear to harmony'. . . .[18]

Duchez quite rightly draws attention to the crucial role of the 'ear'.[19] This concept, indeed, is a nexus for all of the ideas discussed thus far; most importantly, the notion of *sous-entendu*, with its implications of grammaticality and subjectivity, typically occurs in Rameau's discourse linked with an invocation of the musical 'ear' as its agent. 'Do we know what the ear understands in all the successions of sounds which please us?' he asks in the *Préface* to *Génération harmonique*; and in regard to the vocal intonation of a singer accompanied only by a continuo bass line, having pointed out that the latter is an 'artistic bass, in which the fundamental bass occurs only rarely', he goes on to ask, 'what is it that guides the voice in this case, if not the fundamental succession which the ear understands there with its harmony, on the basis of which it [the ear] governs the different inflections of this voice?'[20] For Rameau, it is also the ear that explains how the system of tonal music that he knows and attempts to theorise gradually arose in the first place. This we learn, for example, from those passages in which Rameau attempts to prove one of his central theses, that harmony is prior to melody, by providing a harmonic generation of what he calls 'diatonic succession',

[18] Duchez, 'Valeur épistémologique de la théorie de la basse fondamentale', 123. Duchez here cites *Génération harmonique*, p. 94, and *Démonstration du principe de l'harmonie servant de base à tout l'art musical théorique et pratique* (Paris: Durand, 1750), pp. 47, 57.

[19] Herbert Schneider, explaining Rameau's negative views of Pythagoreanism, also stresses the crucial role played by 'the experience of hearing' in Rameau's thought, particularly his late writings (although he does not consider this from the perspective adopted here), going so far as to claim that Rameau 'is the first theorist who in this way attributed so much significance to hearing, and from this . . . drew in his late theoretical works the far-reaching consequence of reversing the relationship between mathematics and music theory' ('Rameaus musiktheoretisches Vermächtnis', *Musiktheorie* 1/2 (1986), 152). Schneider, it should be noted, overstates the case here, for he overlooks the tradition of empirical music theory stemming from Aristoxenus, including its seventeenth- and eighteenth-century German representatives such as, most prominently, Johann Mattheson; see Thomas Christensen, '*Sensus, Ratio*, and *Phthongos*: Mattheson's Theory of Tone Perception', in *Musical Transformation and Musical Intuition: Eleven Essays in Honor of David Lewin*, ed. Raphael Atlas and Michael Cherlin (Dedham, Mass.: Ovenbird Press, 1994), esp. p. 6.

[20] *Génération harmonique*, *Préface*, fol. [vi]: 'Sçavons-nous ce que l'Oreille sous-entend dans toutes les successions de Sons qui nous plaisent?' (trans. Hayes, p. 24); *ibid.*, Chapter 7, p. 91: 'Qui est plus, la Viole ne donne qu'un Son à chaque fois . . . & la Basse qu'elle fait entendre, étant une Basse de goût, où la fondamentale se trouve rarement, qu'est-ce qui conduit pour lors la Voix, si ce n'est la succession fondamentale que l'Oreille y sous-entend avec son Harmonie, sur laquelle elle gouverne les différentes infléxions de cette Voix?' (see Hayes, p. 116).

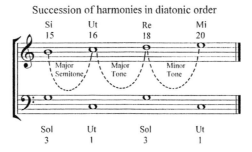

Succession of harmonies in diatonic order

Example 3.2   Jean-Philippe Rameau, *Génération harmonique*, Example 5, *ad* p. 59

the progression by whole tones and semitones that characterises melody and is embodied in the scale. As a first step, Rameau generates the diatonic tetrachord of Greek theory, using only the tonic and dominant chords in alternation, as shown in Example 3.2, where the fundamental bass notes g–c–g–c generate the diatonic tetrachord b-c-d-e.

For Rameau, however, this is not merely a step in a theoretical derivation; it corresponds to a real historical event, revealing both the effectuality of the ear's perception of the *corps sonore* and its insufficiency to produce, by itself, real knowledge thereof:

It is, I say, from precisely this diatonic order that the Greeks formed their diatonic systems, which they gave the name of tetrachords. You see *their origin in the fundamental succession by fifths* . . . It is astonishing that the Ancients thus discovered one of the first *consequences* of the principle, *without being aware of* the principle itself . . . This shows *what the ear can do*, but at the same time, how it can lead us astray when it is the sole guide of our investigations.[21]

Rameau thus believed that the Greeks discovered diatonic succession – one of the 'consequences' deduced from the *corps sonore* – without having recognised this far more basic principle itself. But he is convinced that this discovery could only have been made *as* a deduction from that principle of which the Greeks were unaware. How could they have accomplished this?

In his *Nouveau système* of 1726 Rameau explains the process by which he believed the 'ear' of a man without any prior acquaintance with music would naturally be led to discover diatonic succession as a 'consequence' of the harmonic series generated by any given sung tone of that man's own voice,[22] a topic to which he returns in his

[21] *Génération harmonique*, Chapter 6, p. 60: 'c'est justement, dis-je, de cet ordre Diatonique que les Grecs ont formé leurs Systêmes Diatoniques, auxquels ils ont donné le nom de *Tétracordes*; vous en voïez l'origine dans la succession fondamentale par Quinte . . . Il est étonnant que les Anciens aient ainsi découvert l'une des premieres conséquents du principe, sans s'être apperçus de ce principe, sans l'avoir même suivi dans les rapports qu'ils assignent aux intervalles de leurs Tétracordes: on voit par-là ce que peut l'Oreille, mais en même-tems les égaremens où elle peut nous jetter, quand on n'a point d'autre guide dans ses recherches.' Emphasis added (trans. adapted from Hayes, p. 87).

[22] *Nouveau système*, Chapter 8, p. 48; Chapter 9, pp. 48–9; Chandler, pp. 290, 292: 'The melody that we imagine is suggested by a principle of harmony that is *within us*, and this principle is none other than the chord that we hear in a single sound of the voice [i.e. the *corps sonore*]', for 'melody can be formed only from the progression of fundamental sounds and the constituent [pitches and intervals] of their

Observations sur notre instinct pour la musique of 1754.[23] Also in *Nouveau système*, Rameau suggests that his readers try an experiment that will prove to them that the voice is 'naturally carried' to the fundamental bass note of each 'point of repose' (that is, cadential arrival) in a melody, so that *'without thinking about it* you will intone the true fundamental bass' of a melody note on which a cadential arrival is felt to occur.[24] And later, in the *Observations*, Rameau concludes that 'experiments' such as the one just mentioned 'where the instinct alone acts . . . indeed prove that melody has no other principle than the harmony offered up by the *corps sonore*: a principle by which the ear is so taken up, *without one's realising it,* that by itself [the ear] suffices to make us find the harmonic foundation on which this melody depends'.[25] In short, according to Rameau, it is the ear's unconscious manipulation of the acoustical data of the *corps sonore* that is responsible for music in the first place. This is why a theory that derives its principles as deductions from the *corps sonore* will *ipso facto* explain musical practice: the 'ear' itself *created* musical practice in just that way, except unconsciously; the theory simply makes the ear's accomplishment explicit.

It is clear, then, that Rameau attributes crucial and remarkable powers to what he calls 'the ear'. Indeed, to us, it may appear obvious that Rameau is actually using the word 'ear' metaphorically to signify something that is, to our way of thinking, clearly a faculty of the mind: the mental faculty responsible for what we would call musical 'cognition'; the seat and organ of that unconscious knowledge of musical 'grammar' that he clearly seems to posit, and that we might call musical 'competence'. But to leap to this conclusion would be a mistake, for this is not Rameau's own understanding of the musical ear, as we shall now see.

MIND, KNOWLEDGE AND SENSE EXPERIENCE; SENSUS AND RATIO

Far from regarding the musical 'ear' as an aspect or faculty of the mind, Rameau actually opposes the two: 'That which the mind conceives only after some reflection, the ear seizes first, and grasps that the effect which it experiences is due to the fundamental succession, or to its harmony.'[26] Or consider this passage from a letter of 1736 to Castel, published in the *Journal de Trévoux*:

footnote 22 *(cont.)*

chords. These progressions alone are *natural* to us', he insists, because they are either the consonant intervals directly given by the *corps sonore*, or the stepwise motions that connect the chord-tones generated by each fundamental-bass note in a succession. The first sound to be sung (that is its overtone series), therefore, 'causes the voice to produce after it those sounds which have the greatest rapport with it'.

[23] *Observations sur notre instinct pour la musique*, pp. 2–9; *CTW*, vol. III, pp. 267ff. In this treatise Rameau introduces the term 'instinct' as a new way of designating the faculty which he had formerly always called (and still continues to call) the 'ear'. We shall consider his use of this term below.

[24] *Nouveau système*, Chapter 10, p. 54; Chandler, pp. 306–7. Emphasis added.

[25] *Observations*, pp. 10–11: 'Cette derniere expérience, où le seul Instinct agit, de même que dans les précédentes, prouve bien que la mélodie n'a d'autre principe que l'harmonie rendue par le Corps sonore: principe dont l'oreille est tellement préoccupée, sans qu'on y pense, qu'elle suffit seule pour nous faire trouver sur le champ le fond d'harmonie dont cette mélodie dépend.'

[26] *Génération harmonique*, Chapter 9, pp. 117–18: 'ce que l'esprit n'y conçoit qu'avec un peu de réflexion,

If some have imagined that they *knew* the fundamental bass even before it was announced to them, the *idea* of it, at least, came to them only afterwards. And this should not surprise us, for, since it is the unique compass of the *ear* in harmony, and consequently in melody, it is no sooner presented to the *mind* than |the mind| connects |the fundamental bass| with the operations of this *sense* |the ear|, and, finding it again in those operations, it seems to |the mind| that it actually |already| knew |the fundamental bass|.[27]

Those individuals, Rameau claims here, who upon learning of his revelation of the fundamental bass, think that they already 'knew' it are deceived by the fact that their minds, confronted with Rameau's explicit formulation, immediately recognise the principle that had all along guided their *ears*, but without their conscious awareness of the fact. The mind (*l'esprit*) and its proper possession, knowledge (*connoissance*) are contrasted with, and opposed to, the 'ear', which, since it is a 'sense' (*sens*), produces not knowledge but sensation.

It is important to note that here, and in general when he is distinguishing between the 'sense' of hearing (or later, musical 'instinct') and the 'mind', Rameau presumably understands the latter as denoting specifically the *rational* faculty of the human subject, exclusive of certain other faculties, such as sensation, which are embraced by it in Cartesian usage, since otherwise Rameau's sharp separation of *esprit* and *sens* would relegate the latter to the position of a purely corporeal function, a view which (as we shall see) would not only be contrary to all of the major philosophical psychologies current in his time, but would also make it even more difficult to explain the further, quasi-cognitive abilities that Rameau attributes to the ear.[28] *L'esprit* comprises for Rameau the faculties of rational thought (*raison*) and conceptual understanding (*l'entendement*), and perhaps memory as well, and has as its proper activity the production and possession of 'knowledge'. It stands opposed to the 'sensation' (*sentiment*, sometimes better rendered as 'feeling') produced by the 'ear', which he also characterises as 'experience' in the famous passage from the Preface to *Génération harmonique* from which I quoted earlier:

I am finally able . . . to demonstrate that principle of harmony which until now has only been *suggested* to me by the path of *experience*: that fundamental bass, the ear's unique compass, the musician's *invisible* guide, which has always directed him in all his musical works *without his*

L'Oreille le saisit d'abord, & sçait attribuer à la succession fondamentale, ou à son Harmonie, l'effet qu'elle éprouve' (Hayes, p. 142).

[27] 'Lettre de M. Rameau au R. P. Castel, au sujet de quelques nouvelles réflexions sur la Musique, que le R. P. Castel a insérées dans les mois d'Août (II. Partie), & de Septembre 1735, de ces Mémoires', *Journal de Trévoux, Memoires pour l'histoire des Sciences et des beaux Arts* (July 1736), Pt. II, 1691–1709, 1693: 'Si quelques-uns se sont imaginés qu'ils connoissoient la Basse fondamentale, même avant qu'elle leur fût annoncée, du moins l'idée ne leur en est-elle venuë qu'après; & cela ne doit pas surprendre, parce que, comme c'est l'unique Boussole de l'oreille en harmonie, & par conséquent en mélodie, on ne la présente pas plutôt à l'esprit, qu'il en fait le rapport avec les opérations de ce sens, & que la retrouvant dans ces opérations, il lui semble qu'il la connoissoit effectivement' (ed. *CTW*, vol. VI, pp. 86–92, p. 87). Emphasis added.

[28] Both definitions (among many others) of *l'esprit* are given in both the first (1694) and fifth (1798) editions of the *Dictionnaire de l'Académie Française*. The Cartesian understanding of the 'mind' is discussed below.

having yet noticed it, but of which he no sooner heard spoken than he regarded it as his own property. 'I already *knew* this fundamental bass', he said; however, if he had closely examined himself he would have said simply, 'I *sensed* it.' It is, truly, one of those natural *sensations* which can very easily escape our *thought*, but which unfold to their full extent within us the moment someone reminds us of them.[29]

Later in the same work Rameau gives this set of oppositions its most explicit expression:

I call ignorance all knowledge that comes solely from an experience formed simply from sensation. This knowledge is not, properly speaking, knowledge; it is only a reminiscence of an effect felt on the occasion of a certain arrangement among the parts, the cause of which is not known.[30]

'... the cause of which is not known': this is the crucial point. For Rameau, 'knowledge' in the proper sense denotes what Aristotle sometimes called *episteme*: a reasoned, scientific account (*logos*) of a thing or event in terms of the factors implicated in its existence or occurrence – its 'causes' (*aitia*).[31] Indeed, the whole understanding of the relative roles of sensation, experience and knowledge so clearly implied in this passage is remarkably reminiscent of the discussion that opens the *Metaphysics* of Aristotle. Sensation (*aisthesis*), Aristotle explains there, gives rise to memories, and memories to experience (*empeiria*), which is 'knowledge' (*gnosis*) of individual cases, particulars; finally, 'through experience' human beings arrive at 'scientific knowledge' (*episteme*) and 'art' (*techne*),[32] which involve knowledge of the universal principles, the causes and explanations of the facts that experience has taught with regard to particulars. 'But yet', Aristotle goes on in a passage with which Rameau would surely have agreed, 'we think that *knowledge* [*eidenai*] and *understanding* [*epaiein*] belong to art [*techne*]

[29] *Génération harmonique*, *Préface*, fol. iii: 'Je suis enfin parvenu, si je ne me trompe, à pouvoir démontrer ce principe de l'Harmonie, qui ne m'avoit encore été suggéré que par la voïe de l'expérience, cette Basse fondamentale, l'unique Boussole de l'Oreille, ce guide invisible du Musicien, qui l'a toujours conduit dans toutes ses productions, sans qu'il s'en soit encore apperçû, mais dont il n'a pas plutôt oüi parler, qu'il l'a regardé comme son propre bien; je connoissois déja cette Basse fondamentale, a-t'il dit; cependant s'il se fût bien examiné, il auroit dit simplement, je la sentois: c'est effectivement un de ces sentimens naturels auxquels on peut fort bien ne pas penser, mais qui se développent en nous au moment qu'on nous les rapelle.' Emphasis added (Hayes, p. 16).

[30] *Génération harmonique*, Chapter 19, p. 219: 'J'appelle ignorance, toute connoissance qui ne vient que d'une expérience simplement formée par le sentiment; cette connoissance n'en est pas une, à proprement parler, c'est seulement une réminiscence d'un effet éprouvé à l'occasion d'un certain arrangement entre les parties, dont on ignore la cause' (Hayes, p. 247).

[31] In addition to the 'efficient' cause, which corresponds to 'cause' in our usual usage (that which actively brings about some event or the existence of some entity), Aristotle also regards as 'causes' the 'formal' and 'material' principles of any entity, which are included in a proper determination of its 'essence,' as expressed in its definition, as well as its purpose or 'end', the so-called 'final cause'. See Aristotle, *Physics* II.3 (194b17–195a26) and II.7; *Metaphysics* I.3 (983a24–33). In *Posterior Analytics*, II.11, Aristotle names as the four types of 'explanation' the efficient and final causes, the essence and necessary entailment of the explanandum by something else (94a20–4).

[32] Note that the word *techne*, translated here as 'art', denotes any developed craft, and in particular the organised system of technical knowledge associated with such; Aristotle is using it here as a near-synonym for *episteme*, as the context clearly shows.

rather than to experience . . . For men of experience know *that* the thing is so [*to hoti*], but do not know *why* [*to dioti*], while the others know the "why" and the *cause*.'[33]

This Classical view of knowledge explains, for example, why Rameau can say of his great precursors, Lully and Corelli, that they did not truly 'know' what they were doing, for they did not understand how music is the product of the fundamental bass and its ultimate cause, the *corps sonore*.[34] The fact that each was 'skilled' (*habile*) in composition, that Rameau approves of their music and clearly regards it, particularly that of Lully, as exemplifying his own theoretical principles, does not in Rameau's view mean that they in some sense 'knew' those principles. On the contrary, Rameau writes at one point in his analysis of Lully's recitative 'Enfin il est en ma puissance' from *Armide*: 'Let one reflect on this, after having come into possession of the foundation of the art, and one will see what *Instinct*, by itself, can do; for Lully, guided by *feeling* and by taste, had no *knowledge* of this foundation, which was *unknown* in his day.'[35]

---

[33] Aristotle, *Metaphysics*, I.1, 980a27–981a30; trans. in *The Complete Works of Aristotle: The Revised Oxford Translation*, ed. Jonathan Barnes (Princeton: Princeton University Press, 1984), vol. II, pp. 1552–3. Emphasis partly added, partly in the original. Aristotle's main discussion of scientific knowledge is his *Posterior Analytics*; for a good introductory account, see Timothy A. Robinson, *Aristotle in Outline* (Indianapolis and Cambridge, Mass.: Hackett, 1995), pp. 15–42. The Greek language's many words for 'knowledge' and 'know' perhaps made it easier for Aristotle to acknowledge that there are various kinds and degrees of knowledge. Rameau, on the other hand, does not even seem to make any systematic use of the distinction in French between 'connaître' and 'savoir', using them (as far as I can tell) interchangeably, although in general he uses the former far more frequently than the latter. Of course, Rameau is quite capable of using either word in a less restrictive sense than that pointed out here; in so doing he is simply following common usage, and the resulting inconsistencies will surprise no one who has spent much time with his writings.

[34] For Rameau's discussion of Corelli, which is a critique of the latter's use of figured-bass signatures in his Sonatas Op. 5, see *Nouveau système*, Chapter 23, in which Rameau writes, for example, that his remarks have shown 'that Corelli's figures are worthless, and that he absolutely did not *know* that which his *ear* caused him to practice with such success in this passage' (Chandler, p. 417; *Nouveau Système*, p. 103; *CTW*, vol. II, p. 113). 'On peut juger sur ces remarques que le chiffre de Corelly ne vaut rien, & qu'il n'a pas absolument *connu* ce que son *Oreille* lui a fait pratiquer avec succès en cet endroit.' Emphasis added. See also *Nouveau Système*, pp. 105–6; *CTW*, vol. II, pp. 115–16; Chandler, p. 422.

[35] *Observations*, p. 76: 'Qu'on y fasse réflexion, après s'être bien mis au fait au fonds de l'Art, & l'on verra de quoi le seul Instinct est capable; car Lulli, conduit par le *sentiment*, & par le goût, n'avoit aucune *connoissance* de ce fonds, *inconnu* de son tems.' Emphasis added. Rameau's discussion of Lully's recitative, which occupies pp. 54–125 of the *Observations*, was occasioned by Rousseau's attack on French music in general and Lully's recitative in particular (which Rameau in his *Nouveau système*, as well as others, had singled out as a model of expressive text setting). The treatise is in large part a reassertion of Rameau's conviction that harmony is prior to and generates melody (and a refutation of Rousseau's opposed view), by way of a review of his theory as developed in the *Démonstration* of four years earlier (1750). But much of it is given over to a remarkably sensitive phrase-by-phrase analysis of Lully's recitative, intended to show (*contra* Rousseau) how Lully had subtly employed precisely the right means of 'modulation' to capture the rapidly shifting emotions of the heroine. These means are just the ones that Rameau believes are indicated by his natural principle and the theoretical principles he deduces therefrom. For accounts of Rameau's theory of 'modulation', its development over time and Rameau's application of it in his analysis of the Lully recitative, see Cynthia Verba, 'The Development of Rameau's Thoughts on Modulation and Chromaticism', *Journal of the American Musicological Society* 26 (1973), 69–97, and 'Rameau's Views on Modulation and Their Background in French Theory', *Journal of the American Musicological Society* 31 (1978), 467–79.

Now in the traditional, Aristotelian 'psychology' of the pre-modern West, the 'part' or faculty of the 'soul' (*psyche*) involved in the production of knowledge in this scientific sense was the 'thinking' (*dianoetikon*) part, the mind or intellect (*nous*), which was distinct from (and superior to) the 'sensitive' (*aisthetikon*) part of the soul, responsible for sense perception or sensation (*aisthesis*).[36] As we have seen, Rameau assumes a similar separation of faculties between the rational mind (*l'esprit*) and the sense of hearing, the ear (*l'oreille*). Indeed, his opposition between, on the one hand, 'sensation' (the 'ear'), 'feeling' and 'experience', and on the other hand, 'knowledge' and the 'mind' (or the intellect, 'reflection' or 'reason'), is in essence nothing other than the Classical Greek opposition of the senses and the intellect, familiar from the ancient debates between the Pythagoreans and Aristoxenians, in its latter-day form as the opposition between *sensus* and *ratio*, which had figured in accounts of music from Ptolemy and Boethius until at least Rameau's time.[37]

The ear, as *sensus*, stands for Rameau in essentially the same relation to *l'esprit*, the rational intellect and to knowledge, as it had stood in relation to *ratio* and *scientia* for Ptolemy, Boethius and numerous later musical writers of the Middle Ages and Renaissance. It is necessary, but not sufficient; it perceives correctly, but without clarity; it provides sensory experience, which is, to be sure, the foundation of knowledge as well as the criterion for judging the correctness of theory, but does not itself constitute true knowledge. 'The judgement of the ear is always well founded', Rameau writes, 'and, obscure though it may be without the aid of reason, it nevertheless adds to the light of the latter, once reason has explicated for us the *causes* of [the ear's] judgement. For us, this is a double confirmation: to see Reason and the Ear thus in accord with each other.'[38] Whatever its actual sources may have been, Rameau's tacit understanding of the human subject – or of the soul – is in effect the traditional,

[36] Aristotle, *De anima (On the Soul)*, Bks. II–III, esp. II.2–3; III.3 (427b7–15), III.4–8.

[37] The *locus classicus* is Boethius, *De institutione musica*, esp. I.9 and V.2 (the latter based on Ptolemy, *Harmonics*, I.1). This opposition did not mean, of course, that there was no acknowledgement by the upholders of *ratio* of the role played by sense experience in the production of knowledge. On the contrary, all those whose thought was influenced by Aristotle regarded the deliverances of the senses as the basic and necessary materials (although not the limits) of all knowledge, a view epitomised in the oft-quoted Scholastic maxim that 'there is nothing in the intellect that was not first perceived by the senses' (*nihil in intellectu quod non prius in sensu*) – an axiom taken over and given new significance by Locke; the British empiricists' and high French Enlightenment's grounding of all knowledge in sensation was by no means entirely new. Nonetheless, music-theoretical writings from the Renaissance to the eighteenth century tended to fall back upon the explanations of basic musical phenomena in terms of 'rational' mathematical principles (interval ratios and proportions) that had originally been developed in the Pythagorean-Platonic school of Harmonics and which had always been the main focus of traditional 'speculative' music theory throughout Antiquity and the Middle Ages. This tradition was still strong enough in the first half of the eighteenth century in Germany for Mattheson to feel obliged to devote hundreds of pages to its refutation. See Christensen, '*Sensus, Ratio*, and *Phthongos*' for an account of this late stage of the *sensus/ratio* debate.

[38] *Génération harmonique*, Chapter 7, p. 78: 'Le jugement de l'Oreille est toujours fondé, & tout obscur qu'il est sans le secours de la raison, il ajoute cependant aux lumieres de celle-ci, quand une fois elle nous a développé les causes de ce jugement: c'est pour nous une double confirmation de voir ainsi la Raison & l'Oreille s'accorder ensemble' (Hayes, p. 103). Note the explicit opposition of 'reason' (*la Raison*, i.e. *ratio*) and 'the ear' (*l'oreille*, i.e. *sensus*), and the typical association of the former with knowledge of the *causes* of a phenomenon.

Aristotelian conception of the 'psychology of faculties', which discerns in the soul three distinct 'parts' or 'faculties' (or even three distinct 'souls'), each with its own functions and operations – the 'vegetative', responsible for operations such as nutrition, reproduction and bodily motion; the 'sensitive', responsible for sensation (the perception of both external sense impressions and internal 'feelings') among other things; and the 'understanding' or 'intellect', the highest faculty, responsible for acts of willing, rational thought and conceptual understanding. Such a psychology segregates the operation of sense perception from that of intellection, and thus tends to bar sense experience itself from counting as knowledge properly so called.

MIND, THOUGHT AND SENSE PERCEPTION IN DESCARTES

At this point the question naturally arises, how does Rameau's implicit understanding of the 'soul' relate to the philosophical psychologies current in his own day? In particular, how do his implicit beliefs about the possibility of unconscious sensory perception relate to the psychological views of Descartes, whose influence upon Rameau, at least in other respects, is beyond reasonable doubt?[39]

Descartes, as is well known, defines the human subject as a *res cogitans*, a 'thing that thinks'.[40] More precisely, a human being is, essentially, a *mind* (*mens, esprit*), or *soul* (*anima, âme*) – Descartes uses these words interchangeably – which is both utterly different in essence from, and yet in a mysterious fashion united to, a corporeal 'machine', an animal body. Now the first important point in this for us is that, in his understanding of the respective roles of the soul and the body, Descartes completely rejects the traditional Aristotelian 'psychology of faculties', positing instead a mind or soul that is absolutely unified.[41] Operations such as nutrition and corporeal movement, which the traditional psychology had attributed to the lowest of the three distinct psychic faculties, the 'vegetative soul', Descartes instead regards as activities of the body alone, entirely explicable in terms of the mechanical actions of the nerves, brain and muscles. The mind or soul, however, is defined by its essential and continuous activity of *thought* (*cogitatio, pensée*). This Descartes understands to include, not only acts of the intellect and the will, which had always been attributed to the 'intellectual soul' in traditional psychology, but also faculties and activities which had

---

[39] Rameau's 'Cartesianism' has been a standard topos at least since the work of Charles Paul, 'Rameau's Musical Theories and the Age of Reason' (Ph.D. thesis, University of California, Berkeley, 1966), and 'Jean-Philippe Rameau (1683–1764): The Musician as *Philosophe*', *Proceedings of the American Philosophical Society* 114 (1970), 140–54. For a good introduction to the topic and the issues of historical interpretation it raises, see Christensen, *Rameau and Musical Thought*, Chapter 1, esp. pp. 11–20.

[40] See esp. Descartes, *Meditations*, *The Philosophical Writings of Descartes*, trans. John Cottingham, Robert Stoothoff and Dugald Murdoch, 3 vols. (Cambridge: Cambridge University Press, 1984–91), vol. I, pp. 1–62 (hereafter cited as CSM), II and VI; *Discourse on the Method* (CSM, vol. II, pp. 109–75), IV, sections 1–3.

[41] In a letter to Plempius of 15 February 1638, Descartes writes that it is 'an article of faith (*de fide*) that the rational soul is indivisible and does not have conjoined with it any sensitive or vegetative [part] ...' (ed. in *Œuvres de Descartes*, ed. Charles Adam and Paul Tannery, rev. edn, Paris: Vrin/C.N.R.S., 1964–76), vol. I, p. 523 (hereafter cited as A-T); cited after Geneviève Rodis-Lewis, *Le problème de l'inconscient et le cartésianisme* (Paris: Presses Universitaires de France, 1950), p. 52, n. 4). See Descartes, *Traité de l'homme*, in A-T, vol. IX, p. 202; *The Passions of the Soul*, Pt. I, para. 47.

83

been regarded as belonging to the 'sensitive soul', including, most crucially for us, sense perception, or as I shall sometimes say, 'sensing' (*sentire*). For Descartes the mind, unlike the body, is a thing that is 'utterly indivisible', 'one and entire' and, he goes on: 'Nor can the faculties of willing, of understanding, of *sensing* and so on, be termed parts of the mind, since it is one and the same mind that wills, and senses, and understands.'[42] Descartes thus departs in a fundamental way from the traditional conception of the soul: he explicitly rejects the Aristotelian division of the soul into several distinct 'parts' or faculties, including a 'sensitive' faculty which would be the domain of *sensus* and a separate rational or intellective faculty which would be the domain of *ratio*, and instead conceives of the soul as a unity which is defined by a single activity unique to it, which he calls 'thinking' (*cogitare*, *penser*), which, again, includes acts of sense perception.

The second crucial point is that Descartes regards it as axiomatic that all the operations of the mind or soul are conscious, in the sense that the subject always has some sort of awareness, however attenuated, of the objects of his consciousness – his 'thoughts'. Thought signifies for him 'all that is in us in such a way that we are immediately *conscious* of it. Thus *all* operations of the will, intellect, imagination *and the senses* are thoughts.'[43] Similarly, in *Principles of Philosophy*, Descartes writes: 'By the term "thought", I understand all the things of which we are *conscious* as happening within us, in so far as we *are* conscious of them. Hence *thinking* is to be identified here not merely with understanding, willing and imagining, but also with *sensing*.'[44]

To be sure, Descartes's understanding of sensory perception is more complex than this, for he recognises that (unlike intellection, which he regards as an operation of the mind or soul in its pure activity as *res cogitans* and not, in principle, dependent on the body) sensation, since it is actually a complex psycho-physical activity, necessarily entails corporeal processes, which can themselves be regarded as 'sensation' in a broad sense of the term, in as much as they are the indispensable basis for sensation in the proper sense.[45] Nonetheless, Descartes's most thorough discussion of physical

---

[42] Descartes, *Meditations*, VI; A-T, vol. VII, pp. 85–6: 'Nempe imprimis hic adverto magnam esse differentiam inter mentem & corpus, in eo quod corpus ex natura sua sit semper divisibile, mens autem plane indivisibile; nam sane cum hanc considero, sive meipsum quatenus sum tantum res cogitans, nullas in me partes possum distinguere, sed rem plane unam & integram me esse intelligo . . . neque etiam facultates volendi, sentiendi, intelligendi &c. ejus partes dici possunt, quia una & eadem mens est quae vult, quae sentit, quae intelligit.' Emphasis added. See trans. in CSM, vol. II, p. 59.

[43] Descartes, *Second Replies*, A-T, vol. VII, p. 160: 'Cogitationis nomine complector illud omne quod sic in nobis est, ut ejus immediate conscii sumus. Ita omnes voluntatis, intellectus, imaginationis & sensuum operationes sunt cogitationes' (see CSM, vol. II, p. 113). Emphasis added.

[44] Descartes, *Principles of Philosophy*, I.9; A-T, vol. VIII-1, p. 7: 'Cogitationis nomine, intelligo illa omnia, quae nobis consciis in nobis fiunt, quatenus eorum in nobis conscientia est. Atque ita non modo intelligere, velle, imaginari, sed etiam sentire, idem est hic quod cogitare' (see CSM, vol. I, p. 195). Emphasis added. Descartes goes on to emphasise the point regarding awareness or consciousness, and in so doing makes clear that he does not regard the mechanical functioning of the physical visual apparatus as 'seeing'; there must also be a mental awareness of seeing (i.e. seeing *something*). Without this mental act of awareness, which Descartes calls 'the actual sense', there is no sensation. The same, presumably, is true for sound and hearing, with disastrous consequences for Rameau's beliefs about the 'ear' and the role of the *corps sonore*.

[45] See Descartes, *Sixth Replies*, A-T, vol. VII, pp. 436–8; trans. CSM, vol. II, pp. 294–5, and for more

sensation makes it clear that for him it is only with the 'immediate effects produced *in the mind*' by sensory stimuli that one can properly speak of 'sensations' such as sound.[46] While the operation of the corporeal sense organs, nerves and brain are necessary to it, they are not sufficient to constitute sensation properly so called, for that entails the mind's actual awareness of the sensations, as we learn when Descartes likens sense perception in non-human animals to the automatic, *quasi*-sensory functioning of the organs of sight in those situations in which 'the mind is distracted by something else' and thus does not consciously 'sense' that to which the body may nonetheless react.[47] For Descartes, mechanical reactions of the sense organs to stimuli do not constitute true sensation; if no visual image or 'idea' actually reaches consciousness, it would be self-contradictory to say that sense-perception has occurred, since, although sensation is an act of the soul and body together, 'it is the soul that has perceptions, and not the body'.[48] And there is, of course, no reason whatsoever to suppose that the same would not be true of hearing.[49]

We may supplement our discussion of Cartesian psychology by considering briefly

detailed discussion, see John Cottingham, *Descartes* (Oxford: Blackwell, 1986), pp. 122–34, and Gary Hatfield, 'Descartes' Physiology and its Relation to his Psychology', in *The Cambridge Companion to Descartes*, ed. John Cottingham (Cambridge: Cambridge University Press, 1992), pp. 335–70.

[46] Descartes, *Sixth Replies*, A-T, vol. VII, p. 437; trans. CSM, vol. II, p. 294. Emphasis added.

[47] In such cases, Descartes explains, 'although the images of external objects may impinge upon our retinas, and it may even happen that the resulting impressions on our optic nerves cause various motions of our limbs, nonetheless we *sense nothing* of them; in such a case we are moved just as automata' ('ostendam me non putare bruta videre sicut nos, dum sentimus nos videre; sed tantummodo sicut nos, dum mente alio avocata, licet obiectorum externorum imagines in retinis oculorum nostrorum pingantur, & forte etiam illarum impressiones in nervis opticis factae ad diversos motus membra nostra determinent, *nihil tamen prorsus eorum sentimus*; quo casu etiam nos non aliter movemur, quam automata, ad quorum motus ciendos nemo dixerit vim caloris non sufficere' in 'Letter to Plempius', 3 October 1637; ed. A-T, vol. I, pp. 413–14).

[48] Descartes, *Optics*, Discourse 4; A-T, vol. VI, p. 109; trans. CSM, vol. I, p. 164. Since the influence upon Rameau of one of the most important 'Cartesians', Malebranche, has been urged by some scholars (see, for instance, Christensen, *Rameau and Musical Thought*, pp. 298–301), it may be worth noting that he takes essentially the same view of the matter: 'by the words thought, manner of thinking, or modification of the soul, I understand generally all those things which cannot be in the soul without the soul perceiving [*apperçoive*] them through the inner perception [*intérieur sentiment*] that it has of itself – *such as its sensations*, imaginings, pure intellections, or simply conceptions, as well as its passions and natural inclinations' (Malebranche, *Recherche de la Vérité*, Book III, Chapter 2, section 1; cited after Tad M. Schmaltz, *Malebranche's Theory of the Soul: A Cartesian Interpretation* (New York and Oxford: Oxford University Press, 1996), p. 17). Emphasis added.

[49] In an exhaustive study of the problem of the unconscious in Cartesian thought, Rodis-Lewis shows how Descartes supports his firmly held belief that there is always some sort of 'thinking' activity going in the soul with subtle analyses of various marginal psychological states such as sleep and early infancy, and in so doing clearly indicates his recognition of different 'levels' or 'degrees' (as she puts it) of consciousness, which shade off into attenuated states of awareness some of which could easily be characterised as 'subconscious'. Descartes himself, however, apparently never admitted the existence of truly unconscious mental acts. On the contrary, his point is precisely that, even in the most apparently doubtful cases, it can be shown by close observation and introspective analysis that the soul is not only always thinking, but is always conscious, in however attenuated a manner, of its thoughts. See Rodis-Lewis, *Le problème de l'inconscient et le cartésianisme*, esp. pp. 42–61. See also Catherine Glyn Davies, *Conscience as Consciousness: The Idea of Self-Awareness in French Philosophical Writing from Descartes to Diderot* (Oxford: The Voltaire Foundation, 1990), pp. 1–21.

the second of the two dominant philosophical psychologies of Rameau's time, that of Locke, with whose 'sensationalist' philosophy Rameau's ideas have also been linked.[50] Locke's views with regard to unconscious sensation turn out to be remarkably close to those of Descartes. Indeed, Rameau would have fared no better on this point with Locke, who argued explicitly against those (unfortunately unnamed but presumably Cartesian) thinkers who maintained that 'the soul thinks always', stating categorically that, as he puts it, a man 'cannot think at any time, waking or sleeping, without being sensible of it. Our being sensible of it is not necessary to anything but to our thoughts, and to them it is, and . . . will always be, necessary, till we can think without being conscious of it.'[51] And since for Locke, as for the Cartesians, 'thought' is the general term for all the activities of the mind with regard to its 'ideas', including (most basically for Locke) the 'simple ideas of sensation', it follows that, once again, there can be no unconscious sensations. Indeed, Locke pronounced definitively on a case regarding hearing that is remarkably close both to Descartes's example of reflexive vision and to that of the *corps sonore*, and can serve as a sort of connecting link between the two:

How often may a man observe in himself, that whilst his mind is intently employed in the contemplation of some objects, and curiously surveying the ideas that are there, it takes no notice of impressions of sounding bodies made upon the organ of hearing [despite the fact that these may occur] with the same alteration [of the physical auditory apparatus] that uses to be for the producing the idea of sound! A sufficient impulse there may be upon the organ; but it not reaching the observation of the mind, there follows no perception: and though the motion that uses to produce the idea of sound be made in the ear, yet no sound is heard. Want of sensation in this case is not through any defect in the organ, or that the man's ears are less affected than at other times when he does hear: but that which uses to produce the idea, though conveyed in by the usual organ, not being taken notice of in the understanding, and so imprinting no idea on the mind, there follows no sensation.[52]

Locke's 'sensationalism', then, provides no more comfort than does Descartes's 'rationalism' to Rameau's thesis that music had always been based on the acoustical data of the *corps sonore* despite people's failure actually to hear them. For both Locke and Descartes, this would be an even clearer, and stronger, case of physical stimuli reaching the sense organ but failing to produce an 'idea of sound' in the mind – in this case because they are in themselves simply not 'sufficient' to do so without extraordinary attention on the part of the perceiving subject. And without such a conscious 'idea' of the sensed stimulus there is no sensation.

[50] See Christensen, *Rameau and Musical Thought*, pp. 12–13, 215–18.

[51] John Locke, *An Essay Concerning Human Understanding* (London: George Routledge and Sons, Ltd., and New York: E. P. Dutton and Co., [1910]), II.1.10. It will be noted that, if this attack is directed against Descartes himself, it is misconceived since, as already noted, Descartes does not claim that the soul thinks without being 'sensible', that is conscious, of its thoughts, but rather that consciousness is subject to degrees (see above, n. 49). Locke's remarks may have been directed against other thinkers of basically Cartesian persuasion who had accepted the possibility of truly 'unconscious thoughts' in theological and moral contexts; see Rodis-Lewis, *Le problème de l'inconscient et le cartésianisme*, pp. 188–257.   [52] Locke, *Essay*, II.9.4; see also II.9.3.

The contrast between these views and Rameau's regarding the operations of the ear is indeed striking. For Descartes, sensation is an operation of the mind in its essential, continual activity of thought. For Rameau, the ear, as a sense, is quite distinct from the mind and, perhaps for just that reason, is able to operate without the conscious awareness of its possessor. This would presumably explain, for Rameau, how it could be that musicians had always been influenced by the *corps sonore* without their being aware of the fact. But it also entails that what the ear produces, in its operations of unconscious sensation and deduction, is not *knowledge*, for knowledge, which as we have seen is for Rameau always scientific in nature, and therefore necessarily explicit and conscious, can only be produced by the mind.

In the light of this opposition between the ear or sense perception and the mind, reason and knowledge, Rameau understands his own task to be, not a transmutation of one kind of knowledge (unconscious, inexplicit) into another kind of knowledge (conscious, explicit), as the 'cognitive' interpretation would have it, but rather the transformation by the rational intellect of what had formerly always been, until his own discoveries, a foreshadowing of knowledge furnished by sense experience, into the transparent self-evidence of science, of 'theory': 'Many musicians', he writes in the Dedication to *Génération harmonique*, 'even those who have most successfully used the means their art can provide for them in [producing and judging musical works], have used these means *without knowing them*. Yet there is no doubt that these same means could be reduced to *theory* by people as accustomed as you to joining *reflection* to *sensation*', and he goes on to note, with charming self-deprecation, that he himself has 'made a few discoveries' in this 'territory so little known, although often travelled'.[53]

'INSTINCT' AND THE 'GIFT OF NATURE'

Rameau never abandoned his concept of 'the ear'. But in later writings he supplemented it with another concept, that of 'instinct', which at the time he regarded as sufficiently important to serve as the leading theme of his *Observations sur notre instinct pour la musique*, published in 1754. Characteristically, Rameau never tells us exactly what he means by 'instinct'. His use of the word, however, indicates that he uses it as just another name for that mysterious faculty that he had been calling 'the ear'. But it is a name that allows him to come as close as he ever does to providing an explanation of how it would be possible for the ear to do what he believes it does.

He begins the book by telling us that the 'principle' responsible for the 'effects of music' on us is 'Nature herself', and then immediately goes on:

---

[53] *Génération harmonique, Dédication*, fol. ii: 'Beaucoup de Musiciens, même de ceux qui se sont servis le plus heureusement des moïens que peut leur fournir leur Art dans les cas déja cités, les ont emploïés *sans les connoître*; il n'est pas cependant douteux que ces mêmes moïens ne puissent être réduits en *théorie* par les personnes aussi accoutumées que Vous à joindre la *réflexion* au *sentiment*... si j'ai fait quelques découvertes dan un païs si peu connu, quoique très-fréquenté, j'en suis redevable sur-tout aux lumieres dont quelques-uns de Vous, Messieurs, ont bien voulu m'éclairer' (Hayes, p. 14).

It is from her ['Nature'] that we have that feeling that moves us in all our musical operations; she has made us a gift of it, which we can call Instinct.[54]

A number of points emerge from this passage. First, what Rameau here calls 'instinct' is the same thing as 'the feeling that moves us in all our musical operations', which, as shown above, is also the same as what Rameau calls the 'ear', but what we would call our faculty of musical cognition, which produces what Rameau would call experience but what we would call knowledge; thus it is this faculty that Rameau means by 'instinct'. Second, this faculty, this 'feeling' or 'instinct', is something distinct from the true principle of music, the *corps sonore*, which Rameau here calls 'Nature herself'. Third, this instinct or feeling is a 'gift of Nature'. In making this last claim Rameau, in my view, does not intend a mere rhetorical flourish. The ear's almost divinatory perception – without the conscious awareness of the subject – of the acoustical structure of the *corps sonore* and its deduction, again unconsciously performed, of so many of the 'consequences' thereof, make it clear that to Rameau this faculty, whether he calls it the 'ear', our 'feeling for music', our 'sensitivity to harmony' or, as here, 'our instinct for music', is a most remarkable thing, a miraculous gift. Of course, Rameau offers neither any explanation of how this faculty actually operates, nor any hint as to what it is that enables it to accomplish the remarkable feat of intuiting and deducing from the *corps sonore* all of the 'consequences' (namely all of the principles and 'grammatical' rules of music) that Rameau deduces from it. But the continuation of this passage does make it clear that Rameau believes that there is a *causal* relationship between the *corps sonore* and the 'Instinct'. He intends to show how the natural 'principle', the *corps sonore*, as natural cause, is 'verified by our Instinct', which is the *effect* of that cause.[55]

In other words, Nature, in the form of the 'principle' (the *corps sonore*), gives us the 'gift' of our 'Instinct for music' in that this principle *causes* that instinct in us. This is what Rameau means when he says, a few pages later, that 'Music is *natural* to us', for he immediately adds, 'we owe only to pure *Instinct* the agreeable feeling it makes us experience'.[56] It is this 'instinct' that enables human beings to experience and respond to the *corps sonore*, enabling the latter to be the 'natural principle' of music and indeed of 'all the arts of taste' and 'all the sciences subject to calculation'.[57]

[54] *Observations, Préface*, p. iii (*CTW*, vol. III, p. 259): 'Pour joüir pleinement des effets de la Musique, il faut être dans un pur abandon de soi-même, & pour en juger, c'est au Principe par lequel on est affecté qu'il faut s'en rapporter. Ce Principe est la Nature même, c'est d'elle que nous tenons ce sentiment qui nous meut dans toutes nos Opérations musicales, elle nous en a fait un don qu'on peut appeller *Instinct*.'

[55] *Observations, Préface*, p. vii: 'the principle is verified by our Instinct, and that Instinct by its principle; that is to say . . . the cause is verified by the experienced effect, and that effect by its cause' ('le principe se vérifie par notre Instinct, & cet Instinct par son principe, c'est-à-dire . . . la cause se vérifie par l'effet qu'on éprouve, & cet effet par sa cause'). See *ibid.*, p. xiv, p. 2.

[56] *Observations*, p. 1: 'La Musique nous est naturelle, nous ne devons qu'au pur Instinct le sentiment agréable qu'elle nous fait éprouver . . .'

[57] *Observations, Préface*, p. xv: 'Le Principe dont il s'agit, est non-seulement celui de tous les Arts de goût . . . il l'est encore de toutes les Sciences soumises au calcul: ce qu'on ne peut nier, sans nier en même tems que ces Sciences ne soient fondées sur les proportions & progressions, dont la Nature nous fait part dans le Phénoméne du Corps sonore.'

But what exactly does Rameau mean by 'instinct'? The eighteenth-century *Dictionnaire* of the French Academy defined 'instinct' as 'a feeling or movement *independent of reflection*, which nature has given to the animals to make them know and seek that which is good for them, and avoid that which is harmful', following this up with several examples of common usage, of which the first is 'a natural instinct'. The entry adds that the word 'is also applied to human beings, and is taken to mean *a first movement which precedes reflection*', providing as the first example of such usage the sentence 'he did it more by instinct than by *reason*'.[58] Thus 'instinct' in the normal French usage of Rameau's time seems to have meant more or less what it typically means today: 'an impulse that a living being owes to its nature' rather than to rational thought, or 'the behaviour by which such an impulse manifests itself'.[59] Within this concept of 'instinct' there seem to be two distinct but related ideas that play a key role in Rameau's use of the concept. First, 'instinct' is non- (or sub-, or pre-) rational; it is not an aspect or faculty of the intellect, and hence, for Rameau, not of the mind. This, of course, must be the case if the 'Instinct for music' is to stand as a sort of surrogate for 'the ear'. Second, instinct is a faculty of animals, including human beings, which is implanted in them, or 'given' to them, by 'nature', and which is therefore itself an aspect of the 'natural' in them, and accordingly represents as well an aspect of 'nature' itself. On both counts, instinct is opposed to reason and intellect (and again, for Rameau, to mind and knowledge).[60]

And yet, although instinct is a manifestation of 'nature', it is one that is not 'out there' in the objective world, but *within* the human subject. It is not the 'Nature' represented by the *corps sonore*, the nature that is the object of empirical science, but a

---

[58] *Dictionnaire de l'Académie Française*, 5th edn (Paris, 1798), vol. I, p. 736: 'Sentiment, mouvement <*indépendant de la réflexion*, et> que la nature a donné aux animaux, pour leur faire connoître <et chercher> ce qui leur est bon, et <éviter ce qui leur est> nuisible. *Un instinct naturel* . . . Il se dit aussi De l'homme, et se prend pour un premier mouvement <qui précède> la réflexion. *Il a fait cela plutôt par instinct, que par raison*' (italics here as in the original; emphasis added in translation). Apart from trivial alterations of spelling and diction, these definitions and examples are the same as those in the first edition of 1694 (vol. I, p. 600), with the exception of the phrases enclosed in angled brackets. The 1694 edition lacks the first three of these entirely – most significantly, it lacks the phrase 'indépendant de la réflexion' in the first definition – and in the fourth of them it has 'without reflection'. I have not been able to ascertain exactly when these changes were made.

[59] *Le Nouveau Petit Robert: Dictionnaire de la langue française*, p. 1187. The word is attested in French from 1580, with the sense 'an inborn, powerful tendency common to all living things or to all the individuals of the same species' (*ibid.*). As for contemporary English usage, a popular American dictionary provides the following as the primary definitions of 'instinct': (1) 'a natural or inherent aptitude, impulse, or capacity'; (2) a. 'a largely inheritable and unalterable response to environmental stimuli without involving reason'; b. 'behaviour that is mediated by reactions below the conscious level' in *Webster's Ninth New Collegiate Dictionary* (Springfield, Mass.: Merriam-Webster, Inc., 1991), p. 627.

[60] This concept of instinct, and the sharp division between instinct and intellect, reason and knowledge that it assumes, was criticised shortly after the appearance of Rameau's *Observations* (1754) by Condillac in his *Traité des animaux* (1755), Part II, Chapter 5. Interestingly, at the same time, Rousseau – despite his many sharp disagreements with Rameau on musical issues – expressed views regarding instinct that seem quite close to those of Rameau; see Rousseau, *Discours sur l'origine et les fondements de l'inégalité parmi les hommes* (1755), in *Œuvres complètes*, ed. B. Gagnebin and M. Raymond (Paris: Pléiade, 1959–95), vol. III, pp. 141–4.

special form of nature, presented as a 'gift' by Nature herself. This special form of nature is the correlative faculty, within the human subject, of the *corps sonore*, which enables the human subject to respond to the *corps sonore* and elicit from it at least some of the riches that Rameau believes it has to offer – although not *all* of those riches, of course, since that requires a faculty that is opposed to instinct, namely reason.

These terms thus array themselves in two opposing groups: on the one hand, the mind, reason, intellect, knowledge, science; on the other, the ear, sensation, feeling, experience and instinct. The two series of concepts are mediated by Rameau's concept of 'Nature'.

'NATURE'

It is obvious that nature is the domain of Rameau's fundamental principle, the *corps sonore*. As an acoustical phenomenon, the *corps sonore* represents nature understood from the perspective of post-Newtonian empirical science, as Rameau's attempts at experimental 'verification' of this phenomenon show, and more or less as we still understand it today: as the objective realm of physical phenomena and their laws, the object of the empirico-deductive science produced by the mind in the exercise of its distinctive faculty, reason.[61]

But for many in the eighteenth century, including Rameau, as indeed for many even today, this 'scientific' concept of nature coexists with and indeed is *explained* by and *part of* a concept of 'Nature' as a benevolent, virtually divine force or entity – a *mère bien faisante*.[62] The trope of personification must surely be Rameau's favourite rhetorical device, but even so it is striking how continually in his writings Nature is personified, her good intentions and providential concern for humanity asserted. A portion of the entry on 'Nature' in the *Encyclopédie* is devoted to just such a view. In this sense, 'Nature' signifies 'the action of Providence, the principle of all things, that is to say, that power or spiritual being which acts and operates on all bodies in order to give them their properties or to produce in them certain effects. Nature taken in this sense is nothing other than God himself.'[63]

This is the providential Nature that offers us 'gifts' – the gift of the human 'instinct' for music and the prior gift of the *corps sonore* itself. 'Nature is as fruitful as she is

[61] See esp. *Génération harmonique*, Chapter 1.
[62] See the *Préface* of Rameau's last treatise, the *Vérités intéressantes* of 1763–4: 'What has Nature not done in order to instruct us? She begins by placing in our hands the unique model of all mathematical truth; and this model is the *corps sonore*. Nature herself has taken care to form it; she has communicated in it a language that can be heard and grasped by all nations ... *Nature, that beneficent mother*, does not stop there: she suggests to us easy means of making an instrument with which *the ear* might be able to enlighten *reason*' (ed. Herbert Schneider, *Jean-Philippe Rameaus letzter Musiktraktat 'Vérités également ignorées et intéressantes tirées du sein de la Nature' (1764): kritische Ausgabe mit Kommentar*, Beihefte zum Archiv für Musikwissenschaft, vol. XXV (Wiesbaden and Stuttgart: Franz Steiner, 1986), p. 7). Emphasis added.
[63] Denis Diderot and Jean le Rond d'Alembert (eds.), *Encyclopédie ou Dictionnaire raisonné des sciences, des arts, et des métiers*, 35 vols. (Paris: Briasson, David, Le Breton, Durand, 1751–80; rpt Stuttgart-Bad Cannstatt: Friedrich Frommann, 1988), vol. XI, p. 40, col. 2.

simple', Rameau writes in the Preface to *Génération harmonique*. 'She offers us inexhaustible treasures in her heart', although 'it is up to us discover the paths to them'.[64] But even in our task of discovering Nature's treasures, Nature thoughtfully provides us with the indispensable clue, for 'Nature has taken care to assemble into a harmonic whole, and in this way to communicate to the ear, what judgement also has seized with the aid of other principles.'[65]

To some modern readers, Rameau may perhaps appear to be vacillating between two different and incompatible concepts of nature, the modern 'scientific' one which was already current in his own day, and with which Rameau is typically associated in modern scholarship, and the 'providential' one just discussed, which harks back to a religious conception of the world that many even at the time regarded as outmoded. For Rameau, though, as for others among his contemporaries, the two are merely different aspects of the same phenomenon, force or entity, coexisting without contradiction. And it is this view of nature, finally, that makes possible Rameau's understanding of that which we would call unconscious musical knowledge.

If nature in one sense is the world studied by empirical science, the realm of objective physical laws and events such as the *corps sonore*, it is also, at the same time, that which operates *within* the human subject in the form of musical instinct, the 'gift of nature'. This intra-subjective form of nature renders available to the human subject, at least in a provisional way, that which objective nature in the form of the *corps sonore* has to offer. In other words, because it is the *same* 'Nature' operating in both domains, the objective and the subjective, the problem raised by the 'cognitive' interpretation of Rameau's thought, that of the agency or faculty responsible for the transmutation of the acoustical data provided by the *corps sonore* into unconscious *knowledge*, does not arise. At least in this special instance, there *is* no epistemological gap between subjective knowledge and objective event to be overcome. The selfsame Nature that operates objectively in the *corps sonore* as a physical phenomenon also appears *within* the human subject as the faculty correlative to that phenomenon, by which we may initially and provisionally enjoy the fruits of that first and more fundamental gift, even before, and as the necessary preliminary to, the full possession of that gift by Reason.

While there is surely some warrant for seeing in Rameau's theories the origin of our current interest in questions of musical cognition, Rameau himself seems to have understood his project in very different terms. For him, the faculty that governs the musical operations of human subjects – the 'ear' – is a faculty not of the mind, but of the senses, and what it produces within the human subject is not knowledge, which for Rameau is always scientific, systematic, explicit and conscious, but experience, and indeed unconscious experience. Rameau is able to hold these views about the 'ear' because he holds, implicitly to be sure, certain other views regarding the soul and nature – views which are, in different ways, conservative, even by the standards of his

---

[64] *Génération harmonique, Préface*, fol. [v] (*CTW*, vol. III, p. 11): 'la Nature est aussi féconde que simple, elle nous offre dans son sein des trésors inépuisables; mais c'est à nous de découvrir les routes qui doivent y conduire'.   [65] *Génération harmonique*, Chapter 6, p. 75 (Hayes, p. 100).

own time. It thus appears that it was precisely Rameau's allegiance to concepts of the human subject and of nature which were already regarded as old-fashioned in his own day that made it possible for him to bequeath to music theory the very modern problem of musical cognition, the fascinating question of how the mind 'knows' music.

Chapter Four

▬

Nietzsche, Riemann, Wagner: when music lies

LESLIE DAVID BLASIUS

One of the all-too-common devices of fiction is the unlikely encounter between two historical figures. To be sure, this most often takes the form of an encounter between a fictional and a factual character (Sherlock Holmes and Sigmund Freud), but it can also involve the serendipitous meeting of two factual characters (Mahler and Freud), and the expansion on such a factual (if incidental) meeting. I propose to do the same, to take the one brief mention of the theorist Hugo Riemann in Friedrich Nietzsche's late critique of Richard Wagner and to construct an argument from this encounter. Necessarily, my accounts of Nietzsche and Riemann themselves are underdeveloped, extrapolative rather than interpretative, losing the contrast between these two voices. Nietzsche evolves a style of writing intended to dance around, prick, deflate. Layers of irony compound, circle on themselves; particular themes or leitmotifs – performance, authenticity, health, illness – weave their way in and out of the text. Little is as obvious as it seems, a characteristic that has prompted any number of striking and often conflicting hermeneutics.[1] (Given the almost accidental quality of his reference to the theorist, I trust that my own misappropriation of Nietzsche is no more irresponsible than that of others.) Riemann's writing, by contrast, is straightforward. To say this is not to deny him a real insight into the musical experience, and a flair for abstraction, but merely to note that his work seems to demand exposition rather than explication, to discourage the sort of hermeneutics brought to bear on Nietzsche's writings.[2] In defence of this strategy, I can but plead that the encounter between the

---

[1] Nietzsche has of course prompted an enormous amount of writing, drawing in almost every major philosopher of the century (Heidegger, Bataille, Deleuze and Derrida, to name but a few): what is most interesting is his seeming resistance to interpretation (although that resistance is itself thematicised by later writers). I myself have been influenced by two works, Julian Young's *Nietzsche's Philosophy of Art* (Cambridge: Cambridge University Press, 1992), and Eric Blondel's *Nietzsche, le corps et la culture* (1986), trans. Seán Hand as *Nietzsche: The Body and Culture* (Stanford: Stanford University Press, 1991). The latter, in particular, with its representation of Nietzsche as philologist/physician, has some echoes in this essay. Nevertheless, I would not claim any special insight into the philosopher's work. As quoting Nietzsche is a sort of guilty pleasure, I have tried not to indulge to excess.

[2] This is not to say that Riemann is uninteresting: see Brian Hyer, 'Reimag(in)ing Riemann', *Journal of Music Theory* 39 (1995), 101–38. The best rehearsal of Riemann's development and mature thinking is

mercurial philosopher and the stolid theorist locates an extraordinary moment in the history of theory, one in which the nature and assumptions of our discipline are called profoundly into question, and that the ramifications of this critique have played out in important ways in our own century.

Nietzsche's mention of Riemann is found in the eleventh and penultimate section of the main body of *The Case of Wagner*, one of a series of strange and frantic works composed in 1888, the philosopher's last year of sanity.

> The movement Wagner created even reaches over into the field of knowledge: gradually, relevant sciences emerge from centuries of scholasticism. To give an example, I single out for special commendation the merits of *Riemann* regarding rhythmics: he was the first to establish the validity of the central concept of punctuation for music, too (unfortunately, he used an ugly term, *Phrasierung*).[3]

We may initially find ourselves drawn up short by the notion of 'relevant sciences' – might he be referring to the nascent empirical musicologies of the time? – and then only by the location of Riemann within the Wagnerian orbit. Given Nietzsche's training, his approbation does have a certain logic. Faced with the epigram or text, the first task of the philologist is to establish a grammatical or syntactic sense, and only then to deal with the semantics of the passage. We can easily imagine him relating the classical text with the musical text, conceiving Riemann's rhythmics as a sort of philological exercise.[4] Still, this explanation seems a bit forced, and leaves untouched the central

footnote 2 (*cont.*)

found in his 'Ideen zu einer "Lehre von den Tonvorstellungen"' (1914/15), trans. Robert W. Wason and Elizabeth West Marvin as 'Riemann's "Ideen zu einer 'Lehre von den Tonvorstellungen'": an Annotated Translation', *Journal of Music Theory* 36 (1992), 69–117. In light of the discussion in this article, I would note that much of the technical language of this essay ('mental images' and the like) comes directly from the terminology promulgated by the experimental psychologists of the time.

3   Friedrich Nietzsche, *Der Fall Wagner* (1888), trans. Walter Kaufmann as 'The Case of Wagner', in *Basic Writings of Nietzsche* (New York: The Modern Library, 1992), pp. 609–48; citation p. 635. Nietzsche was preoccupied by Wagner in this last year: his published writings include the volume *Nietzsche contra Wagner: Aktenstücke eines Psychologen* (Leipzig: Naumann, 1895). Even by 1888 Riemann had published widely: his music theoretical works (excluding his historical works) included Hugibert Ries (pseud.), 'Musikalische Logik: Ein Beitrag zur Musiktheorie', *Neue Zeitschrift für Musik* 68/28–9, 36–8 (1872), 279–82, 287–8, 353–5, 363–4, 373–4; Riemann, *Musikalische Logik: Hauptzüge der physiologischen und psychologischen Begründung unseres Musiksystems* (Leipzig: C. F. Kahnt, 1874); 'Die objective Existenz der Untertöne in der Schallwelle', *Allgemeine deutsche Musikzeitung* 2/25–6 (1875), 205–6, 213–15; *Die Hülfsmittel der Modulation* (Kassel: Luckhardt'sche Verlagsbuchhandlung, 1875); *Musikalische Syntaxis: Grundriß der harmonischen Satzbildungslehre* (Leipzig: Breitkopf und Härtel, 1877); *Skizze einer neuen Methode der Harmonielehre* (Leipzig: Breitkopf und Härtel, 1880); 'Die Natur der Harmonik', *Sammlung musikalischer Vorträge* 4 (1882), 157–90; *Neue Schule der Melodik* (Hamburg: Karl Grädener and J. F. Richter, 1883); *Musikalische Dynamik und Agogik: Lehrbuch der musikalischen Phrasierung* (Hamburg: Rahter, 1884); *Systematische Modulationslehre als Grundlage der musikalischen Formenlehre* (Hamburg: J. F. Richter, 1887); *Lehrbuch des einfachen, doppelten und imitierenden Kontrapunkts* (Leipzig: Breitkopf und Härtel, 1888); and *Wie hören wir Musik? Drei Vorträge* (Leipzig: Max Hesse, 1888). Nietzsche's reference is to *Musikalische Dynamik und Agogik: Lehrbuch der musikalischen Phrasierung* (Hamburg: Rahter, 1884).

4   In other words, it is plausible that Nietzsche could draw the analogy between music and those classical manuscripts written without punctuation or gaps between words (*scriptio continua*), and compare Riemann's *Phrasierung* to the philological task of determining the lexical disposition of the text and the

question of the stipulation of this theoretical construct as 'Wagnerian'. Riemannian rhythmics would seem ill-fitted to the Wagnerian musical text, in fact, no more fitted to it than Riemannian harmonics (and neither claims any sort of privilege in reference to Wagner's music).[5] Perhaps Nietzsche means here to characterise Riemannian rhythmics as a means of 'Wagnerising' the entire domain of music (relating it in some fashion to the Wagnerian regimentation of the musical sememe). In context, this reading is perhaps slightly more plausible, and in fact the key to a better reading probably lies in that very context (the entire eleventh and penultimate section of *The Case of Wagner*):

11.

I have explained where Wagner belongs – *not* in the history of music. What does he signify nevertheless in that history? The *emergence of the actor in music*: a capital event that invites thought, perhaps also fear. In a formula: 'Wagner and Liszt'.

Never has the integrity of musicians, their 'authenticity', been put to the test so dangerously. One can grasp it with one's very hands: great success, success with the masses no longer sides with those who are authentic – one has to be an actor to achieve that.

Victor Hugo and Richard Wagner – they signify the same thing: in declining cultures, wherever the decision comes to rest with the masses, authenticity becomes superfluous, disadvantageous, a liability. Only the actor still arouses *great* enthusiasm.

Thus the *golden age* dawns for the actor – for him and for everything related to his kind. Wagner marches with drums and pipes at the head of all artists of delivery, of presentation, or virtuosity; the conductors, machinists, and stage singers were the first he convinced. Not to forget the orchestra musicians – these he 'redeemed' from boredom.

The movement Wagner created even reaches over into the field of knowledge: gradually, relevant sciences emerge from centuries of scholasticism. To give an example, I single out for special commendation the merits of *Riemann* regarding rhythmics: he was the first to establish the validity of the central concept of punctuation for music, too (unfortunately, he used an ugly term, *Phrasierung*).

All these are, as I own gratefully, the best among Wagner's admirers, those most deserving of our respect – they are simply right to admire Wagner. They share the same instinct, they recognize in him the highest representative of their type, they feel changed into a power, even a great power, ever since he kindled them with his own ardor. For here, if anywhere, Wagner's influence has been *beneficial*. Never yet has so much been thought, desired, and worked in this area. Wagner has given all of these artists a new conscience. What they now demand of themselves, *get* from themselves, they never demanded of themselves before Wagner came along – formerly, they were too modest. A new spirit prevails in the theater since Wagner's spirit prevails there: one demands what is most difficult, one censures severely, one praises rarely – what is good, even excellent, is considered the rule. Taste is no longer required, not even a voice.

---

placement of diacritical markings. Less likely is the analogy between Riemann's metrics and those of the classical authors (although the relation between classical metrics and modern music had been drawn by Westphal).

[5] Though Riemann himself does not seriously engage Wagner, this does not mean that his ideas cannot yield spectacular insights into the workings of Wagnerian harmony. See David Lewin, 'Amfortas's Prayer to Titurel and the Role of D in *Parsifal*: The Tonal Spaces of the Drama and the Enharmonic Cb/B', *19th-Century Music* 7 (1984), 336–49.

Wagner is sung only with a ruined voice: the effect is 'dramatic'. Even talent is precluded. *Espressivo* at any cost, as demanded by the Wagnerian ideal, the ideal of decadence, does not get along well with talent. It merely requires *virtue* – meaning training, automatism, 'self-denial'. Neither taste, nor voice, nor talent: Wagner's stage requires one thing only – *Teutons!* – Definition of the Teuton: obedience and long legs. –

It is full of profound significance that the arrival of Wagner coincides in time with the arrival of the 'Reich': both events prove the very same thing: obedience and long legs. – Never has obedience been better, never has commanding. Wagnerian conductors in particular are worthy of an age that posterity will call one day, with awed respect, *the classical age of war*. Wagner understood how to command; in this too, he was the great teacher. He commanded as the inexorable will to himself, as lifelong self-discipline: Wagner who furnishes perhaps the greatest example of self-violation in the history of art (– even Alfieri, otherwise his closest relative, stands surpassed. Note by a Turinese).[6]

The citation of Riemann comes into being amidst a culminating and cumulative tumble of indictments – of Wagnerism as a rupture with music itself, specifically as a 'music' (or better, a representation or simulacrum of music) without a genealogy; of the surrender to spectacle, and ultimately to the authoritarian degradation of the social and spiritual. But what is most interesting is the place the mention of Riemann occupies in the rhetorical trajectory of the passage. It seems to occupy a moment of weightlessness, at the apex of the argument, as it were, before Nietzsche's words take on an increasing force and velocity. I think that the position it holds in this trajectory is the key to gaining an interpretative purchase on this citation. To take the analogy further, if we think of Nietzsche's argument as having a trajectory, we can think of this trajectory as being the product of several functions. These functions, I think, must be read as those ideas which are thematicised, four of which I select to analyse Nietzsche's encounter with Riemann: truth, sickness, discipline and conscience.

TRUTH

The notion of a 'truth' of music theory, it goes almost without saying, is quite complex. Only vulgarly would we hold a music theory to be 'true' if it simply described a musical practice. (I think that the notion of theory as a description of practice is itself an artefact of modern historical musicology.) An early seventeenth-century theory of music may be 'true' in so far as it exploits the hermeneutics of similitude and sympathy, an eighteenth-century theory in so far as it embodies a developed conception of whole-number acoustics, a mid-twentieth-century theory if it is formally consistent and replete.

We might qualify this observation by noting that many theories of music do not thematicise the notion of truth, do not explicitly hazard any strong claims. Yet it is precisely to our point that Riemann's work makes such claims without reservation: it is epistemologically self-conscious. We might ground this consciousness in his historical context. I think that theory through the closing two decades of the eighteenth

[6] *The Case of Wagner*, section 11, pp. 634–6.

century and the first half of the nineteenth century is in some sense epistemologically traumatised by the proto-psychologies of sensation and association (with their assumption of the musical subject as *tabula rasa*), and that Riemann understands his work as a recovery from this trauma.[7] In a sense, we might speak of his project as the reconstruction of a 'naturalistic' theory of music. In this, he draws (and, to be accurate, so do subsequent North German theorists of the latter part of the century) on the prestige of the newly empiricised psycho-acoustics, inaugurated in the mid-1860s by Helmholtz's announcement of a new theory of music grounded in the mechanics of physiology and continued afterwards in the musical phenomenologies of Wundt, Lipps, Stumpf and others.[8]

For example, when Riemann speaks of consonance, he distinguishes it by degrees through the invocation of Stumpf's notion of 'fusion'. This is not to assert, though, that Riemann's theory is somehow a slave to the work of the psycho-acousticians: the relationship between music theory and empirical psychology is at once as much one of tension or of awkward exchange as of derivation or rapport. Helmholtz himself seems to backtrack on the claims of the first two sections of the *Lehre von den Tonempfindungen* in the third section of the work, asserting an autonomy for aesthetics, and distinguishing between the 'pure' situation of the psychological laboratory and the complex world of musical practice – a distinction vigorously reasserted by the second generation of psycho-acousticians. Riemann, reciprocally, puts forward his *musikalische Logik* not as a primary mechanism of sensation, but as a perceptual 'representation' of the sonic world. Yet always with this tension comes the assumption of some sort of sympathy or even correspondence between the empirical and the poetic. Helmholtz's periodicity of sound, Lipps's micro-rhythmic theory of consonance both somehow have a strong resonance in the Riemannian normative *Vier-* or *Achttaktigkeit*. Theory is naturalised: it disciplines itself as a *Wissenschaft* (if not, to be anachronistic, as a *Naturwissenschaft*). In short, for Riemann, the question 'What is music?' is displaced by the question 'How do we hear music?', and music theory as an arbitrary system is superseded by theory as a newly accurate representation of nature as manifested in the structure of the mind.

Wagner too makes triumphal truth claims. His, we might venture, is a 'naturalistic' theatre, one whose power stems from psychological insight transmuted into musical substance. To draw an analogy, his theatre, too, claims in some way to be a recovery from a crisis predicated on an imbalance or incoherence of sensation and association in the musical theatre of the first half of the nineteenth century: *Opera and Drama*, his great theoretical statement, diagnoses the condition of the musical theatre as one in

---

[7] This argument is implicit in my 'The Mechanics of Sensation and the Romantic Construction of Musical Experience', in *Music Theory in the Age of Romanticism*, ed. Ian Bent (Cambridge: Cambridge University Press, 1996), pp. 3–24.

[8] See the discussion in my *Schenker's Argument and the Claims of Music Theory* (Cambridge: Cambridge University Press, 1997), pp. 1–10. Significantly, the full title of Riemann's 1874 exposition of his logic of harmony is *Musikalische Logik: Hauptzüge der physiologischen und psychologischen Begründung unseres Musiksystems*.

which composers strive without purpose after effect, one where every folk and historical tradition is ransacked, one where the whole congeals in empty phenomena.[9] Of course, in attributing such a programme to Wagner we may be going too far. Nonetheless, undergirding and encouraging the whole conception of the *Ring* is Schopenhauer's idealist metaphysics, which makes the strongest possible argument for the essential veracity of music, a veracity beyond the phenomenal, which puts forward an almost exaggerated version of the traditional claims made for music in the Western tradition.

SICKNESS

Yet in what way can a connection be drawn between these two respective projects? Any such rapport would seem to devolve upon a bit of rhetorical legerdemain, a misleading stipulation of two sorts of truth as one and the same. Riemann's theory is 'naturalistic'; Wagner's theatre is 'naturalistic': the first would seem to make its claims on empirical grounds, the second on idealistic grounds. Yet Nietzsche, ever suspicious of such absolute claims, and ever ready to dispute the logical verity of said claims, *would*, I think, draw a connection between these two naturalisms: his peculiar genius is to construct a domain in which such a rapport is more than simply plausible.

Certainly his view of Wagner's truth-claims undergoes an interesting change. One cannot help repeating his wonderful rehearsal of Wagner's appropriation of Schopenhauer in his *Genealogy of Morals*:

With this extraordinary rise in the value of music that appeared to follow from Schopenhauerian philosophy, the value of *the musician* himself all at once went up in the unheard-of manner, too: from now on he became an oracle, a priest, indeed more than a priest, a kind of mouthpiece of the 'in itself' of things, a telephone from the beyond – henceforth he uttered not only music, this ventriloquist of God – he uttered metaphysics . . .[10]

Without question this engaging sense of irony carries through *The Case of Wagner* (although often it mutates into a shrill sarcasm). Yet never can Nietzsche remain the detached observer. The Wagnerian corpus is beyond style, beyond, even, the history of music. It is a music which is not a music, and Wagner a composer who cannot compose. Wagner's successes are spectacular but spectral, a phantasmagoria brought into being by a conjuror, a poseur, an actor. They are seductive precisely because they make vocal claims to insight and veracity. But:

---

[9] Never, of course, is this clearly stated: the 'cure' of critical philosophy is too much part of Wagner's language. Yet it goes without saying that he sees his own work as a 'cure' for that which ails the theatre, the two major symptoms of this illness being 'effect' and 'historicism', or sensation and association without purpose or discipline. See Part 1 ('Opera and the Nature of Music') of *Oper und Drama* (1851), trans. William Ashton Ellis (1893) as *Opera and Drama* (Lincoln: University of Nebraska Press, 1995), pp. 21–115.

[10] Friedrich Nietzsche, *Zur Genealogie der Moral* (1887), trans. Walter Kaufmann as 'On the Genealogy of Morals', in *Basic Writings of Nietzsche*, pp. 449–599; citation from the Third Essay, section 6, p. 539.

One is an actor by virtue of being ahead of the rest of mankind in one insight: what is meant to have the effect of truth must not be true . . . Wagner's music is never true.[11]

Thus, the opening citation, the eleventh section of *The Case of Wagner*, the passage which perhaps is the zenith of Nietzsche's irony, is succeeded by the brief agonic cry of the twelfth section:

12.

The insight that our actors are more deserving of admiration than ever does not imply that they are any less dangerous. – But who could still doubt what I want – what are the *three demands* for which my wrath, my concern, my love of art has this time opened my mouth?

> *That the theater would not lord it over the arts.*
> *That the actor should not seduce those who are authentic.*
> *That music should not become the art of lying.*[12]

Herein lies Wagner's sin: under the avowed goal of giving music a purpose, he has taught it to lie.[13] It is this striking formulation which, I think, puts Nietzsche's citation of Riemann on a different footing. His reasoning perhaps goes like this: at almost precisely that historical moment at which music theory makes what seem to be its most powerful claims to truth, at that moment where it sheds (as Nietzsche notes) 'centuries of scholasticism' and is reborn as a 'science', composition has mastered the art of making music lie. Of course, as noted earlier, it would seem almost too obvious that we speak of different kinds or even registers of 'truth'. When Riemann appeals to the empiricism of the psychological laboratory to rationalise, or at least justify, his project – the 'truth' that he brings to bear on music theory   the 'naturalism' of his endeavour is much different from the 'truth' that Nietzsche finds to be foregrounded and subverted in Wagner's music, the latter being metaphysical or ideological rather than epistemological. Yet in fact this situation is more complex. Riemann, although grounding his argument in some remote appeal to the empirical, ultimately mandates an aesthetic truth; and in Wagner, Nietzsche discovers a break or rupture between the aesthetic and the epistemological, wherein the former comes to make dangerous claims on the latter.

We might perhaps conclude thus that these respective transgressions do but vitiate

---

[11] *The Case of Wagner*, section 8, p. 629.

[12] *Ibid.*, section 12, p. 636. This citation gives this section in its entirety. Obviously it is a fitting conclusion to Nietzsche's entire diatribe, yet he himself felt it necessary to follow this ending with two postscripts and an epilogue.

[13] This notion of a musical capacity for falsehood has occasioned two notable modern readings of Wagner. The first is Lewin's 'Amfortas's Prayer to Titurel'. The second is to be found in the chapter entitled 'Wotan's Monologue and the Morality of Musical Narration' in Carolyn Abbate's *Unsung Voices: Opera and Musical Narrative in the Nineteenth Century* (Princeton: Princeton University Press, 1991), pp. 156–205. Lewin, working from the assumption that Riemannian functional space and *Stufen* space are non-isomorphic, demonstrates how Klingsor's magic has its counterpart in harmonic and enharmonic illusions. (I am grateful to Richard Cohn for pointing this out to me.) Abbate draws a subtle argument from the structural co-option of music by narration in Wotan's monologue, thus making the music complicit in Wotan's deception.

the respective arguments of Riemann and Wagner. Yet Nietzsche makes a strange and subtle move, a move which in taking these appeals at face value co-ordinates them in such a way as to arrive at a deeper truth. One of the more interesting endeavours in his last year of sanity is a projected study of what he calls 'physiological aesthetics'. We get some tenor of this project from his unpublished notes of the same year:

> perhaps we have something more than a metaphor here. Consider the means for producing effects that Wagner prefers to use (– and had for the most part to invent for himself): they are strangely similar to those with which a hypnotist achieves his effect (– his choice of tempo and tonal color for his orchestra; a repellent avoidance of logic and squareness in his rhythm; the lingering, soothing, mysterious, hysteric quality of his 'endless melody'). – And is the condition to which the *Lohengrin* prelude, for example, reduces its hearers, especially women, essentially different from a somnambulistic trance?[14]

Wagner est une névrose. Wagnerism is an aesthetic and ideological illness, a social disease. But it is more. It is the actual agent of physio-psychological sickness, an actual pathology. Listen and you will be changed. Wagner's music is false (be it metaphysically, ideologically, aesthetically, epistemologically), but this falsehood is no simple matter of aesthetics: it is a neurological reality. Music is at once symptom, agent and catalyst through which lying is given revealed substance. 'Some instruments persuade the intestines, some open the marrow of the spine.'[15] Of course, this notion of an actual physiological manifestation of Wagnerism may be dramatic, if not hysterical. Yet in context, it seems less improbable. Without question the critical discourse of the closing years of the nineteenth century thematicises the analogy between infection, illness and music, and (as the sad events of the twentieth century testify) one would be hard pressed to make the case that this analogy is to be read simply as analogy, and not as actual aetiology. Nietzsche advances his case seriously, and for our purposes it makes a certain and stark point. The argument that Wagner's music is ultimately realised in the body draws it into proximity to Riemann's theory. Both look ultimately to a physiological psychology; both create a sort of structural tension between the theoretically and the empirically available, using at least a reference to the latter to justify the former.

DISCIPLINE

The best reason, though, for accepting Nietzsche's argument is that it raises the stakes in an interesting way. To assert that Riemann naturalises music theory is to conceive him as 'disciplining' theory, as opening or reopening possibilities for theory as a discourse. Yet music theory is also deeply – almost peculiarly by comparison to the sister

---

[14] This citation appears in section 839 (1888/1889) of the unpublished writings gathered together posthumously by Nietzsche's sister and published in 1901 as vol. XV of Nietzsche's *Werke* under the title *Nachgelassene Werke: Der Wille zur Macht: Versuch einer Umwerthung aller Werthe*. I am using the translation published by Walter Kaufmann and R. J. Hollingdale under the title *The Will to Power* (New York: Vintage Books, 1968), p. 442. [15] *The Case of Wagner*, section 6, p. 624.

discipline of musicology, systematic or comparative – concerned with a different notion of discipline: pedagogy.

This double definition of 'discipline' has not, I think, always been inherent to music theory (or at least not always as marked). It would be anachronistic to speak of prescriptive and descriptive theories in the nineteenth century, yet we do see a very important tension come to the surface between practice and aesthetics. On the one hand, we witness the creation of a radically simplified, almost industrialised pedagogy at the opening of the nineteenth century, one whose aim is most efficaciously to produce singers, composers for the military band and stage, instrumentalists – whose aim, in short, is to inculcate and assure musical competency. Theory is stripped of the elaborate explication of whole-number acoustics; Rameau's *corps sonore* falls silent in favour of Catel's juxtaposed thirds; rules – the received poetics of music – are justified by pedagogical expediency. Indeed, the practice of pedagogy is not only rationalised but itself prestigiously theorised as a sort of mechanics of character formation by Pestalozzi and Herbart early in the century. On the other hand, by contrast with the mechanisation of pedagogy, we see an aesthetic of Romanticism come into being which values the heroic gesture of transgression, the breaking of 'rules', which values the situation in which (as Nietzsche writes of Wagner) 'virtue prevails even over counterpoint'.[16]

Riemann's naturalisation of music theory solves this problem, allows him both to create an effective pedagogy and to recuperate compositional transgression. In displacing the authority of theory from compositional technique to some (even under-articulated) 'naturalism', Riemannian theory avoids categorical prescription. To return to Riemann's appropriation of Stumpf's mechanism of 'fusion', when speaking of the prohibition of parallel perfect intervals, Riemann notes that parallel octaves and even parallel twelfths are to be found in free composition, and that rather than prohibit such successions, the teacher must inculcate in the student the ability to distinguish between 'reinforcement' (where such successions have a function) and true counterpoint (where they are awkward).[17]

This avoidance of categorical prescription is crucial to the success of Riemannian theory. A scientific conception (or presentation) of music theory alters the nature of the 'rule'. The rule in music theory is no longer *legal* but normative. If a rule is broken compositionally, this is not to be taken as an aesthetic flaw but rather as an excursion into a more complex psycho-acoustic or psychological domain. In terms of the pedagogical situation, the disciplining of students, the authority of the 'rule' is displaced from the teacher, or by extension some inherited body of aesthetic

---

[16] *Ibid.*

[17] See *Schenker's Argument*, pp. 15–16. Riemann's notion of reinforcement signifies a profound reconception of counterpoint as a perceptual rather than a stylistic function. Even conceived as a style or texture, counterpoint held a peculiar authority in the nineteenth century. For evidence of the hold of counterpoint on the compositional imagination earlier in the nineteenth century, a hold which threatened the lyricism of Schubert in which we now recognise his genius, see Richard Kramer, 'Gradus ad Parnassum: Beethoven, Schubert, and the Romance of Counterpoint', *19th-Century Music* 11 (1987), 107–20. Likewise, the Bach revival of the mid-century evidences this authority.

prescriptions, to a 'nature' which does not judge but only explains. Thus the exuberance of the Riemannian moment in music theory rests on the implicit claim that a naturalistic theory can be mapped onto, and in fact made to coincide with, a pedagogical method. Conceived as normative psychological or perceptual functions (rather than as prescriptions), harmony, phrasing, grouping and the like are easily rewritten as a pedagogy.

Not by chance does Nietzsche select Riemann's rhythmics for citation. This is in fact the area where Riemann makes new and marketable claims on musical practice, where theory can extend its pedagogical hegemony. ('*Espressivo* at any cost', 'Obedience and long legs . . .') The selection of this domain of Riemann's theory, however, puts us off the track of a more significant critique, a critique which Nietzsche fails to put forward because were he to consider it he would find the consequences too unsettling. The area of musical practice on which the claims of Riemann are perhaps weakest is composition. Given a naturalistic theory, how might it pedagogically discipline composition, particularly in some new and differently authoritative way?

Certainly the institutional framework for such a programme existed at this time in the form of the *Kompositionslehre*, itself a product of the early nineteenth-century rationalisation of musical pedagogy. I rather doubt, though, that Nietzsche could envision a pedagogy radically altered from one he himself had learned (or, given his musical situation as an auto-didact, a pedagogy he himself had imagined). Nor, indeed could Wagner. The 'artists of delivery' – conductors, machinists, stage singers, orchestral musicians – who precede Riemann in our opening citation correlate fairly well with the projected beneficiaries of a new conservatory proposed by Wagner himself over twenty years before to the King of Bavaria. Wagner's proposal, however, exempts the composer from the programme of this hypothetical conservatory, and in fact would exclude any substantive training in the 'musical sciences': the composer, ironically, is to learn his craft through the traditional apprenticeship.[18]

Yet, recalling the way in which Nietzsche has raised the stakes with his diagnosis of Wagnerism as a physio-psychological condition, the question might be formulated differently. Given a naturalistic music theory, one which makes claims to at least some empirical authorisation, should not this theory take it upon itself to diagnose the 'untruth' of the Wagnerian aesthetic, and then take it upon itself to bring into being (in its disciplinary capacity) some pedagogical prophylaxis? This line of reasoning could not but be unsettling for all parties concerned. The first step in such a theory would be the systematic codification of a Wagnerian poetics, a theory of Wagnerian harmony and form, the second an examination of the physiology and psychology (or psychopathology) of this poetics, and the last an aesthetic prescription for its remedy (or at least a proposal for some system of surveillance). For Nietzsche, the danger would lie in the first step. The systematic formulation of a Wagnerian poetics (the

---

[18] Richard Wagner, 'Bericht an Seine Majestät den König Ludwig II von Bayern über eine in München zu errichtende deutsche Musikschule' (1865), trans. William Ashton Ellis as 'A Music-School for Munich', in *Richard Wagner's Prose Works* (New York: Broude Brothers, 1966), vol. IV, pp. 171–224.

only such formulation which might be useful for psycho-physiological purposes), even if conceived only as a diagnostic protocol, would be almost a legitimation of Wagner's transgression – and an open invitation for composers to sin. However, I think that he would accept this risk in order to discomfit the other parties involved. (In a sense, he views Wagnerism as a sickness from which the recovery leaves the patient ever so much stronger.) More importantly, for Riemann the danger would lie with the third step, with diagnosis and prescription. A naturalistic theory shifts (at least rhetorically) the burden of authority from the theorist to some notion of 'natural law'. The reconception of theory as a prophylaxis could not but test the sincerity of this strategy. Could any amount of psycho-acoustical discovery translate into a theoretical/pedagogical efficacy? Could any theorist relinquish authority (the authority of a carefully nurtured classical tradition) to the empirics of the psycho-acoustician, to become simply (or complexly) a diagnostician, and the architect of a prophylactic regime?

CONSCIENCE

Exaggerated as this argument is, it enables us to formulate an authentically Nietzschean question. Is naturalism (or, particularly, are naturalist arguments for music theory) ever sincere, or, when there is something important at stake, is it always revealed as a rhetorical stratagem?

When it comes time for Riemann to produce his *Große Kompositionslehre*, fourteen years after Nietzsche's critique, the result is remarkably summatory, conservative.[19] It is not by any means the sort of 'naturalistic' *Kompositionslehre* we might have envisioned. Perhaps one would be justified in asserting that this work is symptomatic of a failure of nerve on the part of Riemann, a refusal to engage significant musical questions because such an engagement would entail the surrender of a traditional authority. But we might here misstate the case. Riemann's failure of nerve, in fact, more plausibly stems from another motivation. Would not the specification of some epistemologically pristine truth-regime require from the theorist not an abdication of authority but rather the assumption of a new and frightening authority? Could not Riemann's qualification of naturalism be taken as a defensive strategy, one which allows him to stay on safe ground? Is not the effectiveness of a definition of sickness contingent on a powerful definition of 'health'? And thus would not the theorist, in determining what musical truth is to be and the ways in which it is to be disciplined, in effect be forced into the uncomfortable position of being a composer, yet a composer stripped of the power to transgress rules, the power to create?

Again, we arrive at the sort of dilemma of authority and responsibility in which Nietzsche revels. Even if we are to discount his most outlandish stance – the assumption of some sort of physiological pathology embedded in Wagner's music – we should not deny his insight: the workings of Wagner's music *do* have an unprecedented psychology, one which it would seem a truly naturalistic theory would engage

---

[19] Hugo Riemann, *Große Kompositionslehre*, 3 vols. (Berlin and Stuttgart: W. Spemann, 1902–13).

with in some substantive, even corrective manner, but which instead it deflects. Thus, I believe that Nietzsche's citation of Riemann locates a peculiarly charged moment in the history of music theory, and that the questions he implicitly poses play out in the twentieth century in ways we have not recognised.

The naive naturalism of Riemann's theorising loses its hold on the discourse soon after the turn of the century.[20] (Interestingly enough, the Riemannian notion of function has recently been shown to be remarkably effective in coming to terms with late Romantic harmony, but crucially, this is a theory *de-naturalised*.)[21] This loss of authority is bound up with the sudden collapse (just prior to the Great War) of the dominant psychological methodologies. The idea of a naturalised theory, though, is still very much with us. If, in fact, we draw the Nietzschean analogy further, and think of it as an illness, it is an illness which is chronically recurrent, reappearing in our discourse in the form of various appeals (as aid, accomplice, authority) to available empiricisms (or theories which are made to mediate between music theory and empiricism) such as gestalt psychology, generative grammar, information theory, cognitive science. These naturalisms have always appeared opportunistic, occasions when music theory finds an extra-musical argument so suggestive or prestigious that it must be appropriated, or (to put a better spin on the matter) places where such an argument promises to move the theorising of music to new ground. Nietzsche's reading of Riemann, though, tempts us to read these theoretical moments differently, as reactions (be they attempts to correct or deflect) to perhaps unconsciously perceived threats or crises in composition or in the musical economy as a whole. Yet suggestive as these naturalistic theories have been, none seem to have proved themselves viable over more than a short space of time, and none so completely dominate the discourse. (To be fair, however, I would note that these naturalisations of theory have become increasingly scrupulous about the claims they make.)

Nietzsche gives us a clue as to why this is the case, although in this instance through a failure of his intuitions rather than a success. To the end, he conceives the sole plausible cure for Wagnerism in terms of aesthetics and of the sort of speculation that has served him so well. Hence the following desperate note:

We lack in music an aesthetic that would impose laws on musicians and give them a conscience; we lack, as a consequence, a genuine conflict over 'principles' – for as musicians we laugh at Herbart's velleities in this realm as much as we do at Schopenhauer's. In fact, this results in a great difficulty: we no longer know on what basis to found the concepts 'model', 'mastery', 'perfection' – we grope blindly in the realm of values with the instinct of old love and admiration; we come close to believing 'what is good is what pleases *us*' – [22]

---

[20] Indeed, the notion of a psychologistic basis for any discipline which could be termed a *Geisteswissenschaft* fell quite out of fashion (although the study of music was torn between those who would see it as a human science, and those who saw it as a natural science). The most trenchant critic of psychologism at the turn of the century is Wilhelm Dilthey, who in addition to coining the distinction between the approaches to musical study given above prompted other thinkers such as the philosopher Husserl to reconsider their stances. See *Schenker's Argument*, pp. 10–13.

[21] See Lewin, 'Amfortas's Prayer to Titurel'.   [22] Nietzsche, *The Will to Power*, section 838, pp. 440–1.

His aesthetics is one of nostalgia: for counterpoint, for harmony, for principles — Schopenhauer and music as the mirror of a transcendental reality, Herbart and music as a discipline of character. This is his dilemma: Were he to listen for a twenty-first time to *Carmen*, might he perhaps . . .? To the end, though, he is incapable of excising Herbart and Schopenhauer, of *theorising* a conscience for music from a set of musical preferences.

This dilemma, though, leads us in an interesting direction. The key term in this quotation, I think, is 'conscience'. The notion of a musical discourse of conscience, whether partially or wholly theorised, is not as alien as it might at first seem. We are all familiar with various twentieth-century musical projects that could well qualify, be they ideological (Marxist, nationalist, or otherwise) or stylistic ('composer as artisan', 'return to Bach'). Without question, the greatest critique of Wagner, that of Theodor Adorno, rests precisely on the notion of bad faith and its musical ramifications.[23] Yet this formulation suggests another, one seemingly inconceivable to Nietzsche. Could such a conscience evolve through a music theory, one not subordinated to aesthetics but autonomous?

What would such a music theory entail? Certainly (to repeat myself) it could not entail an appeal to an outside empiricism for epistemological authority. Here, I think, is the flaw in the various naturalised theories of our own time: the appeal to some outside authority for epistemological validation, for 'truth', is an attempt to generate a substitute conscience, to deflect questions about the function and necessity and situation of our discourse. Nor could such a theory be constituted simply as a transparent and rationalised pedagogy (even if this were possible). Nor do I think that it could be constituted by the formally rigorous theories which come into being later in the twentieth century (although these perhaps come close, and certainly carry with them an exquisitely honed, although underarticulated moral sense).[24] 'Conscience', I think, must involve an interrogation of both 'truth' and of 'discipline', a synchronised critique of what defines musical competence and how such competence is to be engineered.

I would suggest, however, that such a theory (or theories) is closer at hand than we might think, and perhaps came into being not long after Nietzsche's critique. The most interesting theories of our century evidence a freshly exquisite and often painful concern with the status of the 'rule'. This is particularly the case with the two great Viennese theorists of the twentieth century. (Perhaps it is significant that both come out of the more conservative traditions of harmonic theory, as does the first true

---

[23] Adorno's lengthy engagement with Wagner, the *Versuch über Wagner* (1952), seems to me one of the classic texts of twentieth-century analysis, and in many ways a model to which our discipline should aspire. The translation given by Rodney Livingstone is quite good: *In Search of Wagner* (London: Verso, 1991).

[24] I think that the moral rhetoric of post-war music theory has too often gone unrecognised. See, though, Martin Brody, '"Music for the Masses": Milton Babbitt's Cold War Music Theory', *Musical Quarterly* 77 (1993), 161–92.

Wagnerian analyst, Karl Mayrberger.)[25] Schenker's *Harmony* (1906), despite its initial invocation of the chimerical 'chord of nature', is anti-naturalistic in sensibility.[26] Harmony is not refined by any appeal to outside empiricism. It is still cast (perhaps rhetorically) as a psychological function, yet a function revealed in the laboratory of actual musical quotations and stripped of its disciplinary mandate, a function whose existence is purely dependent on the musical intuitions of the student. And this conception is reinforced in the first volume of *Counterpoint* (1912), wherein (as has been shown brilliantly by Joseph Dubiel) the status of the 'rule' is even more complex and crucial.[27] (Interestingly enough, Schenker attacks Riemann's discussion of parallel perfect intervals and 'fusion' not on epistemological but rather on pedagogical grounds.) Schoenberg's *Harmony* (1911) likewise stakes out a ramified notion of the rule.[28] Although his appeal is to the ear, seemingly echoing Riemann's question 'How do we hear music?', the ear in question is again that of the *student*. Harmony survives as an extravagant sort of play, one which forms musical sensibility, yet one whose status is radically contingent. Both Schenker and Schoenberg take the traditional disciplines of harmony and counterpoint seriously, yet both resituate them in ways which would have been inconceivable twenty years earlier.

Both, though, come also to complicate the status of the rule in yet another, deeper, anti-naturalist fashion. Even here, Nietzsche perhaps comes to the verge of an insight without taking a crucial final step. We recall the words 'I have explained where Wagner belongs – *not* in the history of music.' Given this statement (or overstatement, although Wagner does seem to constitute a radical break), the reference to Riemann takes on another meaning. Similarly to the way in which both Wagner's music and Riemann's theory are naturalistic, both stand outside of the history of music. Music theory is most often defined as that branch of musical enquiry which stands outside of history. While such a theory might engage the issue of conscience (which, although it has usually been associated with history, has indeed a great resonance with the way in which the notion of 'harmony' is developed in earlier centuries), how might a theory that itself stands outside history diagnose and cure a music which likewise cuts itself off from the tradition? The simple notion of a theory which recuperates the history of music through a reification of 'historical style' is not a viable option, it too resting on the conception of radically synchronic criteria. Rather, we must pursue a different line of reasoning. In material previous to that cited, Nietzsche

[25] Karl Mayrberger, 'Die Harmonik Richard Wagner's an den Leitmotiven aus *Tristan und Isolde* erläutert' (1881), trans. Ian Bent as 'The Harmonic Style of Richard Wagner, Elucidated with Respect to the Leitmotifs of *Tristan and Isolde*', in *Music Analysis in the Nineteenth Century*, 2 vols. (Cambridge: Cambridge University Press, 1994), vol. I, pp. 226–52.

[26] Heinrich Schenker, *Neue musikalische Theorien und Phantasien*, vol. I: *Harmonielehre* (Vienna: Universal Edition, 1906), trans. Elisabeth Mann Borgese as *Harmony* (Chicago: University of Chicago Press, 1954).

[27] Joseph Dubiel, '"When You are a Beethoven": Kinds of Rules in Schenker's "Counterpoint"', *Journal of Music Theory* 34 (1990), 291–340.

[28] See in particular the first three chapters of Arnold Schoenberg, *Harmonielehre* (1911), trans. Roy Carter as *Theory of Harmony* (Berkeley and Los Angeles: University of California Press, 1978).

develops the argument that Wagner metastasises the aesthetic of transgression, and thus steps outside the history of music while profoundly traumatising that history. Nietzsche, though, neglects to follow through on where this argument leads: he refuses to consider a theory of music that is aware of its own historicity, which is *self-conscious*. Our Viennese do not. Both admit a powerful reflexivity: both historicise their projects. Schenker, in his later work, privileges transgression: composers always 'hear' beyond his theoretical predecessors, 'hear' beyond the rules.[29] Thus a striking formulation of the history of music: his theory of music is valid – uniquely valid – because it stands beyond the end of true composition. And Schoenberg is no less certain in claiming the inverse: given a radical contingency of theory, there is no such thing as a transgression in that any compositional move can be theorised. Both *handle* Wagner, Schenker by substantiating Nietzsche's formulation of a Wagnerian break with the history of music, Schoenberg by severing the link between the history of music and theoretical prescription.

In sum, the lesson given in Nietzsche's reference to Riemann is as follows. Riemann stands indicted *not* for any theoretical lapse or deficiency – I think Nietzsche sincere when he speaks of 'relevant sciences' emerging from 'centuries of complacency'. Rather, he stands indicted for a sort of arrogance, an offence both evidenced and compounded by the manner in which he draws natural science into complicity in his descriptive project – his reformulation of music theory on psychologistic grounds – yet hesitates to do the same in his prescriptive project. For Nietzsche, he makes *too much* of music theory: he claims truth, yet refuses to hazard that claim through any meaningful engagement with the musical culture at large, a project which he cannot undertake because it is one beyond the power of music theory. While the lesson Nietzsche gives to us about the fatal limits of a naturalised theory is one I would accept, I think that Nietzsche makes *too little* of music theory. He himself regarded Wagnerism as a necessary illness, in so far as his mature work could only have come through a recovery from this illness. Perhaps Riemannian naturalism could likewise be said to have constituted a sort of illness, one from whose recovery was born in the work of Schoenberg and Schenker a self-conscious and conscientious music theory, one which revealed itself in a refusal of complacency, in a deep and continuing process of self-examination, in an engagement with the complex and intertwined knot of epistemic and pedagogical disciplines that is the nature of our discourse.

---

[29] See *Schenker's Argument*, pp. 36–9.

Part II

Natural forms – forming nature

Chapter Five

The second nature of sonata form

SCOTT BURNHAM

SONATA FORM AND US

Tonality is often assumed to be the natural modality of music, sonata form the natural expression of tonality. Why should this be so? Why is sonata form second nature for so many of us? On the face of it, it is not so hard to see why sonata form appears to be an innate expression of tonality: the form, as we like to understand it, makes a central issue of resolution and of return, just as tonal harmony does. In dramatising the return from dominant to tonic (so often conceptualised as the 'chord of nature'), sonata form performs not just a return but a return to nature, in the same way that the dominant–tonic cadence does. This is a broadly resonant scenario, and hard to resist – sonata form brings us home, and who among us does not long for some sense of home?

Within the academy, sonata form has proved an extremely serviceable pedagogical construct: it allows us to be at once taxonomical and beyond mere taxonomy. We can find a name for a great many things ('sonata form') and we can, at the same time, relish making the claim that 'there's no such thing as a textbook sonata form'. Related to this latter notion is the suggestion that one can never know too many sonata forms, for each one is different. In the preface to the revised edition of *Sonata Forms* (a book whose title encapsulates this view) Charles Rosen compares sonata forms to chimpanzees, citing Stephen Jay Gould's claim that there is no such thing as 'the chimpanzee', but only chimpanzees. As Gould puts it: 'Individuality does more than matter; it is of the essence.'[1] But when we assess the degree of individuality of something with reference to a fundamental organising strategy like sonata form, we are addressing ourselves not only to the individual but also to the abstraction.

What are some of the things we like to do with this abstraction we call sonata form? As I see it, there are two broad types of things that we do with sonata form: we like to read different things into sonata form and we like to read sonata form into

I would like to offer warm thanks to my friend David E. Cohen, for his ready insights on sonata form, Vergil and any number of things else.

[1] Charles Rosen, *Sonata Forms*, rev. edn (New York: W. W. Norton, 1988), p. viii.

111

different things. For instance, we can read a quest plot (the hero's journey) and a suppression-of-the-Other plot (Animus versus Anima) into sonata form. And we often read sonata form into different pieces, such as Chopin's *Ballades* and Liszt's B minor Sonata. Through sonata form, we hear different musics enacting the same underlying plot, and we interpret this underlying plot as telling stories that we feel we need to hear (or are tired of hearing).

We also do something like this with the archetypal plots of myth, as in, say, the quest plot: we might interpret the underlying structure of the quest plot in a psychoanalytical manner or in an allegorical manner, we may read into such a mythic plot an ideological agenda or a psychological conflict, or we may be satisfied to see it simply as a structure articulated by binary oppositions. And we might choose to read such a mythic plot into any number of stories – as we could read a messianic plot into the films *E.T.* or *Blade Runner*, or the quest plot into almost any Hollywood action picture. Both the archetypal plot and our construction of sonata form offer a compelling modality for grounding a variety of new experiences, for bringing them into line with more stabilised experiences. Sonata form may thus be said to be the closest analogue of music to the function of an overarching, archetypal plot in literature.[2]

A great many literary works can be understood to enact the basic, 'textbook' functions of plot: exposition, initiating action, rising action, falling action and denouement. As in our notion of sonata form, such plots rely on the idea of conflict; conflict is the mainspring, the 'unifying principle of action'. This type of plot has been enacted in numberless ways; it feels natural, beyond question. However, sonata form has an advantage even beyond this, for it boasts a distinct link to nature itself: from the overtone series and the 'chord of nature' to the dominant–tonic resolution. Encompassing conflict and enfranchised by nature, sonata form offers a sense of protagonist and world, subject and object, journey and home.

Sonata form offers a whole story, and in the musics that we hear in this way it is, more probably than not, the whole story. We trade heavily on the conceit that fulfilling the demands of the so-called sonata principle[3] is the all-consuming job undertaken by pieces in this form: the interest we take in them is proportional to the interest we take in the way they fulfil this contract, the way they do their job, the way they work. The most satisfying exemplars are often those which end by leaving us with a sense that they are indeed finished, that there is nothing more to do, that no loose ends remain.

In this essay, I want to dwell on some loose ends. I want to consider several pas-

---

[2] For a sturdy and illuminating treatment of sonata form as plot, see Anthony Newcomb, 'Schumann and Late Eighteenth-Century Narrative Strategies', *19th-Century Music* 11 (1987), 164–75. For a more general interpretation of musical form and paradigmatic plot see Mark Evan Bonds, *Wordless Rhetoric: Musical Form and the Metaphor of the Oration* (Cambridge, Mass. and London: Harvard University Press, 1991), pp. 186–91.

[3] The 'sonata principle' was enunciated by Edward T. Cone, as follows: '[I]mportant statements made in a key other than the tonic must either be restated in the tonic, or brought into a closer relation with the tonic, before the movement ends', in *Musical Form and Musical Performance* (New York: Norton, 1968), pp. 76–7.

sages in the music of Haydn and Beethoven that may be said to question – and lighten – the fundamental burden of our sense of sonata form: the idea of return as resolution and the closely related ideas of teleological process and unequivocal completion. In the final section, I will take up the question of how hard we have been asking sonata form to work – as a mechanism of harmonic closure, as the culmination of music history, and as a resonant archetype for human experience.

In several recent essays, Peter A. Hoyt has been encouraging us towards a renewed investigation of our sense of sonata form and Classical style.[4] He has illuminated the extent to which the sonata principle, as we have inherited it, relies on the idea of conflict and resolution. In particular, his study of Anton Reicha's early nineteenth-century theory of form suggests that this emphasis is problematic, even anachronistic. The conflict–resolution scenario, however, is crucial to the current mainstream accounts of sonata form that have been offered by writers such as Leonard B. Meyer, Leonard Ratner, Charles Rosen and James Webster. For Webster, the so-called double return – the return of both home key and first theme – stands as the 'central aesthetic event' of the form. (Meyer refers to this moment as the syntactic climax of the form.)[5] Perhaps the ultimate aggrandisement of this scenario can be found in Webster's book on through-composition in Haydn, where he extends the conflict–resolution model of sonata form to the level of an entire multi-movement work. For Webster, through-composition makes possible '[a] progression from paradoxical disorder to triumphant order' that now may span more than a single movement.[6]

The central and catalysing event in Webster's book is the D major interlude that appears within the development section of the first movement of Haydn's *Farewell* Symphony, No. 45 in F♯ minor (Example 5.1).

It is instructive to compare the views of Rosen and Webster on this D major interlude. Rosen downplays its radicality by showing how it enacts an available form, a pre-Classical formal procedure, that of the central trio (which he finds in Sammartini, J. C. Bach and early Mozart).[7]

Rosen's view of the interlude is a red herring, claims Webster, who instead takes the opposite stance, highlighting the interlude's radicality, as a primary argument for his view of Haydn's music as the *locus primus* of the through-compositional impulse we

---

[4] Peter A. Hoyt, 'The Concept of *développement* in the Early Nineteenth Century', in *Music Theory in the Age of Romanticism*, ed. Ian Bent (Cambridge: Cambridge University Press, 1996), pp. 141–62, and a Review Essay of books by Ethan Haimo, Elaine Sisman, James Webster and Gretchen Wheelock, entitled 'Haydn's New Incoherence', *Music Theory Spectrum* 19 (1997), 264–84.

[5] James Webster, 'Sonata Form', in *The New Grove Dictionary of Music and Musicians*, ed. Stanley Sadie (London: Macmillan, 1980), and Leonard B. Meyer, 'Exploiting Limits: Creation, Archetypes, and Style Change', *Daedalus* 109/2 (1980), 189.

[6] Webster, *Haydn's 'Farewell' Symphony and the Idea of Classical Style* (Cambridge: Cambridge University Press, 1991), p. 127.   [7] Rosen, *Sonata Forms*, p. 167.

Example 5.1 Joseph Haydn, Symphony No. 45: development section of first movement

Example 5.1   (cont.)

Example 5.1   (*cont.*)

most readily associate with Beethoven. For the interlude needs to be assimilated, and this does not happen within the confines of the first movement alone (in the way that, for example, the new theme in the development of the first movement of the *Eroica* is recapitulated in the coda of that movement). Instead, Haydn's interlude requires the entire symphony for its assimilation – thus giving the entire symphony an overall, through-composed trajectory.

Both Rosen's and Webster's views of the interlude are shaped by an evolutionary sense of the Classical style: for Rosen, on the one hand, Symphony No. 45 is pre-Classical, and, as such, its D major interlude is not anomalous and, though 'a brilliant inspiration', not terribly interesting from the point of view of form. For Webster, on the other, the symphony is forward-looking and proto-Beethovenian (because for him, Haydn is the heretofore little-suspected origin of much that we have come to revere in Beethoven).

But to understand the D major interlude as either proto-Classical or proto-Beethovenian is to miss the opportunity of hearing it less as a challenge and more as an invitation, a chance to learn a new sensibility. This is where Hoyt's argument comes in. For him, one of the natural results of our emphasis on resolution is to increase the level of opposition between development and recapitulation. The development is viewed almost exclusively as the site of maximal tension and instability, so that the return of the main theme and the home key can then be maximally stabilising.[8] This is why we are thrown by appearances of the tonic within a development section, or by interludes such as the one in the *Farewell* Symphony, whose thematic stability seems to create an unwonted (and unwanted) sense of decompression in the context of the development section. Such intrusions have then to be treated as creative anomalies that can be tied to larger scenarios, saving the fundamental model of conflict and resolution. Thus for Webster, the development of the first movement of the *Farewell* Symphony, while locally puzzling with its stable thematic interlude, acts globally as a source of even greater tension, tension that now requires an entire symphony for its resolution.[9]

Haydn marks the interlude as a return. Note the immediately preceding pedal point on the V of B minor. This stands in relation to the following D major as a V/vi. The V/vi is a very common point from which to head into a recapitulation, often without an intervening transition. (This practice was described by Heinrich Christoph Koch in the *Versuch einer Anleitung zur Composition* (1793) and has featured in the writings of Ratner, Rosen and Webster, among others.[10]) Thus we have a development that

---

[8] This is not the sense of development that emerges from Reicha's view of sonata form (the *grande coupe binaire*). For Reicha, thematic material is not so much transformed and re-established as progressively revealed, with the result that Reichian development takes place throughout the movement. This effectively attenuates the contrastive, destabilising role of what we would call the development section. See Hoyt, 'The Concept of *développement*'. [9] Webster, *Haydn's 'Farewell' Symphony*, p. 45.

[10] Heinrich C. Koch, *Versuch einer Anleitung zur Composition*, 3 vols. (Leipzig: A. F. Böhme, 1793; rpt Hildesheim: Georg Olms, 1969), vol. III, pp. 307–11. See also Charles Rosen's history of this convention in *Sonata Forms*, Chapter 10 'Development', pp. 262–83.

moves to a dominant pedal point and proceeds to a locally plausible but wrong key – but just how wrong is it? Remember that the development starts in A major. Developments often start in the dominant; A is the dominant of D; hence a 'return' to D. But in the overarching context of F♯ minor, this can only come across as a strange return.[11] Though the D major interlude is thus both harmonically marked and formally positioned as if it were a return, it is almost impossible to hear it as one, for the obvious reason that it presents new thematic material in utter contrast with the rest of the movement. If anything, it acts as the very opposite of resolution, asking us to step into some other realm at the very point where we would reasonably expect to step back into the place whence we came.[12] The grand pause after the pedal point only enhances this effect of crossing an unexpected threshold. Finally, it is worth pointing out that the transition to the A major section in the finale (the 'farewell' music) is effected in the same way: the dominant of F♯ minor acts as a V/vi that moves into the following A major music, again with a grand pause (that dominant will later act as a V, resolving to the F♯ major closing section).[13] Thus this programmatically charged 'return' near the end of the symphony reminds us of the strange step taken in the development of the first movement. Both passages are marked as returns and yet introduce new and different music. Both open up and lighten the terms of our sense of closure and resolution in the Classical style. After all, what could be lighter or more open than the evaporating orchestra at the end of this symphony?

Another kind of strange return in Classical-style musical practice is the literal (or near-literal) recall, in a subsequent movement, of music from an earlier movement. The most famous instance of this is the recall of the scherzo in the finale of Beethoven's Symphony No. 5. But a case that has earned much recent attention is that of Haydn's Symphony in B major, No. 46, in which the music of the minuet movement returns within the coda of the finale.

Both Rosen and Webster point out thematic resemblances between the minuet and the finale, an analytical move that helps justify the interpenetration of these movements.[14] Indeed, it is not hard to hear the opening of the finale as a kind of comic variant of the closing strain of the minuet (Example 5.2).

The finale makes a play of closure throughout, interspersing garrulously ineffective cadential figures with numerous grand pauses – in fact, taking all the repeats gives one a feeling of not knowing what may happen after any given pause. The development

[11] D major stands in an interesting relation to F♯ minor here. At the outset of the development, A major is clearly heard as the relative major of F♯ minor; it then proceeds as if it were the dominant of D major. This puts special emphasis on the fact that A major is related to both F♯ minor and D major as the first key to which both would habitually move.
[12] Webster has some wonderful analytical pages on the paradoxical Otherness of the interlude. He hears it as detached, ethereal, offering lyrical coherence and yet subtly (if not fundamentally) unsettling: 'In short, the interlude will not parse.' Webster, *Haydn's 'Farewell' Symphony*, pp. 43–5.
[13] Webster refers to the passage before the interlude as a 'close aesthetic counterpart' of the later transition in the finale. *Ibid.*, p. 20.
[14] Rosen, *The Classical Style* (New York: Norton, 1971), p. 148; Webster, *Haydn's 'Farewell' Symphony*, p. 280; see also Webster's annotated musical examples on pp. 268–72.

Example 5.2   Joseph Haydn, Symphony No. 46: minuet to opening of finale

Finale   IV

Example 5.2   *(cont.)*

section goes by quickly, slipping into the recapitulation without a noticeable sense of retransition. Soon thereafter the recapitulation itself lands on a dominant pedal point that sounds like a retransition – and in comes the recalled minuet, starting from the middle of its B section and including the reprised reference to its A section. (The reference to the A section is very clear, even though the contours of the initial minuet theme are played backwards.) The interposed minuet music is followed by a Presto that eventually musters a final cadence (Example 5.3).

For Webster, the reprise of the minuet at the end of the finale creates what he calls a meta-reprise: since it reprises the reprise part of the minuet theme, it is music about a reprise. The effect is one of reminiscence and not merely one of recall.[15] Both movements are heard to constitute a single complex, a structural and psychological interpenetration, which expresses the cyclic function 'finale'.[16] The return of the minuet allows us to make such an observation about the two movements; indeed, it forces the issue. The idea of meta-reprise works well for Webster, as the sonata principle itself is primarily about reprise and closure. Here Haydn is heard to touch ironically upon the very nub of the sonata-form ethos.

Webster goes one step further: he hears both Symphonies Nos. 46 and 45 as a pair, as part of a bigger, collective story, having to do with a partly anecdotal scenario of leave-taking and homecoming, the story of musicians at Esterháza, dreaming of happier days. In this context, Webster hears the return of the minuet as an idealised memory. As such, the minuet reprise cannot effect closure in the real time of the finale. Webster points out that the minuet reprise leads to an important root-position cadence in the concluding Presto (bar 189), important because this movement has not to this point summoned the wherewithal to make a strong cadence. Thus Webster analytically subsumes the minuet recall within a dominant pedal point[17] – its own rather strongly articulated root-position cadences are apparently not real; they take place not on the plane of the finale but only in some 'meta' land of reminiscence. What we need are 'here and now' cadences, which the ensuing Presto provides. For Webster, then, the recalled minuet does not effect a true return; it is only a reminiscence.

I would argue, however, that the cadences in the minuet citation *are* real, and that they contribute to the effect of making the finale issue into the minuet. Note how the dominant pedal point is taken up and resolved by the minuet music. Nevertheless, the recalled minuet itself is not permitted to close with a cadence on the tonic; instead, it drifts off on an unresolved vii$_3^4$ chord, thus seeming to ask the finale music to resolve it. The theme of the finale does indeed resolve the hanging G♯ from that wonderful chord. Yet what is the effect of the root position V–I cadence that Webster points to

[15] Webster, *Haydn's 'Farewell' Symphony*, p. 284.
[16] *Ibid.*, p. 280. Mark Evan Bonds relates the recalled minuet to a strategy of interruption and interpolation he hears operating throughout the entire symphony. For Bonds, the 'return of the minuet within the finale (as well as its abrupt dismissal) marks the culmination of an attempt to create a coherence between movements that goes beyond the mere recycling of similar themes'. Bonds, *Wordless Rhetoric*, p. 204.   [17] Webster, *Haydn's 'Farewell' Symphony*, p. 275.

Example 5.3   Joseph Haydn, Symphony No. 46: end of finale

Example 5.3   (*cont.*)

Example 5.3   (cont.)

Example 5.3   (*cont.*)

in bar 189? Note how the first violins subsequently echo the 5–1 motion in the bass: Webster's cadence is dissipated by the violins, slowed down and finally resolved disjointedly by the horns after the grand pause. The only strong cadences in the movement come in the minuet recall, and then in the very last bars, where the emphatic V–I sounds almost out of place and certainly ironic. (It is essential to take the repeat of the second half of the movement to get the full effect of this irony.) What this means is that the recalled minuet does even more than Webster says it does: it is not simply a reminiscence over a dominant pedal holding up the business of cadential closure. It confuses our sense of an ending in a way that can liberate us from how we usually think of finales.

Hoyt argues that the minuet may reprise simply in order to be heard once again, in a context that will now bring out (or 'develop', in the Reichian sense) its expressive potential.[18] Webster's hearing of the return of the minuet as an idealised memory resonates to some degree with Hoyt's sense of the 'expressive potential' of the minuet. Yet Webster is looking for the recalled minuet to perform and consolidate the important work of through-composition and multi-movement coherence. To put their two views into crass opposition: for Webster, the minuet returns in order to do; for Hoyt, the minuet returns in order to be.

I like to hear the minuet in a way that combines these views. I agree with Hoyt that the minuet stands revealed in the finale as something more expressive than one had imagined. It seems clear, to my ear at least, that this minuet 'never had it so good' as when it returns at the end of the finale. In fact, I would say that its return prompts the inviting feeling of arriving back home, not the home implied by the all-important double return of sonata form, but home in a more sentimental sense. Given the choice, one would rather live in that minuet than in that finale, especially as the minuet sounds within the finale. (This latter point is more or less the burden of Webster's

---

[18] Hoyt, 'Haydn's New Incoherence', 275. On Reichian *développement*, see note 8 above.

extramusical interpretation.) Moreover, the finale seems to get folded into the minuet – with the result that the finale itself stands revealed as a loose end, especially when it comes back after the reprised minuet. Thus the overall impression of the finale resembles all those loose ends heard at so many junctures within it, cadence figures that flap in the wind without firmly closing anything off. The effect of all this is complex: the finale is problematised as a final term, a consummating endpoint. An interesting emotional twist is applied to the minuet, now heard as somehow containing the finale, but not quite ending the piece. The reminiscence of the minuet enacts a return, but it is a return without an unequivocal sense of resolution.

Haydn marks both the D major interlude in the *Farewell* Symphony and the minuet recall in Symphony No. 46 as returns. The D major interlude is set up with its own V/vi, and the reprise of the minuet in Symphony No. 46 is furnished with a pedal point on the dominant of the home key, another common strategy for preparing the recapitulation. Both episodes are fashioned as returns, but not as resolutions in the strong sense. They demonstrate that the act of reprise may not always mean resolution: we may return at the right time but to an unfamiliar place, and we may return to a familiar place but at the wrong time.

So why do we tend to associate reprise with strong resolution? Consider the case of that other famous instance of a third movement reappearing in the finale, namely Beethoven's Symphony No. 5. Where does Beethoven choose to reprise his scherzo theme? Right before the recapitulation. In other words, the scherzo citation is followed by the first theme of the finale. As we have seen, Haydn did this too but at the end of the movement. Like Haydn's, Beethoven's recall of the third movement within the finale reprises the link between third and fourth movements – but with an utterly different effect. Instead of moving from a reassuring minuet into a finale that turns out to be anything but reassuring, Beethoven reprises perhaps the most famous resolution in all Western music, the long transitional pedal point from C minor to C major, the turning point of the entire symphony.

Obviously enough, Beethoven folds the recalled scherzo into the resolution of the finale, rather than the other way round. This move may be said to have an imposing effect on the history of sonata form. By recalling the earlier transition to the finale at the moment of the finale's retransition, he replays that earlier transition as a literal retransition. This confirms our sense that the earlier transition in fact sounds like a retransition. Marked as such, it has the effect of folding the entire symphony into the rhetoric of sonata form: the onset of the finale is marked as a return, and the finale seems to resolve the entire work. This specifically marks the sonata-form recapitulation as a large-scale and momentous resolution.[19] In other words, Beethoven's recall of the third movement works to galvanise sonata form as a procedure of resolution; sonata form and the through-composed symphony are heard to validate each other.

[19] I have taken up this point in an earlier essay. See 'How Music Matters: Poetic Content Revisited', in *Rethinking Music*, ed. Mark Everist and Nicholas Cook (Oxford: Oxford University Press, 1999), pp. 207–8.

In Haydn's Symphony, the overall effect is anything but resolved. Instead, it is more retrospective, more open-ended: the reprise of the minuet comes at the end, not at the retransition, and the finale issues into the minuet rather than the other way round. In Beethoven's Fifth Symphony, the recall is a means towards a larger end; in the *Farewell* Symphony, the recall *is* the end, and it is an open end at that.

Beethoven's telling of sonata form as a grandiose resolution is arguably the telling to which we adhere these days, the telling that promotes the whole idea of the primacy of the double return and the reconciliation of tonal opposition, the telling that presents a denouement with no loose ends and that gives us licence to think of whole symphonies as dramas of conflict and resolution.

TAILS WAG

No loose ends? Even by virtue of its name, the phenomenon of the coda (or tail) would seem to indicate something tacked on, a loose end, something not strictly necessary. It may even have been deemed so at one point by Charles Rosen, for the otherwise taxonomically replete first edition of his book *Sonata Forms* contained no section on codas (he made good on this in later editions, as we shall see).

Such a thing as a coda can only spell trouble for the mainstream view of sonata form. As the concept of denouement, of conflict and resolution, became all-important, the so-called double return became, as Webster put it, 'the central aesthetic event of the entire movement'.[20] For the double return allows sonata form to consolidate its various knots: the thematic knot and the tonal knot are untied together, encouraging a sense of a single, unitary dramatic process. But to all this the coda, and particularly the Beethovenian coda, seems to say 'not so fast – we've only just begun untying the knots around here'. In fact, many of his codas are heard to create new knots – imagine a drama that did this! (As Hamlet expires in Horatio's arms, Fortinbras rushes in to explain that poor Yorick is really Horatio's long lost father, and that his ghost expects Horatio to kill the gravedigger who so rudely tossed his skull around earlier in the play. But Horatio's vengeful access to the gravedigger is checked by the discovery that the gravedigger is actually the long lost father of Fortinbras. Madness ensues, etc., etc.)

For years, many critics thought of the Beethovenian coda as something like this, as a second development section. This view soon proved troubling, for it obviously undermines the sense of one unitary process of tension and resolution. The idea of the coda as a supplementary recapitulation, on the other hand, has found somewhat more support, and is in fact more congenial to our view of the form. In this conception, the coda is said to realise some latent aspect of the material, or to recapitulate some new and undigested material from the development section. The 'sonata principle' continues to be honoured in such a scenario: everything not in the tonic shall be reprised in the tonic (i.e. everything not stabilised shall find stability, shall be played

[20] Webster, 'Sonata Form'.

out). Again, sonata form, as we like to construct it, leaves nothing dangling, nothing incomplete.

Thus the coda is now commonly understood to be taking care of unfinished business. But this clouds the picture as well: are there now two big jobs to do? Are there two knots to untie – the mega-knot, untied at the double return, and now some new knot, or knots? If the knots of the coda were large and imposing, it would seem to question the primacy of the double return (which no longer unties the biggest knot); if they were diminutive, it would make the coda a rather small-time operation, rendered particularly absurd when it consists of hundreds of bars, as Beethoven's are wont to do. Or do Beethoven's codas demonstrate that the goal-orientated process of his sonata form has less to do with the underlying form and its double return, and more with 'developing' a facet of its thematic material? Would any self-respecting organicist conceive thematic content in this way, as working against the grain of the form? Either way, the coda is troubling to our prevailing sense of sonata form.

Let us consider a coda whose sheer size has triggered debates among formal analysts. The finale of Beethoven's Eighth Symphony is 502 bars long; the section we generally refer to as its coda begins at bar 267. Thus very nearly half of the movement is coda. Coming as it does after a fully realised recapitulation, the section in question clearly sets out as if it were a coda. It is so lengthy, however, that some have preferred to think of it as a second development followed by its own recapitulation.

For Rosen, writing in the revised edition of *Sonata Forms*, the section is most definitely a coda, and it 'realizes the remaining dynamic potential'[21] of the movement to which it is appended first and foremost by working to resolve the famous C♯ in bar 17, a *fortissimo* intrusion that is left unresolved in its first two appearances (Example 5.4).

The coda performs this task with an outspoken climax in F♯ minor. As Rosen puts it: 'When we consider the violence of this climax, we no longer may judge the length of the coda as unprovoked; we may see it as justified and even demanded by the material. From bar 17 on, the grandest of all Beethoven's codas is a necessity.'[22] Rosen's argument assumes the following steps: (1) the C♯ in bar 17 needs a momentous climax in F♯ minor; (2) the climax is so momentous that it needs 100 bars of preparation; (3) the climax is so momentous that it needs another 100 bars of tonic resolution afterwards. The preparation and aftermath of this climax are heard to justify the great length of this 'coda'.

This is not all that the coda does in Rosen's view: it also resolves the presence of the mediant key in the development by the presence of the submediant in the coda (a common recapitulatory key-centre transaction in Beethoven), and it presents the second theme of the movement for the first time wholly in the tonic (which did not quite happen in the recapitulation proper – there it appears in the tonic only after being initiated in D♭ major). Can these somewhat oblique resolutions be deemed absolutely necessary?

[21] Rosen, *Sonata Forms*, p. 324.   [22] *Ibid.*, p. 342.

Example 5.4   Ludwig van Beethoven, Symphony No. 8: opening of finale

Example 5.4   (*cont.*)

Rosen himself is uncomfortable with the idea of necessity: he immediately qualifies his assertion that 'the grandest of all Beethoven's codas is a necessity' by admitting that

Such necessity is always post facto. Whatever is, is right – at least when it comes to the work of a composer in whom we have put our trust. The coda was obviously necessary to Beethoven, because that is the way he wrote it. It seems necessary to us when we have persuaded ourselves that we perceive his reasons, understand his logic . . . We must not hide the inconvenient fact that it is analysis that tells us how to hear the music, counsels a certain kind of attention.[23]

If Rosen were fully comfortable with the idea of necessity in this coda he would not characterise as *inconvenient* the 'fact that it is analysis that tells us how to hear' the coda as performing the work of coherence; he would not encourage us to be brave enough to admit this fact openly. I cannot blame him for feeling uncomfortable. For he has just gone to great lengths to justify the great length of this section of the music – which only needs justification because we have decided to call it a coda. And we

[23] *Ibid.*

130

Example 5.4 *(cont.)*

have only decided to call it a coda because of a sonata-form construction that dictates when the movement proper is over.

In fact, maybe the 'second development' view of the coda is not so far off the mark. The idea of a second development at least allows for more than one process of recapitulation. This would be more in the spirit of the rondo-like nature of the Classical finale, where the 'double return' is clearly attenuated.[24] Moreover, to see the F♯ minor climax as a necessary goal of the entire movement is to miss the comedy of it, which produces its effect because this climax is, strictly speaking, not necessary. The resolution from F♯ minor back to F major is the work of high spirits, a lateral shift that is genial and unbuttoned – the very opposite of laboured. If we can hear the C♯ of bar 17 as a Bronx cheer, the F♯ minor climax draws unseemly and comic attention to it, turning it into an absurd moment through which the theme itself is turned inside out, as it were (F♯ minor preserves the A of F major). The resolution back to F turns on a screaming pun – F♮ for E♯, tonic for leading tone (Example 5.5).[25]

[24] Leonard Ratner subscribes to the 'second development' view of this movement, and he puts a special emphasis on its rondo-like nature. Ratner, *Classic Music: Expression, Form, and Style* (New York: Schirmer Books, 1980), pp. 254–5.

[25] Tovey, in one of his more high-spirited essays, characterises this coda as a profusion of enharmonic jokes ending with a surge of Homeric laughter that 'has all the vaults of heaven wherein to disperse itself'. Donald Francis Tovey, *Essays in Musical Analysis: Symphonies and other Orchestral Works* (Oxford: Oxford University Press, 1989), p. 82.

Example 5.5   Ludwig van Beethoven, Symphony No. 8: finale, climax of coda

Example 5.5 (cont.)

Example 5.5 (cont.)

Example 5.5   (cont.)

I must admit that hearing this climax as comic allows me to attenuate its role as a necessary goal, just as attenuating its necessity allows me to hear it as comic. Rosen, however, speaks of the brutality and violence of Beethoven's emphatic motion into and out of F♯ minor and believes that the initial C♯ back in bar 17 'acts almost as an irritant'.[26] These interpretative notions do seem to warrant a more plot-driven type of narrative, in which an irritating feature builds up pressure (is repressed) and finally bursts out violently (and is just as violently re-repressed). I prefer to hear the initial C♯ less as a portentous irritant and more as a musical pratfall. The suddenness both of its onset and its disappearance renders the C♯ more a potentially comic interjection than a real threat (compare, for example, the equally famous D♯s at the outset of the Violin Concerto), although one could make a case for the reactive vehemence of the statement of the theme that immediately follows. Perhaps a conflation of both views comes out about right: brutal humour.[27]

[26] Rosen, *Sonata Forms*, p. 337.
[27] To see which kind of interpretation you prefer, try setting different words to the initial C♯. First, in the melodramatic spirit of the 'maledizione' from Verdi's *Rigoletto*: 'Die!' Next, in the blasé contrarian spirit of a late-twentieth-century Valley Girl: 'Not!' Or finally, here is a scenario not lacking in a certain pertinent irony: imagine a nearly deaf man reacting with pique to a conversation that has fallen out of his range of hearing: 'What?!'

Example 5.5   (*cont.*)

In any event, Rosen's ironic caveat about necessity reminds us that we must be careful about conflating the composer's sense of compositional necessity with our own sense of intrawork structural necessity and inevitability. Beethoven generally works so hard that we automatically assume that anomalous or non-normative aspects of his music are performing some important life-support work, as that done by an important organ of the body. In the case of the Eighth Symphony, however, perhaps the coda of the finale is more like the proverbial tail wagging the dog.

SONATA FORM WORKS

Sonata form works, in both senses of the word. It is effective, and it performs work. What kind of work do we understand it to do? Sonata form both sets up and resolves a consequential long-range tonal opposition, one which is said to reside in the very syntax of tonal music.[28] It creates thereby a dialectical process: tonic begets dominant which begets tonic-again. Dominant and tonic are synthesised within a large-scale cyclic rhythm, like the great cyclic processes of nature, but with one big difference: this process closes; it is unitary and all-consuming.

---

[28] In Ratner's formulation: '[C]lassic style . . . is made possible by the specific action of classic harmony.' Ratner, 'Harmonic Aspects of Classic Form', *Journal of the American Musicological Society* 2 (1949), 167.

Example 5.5   (*cont.*)

The predominant sense of sonata form as enacting a large-scale harmonic resolution itself arose in the manner of a sonata-form reprise: namely, twentieth-century theorists of the form self-consciously returned to the eighteenth-century harmonic view of the form, overcoming the thematic view that tenaciously prevailed throughout the nineteenth century.[29] They did so with a vengeance, now bolstered not only by harmonic theory but by the manifest attractions of the Schenkerian background. The unitary, unequivocal closure of the textbook cadence (or closure of the background structure) came to be transferred onto the much looser expanse of an entire movement or even an entire multi-movement piece. But comparing the closure of a harmonic cadence with the closure of a large-scale, highly differentiated piece of music is a risky proposition: the change in scale results in a more open-ended phenomenon, bringing on a much greater level of complexity.[30] In effect, we have asked sonata form to bear an impossible burden of harmonic closure: nothing as large as that can resolve and close quite so unequivocally.

Sonata form has also been asked to perform important historical work. Our

[29] A decisive early move in this direction is Ratner, 'Harmonic Aspects of Classic Form'.
[30] Such disparities of scale are routinely taken into account in more practical matters. Nobody would attempt to dispatch an elephant with a gigantically proportioned mousetrap. But to take the harmonic conflict/resolution assumption fully seriously is to accord to pieces in sonata form the single-minded agenda of such a trap: open with strain, quiver with tension, slam shut with consequence.

Example 5.5 (*cont.*)

construction of sonata form is inextricably tied to our construction of the Classical style. Any account of the Classical style will read like a story of the genesis of sonata form out of the chaos of the pre-Classical generation, a story of synthesis and realisation. In Webster's article on sonata form in the *New Grove*,[31] we read of various earlier forms as so many independent agents gradually working towards a solution: each earlier form held some piece of the solution, but only sonata form was able to put it all together; only sonata form closed the case.[32]

Rosen defines the Classical style in terms strikingly similar to those in which T. S. Eliot defined the literary classic, in his essay 'What is a Classic?'[33] Both writers emphasise as classic the culminating realisation of a language. The values that come to the fore in both cases are maturity, universality and comprehensiveness: the classic language realises a 'common style' which is unmannered, uneccentric. For Eliot, the true classic not only fully realises a language but exhausts it as well (he considers Vergil to

[31] See note 5.
[32] We would do well to remember, however, that in his later book on the *Farewell* Symphony, Webster mounts a sustained critique of evolutionary views of the Classical style, views that banish 'Haydn's early and middle music, indeed all pre-1780 music, to a pre-Classical ghetto'. Webster, *Haydn's 'Farewell' Symphony*, pp. 349–56.   [33] T. S. Eliot, *What is a Classic?* (London: Faber and Faber, 1945).

be the only true classic, and Latin the language both realised and exhausted). There is a strong sense in which we tend to consider the tonal language to be both realised and exhausted in the Viennese Classical style. Accounts of later tonal usage almost always trace the fomenting seeds of atonality. This is hardly surprising: just as the Classical style needs a germinating pre-history, it also needs a decaying post-history.

Even ahistorical accounts of sonata form emphasise its power to resolve the problems of other, lesser forms. Consider how hard A. B. Marx works to establish sonata form as a telos in his derivation of forms: he treats the form as a resolution of a series of problems, the final denouement of a long train of knots, leading from the simple *Satz*, through various minuet and rondo forms, to the fully realised sonata form.[34] Marx's scenario is markedly different from those of our own century – it is more strictly constructed and completely ahistorical – but the basic idea is the same: sonata form is understood to realise the language of tonality.

The work of closure haunts all these constructions. At the heart of our notion of sonata form, we find again and again this idea of work; we have clearly been chiefly concerned with what sonata form does, how it works to close a harmonic circuit and/or a historical circuit, how it performs the work of resolution. Thinking about such musical work, we find ourselves faced with the very notion of the musical work, pun emphatically intended. For it is no accident that the 'work-concept' became distinctly foregrounded around the same time as the recognition of sonata form.[35]

It seems natural enough to call pieces of music 'works'; a musical work is a form of ergon, it is something that is made or produced. A composer's life work is a life in works;[36] the word oeuvre is related to words like 'ouvrage' or 'ouvrier'. The Latin word 'opus' originally meant 'work', in the sense of toil; later it came to mean a finished work. But I think that our prepossession about how sonata form works runs deeper than the unthinking conflation of the work (toil) of the composer with the composer's work (piece). For to that conflation we add another kind of work: the work we imagine is performed by the piece and vicariously performed by us as we listen to the piece.

Let us return to that word opus. Probably the most well known Classical usage of opus occurs in Book VI of Vergil's *Aeneid*, in the line that begins: 'hoc opus, hic labor est' (literally: 'there's the toil, there's the work'). This is a paratactic structure, and it clearly establishes the identity of opus and labour. But we need to go further: recovering the original context of Vergil's words may actually help us characterise our attachment to sonata form and the idea of work.

In Book VI, Aeneas undertakes to visit the realm of Hades, where he wishes above

---

[34] Adolf Bernhard Marx, *Die Lehre von der musikalischen Komposition, praktisch-theoretisch*, 2nd edn, 4 vols. (Leipzig: Breitkopf und Härtel, 1848), vol. III.

[35] On the history and philosophy of the work-concept, see Lydia Goehr, *The Imaginary Museum of Musical Works: An Essay in the Philosophy of Music* (Oxford: Oxford University Press, 1992).

[36] For a characteristically dialectical discussion of this notion, see Chapter 1, 'Life and Work', of Carl Dahlhaus, *Ludwig van Beethoven: Approaches to his Music*, trans. Mary Whittall (Oxford: Clarendon Press, 1991), pp. 1–42.

all to speak to his father Anchises about his destiny and the destiny of Rome. However, one does not arrive at the underworld just for a visit. In fact, only epic heroes have ever gone there and attempted to return (it is one of the things that defines them as epic heroes). Aeneas is assisted in this treacherous passage by the Cumaean Sybil, who issues this dire warning:

> O son of Anchises, the descent to the underworld is easy
> the gates of darkest Hades stand open night and day;
> but to retrace one's steps, to climb back out to the upper air,
> there's the toil, there's the work (*hoc opus, hic labor est*).[37]

I would like to offer this passage as lending specific mythological resonance to our prevailing sense of the archetypal work of sonata form. In this reading of sonata form, the double return is a return from the underworld, a toilsome, precarious journey. The development section thus becomes a place of maximum tension, even personal disintegration; it entails a symbolic loss of identity, a symbolic death. Rebirth occurs in that wonderfully aggrandising passage to the recapitulation that would make epic heroes of us all.

Still, the act of returning to the home key in Classical tonal language, particularly the return from the dominant, is the easiest thing in the world. This is obvious to anyone who has ever heard the repeat of an exposition (hence such repeats play no significant role in anyone's view of the form). The trick of sonata form seems to be to make this easy return sound like work. In fact, the return to the tonic sounds never so exalted as it does in sonata form. Hearing that return as a supreme resolution gives sonata form a single, archetypal rhythm, an inclusive autonomy.

Our emphasis on conflict and resolution in sonata form has allowed us to treat sonata form as a mythic archetype, with the full range of uses that such archetypes invite. The rewards of this emphasis, like the rewards of work well done, are manifest and not to be dismissed. But sonata form can be so much less! Haydn reminds us that return is not always a return from the underworld, that we do not have to keep working so hard to hear it that way: sonata form need not always be a psychodrama with a single, destined outcome. Beethoven reminds us that even his fabled endings often simply end, forsaking (or lampooning) the laboured glories of absolute closure. Return can be a moveable feast, and loose ends can encourage a welcome form of lightness, the loose weave of human possibility.

I opened by commenting on how the Western theoretical tradition has heard the dominant–tonic cadence as a return to the chord of nature, and how, by dramatising and centralising this resolution, sonata form can be heard to enact a homecoming, a

---

[37] Tros Anchisiade, facilis descensus Auerno:
noctes atque dies patet atri ianua Ditis;
sed revocare gradum superasque evadere ad auras,
hoc opus, hic labor est.

Vergil, *Aeneid*, Book VI, 126–9. In *P. Vergilius Maronis Opera*, ed. R. A. B. Mynors (Oxford: Oxford University Press, 1969, rpt with corr. 1972), p. 231. My translation.

renewal of our natural beginnings. But the nature of sonata form may in fact be broader than this exclusive renewal of a central tonic, broader than that fraught journey home: the nature of sonata form may teach us that renewal is a basic rhythm of life, as momentous as the new millennium, as available as the next sunrise, or as easy and unpredictable as one's next step.

Chapter Six

—

August Halm's two cultures as nature

ALEXANDER REHDING

On the surface, August Halm's study *Von zwei Kulturen der Musik* (*On Two Cultures of Music*) of 1913 is a textbook in the venerable, some might say notorious, German tradition of *Formenlehre*. However, in spite of many highly perceptive observations about the 'two musical cultures', fugue and sonata, the book on the whole would scarcely qualify as a theory of forms: there is no clear-cut definition or characterisation – or even an attempt at it – of either fugue or sonata form. In fact, Halm deliberately defies definitions of these terms: 'It appears that one cannot say what a fugue, or a sonata, is. All we can say is what happens in either form and what each form demands: as yet, I have never encountered, or succeeded in formulating, a definition of fugue or sonata.'[1] Despite the professed inability to pin down the essence of the 'two cultures', this claim points precisely towards Halm's central ambition, to formulate a theory approaching an ontology of sonata and fugue.

Perhaps the foremost obstacle that has prevented Halm, whom the philosopher Theodor W. Adorno lamented as 'now disgracefully forgotten',[2] from being more widely known is that his theory is steeped in the German Idealist tradition, to a degree that makes it hard – from our present viewpoint – to sympathise with his premises and conclusions. For Halm's theory does not lend itself readily to broader, practical application.[3] In Halm's philosophical framework, which, perhaps misleadingly, he calls 'phenomenological',[4] musical works are not simply sounding phenomena in their own

---

[1] August Halm, *Von zwei Kulturen der Musik*, ed. Gustav Wyneken, 3rd edn (Stuttgart: Ernst Klett, 1947), p. 9: 'Was eine Fuge, was eine Sonate sei, scheint nicht gesagt werden zu können, sondern nur, was in jeder der beiden Formen vorgeht und was eine jede verlangt: eine Definition der Fuge oder der Sonate ist mir bis jetzt weder gelungen noch begegnet.' All translations used here are mine, unless marked otherwise. Some passages from Halm's work are translated in Edward A. Lippmann, *Musical Aesthetics: A Historical Reader*, 4 vols. (Stuyvesant, NY: Pendragon, 1986–90), vol. III, pp. 51–69.

[2] Theodor W. Adorno, *Aesthetic Theory*, trans. Robert Hullot-Kentor (London: Athlone Press, 1997), p. 201.

[3] That two musicological writers, Carl Dahlhaus and Theodor W. Adorno, have drawn on Halm to no small extent is ultimately a reflection upon their own Idealist background.

[4] Halm's phenomenology has less to do with Husserl's contemporaneous approach than with Hegel's notion of the 'journey of the World Spirit through history towards itself'. See also August Halm, *Von*

right, but rather representations of a musical Hegelian Spirit that evolves teleologically. (In this sense, Halm speaks of 'Bach's Fugue' and 'Beethoven's Sonata' – using both in the singular – as manifestations of this musical spirit in the first place, not as individual works.) In fact, his musical universe consists of only three composers: Bach, Beethoven and Bruckner. Other composers, such as Mozart and Handel, do feature in his books, but mainly to serve as negative examples. This view would certainly raise some eyebrows; however, what may at first appear as hubris is in fact part of an all-embracing conception of absolute, instrumental music, where the works of Handel, whom Halm thought to be primarily a dramatic composer, simply have no place.

The supreme role in which absolute music features in Halm's thought is reflected in the formalist stance he assumes in his musical analyses, coupled with an intransigent opposition towards the then prominent hermeneutic school of musicology.[5] In stark contrast with this position, however, the language that Halm employs throughout his writings is richly metaphorical. His imagery, which draws, apparently arbitrarily, on theology, mythology and politics, has caused bewilderment among many commentators and resulted in a variety of responses, ranging from incidental acknowledgement to outright rejection.[6]

And yet, these diverse and seemingly incongruous aspects of *Formenlehre* and ontology, of formalist analysis and metaphorical representation, and indeed of politics, theology and absolute music, belong together inseparably. It is indicative in this respect that a crucial element in Halm's thinking, his somewhat arcane conception of nature, which will be explored in greater depth in the following, is mentioned as if in passing, in only a couple of places, and is exclusively employed to describe Beethoven's music. Its implications, like the edifice of Halm's theory as a whole, must be pieced together. Once this is done, Halm's concept of nature can be read as a kind of *basso continuo* that pervades Halm's whole musical philosophy and unlocks the connections between the diverse aspects of his theory.

THE NATURE OF BACH'S AND BEETHOVEN'S THEMES

Halm concludes the first part of *Von zwei Kulturen* with a mysterious characterisation of Beethoven's sonatas:

Form und Sinn der Musik, ed. Siegfried Schmalzriedt (Wiesbaden: Breitkopf und Härtel, 1978), p. 35, and Lee A. Rothfarb, 'Beethoven's Formal Dynamics: August Halm's Phenomenological Perspective', in *Beethoven Forum IV*, ed. James Webster and Lewis Lockwood (Lincoln: University of Nebraska Press, 1995), pp. 65–84.

5 On Halm's debate with the hermeneuticists, see Lee A. Rothfarb, 'Music Analysis, Cultural Morality and Sociology in the Writings of August Halm', *Indiana Theory Review* 16/1–2 (1995), 171–96, and Halm, *Von Form und Sinn in der Musik*, pp. 33–5. See also the section 'Reclaiming Beethoven' in this chapter.

6 See Schmalzriedt's introduction in Halm, *Von Form und Sinn der Musik*, and Lotte Thaler, *Organische Form in der Musiktheorie des 19. und beginnenden 20. Jahrhunderts*, Berliner musikwissenschaftliche Arbeiten, vol. XXV, ed. Carl Dahlhaus and Rudolf Stephan (Munich and Salzburg: Katzbichler, 1984), pp. 114–17.

What appear before us are not animate figures but relations between opposites which seem alive and whose unity is only achieved in their total effect. Thus it is not a living, created nature that is presented to us. What is proffered instead is the law of nature, the unity of the diverse forces, in an abstract process, without coincidences, without anything incidental. *Natura naturans*, which the Scholastic philosophers believed had to be interpolated as an opposition to *natura naturata* between God and the created world, seems to speak to us here.[7]

The whole passage sits uncomfortably with the received wisdom of music theory that 'Beethoven's music most closely resembles the way music ought to go.'[8] While Beethoven conventionally serves as a theoretical paradigm for organicism,[9] Halm detects here 'not a living, created nature' but only a schematic representation of it, as 'laws of nature' – the epitome of the mechanical. Beethoven's music seems to have little to do with organic nature itself. Despite this alleged lifelessness, Halm implies that Beethoven's music nevertheless has a certain fertility: in drawing on the two-tiered Scholastic conception of nature, its creative potential (*natura naturans*) on the one hand, and its creation, its potential realised (*natura naturata*) on the other, Halm designates Beethoven's sonata as a creative force. However, Halm remains suspiciously silent as to what it is that Beethoven's sonata creates. One must ask, in other words, what does Halm mean by *natura naturata*?

A rash answer to this question has been to take the duality at the foundation of Halm's book as a guideline and to suggest that if Beethoven's sonata is *natura naturans*, then Bach's fugue must be *natura naturata*.[10] Appealing though this analogy might seem, it is in fact not tenable, for the simple reason that fugue precedes sonata. It does so in two ways: historically and logically. Even though Halm is not interested in accurate music history, as he repeatedly emphasises, the succession of fugue and sonata cannot be inverted, as the Scholastic concept of nature implies that *natura naturans* is the source of *natura naturata*, not vice versa. As we shall see, Bach's fugue cannot be 'created nature'; it is not contingent upon Beethoven's sonata – *natura naturata* must be something else.

Even so, it is advisable to study in some detail what Halm regards as essential in fugue, by re-examining an example that Halm discusses at some length in his book. Example 6.1 shows the theme of the B♭ minor fugue from the second volume of *Das wohltemperierte Klavier*. This theme is of particular interest to Halm, he explains, because it is one of the 'most animate' – that is to say, most un-Beethovenian – 'and hence most instructive themes'.[11] Accordingly, he uses it as an exemplar of Bach's thematic work.

[7] Halm, *Zwei Kulturen*, p. 139: 'Keine lebensvollen Gestalten, sondern lebendig wirkende Beziehungen von Gegensätzen treten vor uns, deren Einheitlichkeit erst in ihrer gesamten Wirkung erreicht wird. Also nicht eine lebendige, geschaffene Natur, sondern das Naturgesetz wird uns vorgestellt, die Einheit der verschiedenen Kräfte dargetan; in einem abstrakten Geschehen, ohne Zufälliges, ohne Akzidentielles. Die natura naturans der Scholastiker, die sie als Gegensatz zur natura naturata noch zwischen Gott und die geschaffene Welt einschieben zu müssen glaubten, scheint hier zu uns zu sprechen.'
[8] Scott Burnham, *Beethoven Hero* (Princeton: Princeton University Press, 1995), p. 112.
[9] *Ibid.*, pp. 66–111.   [10] See Schmalzriedt's introduction in Halm, *Von Form und Sinn der Musik*, p. 39.
[11] Halm, *Zwei Kulturen*, p. 207.

Example 6.1   Halm's analysis of Johann Sebastian Bach, Fugue in B♭ minor (BWV 891)

The full theme, Halm explains, grows out of a motive that is stated explicitly at the beginning. In bars 3–4 he observes a further statement of this motive in transposition, which is written out in Example 6.1b. The decorated manner in which the motive appears in the fugue with quaver figuration (compare the first and second lines of the example), however, lacks the characteristic crotchet rest. He notes that the absence of the rest is motivated by the sheer kinetic force of the quaver figuration; the rest is overrun, so to speak. The heightened movement of these bars was in turn initiated by the upbeat that was added to the motive at the end of bar 2. This final crotchet of bar 2 and the preceding crotchet rest, however, are also a reference back to the first bar. Consequently, as is shown in Example 6.1c, bar 2 can also be heard as a sequence to bar 1. The two phrases must be understood, in this case, as effectively overlapping. Halm makes the fine observation that in this form the tritone A♮–E♭ requires resolution. He finds the resolution of E♭ in the D♭ at bar 3, at the start of the restatement of the motive.[12] This *Fernhören* motivates an alternative phrasing where the crotchet rest of bar 2 is no longer a division between phrases but rather an *Innenpause*, as Riemann would call it, a rest within the phrase. The harmonic need to resolve the E♭ overrides the motivic break which the crotchet rest would mark on a merely rhythmic level. The equivocal nature of the phrasing, where harmonic considerations interact with the rhythmic-melodic aspects, Halm concludes, lends the theme its impetus.

This impetus causes the rising quavers to shoot over the goal so that the G♭ at bar 4 returns to F. While it is possible to draw an analogy from this bar to elements of bar 2 – and Halm proceeds to discuss this in detail – it becomes apparent in the course of

---

[12] It should come as no surprise that Halm was to become a fervent admirer of Schenker, their differences over the stature of Bruckner notwithstanding. See *Von Form und Sinn der Musik*, pp. 30–1 and pp. 271–4.

his fourteen-page discussion of this four-bar theme that the very notion of a motive has gradually shifted. To begin with, Halm adheres to a conventional idea, where the principal motive encompasses the first phrase of the theme, across the dividing crotchet rest, spanning from B♭ in bar 1 to B♭ in bar 2. However, his discussion of the more subtle relationships between the bars reveals that the notion of a motive as a surface phenomenon is abandoned in that the motive is progressively equated with linear motion, so much so that Halm concludes his discussion by suggesting that the final bar of the theme should be heard as depicted in Example 6.1d, as a descending line G♭–F–E♭–D♭ intertwined with the ascending line C–D♭–E♭–F. The final F is in fact not sounded as part of the theme, but should be heard as implied because the tritone C–G♭ needs resolution, in analogy to bar 2. (The reason Bach chose not to explicate this resolution in this instance is, Halm explains, that a total resolution of the theme is not desirable in a fugal subject, which rather dwells on its continuous impetus.) In this way, Halm manages to read two scalic motives into the final bar of the theme. The scale is for him 'the primordial' (*das Ursprüngliche*) and hence represents ideal motion.[13]

The multiplicity of levels at which this theme seems to work, due to the inter-penetration of harmony and melody, is for Halm a sign of its organic nature. In his eyes it possesses 'eternal life'.[14] Its long line and forward drive, as we have seen, is due to the concordant interaction between melody and harmony: where the melodic phrase stops, the urge for harmonic resolution carries the flow across the boundaries. This theme, Halm concludes, is an individual: in its literal sense, this means that the theme cannot be divided; following a commonplace of organicism, any change made to the theme would be at the expense of the entire organism.[15] In a more general sense, by calling the theme an individual Halm alludes to the self-contained, unique nature of Bach's themes, where harmony and melody form an inextricable unity. The theme is, in other words, described as a fully rounded personality. This may sound odd at first, given that Halm stresses that at the bottom of the B♭ minor theme is only the scale. But it is the ambiguity of the term 'primordial' that allows him to make this leap of thought: the primordial is not simply the ordinary, but rather the original and sem-piternal, which is irreducible, and becomes, so to speak, indivisible. The virtue of Bach's theme lies for Halm in its 'free, that is organically grown symmetry', as opposed to the static, utilitarian symmetry of Classical four-square themes of Mozart and Beethoven.[16] The form of fugue itself, Halm asserts, builds on nothing but the theme; the theme is not changed or developed in any way, it is simply restated. The fugue as form is thus no more than an elaboration of the theme, a thorough explora-tion of the individual: 'A Bach theme is a form unto itself.'[17] The fugal theme sub-

[13] Halm, *Zwei Kulturen*, p. 221.   [14] *Ibid.*, p. 218.
[15] Halm has to concede, however, that the *Abgesang* of bar 4 develops a small degree of independence: in bar 81 of the fugue the last part occurs without its beginning (*ibid.*).
[16] *Ibid.*, pp. 211 and 190. He regards the symmetry of Tamino's aria 'Dies Bildnis ist bezaubernd schön', with its tonic–dominant antecedent and dominant–tonic answer, as trivial.
[17] *Ibid.*, p. 130.

Theme 1:'moving chord' Theme 2:'stationary scale'

Example 6.2   Halm's 'themes' in Ludwig van Beethoven, *Tempest* Sonata, Op. 31 No. 2

ordinates both melody and harmony and organises them. 'The more a theme absorbs the fundamental forces of music and uses them in its spiritual constitution', he sums up, 'the more life and life values it has.'[18]

Beethoven's themes, by contrast, could not be further removed from this organic ideal: they show none of the absorption that Halm discovers in Bach's thematic invention. If Halm's discussion of Beethoven's themes strikes one as technically unsophisticated in comparison with Bach's, then this is in no small part a deliberate ploy aimed at exposing the rudimentary nature of Beethoven's thematic invention. These themes are what Halm pointedly classifies as 'dividuals'. In Beethoven's Op. 31 No. 2, the so-called *Tempest* Sonata, Halm identifies the principal themes in the opening passage, as shown in Example 6.2. The Largo opening of the sonata is an arpeggiated dominant chord, the following Allegro is a scale, spanning from A down to D, and from the D an octave above back to the original A. On account of the circular nature of the Allegro theme, beginning and ending on the same note, Halm explains that the scalic theme possesses an essentially 'stationary' quality, in contradiction with the dynamic character conventionally associated with scalic movement. The chordal theme, conversely, is assigned a latent 'moving' character.[19]

Although Halm introduces these two as themes, they are so de-individualised that they are described interchangeably, and seemingly indiscriminately, as motives, and motives of the most ordinary kind at that: a chord and a scale.[20] Even when, in the course of the movement, the two combine in the passage after bar 21 (see Example 6.3) the combination is not an organic integration or synthesis, as in Bach's example, but an 'industrial, machine-like unity'.[21] The two themes, chord and scale (the latter now reduced to the figure of a turn in bar 23, which underscores the essential 'stationary' quality that Halm hears in the scalic theme) do not concur but follow each other in opposition.

The question of identifying the formal parts in Op. 31 No. 2 is a vexed one.[22] Carl

[18] *Ibid.*, p. 206.

[19] Halm does not explain this in any greater detail. It is possible that the 'moving character' is brought about by the circumstance that the arpeggiated A major chord turns out to function as the dominant, which would require a motion towards resolution.   [20] *Ibid.*, p. 76.   [21] *Ibid.*

[22] See Janet Schmalfeldt, 'Form as the Process of Becoming: The Beethovenian-Hegelian Tradition and the "Tempest" Sonata', in *Beethoven Forum V*, ed. James Webster and Lewis Lockwood (Lincoln: University of Nebraska Press, 1996), pp. 37–71.

Example 6.3   Excerpt from the exposition of the *Tempest* Sonata

Dahlhaus, in particular, has wrestled with the movement in a variety of contexts, largely, as Janet Schmalfeldt rightly observes, in response to Halm's analytical comments on this sonata. The chief problem, which Dahlhaus discusses again and again in a variety of contexts, is where the first subject resides: is it in the introductory, quasi-improvisatory opening, or in the transitional passage after bar 21? The answer Dahlhaus proposes is that the introduction is 'not yet' thematic, and the transition is 'no longer' the subject.[23] For Halm, however, this particular question seems quite

23 See, for instance, Carl Dahlhaus, *Ludwig van Beethoven: Approaches to his Music*, trans. Mary Whittall (Oxford: Clarendon Press, 1991), pp. 117 and 177. A detailed discussion of Halm's analysis of the movement, focusing on the exposition, is found in Rothfarb, 'Music Analysis, Cultural Morality and Sociology', 183–93.

irrelevant. His approach takes the processual development of the material for granted. The two subjects of the sonata play only a subsidiary role in Halm's account besides these two principal themes (or rather, thematic principles), the arpeggiated Largo chord and the scalic Allegro.[24] He underlines his bias against the search for subjects by referring to an anecdote where the composer is reported to have said: 'Two principles – thousands do not grasp this!'[25] These two principles, Halm interprets, are not simply to be equated with the two subjects, as would conventionally be done; rather, they symbolise abstract forces. The sonata itself builds on the fundamental opposition between the principles – chord and scale – not between the subjects. This decision will have considerable consequences for Halm's conception of form of this movement on the whole.

When Halm refers to the two principles as 'symbols of force',[26] he alludes to its essentially mechanical nature: the arpeggio represents 'the harmonic', and the scale 'the melodic'. To adopt Halm's apocalyptic prose, in juxtaposing and deploying those two forces, Beethoven has achieved a formidable deed: he has rent asunder the primordial unity of harmony and melody that prevailed in Bach's theme. In this way he has brought about the fundamental separation of elements, as a veritable division of labour.[27] These elements now function as an opposition, although not as a hostile one, as Halm is eager to point out: as we shall see later, the self-contradictory character that he ascribes to the themes – as 'moving chord' and 'stationary scale' – implies some latent force of attraction. The themes are not personalities, as Bach's theme was, but signals of a dynamic situation within the form.

In this way Halm demonstrates how the separation of the fundamental elements of music, harmony and melody, has a dramatic effect on musical form: in Bach, the theme relied on the use of the fundamental elements to flourish. However, the very same forces, once released, as is the case in Beethoven, weaken and even annihilate the individual nature of the theme.[28] Whereas in his analysis of Bach's fugue the scale was upheld as the glorious discovery at the heart of the complex fugal theme, the very same scale featured in Beethoven's sonata as raw material, as one of the 'two principles' – *qua* scale, as it were – to demonstrate the impoverishment of Beethoven's themes.

When Halm speaks of the release of forces this does not mean that harmony and melody are left to their own devices. On the contrary, in the hands of Beethoven they

[24] Halm goes so far as to maintain that the two subjects, like many of Beethoven's themes, are so devoid of individuality that one might as well exchange them for others without doing much damage. See *Zwei Kulturen*, p. 78.

[25] *Ibid.*, p. 79. This remark goes back to a comment, which is probably apocryphal, found in Anton F. Schindler's *Beethoven As I Knew Him*, ed. Donald W. MacArdle, trans. Constance S. Jolly (London: Faber and Faber, 1956), p. 406. See also Arnold Schmitz, *Beethovens zwei Principe: Ihre Bedeutung für Themen- und Satzbau* (Bonn and Berlin: Ferdinand Dümmler, 1923).

[26] Halm, *Zwei Kulturen*, p. 77.   [27] Halm uses this term in *ibid.*, p. 253.

[28] *Ibid.*, p. 206. It is noteworthy that at this stage in the book rhythm also counted as a fundamental force. The role of rhythm was much reduced in the corresponding passages in the sequel to *Zwei Kulturen*, the *Bruckner* monograph, 2nd edn (Munich: Georg Müller, 1923; rpt Hildesheim: Georg Olms, 1978). It seems that Halm was only gradually becoming aware of the full implications of his views of music theory.

must be understood as sublated, or *aufgehoben*, in Hegel's sense: cancelled and preserved at the same time, and in this way restored at a higher level. In Beethoven's sonata, the fundamental elements are no longer subjugated to the theme but to the form as a whole. In the final analysis, then, Halm's dialectic between theme and form can be understood as follows: fugal form is engendered by its theme, while sonata in turn engenders its themes in the service of the form. Halm couches the condition of the sonata in another simile: 'The sonata, by contrast, is the formula of the collaboration of many individuals, it is an organism writ large: it is like the State.'[29]

BEETHOVEN'S SONATA AND THE PROMISE OF THE IDEAL STATE

The idea that the State should be regarded as one great individual was part and parcel of organicist theories of the State, which aimed to oppose an atomistic kind of individualism.[30] Individuals are formed, according to organicist doctrine, within the social group to which they belong, which at the same time shapes their needs, aims and ways of thinking. The organic view can, as a rule, be seen as conservative when it further posits that outside their group individuals cannot gain a concept of themselves, in other words, when it maintains that society suits individuals, precisely because it formed them through its institutions.[31] This would be the case in the State that Beethoven's sonata represents. Halm describes it as a 'State of ants',[32] referring not only to the division of labour between the melodic and harmonic forces but also to the crippled themes. It is certain that he does not regard Beethoven's music as the ideal State.

Rather, the dualism of Bach's fugue and Beethoven's sonata reflects the basic dichotomy that lies at the heart of traditional political philosophy: are the principles on which society works shaped by the wills of individuals (at the risk of solipsism), or is, conversely, society prior to human individuals? This is, in other words, the chicken-and-egg question: which is more fundamental, the individual or society?

Bach's fugue and Beethoven's sonata present alternative means of organisation – or 'cultures', as Halm refers to them in the title of his book. However, neither seems to satisfy him fully. Whilst Bach appears to fare better on the whole, as he is criticised in less harsh terms, Halm nonetheless regards Beethoven as the arbiter of harmony and rhythm, and the sonata as superior to the fugue.[33] This is because Halm regards the existence of the State as a fundamental necessity, which is directly related to his notion of progress: 'Bach's music is more musical than that of the classical compos-

[29] Halm, *Zwei Kulturen*, p. 33: 'Die Sonate dagegen ist die Formel des Zusammenwirkens vieler Individuen, ist ein Organismus im grossen: sie gleicht dem Staat.'
[30] Kenneth Dyson, *The State Tradition in Western Europe* (Oxford: Martin Robertson, 1980), p. 165.
[31] Kenneth Westphal, 'The Basic Context and Structure of Hegel's *Philosophy of Right*', in *The Cambridge Companion to Hegel*, ed. Frederick C. Beiser (Cambridge: Cambridge University Press, 1993), p. 236.
[32] Halm, *Zwei Kulturen*, p. 253.
[33] *Ibid.*, p. 117 and *Bruckner*, p. 28. Originally, his distinction between the two cultures was that Bach's fugue represented 'style', whereas Beethoven's sonata represented the lesser 'form' (*Zwei Kulturen*, p. xlvi). In the course of the book, however, this evaluation shifted considerably.

ers. However, what we still miss in it is the grand idea of the State, which, once it has appeared, never lets go of our minds again.'[34]

This last thought Halm shares with Hegel, who in his *Philosophy of Right* declares the dichotomy between the priority of the individual and that of society to be false. Instead, Hegel resolves the dichotomy dialectically: individuals are social practitioners; their desires and needs are conditioned by society, as are the means of realising these objectives. At the same time, however, social practice is in turn shaped by individuals' own actions. In this way, social procedures and individual action are mutually dependent and modify each other in Hegel's model.

For Hegel, the presence of the State is the manifestation of objectified, actual freedom. Freedom in Hegel's special sense, however, is not the ability to do whatever the individual wants, but could rather be described as the happy coincidence that the individual's own will is in agreement with the ethical institutions of the State.[35] In other words, freedom can only be attained within the State. Translated into Halm's terms, this would mean that while sonata form is the necessary precondition for freedom, actual freedom only exists where thematic individuality is not suppressed. It is only with this Hegelian concept of freedom in mind that we can understand Halm's assertion:

One hears the announcement in the streets that with the sonata freedom in music has begun. We recognise that it is illegitimate to say so in general. Such talk is thoughtless in this generality, and with our distinction of waxing harmonic power and waning thematic power we have already given an answer to such gibberish.[36]

In other words, as Beethoven has elevated harmony to form-bearing status, but at the expense of the themes, which are now maimed and oppressed, his sonata cannot be heard as a manifestation of freedom. In Hegel's terms, a 'bad State is one which merely exists; a sick body also exists, but it has no true reality'.[37] Nevertheless, the foundations of freedom have been created with Beethoven's sonatas; an idea of future freedom can be glimpsed in them through the oppressed themes.

---

[34] Halm, *Zwei Kulturen*, p. 253: 'Bachs Musik ist mehr Musik als die der Klassiker. Was uns dennoch an ihr fehlt, ist eben der große Staatsgedanke, der, einmal erschienen, unser Denken nie mehr freigibt.'

[35] See Georg W. F. Hegel, *Grundlinien der Philosophie des Rechts* (Stuttgart: Reclam, 1970); trans. H. B. Nisbet as *Elements of the Philosophy of Right* (Cambridge: Cambridge University Press, 1991), particularly par. 258, pp. 275–9, and *Zusatz*. Hegel is scathing about the notion that freedom consists merely of rights (see par. 15, p. 48) – the notion of rights, he posits in dialectical fashion, is meaningless without a notion of duties. True freedom must also encompass these duties: in this sense, doing one's duty is an assertion of freedom (see par. 155, p. 197; par. 261, pp. 284–5). It is worth noting, as Paul Lakeland reminds us in *The Politics of Salvation: The Hegelian Idea of the State* (Albany, NY: State University of New York Press, 1984), that Hegel's understanding of the State resembles in many ways what other thinkers call 'civil society'.

[36] Halm, *Zwei Kulturen*, pp. 140–1: 'Man hört es auf den Gassen verkündigen, dass mit der Sonate die Freiheit der Musik angebrochen sei. Wir erkennen, dass das so im ganzen zu sagen unberechtigt ist, und haben mit unserem Unterscheiden des Wachsens der harmonischen und des Abnehmens der thematischen Kraft schon die Antwort auf ein in solcher Allgemeinheit gedankenloses Gerede gegeben.'

[37] Hegel, *Philosophy of Right*, par. 270, *Zusatz*, p. 306.

For Hegel, whom many commentators believe to have written a legitimation for the status quo,[38] the ideal State was already in existence, in the form of the Prussian monarchy. For Halm, by contrast, it seems Beethoven's sonata does not represent the musical equivalent of the Prussian State; the ideal musical State was yet to come. In this sense, Halm's employment of the category of nature must be understood as a promissory concept: Beethoven's sonata is *natura naturans*, creative potential, in that it cannot yet be the end of a development; rather it refers beyond itself. Unlike the passive concept of nature, as the object of scientific investigation, that according to the historian Carolyn Merchant became predominant from the Renaissance onwards,[39] Halm's pre-Renaissance notion of *natura naturans* is a pointedly active concept. It requires that something else follow it, a music heralding the advent of the perfect State. It is creative by establishing an expectation of the future of music where the dichotomy between fugue and sonata will be resolved. Elsewhere Halm writes about sonata in terms of a 'prophecy', or even *Schuld* (which can be rendered in English as either 'guilt' or 'debt') that Beethoven's sonata owes.[40] All these images, despite their qualitatively different connotations, seem to point to the same thing: sonata is a crucial stepping stone in an eschatological process that is as yet incomplete. As such, Beethoven's sonata has a cosmological significance. However, in contrast to the Scholastic philosophers from whose cosmology he ostensibly borrows the term *natura naturans*, Halm uses it to make a statement about the logic of history.

Halm himself confirms this thought: sonata, he says, is 'the mother . . . of form as a parallel to "history"'.[41] This statement must be read through Hegel again, for whom history is progress in the self-consciousness of freedom.[42] Since the State is the phenomenal manifestation of freedom, history proper only starts with the existence of the State, even in its most incomplete form. Any events that precede the existence of the State are consequently relegated to pre-history.[43] In this sense, Bach's fugue must be seen as a pre-historical condition. Halm (who was, not surprisingly, a theologian by training) expresses this in biblical terms when he explains that this pre-history mani-

38 Note above all his notorious, but often misrepresented dictum 'What is rational is actual, and what is actual is rational' (*ibid.*, p. 20).
39 Carolyn Merchant, *The Death of Nature: Women, Ecology, and the Scientific Revolution* (San Francisco: Harper and Row, 1980). See Peter Burke, 'Fables of the Bees: A Case-Study of Views of Nature and Society', in *Nature and Society in Historical Context*, ed. Mikuláš Teich, Roy Porter and Bo Gustafsson (Cambridge: Cambridge University Press, 1997), p. 114.
40 Halm, *Bruckner*, pp. 217 and 210. Busoni speaks of Beethoven in similar terms when he contends that 'Beethoven is no master . . . because his art foreshadows a greater as yet incomplete' (Ferruccio Busoni, *Sketch of a New Esthetic of Music*, in *Three Classics in the Aesthetics of Music*, trans. Th. Baker (New York: Dover, 1962), p. 80 n. 2.) I am grateful to Benjamin Earle for bringing this parallel to my attention. Lee A. Rothfarb, by contrast, portrays the aesthetic stances of Busoni and Halm as essentially antagonistic and allies Halm with Pfitzner, in 'Music Analysis, Cultural Morality and Sociology', 193–6. In light of this parallel, however, it seems that Halm's position fully conforms neither with Pfitzner's nor with Busoni's views.   41 Halm, *Bruckner*, p. 76.
42 Hegel, *Vorlesungen über die Philosophie der Geschichte*, in *Theorie Werkausgabe*, vol. XII, 4th edn (Frankfurt am Main: Suhrkamp, 1995), p. 32.
43 Hegel, *Enzyklopädie. III. Philosophie des Geistes*, ed. Hermann Glockner, *Jubiläumsausgabe* vol. X, 4th edn (Stuttgart-Bad Cannstadt: Friedrich Frommann, 1965), p. 429, and *Philosophie der Geschichte*, p. 82.

fests itself in an ideal situation of innocence,[44] where harmony and melody were still in unity. Their separation ended this paradisiacal 'age of innocence'. Just as Adam and Eve's earthly existence after the expulsion from paradise consisted in labour, so the themes of Beethoven's sonata are condemned to labour.

At the same time, however, Halm has to concede that only with this separation, the musical division of labour, could real progress begin in Beethoven's sonata,[45] and history proper start. This admission testifies to a significant moment of reorientation in Halm's argument: although 'sonata form did not do the art of thematic invention much good',[46] as he complains more than once, its inception was nevertheless necessary and inevitable in the grand plan of the world. Like the biblical history of humankind as described in Genesis, the history of musical forms begins with the original sin, namely with the *Schuld* – and it is clear that *both* economic debt *and* spiritual guilt are encompassed here – that the sonata had brought upon music when it separated the fundamental elements.

The musical division of labour is in this account both the cause of music's expulsion from paradise and its atonement. In a metaphor not dissimilar from Max Weber's interpretation of Protestantism, sonata labours to prosper;[47] the resulting progress means for Halm a move towards formal expansion. The basis of this formal expansion, however, is given in precisely the separation of the fundamental elements of music and the ensuing *Aufhebung* of their function. For Halm, this form of progress manifests itself in Beethoven's *Tempest* Sonata.

RECLAIMING BEETHOVEN

It is conspicuous that in his entire book Halm draws only on a very small number of works to illustrate his points. Apart from a few compositions by Beethoven that Halm briefly discusses in *Von zwei Kulturen der Musik*, notably the *Waldstein* Sonata and the Sonata in F minor, Op. 2 No. 1, only two works receive more detailed commentary: the *Tempest* Sonata and the *Pastoral* Symphony. The choice of pieces seems unusual, given the formalist stance Halm takes in his analyses. Not least because of their suggestive titles, both the *Pastoral* Symphony and the *Tempest* Sonata were in the firm grip of hermeneutic Beethoven scholars of the turn of the century, such as Hermann Kretzschmar, Arnold Schering and Paul Bekker. Indeed, it is Bekker's work that Halm criticises relentlessly. In a fundamental critique of Bekker's exploration of the 'poetic idea'[48] in the *Tempest* Sonata, which takes up a significant part of *Von zwei Kulturen*, Halm ridicules Bekker's mixture of technicalities with anthropomorphisms and

---

[44] See Halm, *Bruckner*, p. 102.   [45] Halm, *Zwei Kulturen*, p. 16.

[46] Halm, *Bruckner*, p. 27, and similarly, p. 213.

[47] See Max Weber, *The Protestant Ethic and the Spirit of Capitalism*, trans. Talcott Parsons (London: George Allen and Unwin, 1976).

[48] It is perhaps no coincidence that Bekker mentions both the *Pastoral* and the *Tempest* in his introductory chapter in which he explains the nature of Beethoven's 'poetic idea'; see Paul Bekker, *Beethoven* (Berlin: Schuster und Loeffler, 1912), pp. 81–2.

psychologisms. In particular, Halm is averse to the rhetoric of pathos that Bekker employs to describe the beginning of the recapitulation:

There! – at the . . . return of the opening, the spell seems to be broken. The theme begins to speak. A recitative of plaintively supplicating expression wrestles itself away from the chordal motive. In vain. In sombrely pounding chords and sudden arpeggiations, only a suppressed, not a calmed, emotion is expressed.[49]

The exclamation 'In vain' is quoted sarcastically against Bekker throughout the book at strategic moments. Halm argues that Bekker's hermeneutic approach is wrong-headed, as it is merely allusive rather than explanatory. His main criticism of Bekker's poetic rendition of this moment is that it does not give a sense of formal necessity: the description is unclear and makes its own lack of clarity into its content. *Contra* the hermeneuticists, Halm insists that the *Tempest* is not a wishy-washy 'Fantasy Sonata' but rather a paragon of formal clarity.[50]

There is one element in Halm's adamant rejection of Bekker's hermeneutic approach that seems particularly curious: why did Halm choose this paradigm of musical hermeneutics – did not Beethoven himself, according to Schindler's famous anecdote, advise his listeners to read Shakespeare's *Tempest* in order to understand the sonata?[51] Halm could easily have made his points about the poverty of thematic invention in Beethoven using another piece.[52] The choice of the *Tempest* Sonata, however, seems to suggest that there was a lot more at stake for Halm than meets the eye.

The reason for Halm's choice can be pinpointed to the very 'In vain' moment, the occurrence of the recitatives in the recapitulation at bar 143 (Example 6.4). On the surface, Halm claims to demonstrate how there are compelling formal arguments for the occurrence of the recitative at this point rather than anywhere else, but it seems that his real objectives are rather different.

The moment in which the theme comes into its own, at the beginning of the recapitulation, is formally the moment of synthesis. In this movement, however, the idea of synthesis refers not only to the conventional coming-together of two tonal areas, but rather to the eventual coming-together of the two principles on which the sonata builds. Halm is anxious to show that this moment of synthesis could not possibly have happened at any other point in the movement: in the exposition it would sound out of place; in the development the theme is still undergoing the processual metamorphosis that will eventually lead to its liberation. In this sense, the recapitulation is presented as the *result* of the development:

[49] *Ibid.*, p. 151, quoted in Halm, *Zwei Kulturen*, p. 44: 'Da – bei der . . . Wiederkehr des Anfanges scheint der Bann gebrochen zu sein. Das Thema beginnt zu sprechen. Aus dem Akkordmotiv ringt sich ein Rezitativ von schmerzlich bittendem Ausdruck hervor. Umsonst. In dumpf pochenden Akkorden und sich aufbäumenden Akkordgängen verkündet sich nur eine unterdrückte, nicht beruhigte Erregung.' [50] Halm, *Zwei Kulturen*, pp. 47–86.
[51] See Schindler, *Beethoven As I Knew Him*, p. 406.
[52] Subsequently, Dahlhaus has applied Halm's ideas to other works by Beethoven. See '"Von zwei Kulturen der Musik": Die Schlußfuge aus Beethovens Cellosonate opus 102,2', *Die Musikforschung* 31 (1978), 397–405.

Example 6.4   End of the development and beginning of the recapitulation in the *Tempest* Sonata

We should regard [the recitatives] as liberated melody, previously covered up or suppressed and dependent. Its thus far greatest freedom awoke in the final descent of the development section, where it still had to be supported by a choir-like octave unison. Also, it appeared semi-unconscious, dreamy, without the activity of elastic rhythm. In the first recitative, it finally awoke, it recognised itself, and became an individual.[53]

On considering his last remark in detail, it becomes apparent that Halm is concerned not merely with the *formal* function of the recitative, which he set out to discuss, but just as much with its representational *content*. The manner in which he describes this moment is as incipient self-consciousness and the beginning process of (re)individuation of the musical material. The progressive development of the thematic material – the 'story of a theme', as he calls it once – is crucial for him.[54] For Halm, the recapitulation is indeed fundamentally different from the exposition. He places great emphasis on the fact that the thematic-transitional passage of bars 21–41, shown in Example 6.3 above, is not recapitulated: its 'industrial, machine-like unity' is no longer required; it has been replaced by something better, a higher unity.[55] In this sense, the recapitulation, the result of the development, presents something qualitatively new; it is a genuine synthesis. Only if the processual thematic development is understood in its temporal unfolding, Halm concludes, can one understand 'that the position "after the double bar" is really very meaningful'.[56]

In the recapitulation – which Halm would no doubt hear as beginning with a very meaningful double bar – it is as though the schism that pervades Beethoven's music and that has caused the suppression of the individuality of themes has begun to heal itself. For a brief moment the liberated melody supplants the formulaic, scalic melody. In the recapitulation 'dead', scalic melody gives way to 'living' melody. The liberated melody transgresses the constraints of the material and creeps out of the formal plan. The lacuna in the form of the *Tempest* Sonata offers us a glimpse of the music that is to come, the music of historical synthesis, which parallels the moment of reconciliation between the individual and the state.

When Halm asks himself: 'So would Bekker ultimately be right in saying that the spell was broken?',[57] it seems the answer would have to be yes, though for all the wrong reasons. Despite his overt criticism of musical hermeneutics, the real problem is not that the hermeneuticists draw on extra-musical programmes to understand

[53] Halm, *Zwei Kulturen*, p. 65: 'Wir haben in ihnen die befreite Melodik zu sehen, welche bisher verhüllt oder beengt und unselbständig geblieben war. Ihre bis dahin größte Freiheit war eben in dem Schlußgang der Durchführung erwacht, wo sie selbst aber durch ein chorartiges Oktaven-Unisono gestützt, auch noch halb unbewußt, träumerisch, ohne die Aktivität eines elastischen Rhythmus erschienen war. In dem ersten Rezitativ ist sie endlich erwacht, hat sich erkannt, ist Individuum geworden.'
[54] *Ibid.*, p. 227, see also pp. 56–7. It is intriguing that Adorno seems wrongly to attribute this dictum to Schoenberg. See his *Beethoven: Philosophie der Musik* (Frankfurt am Main: Suhrkamp, 1993); trans. Edmund Jephcott as *Beethoven: The Philosophy of Music* (Cambridge: Polity Press, 1998), fragments 29 and 31.
[55] By contrast, Halm is quite nonchalant about the return of the 'scalic' theme at bar 152, which would in fact question his interpretation.   [56] Halm, *Bruckner*, p. 35.   [57] Halm, *Zwei Kulturen*, p. 65.

music. (Indeed, Bekker is not wholly unjustified in retaliating that Halm's language is hardly less metaphorical than those of the hermeneuticists.[58]) Both Halm and the hermeneuticists are essentially concerned with the search for meaning behind the music. However, the problem for Halm is that the hermeneuticists do not go far enough. Their merely illustrative and programmatic readings pay too much attention to the sounding phenomena as gestures. Their 'translation' from the musical into the verbal medium misses what Halm considers to be the spirit of music, as it ignores the transcendent level that he himself uncovers in the musical form.

Halm's choice of the *Tempest* Sonata must be seen as an act of reclamation, a reappropriation of the sonata for his own cause. Its recitative is not merely the expression of an emotion that can be clothed in descriptive words, but it is the articulation of spiritual life in music itself. The 'broken spell' which Bekker hears in the recitative marks for Halm a historical turning point: the thematic element is becoming individualised again, this time, however, within the expansive 'state-like' confines of sonata form. In this sense, Beethoven's *Tempest* is no less than a microcosm of Halm's conception of music.

PARADISE REGAINED

There is a second reason that Halm draws on the *Tempest* as his paradigm of Beethoven's sonata. He writes:

[I]ndeed, this Op. 31, and particularly its most consummate part, the D minor sonata, may rightly be juxtaposed, as a New Testament of form to the Old, to Beethoven's first piano sonata. Conceived with the same stringency, no less an extract than the former, it is nevertheless designed more towards breadth. In it, Beethoven finds the deep necessity for expansion for the first time.[59]

As seen above, Halm associates formal expansion with progress in history; when he detects Beethoven's concern with expanding form in this sonata, this reconfirms the historical importance of the work. However, the overtly religious comparison, suggesting a re-interpretation of the sonata principle that he had first determined in his Op. 2 No. 1, opens up another dimension: if the Old Testament prophesied the advent of the Redeemer, then the New Testament names Him and is directly concerned with His works in the world. But who is this Redeemer of whose works Beethoven's *Tempest* Sonata tells us? Halm makes no secret of whom he means by this reference:

---

[58] Paul Bekker, 'Wohin treiben wir?', in *Kritische Zeitbilder* (Berlin: Schuster und Loeffler, 1921), p. 256. On the convergence between formalist and hermeneutic analysis see Scott Burnham, 'How Music Matters: Poetic Content Revisited', in *Rethinking Music*, ed. Nicholas Cook and Mark Everist (Oxford: Oxford University Press, 1999), pp. 193–216.

[59] Halm, *Bruckner*, p. 42: '[W]ahrhaftig, dieses op. 31, und insbesondere sein vollkommenster Teil, die D-moll-Sonate, darf mit Recht der ersten Klaviersonate Beethovens, gleichwie ein neues Testament von Form dem alten gegenübergestellt werden. Mit der gleichen Straffheit konzipiert, nicht minder Extrakt wie jene, ist sie doch mehr auf das Breite angelegt; in ihr findet Beethoven zum erstenmal die tiefe Notwendigkeit der Ausdehnung.'

I am convinced that the classical composers would have hailed Anton Bruckner as their King, and worshipped him. To doubt this would mean to group them together with those who use their works as a shield to ward off the superior . . . But I also imagine something else, which at least I consider possible. These great predecessors would not only have recognised in their greater pupil the King but indeed the Redeemer.[60]

In this relationship between Beethoven and Bruckner, we finally have an answer to our initial question: the evasive *natura naturata* is found in Bruckner's symphony (again, symphony in the generic sense). In Bruckner's work, Bach's thematic individuality and Beethoven's formal organisation are synthesised, and the antithetical relationship between the two is reconciled. Bruckner's work fulfils the promise of the perfect state that Beethoven's sonata made but could not keep. It was a cosmological necessity that Bruckner's symphony had to succeed where Beethoven's sonata fell short. 'Only with Bruckner', Halm sums up, 'do we understand the destination and the sense of the history of the sonata.'[61]

Halm's dialectical description of the historical process clearly refers to the Hegelian concept of self-consciousness as a historical process towards the Absolute Spirit. Hegel explains that the unity of objectivity and subjectivity can occur in three guises – as religion, as philosophy and as art.[62] It would be perfectly possible to relate Halm's extensive and wide-ranging use of metaphor and imagery, which all draws on these three guises, to this condition in Hegel's metaphysical framework. However, the inherent danger in doing so is that the immediate impact of Halm's rhetoric would be qualified. The determination and consistency with which Halm employs the metaphors of nature, the state and Christian redemption leave us in no doubt that they are not merely accidental, but rather the very essence of Halm's metaphysical music theory. Indeed, it is perhaps even inappropriate to categorise them as metaphors: they lack the semantic tension that is, according to the literary theorist Hugo Friedrich, at the base of the modern metaphor, which tries to force two things together that do not appear to belong together.[63] Rather, Halm's rhetorical relations are analogies, articulating processes that have always belonged together inseparably.

In this sense, Halm's *Bruckner* monograph, the sequel to *Von zwei Kulturen der Musik*, describes this 'third culture', which is nothing short of the Everlasting Kingdom, in overtly soteriological terms throughout. Bruckner's symphony leads music to a state of salvation that had been lost when Beethoven separated harmony and melody.[64] The original sin is forgiven, paradise is regained. Although this unabashed apotheosis of the composer, one imagines, would not necessarily coincide with our views of

[60] *Ibid.*, pp. 209–10: 'Ich bin dessen sicher, daß die Klassiker Anton Bruckner als ihren König begrüßt und verehrt hätten. Daran zweifeln hieße mir sie mit denen zusammentun, die ihre Werke als Schild mißbrauchen, um das Bessere abzuwehren . . . Ich denke mir aber noch ein anderes, das ich immerhin für zum mindesten möglich halte. Nicht nur den König, nein auch den Erlöser hätten jene großen Vorbilder in ihrem größeren Schüler erkannt.'

[61] *Ibid.*, p. 218. I reserve a fuller discussion of Halm's treatment of Bruckner for a separate essay.

[62] Hegel, *Philosophie der Geschichte*, pp. 68–9.

[63] See Harald Weinrich, 'Semantik der kühnen Metapher', in *Theorie der Metapher*, ed. Anselm Haverkamp, 2nd edn (Darmstadt: Wissenschaftliche Buchgesellschaft, 1996), p. 317.

[64] Halm, *Bruckner*, p. 102.

Bruckner's symphonies, nothing would be more inappropriate than to dismiss Halm's rhetoric as incidental imagery. (Indeed, Bekker chastises him, not without justification, for his music-aesthetic dogmatism.)

Halm's employment of the *natura naturans – natura naturata* pair is not only an indication of his cosmological conception, but rather it is the 'master trope', which co-ordinates the various strands of analogies and motivates the dialectically unfolding logos. This is partly an effect of Halm's idiosyncratic adaptation of Hegelian principles. It would be wrong simply to equate the three-step dialectic with the two part concept of nature: Bach's fugue in fact precedes *natura naturans* and is therefore not part of history in Halm's sense. Yet, without this understanding of nature, the State could remain tyrannical, the prophet could preach in the desert and the themes of the sonata could remain oppressed 'dividuals'. Only with this forward-looking force of nature can Halm argue for the inevitable logic of his cosmology, which calls for a Bruckner to bring music history to its consummation and its end. Only with this concept of nature can he substantiate his account of music as a social and religious indicator.

Yet this is not the whole story: it would clearly be wrong-headed to insist that the *natura naturans – natura naturata* pair has only structural function within Halm's music-theoretical oeuvre. While on the surface Halm is a fervent advocate of absolute music, as his repeated attacks against dramatic and programmatic music demonstrate, he nonetheless assigns absolute music an eminently social function. At the end of his *Bruckner* monograph, Halm states suggestively:

Art, however, is a symbol not of a magical deed, i.e. an act of force, but of the transfiguration, the becoming-divine [apotheosis] as in one's own desires and in freedom. Indeed, it is possibly something better than a mere symbol.[65]

The significance of this last sentence, which alludes to the celebration of the Eucharist, can hardly be overestimated. In particular, his reading of Beethoven's *Tempest* as a microcosm is an indication of the close relation – more than metaphorical relation – between music and society behind his essentially cosmological view of music. This ostensibly goes hand in hand with the arcane concepts of *natura naturans* and *natura naturata* whereby Halm presents the history of musical forms. However, Halm's reference back to Scholastic philosophy is a red herring: in fact, in the long history of the term, stretching back to neo-Platonic thought, there is no definition of this paired nature that would match Halm's application.[66] Like his understanding of

---

[65] *Ibid.*, p. 240: 'Die Kunst aber ist Symbol nicht für eine Zaubertat, d.h. einen Gewaltakt, sondern für das Sich-wandeln, das Göttlich-werden als in eigenem Verlangen und in Freiheit. Ja, sie ist wohl noch Besseres als nur Symbol dafür.'

[66] The term *natura naturata* (without its double *natura naturans*) is first mentioned in the late twelfth-century commentary of Averroës on the works of Aristotle. The concepts themselves, however, are older, going back as far as the ninth century, where they are found in John Scotus Erigena's *De divisione naturae*. I am grateful to David E. Cohen for drawing my attention to this work. The terms *natura naturans/naturata* have an almost continuous history up to Spinoza. (For further information on the history of the terms, see Henry A. Lucks, 'Natura Naturans/Natura Naturata', *The New Scholasticism* 9/1 (January 1935), 1–24.) Hegel, too, discusses the terms in a critique of Spinoza; however, his use bears no obvious relation to Halm's understanding of the nature pair.

Hegel, his use of these terms is not philosophically accurate, but rather reflects a cultural attitude. Rather, the crucial point in Halm's use of the *natura naturans – natura naturata* pair is the reference back to pre-modern modes of thinking, which disguises the pressingly topical concerns behind this apparently irrelevant and archaic cosmology.

It must be borne in mind that Halm's generation produced such personalities as Oswald Spengler, the author of the influential *Decline of the West*, and the sinister *Rembrandtdeutscher* Julius Langbehn, whose historical thinking, their different approaches notwithstanding, was dominated by the intentionalisation of world history by means of transcendental analogies.[67] Thinking in terms of macrocosm and microcosm was the privilege of Halm's generation, and, as in Spengler's case, a desperate attempt to impose order in an increasingly fragmentary world. It is in this context of cultural pessimism that we must ultimately consider Halm's cosmology: around the turn of the century this kind of world consciousness generated an upsurge of hardly fathomable dimensions, which can only be explained against the background of the precarious state of subjectivity in post-Nietzschean Germany.[68] Halm's profession as an educator at the German reform boarding school, the *freie Schulgemeinde* Wickersdorf, is crucial in this respect.[69] The music that Halm played at assembly every day – by Bach, Beethoven or Bruckner[70] – did not merely serve the purpose of musical education, but had a strongly metaphysical, theological and political flavour to it, which served education in a much broader, spiritual sense.[71]

It seems that Gustav Wyneken, the founder of the *Schulgemeinde* at Wickersdorf, who was also Halm's brother-in-law and editor, is wholly correct when he claims that Halm's music theory is the 'precipitation of a *Weltanschauung*',[72] born of the spirit of music. In this sense, it is no empty talk but rather an expression of his conviction, manifest in his consciousness of a totality of which musical forms are the supreme part, when Halm asserts: 'at the very end and at the very beginning, the fugue and the sonata exist'.[73]

[67] Oswald Spengler's influential *Decline of the West* (1922), trans. Charles Francis Atkinson (London: Allen and Unwin, 1926), largely written before the First World War, compared the world cultures and concluded that they all followed parallel processes of acculturation from 'barbarism' to 'civilisation'. Civilisation, the ultimate stage of any culture under consideration, was tantamount to that age's decline. Julius Langbehn (pseudonym *Ein Deutscher*), in his phenomenally successful *Rembrandt als Erzieher* (Leipzig: C. L. Hirschfeld, 1890), made a plea for national renewal and the purification of the German spirit through the contemplation of great art, such as Rembrandt's. Lee A. Rothfarb assesses Langbehn's impact on Halm's friend Ernst Kurth in *Ernst Kurth: Selected Writings* (Cambridge: Cambridge University Press, 1991), pp. 8–10.

[68] See Wolfgang Gebhard, *Der Zusammenhang der Dinge: Weltgleichnis und Naturverklärung im Totalitätsbewußtsein des 19. Jahrhunderts*, Hermaea Germanistische Forschungen, Neue Folge, ed. Hans Fromm and Hans-Joachim Mähl, vol. XLVII (Tübingen: Max Niemeyer, 1984), p. 536.

[69] Lee A. Rothfarb has written about Halm's work at Wickersdorf in 'The "New Education" and Music Theory, 1900–1925', in *Music Theory and the Exploration of the Past*, ed. Christopher Hatch and David W. Bernstein (Chicago: Chicago University Press, 1993), pp. 449–72.

[70] See Halm, *Von Form und Sinn der Musik*, p. 52.

[71] Although the political aspect is seductive, particularly in light of subsequent German history, it would seem precarious to single out one dimension as separate from the totality, as Thaler does in her *Organische Form*, pp. 114–17.   [72] Halm, *Zwei Kulturen*, p. viii.   [73] *Ibid.*, p. 32.

Chapter Seven

—

Seduced by notation: Oettingen's topography
of the major-minor system

SUZANNAH CLARK

Arthur von Oettingen begins his treatise *Harmoniesystem in dualer Entwickelung* (1866) with what looks to be a potted history of the development of tonal theory.[1] His account begins with Jean-Philippe Rameau, whom he singles out for his notion of the fundamental bass. Next are Jean le Rond d'Alembert, whose contribution was a description of the construction of scales, and Leonhard Euler for his ideas on the properties of intervals. No progress was made, Oettingen claims, until the work of the physicist Hermann Helmholtz, who put music theory on an entirely new footing. We soon discover, however, that Oettingen's theoretical sympathies lie with Moritz Hauptmann, author of *The Nature of Harmony and Metre*.[2] Hauptmann developed a system based on a symmetrical opposition between the major and minor triads, a theory which, thanks to Oettingen who coined the term, is known as harmonic 'dualism'.[3] Although the symmetry between the major and minor triads had been noted before, Hauptmann was the first to go beyond this observation by fashioning the rest of the major-minor system symmetrically.

Hauptmann's theory was grounded in quasi-Hegelian dialectics, where each aspect of the tonal system was construed as part of the process of thesis–antithesis–synthesis.[4] The attraction of dialectics as a founding principle for a music theory was

I am grateful to Scott Burnham and Roger Parker for their comments on this article.

[1] Arthur von Oettingen, *Harmoniesystem in dualer Entwickelung: Studien zur Theorie der Musik* (Dorpat and Leipzig: W. Glaser, 1866). Although many other things were to change by the publication of Oettingen's third treatise on tonal theory, *Das duale Harmoniesystem* (Leipzig: Linnemann, 1913), his introduction to the 1913 treatise recounts the same historical lineage.

[2] *The Nature of Harmony and Metre*, trans. William Edward Heathcote (London: Swan Sonnenschein, 1888; rpt New York: Da Capo Press, 1989).

[3] Oettingen, *Harmoniesystem in dualer Entwickelung* (1866), p. iv.

[4] This is hardly exclusive to Hegel, though it is generally assumed that Hegelianism inspired Hauptmann. He apparently had no first-hand knowledge of Hegel's work. Peter Rummenhöller has suggested on the basis of a letter from Hauptmann to Franz Hauser that it would be more accurate to speak of an indirect influence that came through Gustav Andreas Lautier. Rummenhöller, *Moritz Hauptmann als Theoretiker: Eine Studie zum erkenntniskritischen Theoriebegriff in der Musik* (Wiesbaden: Breitkopf und Härtel, 1963), pp. 123–4. See also Mark McCune, 'Moritz Hauptmann: *Ein Haupt Mann* in Nineteenth Century Music Theory', *Indiana Theory Review* 7 (1986), 3 n. 6.

undoubtedly its 'threeness', which promised to allow the triad to be the centre of the system. Equally, he also saw in the organic nature of dialectics potential to shape all levels of his theory from the construction of the major and minor triads to their respective key systems. It even governs all rhythmic and metrical aspects, which are detailed in the second half of his treatise. With regard to its ability to structure pitch material, one might assume that Hauptmann took the three pitches of the triad to fulfil the three dialectical functions. In fact he constructed the triad as three intervals: the octave, fifth and major third, seeing the octave as unity or thesis, the fifth as division or antithesis and the third as synthesis.[5] In this way, both the major and minor triads were derived from an identical dialectical process with identical intervals. While each component of the process was assigned a fixed interval, the triads themselves were understood differently, the major triad as generated from the bottom, the minor triad from the top. This reading of the two triads is the most basic defining feature of dualism. Hauptmann continued the dialectical derivation of the tonal system by arguing that the major and minor triads, now ready for the next dialectical stage, form the thesis of their respective 'Triad of Triads'. These consist of the tonic, subdominant and dominant of each mode and in turn form the collective thesis for the modulatory system, the 'Triad of Keys'.

Hauptmann's purpose in applying a single principle was to create a consistent, coherent system. Furthermore, by suggesting that the two tonal modes are antithetical and have the same origin, he could claim that they are equal. This conclusion appealed to Oettingen, who also attempted to find a singular structuring pattern for both modes. Hauptmann and Oettingen recognised that the dualist's interpretation of the minor triad – as a triad constructed from the top – is at odds with its accepted aural perception – as a triad whose root is at the bottom. Hauptmann's way of treating this discrepancy in *The Nature of Harmony and Metre* was a disappointment to Oettingen, who felt that Hauptmann should have questioned accepted aural perception rather than his dualistic tenet. A letter Hauptmann wrote to Spohr reveals his attitude towards the place of theory and accepted practice: curiously, he pointed out that his treatise was concerned not with musical practice but only with 'natürliche Bildungsgesetze'.[6] This split was foreshadowed but not explained in his treatise, where he announced that the ear should ultimately be the judge of what is musically correct. As far as Hauptmann saw it, hearing chords as rooted at the bottom – that is according to Rameau's theory of the fundamental bass – was 'correct'.[7]

The significance of the explicit schism between his dialectic imagination and what he saw as the auditory principle of the fundamental bass extends far beyond the customary tension between theory and practice. Although Hauptmann readily aban-

[5] For a possible explanation of why Hauptmann chose the octave rather than the fundamental as unity, see Michael Cherlin, 'Hauptmann and Schenker: Two Adaptations of Hegelian Dialectics', *Theory and Practice* 13 (1988), 124–6.

[6] Mentioned in Rummenhöller, *Moritz Hauptmann als Theoretiker*, p. 103 n. 2. Indeed, in Hauptmann's view a musical system is 'born in us' and 'the notion of an artificial system of notes is a thoroughly worthless one'. See *Harmony and Metre*, p. xl.   [7] Hauptmann, *Harmony and Metre*, p. xl.

doned the dialectic when its consequences seemed to be counterintuitive,[8] his letter to Spohr suggests that he accepted the fact that a theory about the foundations of music might differ from the way musical practice should be understood. Why write a theory that you know does not – or cannot – correspond to practice? While one might question the integrity of a theorist who writes such a theory, Hauptmann seems to suggest that the split is inevitable because theory explains the natural 'Bildungsgesetze' while musical practice is based on something else. Unfortunately, Hauptmann is not forthcoming on what the latter might be, though he does see it as also 'natural'.

Soon after publishing *Harmoniesystem in dualer Entwickelung* in 1866, Oettingen, like Hauptmann before him, was also accused of writing a theory that bears no relation to musical practice, a view that persists in modern commentaries.[9] Apart from advocating a different tuning system, Oettingen remained closer to musical practice than most critics have suggested.[10] Indeed, as this chapter will demonstrate, Oettingen attempted to shift our *perception* of musical practice rather than musical practice itself, reckoning that his theory, which was to be the natural explanation of tonality, would be truth enough to make us want to change our understanding of how the tonal system worked. Most significantly, we would want to understand minor triads from the top, re-imagine the tonal relationship between cadences and scales, re-tune our instruments, and have our orchestras tune (their new tunings) to D rather than A. This last, seemingly innocuous suggestion was in fact the final touch to his radical attempt to reorganise our understanding of music.

Oettingen produced three treatises on harmonic dualism: *Harmoniesystem in dualer Entwickelung* (1866) is the earliest; then 'Das duale System der Harmonie' appeared in six instalments in *Annalen der Naturphilosophie* (1902–6); and finally *Das duale*

---

[8] In addition to demonstrating how the minor triad could be constructed from upward intervals (*Harmony and Metre*, p. 17), he suggested, for example, that the Triad of Triads in the minor key 'cannot issue from negation without positive premise' and therefore it requires a major rather than a minor dominant (p. 18–19).

[9] One of Oettingen's main contemporary opponents was Carl Stumpf, and Oettingen replied to the criticisms in Stumpf's *Beiträge zur Akustik und Musikwissenschaft* (Leipzig: Johann Ambrosius Barth, 1898) in his second treatise, 'Das duale Harmoniesystem', esp. pp. 116–36. The criticisms of more recent commentators will be discussed during the course of the rest of this chapter.

[10] While Oettingen questions several aspects of practice, he rarely attempts to change it. In the introduction to his 1866 treatise Oettingen stresses that its second part is about the normal construction of tonality and normal cadences: 'Der zweite Abschnitt behandelt die Construction der normalen Tonsysteme, die Normalcadenzen und consonanten Gebilde', *Harmoniesystem in dualer Entwickelung* (1866), p. 5. However, Oettingen wonders whether the cadence that ends dominant–tonic in what resembles our minor mode should have a raised leading note in the penultimate chord; see *Harmoniesystem in dualer Entwickelung* (1866), pp. 77–8. He wonders here, as he does elsewhere, whether the desire for the raised leading note and perhaps even a *tierce de picardie* in the final chord is due to physical and physiological demands or to learned behaviour. He surmises it should be a minor chord and predicts that, with enough repetition, we could unlearn our mistaken way of listening to and thinking of this cadence and we could become accustomed to hearing it in its pure, natural form. However, this is a rare instance in which Oettingen argues for a change in practice; significantly, too, it is on a subject that occupies many theorists.

Harmoniesystem was published in 1913.[11] Although his ideas on the structure of the tonal system remained relatively constant through his career, each treatise shows a greater refinement of the manifestations of symmetry and, importantly, an increasing affinity with existing musical practice, at least as far as the musical rudiments are concerned. This view of Oettingen's theoretical career is contrary to the general view of his development. Nearly every commentator questions his concern for accounting for musical practice, a view which is propagated most forcefully by Daniel Harrison, who writes, 'In truth we must indict Oettingen for failing to deal properly with the minor mode. Although he does present a theory that makes the minor *triad* the consonant dual of the major triad, he is unable to reach the traditional minor system of triads, keys, and tonics.' On Oettingen's presentation of the scales, he argues, 'The fusion of musical and visual space, encouraged by Hauptmann, is here completed with a rhapsodic flourish of inanity; Oettingen's dualism threatens now to lose all relationship to musical art.' Harrison also suggests that Oettingen departs from accepted theoretical practice: 'The relentless pursuit of symmetry takes Oettingen further and further from accepted methods of theorizing; indeed, he seems at times to glory in the most bizarre manifestation of symmetry.'[12] Contrary to this common assumption, as the manifestation of symmetry increased in Oettingen's treatises, so did his attention to musical practice. Moreover, the general assertion that he lost sight of the traditional major-minor system, or was unable even to attain it, stems from a misreading of another (consistent) aspect of Oettingen's theory, a misreading which, as we shall see, is not exclusive to Harrison but dates back to the beginning of English-language accounts of his theory.[13]

Oettingen aimed to revise the traditional manner of construing the tonal system, and, in particular, he restructured elements of the minor mode. Borrowing from Hauptmann, his application of symmetry was more consistent and exhaustive. The problem is that most accounts have suggested that, when it came to the minor scale, Oettingen's proposed scale is, as one commentator put it, 'not the minor mode, nor do the harmonic combinations possible in it come within the scope or treatment of the modern European system of harmony, and therefore as a creation it stands apart

[11] 'Das duale System der Harmonie', *Annalen der Naturphilosophie* 1–5 (1902–6), 1: 62–75, 2: 375–403, 3: 241–69, 4: 116–36, 301–38, 5: 449–503. The serialised treatise is listed in the entry 'Oettingen', in *The New Grove Dictionary of Music and Musicians*, ed. Stanley Sadie (London: Macmillan, 1980) as a reprint of the 1866 treatise, which is not the case. The two texts are substantially different.

[12] Daniel Harrison, *Harmonic Function in Chromatic Music: A Renewed Dualist Theory and an Account of Its Precedents* (Chicago: University of Chicago Press, 1994), pp. 249–50.

[13] These include Herbert Westerby, 'The Dual Theory of Harmony', *Proceedings of the Musical Association* 29 (1902–3), 21–72; Matthew Shirlaw, *The Theory of Harmony: An Inquiry into the Natural Principles of Harmony, with an Examination of the Chief Systems of Harmony from Rameau to the Present Day* (London: Novello, 1917); Dale Jorgenson, 'A Résumé of Harmonic Dualism', *Music and Letters* 44 (1963), 31–42; William Cooper Mickelsen, *Hugo Riemann's Theory of Harmony, with a Translation of Riemann's 'History of Music Theory', Book 3* (Lincoln, Nebraska: Nebraska University Press, 1977); David W. Bernstein, 'Symmetry and Symmetrical Inversion in Turn-of-the-Century Theory and Practice', in *Music Theory and the Exploration of the Past*, ed. Christopher Hatch and David W. Bernstein (Chicago: University of Chicago Press, 1993), pp. 377–407; and Harrison, *Harmonic Function in Chromatic Music*.

in itself, and proves nothing'.[14] However, as will be shown in this chapter, Oettingen preserved the pitch content of all aspects of the major-minor system, altering only their structure. Indeed, his purpose was to show that the principle of the fundamental bass is so ingrained in our collective thinking as to seem natural – its all-encompassing application to tonal music is what he wanted to challenge. Ironically it is the persistence of this deeply ingrained thinking that has led to the misreading of Oettingen's vision of tonality. Those who describe his system as outside the realm of major-minor tonality have viewed it through the very fundamental-bass spectacles that he was aiming to remove. For this reason, I shall begin by explaining in detail how he envisioned the basic tonal components – the triad, primary triads, cadences and scales. Then I shall explore briefly how and why these misreadings occurred in order to address a potential benefit of Oettingen's theory.

The two principal triads of Oettingen's system contain the same pitches as those described in any theoretical treatise about tonal music: C–E–G and C–E♭–G. It is our understanding of the second triad that Oettingen hoped to refashion. With regard to the first triad, Oettingen more or less concurs with his contemporaries and immediate predecessors. The triad bears a striking resemblance to partials found in the overtone series – the note C, as the fundamental, produces the other two notes, E and G, in the first few partials of the series. For this reason, he interprets it as a triad that emanates from its root: to put it in Rameau's terms, it is understood according to the principles of the fundamental bass.

As Oettingen explains, his predecessors have explored many derivations for the other triad, C–E♭–G. There are two important new influences on Oettingen's reading: the manner in which Hauptmann construed the relationship between the major and minor elements in tonality, and the physical observations made by Hermann Helmholtz. Indeed, Oettingen saw Hauptmann's ideas as the proper theoretical conclusion to Helmholtz's physical observations, and thought of himself as placing Hauptmann's ideas in their rightful physical setting: 'With the help of our principle all of Hauptmann's philosophical definitions gain the ground of reality.'[15]

Oettingen builds on an explanation offered by Helmholtz when he regards the notes C and E♭ as converging on the note G.[16] Helmholtz argued that the minor triad is made up of two overtone series, one generated from C, the other from E♭. The third note of the triad, G, represents the point of intersection between these series. The two fundamentals were therefore said to be united through the fifth. For

---

[14] Westerby, 'The Dual Theory of Harmony', 64.

[15] Oettingen, *Harmoniesystem in dualer Entwickelung* (1866), p. 40. Helmholtz's treatise, dating from 1863, is *On the Sensations of Tone*, trans. Alexander J. Ellis, rpt (New York: Dover, 1954).

[16] This is one of two explanations Helmholtz contemplated for the origin of the minor triad in *On the Sensations of Tone*, pp. 294–5. The other explanation, not adopted by Oettingen, uses only one overtone series and sees the minor third as a 'foreign tone'.

Helmholtz, G is simultaneously a uniting force and a 'dependent tone'. Undoing this sense of dependency, Oettingen latched onto the idea that G was a point of unity and saw it as the tone that defined the triad. In much the same way as we would label a major triad from its root, Oettingen suggested that the minor triad should be labelled from its point of unity, the top note. This means that, for Oettingen as for Hauptmann, both triads are made up of the same interval structure but are distinguished by direction.

However, in other respects Oettingen differs from Hauptmann, particularly in how he described the intervallic structure of the triads. Avoiding any use of dialectics, he observes that both triads contain a perfect fifth between their two outer notes. Though similar in distance, the direction in which the fifth is built in each triad – from the lower note to the higher note or vice versa – is, he argues, dependent on the position of their respective middle tones. Accordingly, any single interval in a triad is ambiguous until the triad is filled out; both the fifth and the major or minor third could be part of either triad. This is not in itself a new concept: the famous review of Beethoven's Fifth Symphony, by E. T. A. Hoffmann, makes the point that the first motive is ambiguous and that the impatient first-time listener might ask, after hearing the opening interval G–E♭, 'is this symphony in E♭ major or C minor?'[17] Thus, while it is true that any one of the above intervals could belong to either a major or a minor triad, for Oettingen the additional tone not only clarifies the type of triad and mode to which the interval belongs but, more importantly, it clarifies the direction in which it must be understood. For example, a perfect fifth C–G, filled in with an E, can be identified as part of the C major triad and must therefore be understood, as all major triads are, from the bottom up. However, if that same fifth (C–G) were filled in with an E♭, the resulting triad would be called C minor by a fundamental-bass theorist and would be understood from the bottom up, while Oettingen would call it something else and would understand it, as Hauptmann did, from the top. (I shall return to Oettingen's nomenclature shortly.)

It is clear, then, that Oettingen believed that not all harmonic elements or intervals are subject to Rameau's theory of the fundamental bass. Rather, Rameau's theory applied only to major elements because only they have the support of the rising harmonic series. What is more, Oettingen asserts that constructing the major-minor system entirely according to the principles of the fundamental bass had led theorists to admit that the minor triad and its mode as a whole could not be said to stem from nature. In a brief chapter on the history of conceptions of the minor mode, Oettingen's discussion of A. B. Marx points out that although Marx clearly derived all harmony from nature, he was forced to conclude that minor was different. According to Marx, minor has 'no origin in the nature of tonal essence', rather it 'has been created from it and according to its image by the spirit and the needs of art'.[18]

[17] E. T. A. Hoffmann, review of Beethoven's Fifth Symphony, in *Allgemeine musikalische Zeitung* 12/40–1 (1810), 630–42, 652–9.
[18] Quoted in Oettingen, *Harmoniesystem in dualer Entwickelung* (1866), p. 84 from A. B. Marx, *Die Lehre von der musikalischen Composition*, 2 vols (Leipzig: Breitkopf und Härtel, 1863, vol. I).

Oettingen's solution was to conclude that although the principles of the fundamental bass were a natural way of reading major sounds, they were a learned behaviour for minor. In other words, it was the explanation and not the mode that was non-natural. Oettingen's purpose, thus, was to find the natural order for tonality that included minor, though he never clarifies explicitly why the system of complete symmetry that he adopted should mark the way forward. In perusing the history of attitudes towards the minor mode, he proposed a return to the Greek modal system, where a proper identification of modal properties would allow the modern major and minor scales to stand in the same perfect symmetry he also identified for the triads and cadences.

To match the untraditional way of reading minor elements, Oettingen introduced new terminology. It is not possible, he argued, simply to re-educate our minds while keeping the old terms. He was convinced that new terms would replace the old associations of the fundamental bass as the essential and natural principle behind the structure and reading of all tonal elements, whether major or minor.[19] The most significant of these new terms related to the modes themselves: *Tonicität* and *Phonicität* were coupled with *Tonalität* and *Phonalität*. *Tonicität* and *Tonalität* replaced *Dur* or major, and *Phonicität* and *Phonalität* replaced *Moll* or minor.

PRIMARY TRIADS

The distinction between *Tonicität* and *Phonicität* on the one hand, and *Tonalität* and *Phonalität* on the other, begins to emerge at the level of the primary triads. The former ('*–icität*') refer to single elements, such as intervals, triads or scales, the latter ('*–alität*') refer to the collection of the triads and tones of the closed tonal system. The primary triads are described on a number of occasions in each of Oettingen's three treatises. The consistent feature among his treatises is the arrangement of tones: each mode has a central triad, with two triads on either side of it, one a fifth above, the other a fifth below. The variable element is the starting pitch of the central triad of each mode, which is sometimes C for both modes, with the other two triads of each mode built around F and G; sometimes, the notes are C and E for *Tonalität* and *Phonalität* respectively, again with fifths on either side of each centre; at other times, the central triads both begin from D, with the other triads then built around G and A. Because these different starting pitches have more to do with how the two modes are said to relate to each other than with how the primary triads interrelate within their respective modes, the reasons for these different starting points will be explored later in this chapter, during the discussion on the scale. For now, I shall describe how Oettingen envisioned the relationship between the primary triads beginning, as he first did, from the note C.

[19] Oettingen makes his reasons for the change in terminology very clear in the introduction to *Harmoniesystem in dualer Entwickelung* (1866), p. 6. He wrote: 'Wenn in hergebrachter Weise Moll den absoluten Gegensatz von Dur bezeichnet, so *musste* ich den Namen Moll, um Verwirrung zu vermeiden, verwerfen ... Dass die jetzt gebräuchliche Nomenclatur, die an die Begriffe des Fundamental-basses *gekettet* ist, nicht lange mehr wird genügen können, das, scheint mir, liegt auf der Hand' (emphasis in original).

Both *Tonalität* and *Phonalität* have three primary triads, built from C, F and G. Each generates two different triads, one built according to the principle of *Tonicität* (that is, upwards), the other according to *Phonicität* (that is, downwards). C-*Tonalität* therefore contains the triads 'f+, c+ and g+' (F–A–C, C–E–G, G–B–D respectively), and the C-*Phonalität* will contain the triads 'f°, c° and g°' (Bb–Db–F, F–Ab–C, C–Eb–G respectively).[20] The terms for the 'tonic' triads are familiar: f+ is called the *Unterdominante*, c+ the *Tonica* and g+ the *Oberdominante*. Meanwhile, not surprisingly, the triads in the 'phonic' set are assigned new terminology: f° is called the *Unterregnante*, c° the *Phonica* and g° the *Oberregnante*.

The names thus describe the position of the triads in relation to the central tonic or phonic triad – in both cases, the triads a fifth below are 'Unter-' and a fifth above 'Ober-'. An obvious point perhaps, but Oettingen's manner of abbreviating two of the triads to *Dominante* and *Regnante* has caused confusion. Oettingen followed Rameau's lead, who in coining the term for the subdominant left the other dominant without a prefix; 'dominant' has always been understood to mean the upper dominant. Similarly, Oettingen dispensed with the prefix for the chord that matches what he saw as the 'dominant' function in the two modes. This is the *Oberdominante* in the tonic system and, notably, the *Unterregnante* in the phonic system; the *Dominante* is the upper fifth in *Tonicität* but the *Regnante* is the lower fifth in *Phonicität*. Perhaps because Oettingen's intellectual successor Hugo Riemann was criticised for not reversing the functions of the *Ober-* and *Unter-* triads in the two modes, Oettingen was assumed to have done the same.[21] Why did Oettingen link the *Oberdominante* and the *Unterregnante*? Not, as one might legitimately assume, because their respective systems are construed in opposite directions. Rather the link stems from a 'symmetrical manifestation' of the tonic and phonic cadences, to which we now turn. It is, as we shall see, a notational rather than a strictly intervallic symmetry that governs his thinking.

CADENCES

In the 1866 treatise Oettingen did not use notation to illustrate his explanation of the structure of the triads or scales; instead he used abecedarian letters. The only components of the system to be accompanied by musical notation were the cadences. Their visual representation was the mechanism through which Oettingen determined their structure and the relationship between the two modes. Although given no notation,

[20] Oettingen uses minuscules throughout his treatise and adds strokes above or below the letters to specify tuning, a tuning based on pure thirds and fifths. In listing the pitches, I will use capitals and will not indicate tuning as my argument pertains to the structure rather than the tuning of Oettingen's system. However, I will use minuscules with the appropriate symbols for triads and keys.

[21] For Riemann, the subdominant function always stands for the lower fifth and its relatives and the dominant function for the upper fifth and its relatives. It is presumably for this reason that Harrison assumed that *Regnante* is short for the *Oberregnant* in his 'Flow chart of Oettingen's theory' (*Harmonic Function in Chromatic Music*, p. 248). See, however, Oettingen, *Harmoniesystem in dualer Entwickelung* (1866), p. 67, 'Das duale System der Harmonie' (1902–6), 303, and *Das duale Harmoniesystem* (1913), p. 47.

the visual aspect of his presentation of the intervals, triads and scales is nevertheless telling: he always wrote out their letter names from left to right but expected the tonic and phonic triads to be read in opposite directions. While it might have seemed sensible to write the notes in the order in which they were to be understood – the tonic as C–E–G, the phonic as C–A♭–F – he continued to write F–A♭–C for the latter. In order to emphasise that he was interested not in creating an entirely new system of tonality but simply in re-imagining its existing contents, he did not alter the way these triads are *written* but rather the way they are *read*, a fact he occasionally clarifies by including arrows above the note names.[22]

The notation of the cadences enabled Oettingen to speak for the first time of genuine mirrored symmetry. He could claim more than a mere structural symmetry between their intervallic contents. Indeed, he could take his theory out of the spatial realm and pin down his symmetrical proposition to something visual and apparently musical. Significantly, his means was notation. While it could be claimed that this is an inevitable manoeuvre (cadences are already 'real' music, and thus it is natural to scrutinise them in a notated form), Oettingen was seduced by their notation. Indeed, just as that problematic 'the music itself' was long assumed to be stored in the notation, so Oettingen thought he found 'the theory itself' in the score. In 1866, he hit on a way of showing that tonal cadences could actually be transformed into one another when their written incarnation was reflected in a mirror, and it is precisely the act of writing that brings about this possibility.

Example 7.1a shows the authentic cadence in both the tonic and phonic modes. They are, as Oettingen put it, 'complete opposites', using such terms as 'vollkommener Gegensatz', 'analoger Gegensatz' and 'vollkommenes Spiegelbild'.[23] If one were to position a mirror between the staves in the example, facing it towards the tonic cadence, the phonic cadence would be reflected in it. Similarly, if it were facing the phonic cadence, the tonic version would show in the mirror. Because of the position of tones and semitones and the interval structure suggested by lines and spaces in the staff, as organised by the bass clef, Example 7.1a is the only available notation that creates this effect. The relationship between tonic and phonic in this special arrangement is specifically between C-*Tonalität* (whose tonic triad is C–E–G) and E-*Phonalität* (whose tonic triad is A–C–E). A connection between these will come as no surprise to the music theorist, for C major and A minor are generally taken to be related. Undoubtedly much of what must have convinced Oettingen to pursue his investigation into notational symmetry is that it upheld the traditional idea that these keys are related.

In his first treatise, Oettingen was particularly ambitious about teasing out the symmetries in the notation of cadences, often putting his theory in a precarious position with regard to existing musical practice. While in his first treatise he was prepared to

---

[22] See, for example, his explanation of the tonic and phonic triads in 'Das duale System der Harmonie' (1902–6), 117.

[23] See in particular the chapter on 'Cadenzen der reinen Tonsysteme', *Harmoniesystem in dualer Entwickelung* (1866), pp. 72–82.

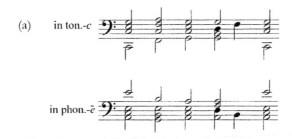

Example 7.1   Tonic and phonic cadences from Oettingen, *Harmoniesystem in dualer Entwickelung*, p. 74

suggest that practice should adjust to his findings, his subsequent treatises seem more sensitive to it. Indeed, the refinements to his explanation of the structure of the tonal system in his later treatises seem designed precisely to bring his theory closer to existing practice. To be sure, even in his first treatise, he seemed always to begin with formulas that are common enough in practice. For example, the rhythmic and contrapuntal presentation of Example 7.1a gives the impression that these cadences were plucked out of 'real' musical literature. Beginning as he did inevitably with formulas in the major key, their mirror inversion, meant to be the phonic version of the formula, often did not 'reflect' musical practice. Indeed, when critics accuse him of not coming up with 'our' major-minor system, they seem at first to be right. The cadences in Example 7.1a are a case in point. By including the dominant seventh as part of the tonic system's cadential formula, Oettingen leaves the phonic system with its own version of the dominant seventh. This phonic seventh chord creates a peculiarity as far as musical practice is concerned but is logical within Oettingen's system, as is demonstrated by the symmetrical figuring in Example 7.1b, which Oettingen calls figured bass (*Generalbassschrift*) in the tonic system and figured discant (*Generaldiscantschrift*) in the phonic.[24] The dominant seventh of C-*Tonalität* consists of the notes G–B–D–F, where the seventh is the highest pitch; the equivalent phonic 'seventh' chord consists of the notes B–D–F–A and the dissonant seventh is the lowest pitch, B. Quite apart from the inclusion of this phonic seventh chord, however, the cadence e°–b°–e°–a°–e° in Example 7.1 does not correspond to the one most commonly found in musical literature, for it charts (in our terms) the progres-

[24] *Ibid.*, p.74.

Example 7.2   Symmetrical authentic and plagal tonic and phonic cadences from Oettingen, *Harmoniesystem in dualer Entwickelung*, p. 77

sion tonic–dominant–subdominant–tonic or, in Oettingen's terms, *Phonica–Oberregnante–Unterregnante–Phonica*. Minor-key pieces (as we would term them) generally also use dominant–tonic endings. It was undoubtedly musical practice that forced Oettingen to expand the authentic cadences in Example 7.1 to find a phonic cadence like the one most familiar to listeners of tonal music.

He achieved this by probing further into notational symmetries, seeking a retrograde, which he would term plagal. Clearly, the seventh posed a problem, for it ought to remain a penultimate chord. Already in 1866, he had explored the possibility of a retrograde without this seventh, producing Example 7.2, which is an arhythmic set of chords, the right-hand column containing the retrograde or 'plagal' cadential progression. Most significantly, the seventh was removed. In his later two treatises, Oettingen presented these cadences more succinctly still. Significantly, he also completely dropped the use of the seventh from his display of cadence types. Example 7.1a never surfaces again; instead he reshaped Example 7.2.[25]

His new diagram would look like Example 7.3,[26] emphasising a symmetry that must have delighted this nineteenth-century scientist, who would undoubtedly have become acquainted with the newly developing field of group theory. The whole set of cadences emanates from one: operations performed on the cadence that I have labelled (a) in Example 7.3 produce the other three cadences: (a) flipped over on its horizontal axis produces (b), which flipped over on its vertical axis produces (d), which in turn produces (c) when flipped over on its horizontal axis again. Thus, every possible operation has been performed on the initial cadence (a). Or, using a mirror placed on the horizontal axis in Example 7.3, the cadence is transformed into its opposite mode, while a mirror placed on the vertical axis maintains the mode but transforms the cadence into its authentic or plagal counterpart.

---

[25] The cadences in Example 7.1a are the ones that sparked Harrison's comments, discussed at the outset of this chapter. See note 12 above. These are the only cadences from Oettingen's treatises that Harrison cites (indeed, he bases his account of Oettingen's theory on his first treatise). It is perhaps unfair to 'indict' Oettingen for a failure here, for it is surely more significant that he dropped their use than it is that he used them as a prototype in the first place.

[26] This diagram remains basically the same in his final treatise; the only difference is that he adds signs to indicate the tuning. See Oettingen, *Das duale Harmoniesystem* (1913), pp. 49–50.

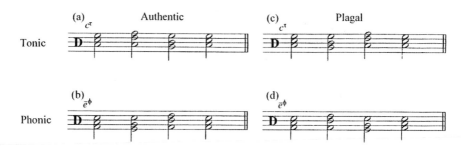

Example 7.3   Symmetrical authentic and plagal tonic and phonic cadences from Oettingen, 'Das duale System der Harmonie', 305–6

Apart from being more compact, Example 7.3 shows two new features in comparison with Example 7.2. First is a new clef, a crucial feature that I mention here but will return to later. Second are the Greek symbols he used to signify *Tonalität* and *Phonalität*, ᵀ (Tau) for the former and ᵠ (Phi) for the latter.[27] These complemented the symbols + and ° used to designate *Tonicität* and *Phonicität*. Thus, for example, one would speak of c^τ as having $c+$, $g+$ and $f+$ as its *Tonica, Dominante* and *Unterdominante* and e^ϕ as having $e°$, $a°$ and $b°$ as its *Phonica, Regnante* and *Oberregnante*.

Finally, note how the various triads in the two modes came to be associated with each other: the authentic progressions *Tonica–Unterdominante–Oberdominante–Tonica* and *Phonica–Oberregnante–Unterregnante–Phonica* have the 'strong' (*stark*) side of their respective systems as their penultimate chords, namely the *Oberdominante* and *Unterregnante*, while the plagal progressions *Tonica–Oberdominante–Unterdominante–Tonica* and *Phonica–Unterregnante–Oberregnante–Phonica* have the 'weak' (*schwach*) side of the systems as their penultimate chords, namely the *Unterdominante* and *Oberregnante*. Thus, both the *Oberdominante* and *Unterregnante* and the *Unterdominante* and *Oberregnante* are analogues. It is for this reason that Oettingen suggested that *Oberdominante* be shortened to *Dominante* and *Unterregnante* to *Regnante*.

Having shown that c^τ and e^ϕ are related to each other through mirrored symmetry, Oettingen next found a way to assert that keys that share their tonic and phonic are also related through symmetry. Although there were visual displays of this symmetry towards the end of his first treatise, it is not until the second that he included them in the section on the structure of the tonal rudiments. Oettingen could thus speak, for example, of c^τ and e^ϕ as parallel tonalities (*Parallel-Tonarten*) and c^τ and c^ϕ (or, as Oettingen would eventually favour, d^τ and d^ϕ) as antinome tonalities (*antinome*

---

[27] Although Rummenhöller states in *Musiktheoretisches Denken im 19. Jahrhundert: Versuch einer Interpretation erkenntnistheoretischer Zeugnisse in der Musiktheorie*, Studien zur Musikgeschichte des 19. Jahrhunderts, vol. XII (Regensburg: Gustav Bosse Verlag, 1967), p. 86 that Greek symbols were first used in Oettingen's 1913 treatise, they were introduced in 'Das duale System der Harmonie' (1902–6), and in this example.

$$c — d —\overline{e}— f — g —\overline{a}—\overline{h}— c$$
$$c – \underline{des} – \underline{es} – f — g — \underline{as}— b — c$$

Example 7.4   Tonic and phonic scales from the common tone C from Oettingen,
Harmoniesystem in dualer Entwickelung, p. 65

Tonarten). The 'proof' of this last relationship would be in one particular – symmetrical – way of notating the scale, to which we now turn.

SCALE

It is at the level of the scale that Oettingen is most often accused of losing sight of 'our' major-minor system. As seen thus far in relation to the triads and cadences, he sets out the traditional tonal components, configuring them in a new symmetrical pattern. Similarly, he considered the tonic and phonic scales to be mirror reflections of each other. The criticism that the phonic scale is not the traditional minor one stems, as we shall see, from a misreading.

In all three treatises Oettingen introduced the scale after the three primary triads (and before the presentation of the cadences). While there are significant differences in the way he presented the tonic and phonic scales in each volume, the structure of the scales themselves remains the same. In each treatise, the scales are presented at least twice, once from a major third apart and also from a common starting tone. Only at the beginning of the first treatise are the scales presented exclusively in letter notation, first from the common tone C (such as in Example 7.4), then from C and E.[28] Again, the scales in Example 7.4 are meant to be read in opposite directions, the tonic scale from left to right, the phonic scale from right to left. Towards the end of this treatise, in a discussion about the harmonic foundation of pure and mixed scales, Oettingen arranges the scales from the note D, presenting them in a notated form (Examples 7.5a and b).[29] It is this last method of structuring and envisioning the anti-nome relationship that has the greatest impact on the final incarnation of the presentation of the musical rudiments in his next two treatises. While Oettingen continues to explore parallel relationships using C and E, D supplants all explanations that previously relied on C as a common tone. Why this new detail?

Most theorists demonstrate the principles of their theory with the note C as a starting point or, when describing minor, the note A. This is largely a matter of convenience, since neither scale has accidentals. Throughout his career, Oettingen focused on c^{τ} and e^{φ} for his cadential prototypes because only in this notational set-up did they lend themselves to the kind of reversals and mirror reflection demonstrated in Examples 7.2 and 7.3. The primary triads and scales would be reworked after his 1866 treatise in order to achieve a similar symmetrical impact in notation. It is important to

[28] *Harmoniesystem in dualer Entwickelung* (1866), pp. 65 and 71.
[29] *Ibid.*, pp. 216 and 218.

Example 7.5   Various presentations of scales in notation
(a) and (b) from Oettingen, *Harmoniesystem in dualer Entwickelung*, pp. 216, 218
(c) from 'Das duale System der Harmonie', 66
(d) from *Das duale Harmoniesystem*, p. 46

map out how Oettingen understood the structure of these scales because, with the exception of a brief description in *The New Grove Dictionary*,[30] no English-language discussion of Oettingen's theory reads the scales from any of his treatises accurately.

Oettingen imbued the note D with great significance, arguing that its unique properties make it best able to convey his system of comprehensive opposition. It is the only pitch for which symmetrical major-minor scales produce 'opposite' accidentals on the same scale steps, namely: where there is a sharp in one scale, there is a flat in the other. That is to say, the third and seventh tones in the ascending scale are sharpened, whereas the third and seventh tones in the descending scale are flattened. Starting from a D in any octave will produce the same results. It is interesting how Oettingen inches his way towards a clear visual symmetry. Example 7.5 shows this process: Example 7.5a is the first appearance of the scales beginning on D in his 1866 treatise. The tonic scale begins on D below middle C and the phonic scale on the D above it. In Example 7.5b, Oettingen brings the octave together, a decisive move but, curiously, one not repeated in his second treatise, where the scale is instead represented as Example 7.5c. Here there are no clef signs, again an important gesture, although the bass clef is assumed. In Example 7.5c, Oettingen attains a certain visual symmetry, since the lines and spaces of each scale degree match, but the scales do not start from the same octave – the *Tonica* starts two octaves below middle C and the *Phonica* a tone above it. It is not until his third treatise that sound and notation come together, as it were, in perfect symmetry. As illustrated by Example 7.5d, a single pitch launches both scales, drawn on a single stave. The example not only shows the symmetrical location of the sharps and flats, it also turns about a central axis. For Oettingen's new

---

[30] See 'Oettingen', in *The New Grove*.

visual and sonic symmetrical purposes, only one D will perform the task: the one in the bass clef. So special is its location – the middle line – that Oettingen developed a new clef to express its singularity: the D-clef. While this might seem a mere substitution for the F-clef (or bass clef),[31] Oettingen uses it sparingly. When he quotes musical examples (as he does from the music of Bach, Beethoven, Liszt, Schubert, Schumann, Wagner and Reger), he uses conventional clefs. The D-clef has, one must conclude, a strictly theoretical purpose: in Oettingen's mind it is the clef that fixes the pitch that is going to help unlock the laws of the tonal universe. The key, as it were, is Example 7.5d. There has never been any question that its ascending scale matches the major scale of traditional tonal theory; but exactly which scale does the descending collection of notes represent? Many have interpreted it as phrygian, although Oettingen warned against interpreting it as such.[32]

William Mickelsen's book on Riemann takes his description of Oettingen's scales from an article by Martin Vogel, translating the following from the article:

Oettingen points out that the two most important scales historically, the Dorian as the main scale of antiquity and the major scale as the main scale of modern times, are antagonistically opposite. Moreover, they are constructed equally and joined together with the same scale steps.[33]

One might have assumed that Mickelsen had successfully understood the structure of the scale had he not created and annotated a musical example which, incidentally, draws both scales from C as common tone.[34] Mickelsen's quotation from Vogel's article mentions the dorian mode (which is correct), but Mickelsen glosses his musical example as phrygian.[35]

Mickelsen is not alone: Dale Jorgenson, in his article 'A Résumé of Harmonic Dualism', equates Oettingen and Vincent d'Indy, arguing that the topography of their major-minor systems is the same (which we can essentially agree with) but he incorrectly concludes that for both theorists the opposite of the major scale is phrygian.[36] Similarly, David W. Bernstein in a study dedicated to use of symmetry by Hauptmann,

[31] In 'Das duale System der Harmonic' (1902–6), 246, Oettingen explains that the middle line in his D-clef is intended to refer to the D above middle C. This is in order to accommodate the wide range of some symmetries he discusses, such as the overtone series and its mirror reflection (see 'Das duale System der Harmonie' (1902–6), 245).

[32] Oettingen explained the dangers of reading the scale incorrectly in each treatise: Oettingen, *Harmoniesystem in dualer Entwickelung* (1866), p. 66, 'Das duale System der Harmonie'(1902–6), 302, and *Das duale Harmoniesystem* (1913), pp. 46 and 49. In the last two treatises, he explicitly warned against seeing it as phrygian.

[33] Martin Vogel, 'Arthur v. Oettingen und der harmonische Dualismus', in *Beiträge zur Musiktheorie des 19. Jahrhunderts*, ed. Martin Vogel, Studien zur Musikgeschichte des 19. Jahrhunderts, vol. IV (Regensburg: Gustav Bosse Verlag, 1966), p. 128.

[34] Mickelsen, *Hugo Riemann's Theory of Harmony*, his Example 7, p. 16.

[35] *Ibid.*, p. 16.

[36] Dale Jorgenson, 'A Résumé of Harmonic Dualism', pp. 39–40. D'Indy kept the names major and minor for his scales and labelled the degrees of the latter from the top: E is I, D is II, C is III, B is IV and so on; the phrygian ♭II is VII of d'Indy's minor scale. Clearly thus he did not intend to imply the phrygian scale. See Vincent d'Indy, *Cours de composition musicale*, 3rd edn (Paris: A. Durand, 1912), vol. I, p. 101.

Oettingen, Riemann, Cappellen and Ziehn reports that Oettingen uses the phrygian mode to oppose the major scale.[37]

Matthew Shirlaw is another to write on the dualists; the section dedicated to Oettingen is very brief and characterises only the way in which Oettingen derived the triads but not the scales. His misreading can be found in the section on Riemann, whose structure of the scales stems directly from Oettingen's:

> It is unfortunate that the minor scale which Dr. Riemann presents to us as the direct antithesis of the major is not our minor scale at all. Dr. Riemann considers it to represent the Dorian Mode of the Greeks. This however it does not do. The Greek Dorian Mode had Pythagorean tuning, with dissonant Thirds and Sixths.[38]

Again, the dorian mode of the Greeks is indeed the one that Oettingen and Riemann intended us to read but Shirlaw is wrong to conclude that Riemann does not present 'our minor scale'. Indeed, Shirlaw missed why Oettingen and Riemann would want to mention the dorian mode. Neither of them is interested in tuning here; rather they are interested in the structure of the dorian scale. The thirds and sixths in Pythagorean tuning might well be dissonant, as Shirlaw points out, but this is of little consequence to Oettingen's or Riemann's argument about the scale. Both were interested in conveying how the symmetry of the major scale does indeed produce 'our' minor scale. Both, in other words, meant to come up with the traditional major-minor system.

Most recently, Daniel Harrison repeated the misinterpretation of this symmetry, also concluding that 'Oettingen is forced to create not a traditional major-minor system but a major-phrygian system.'[39] His 'Flow chart of Oettingen's Theory'[40] uses C as the central pitch and uses letters rather than notation. Unlike either Oettingen's own abecedarian characterisation of the scale or the notated examples (Examples 7.4 and 7.5d), Harrison provides the scale without repeating the octave C: he writes, C Db Eb F G Ab Bb. Thus, while in his flow chart, Harrison correctly identifies all other phonic aspects of Oettingen's system, he presents only the phonic scale as though it starts from the bottom or from left to right. Phonic elements are to be read from right to left, which means the starting pitch is missing from Harrison's version. Even so, one might ask, how would a C at the other end of the collection of pitches listed in Harrison's chart (as above) make a difference to its modal identity? The special feature of scales, so we are usually taught, is that they are the same going up as going down, with, however, the exception of the melodic minor scale, where the pitches change depending on whether one is approaching or leaving the tonic. Even so, a melodic minor scale is known as 'D minor' despite having different pitches on the way up and on the way down. How, then, could a scale with no change in pitch be phrygian in one direction but dorian in the other? The difference – an all-important one for Oettingen – lies in how the pitches are taken to define the tonal system. The primary triads extracted from each scale will vary depending on how its contents are assumed to be

[37] Bernstein, 'Symmetry and Symmetrical Inversion', p. 385.
[38] Shirlaw, The Theory of Harmony, p. 394.
[39] Harrison, Harmonic Function in Chromatic Music, pp. 247–8.   [40] Ibid., p. 248.

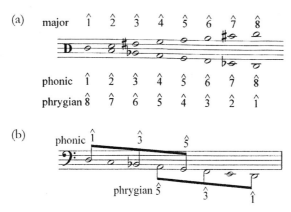

Example 7.6   Comparison of tonic, phrygian and dorian readings of scales

organised. For Oettingen, this difference distinguishes theories founded on Rameau's fundamental bass from dualism.

Thus, the descending scale in Example 7.5d could be phrygian, dorian or 'our minor scale' depending on how you look at it. Oettingen insisted it was dorian, advising readers not to interpret the note D as a tonic but as the 'phonic' of the scale. Example 7.6a uses scale degrees in order to illustrate the difference between a phrygian and dorian reading of the starting pitch of the descending scale. Example 7.6b shows the primary triad (the tonic in our terms) of each of the these scales. However, even Oettingen's reference to the phonic scale as dorian has caused some confusion, additional to that mentioned in the quotations from Mickelsen and Shirlaw above. Harrison assumes Oettingen meant the 'white-note' D-dorian mode, which, as he rightly points out, has a unique symmetrical feature: it is the only church mode that inverts into itself, as shown in Example 7.7.[41] However, this scale is clearly not the one in Example 7.6, and, moreover, Oettingen was not interested in any scale that inverts into *itself*; rather he was interested in a scale that would invert into *another*. The special feature of Oettingen's dorian scale was that it inverts into the major scale. How?

Oettingen's scale was not the so-called church or 'white-note' dorian but the Boethian dorian, which at the transposition D–D has its *mese* on G, a fifth from the top.[42] It is

---

[41] *Ibid.*, p. 250 n. 65.

[42] In the discussion that follows all modes have been transposed to D–D. The untransposed level for Boethius' dorian, the so-called 'church-mode' phrygian and the hypoacolian modes is E–E; all of these use the white notes between E–E. The modes are distinguished by the relative importance of different notes within this same collection of pitches. My discussion here transposes the collection to D–D simply to match Oettingen's musical examples. My purpose in this discussion is not to come to conclusions about what these modes actually are (that is a debate for modal scholars) but rather to investigate what aspects of structure Oettingen himself saw in these modes and what encouraged him to envisage the descending scale in example 7.5d as the legitimate opposite to the major scale. Oettingen's declared source on the structure of Greek modes and the significance of the dorian was Karl Fortlage, *Das musikalische System der Griechen in seiner Urgestalt* (Leipzig, 1847) and Heinrich Bellermann, *Der Contrapunct* (Berlin: Julius Springer, 1862). See *Harmoniesystem in dualer Entwickelung* (1866), pp. 82–9. For a concise account of the history of these modal terms, see Harold S. Powers, 'Mode', in *The New Grove Dictionary of Music and Musicians*, ed. Stanley Sadie (London: Macmillan, 1980).

Example 7.7   Symmetry of 'white-note' dorian

different from the 'white-note' dorian, whose secondary pitch is a fourth from the top; untransposed, its primary pitch would be D and the secondary A. However, there is another mode besides the Boethian dorian that emphasises the notes D and G: the hypoaeolian mode. So why didn't Oettingen make life simple and refer to his descending scale as the hypoaeolian? At least then we might have recognised it more easily as our own minor scale, with the tonic in the middle.

Oettingen could not call it hypoaeolian because there is an all-important difference between the structure of the Boethian dorian and the hypoaeolian modes. Although they both emphasise D and G, these pitches have a different hierarchy in each mode. As illustrated by Example 7.8, in the Boethian dorian, D is the primary pitch and G is the secondary pitch, while in hypoaeolian, D is the secondary pitch and G, the finalis, is the primary pitch. Oettingen would naturally be attracted to the dorian mode because it mirrors the location of the primary and secondary tones of the major scale (see Example 7.8). Indeed, to call the descending scale hypoaeolian would be to envision it in terms of the fundamental bass, with D as a fifth above the tonic or final. Oettingen wanted D to be a 'starting' or generating pitch, and G the *Regnante*. As can also be seen from Example 7.8, neither the phrygian nor the 'white-note' dorian matches the major scale: in this transposition, the primary and secondary pitches of the phrygian mode are D and A, and C and G in the 'white-note' dorian.

To get 'our' minor scale, then, Oettingen's primary axiom of mirror opposition must go hand in hand with the axiom's corollary – that all minor elements are defined from the top. As such, Oettingen was the first dualist to find a logical means to connect the triad, the cadence and the scale with identical structuring principles. We can also see from this why Oettingen would, in his later treatises, revise various other charts to have them centre on the note D too.[43]

I could end here and claim to have properly demonstrated Oettingen's system. But I want to make a different point. Before doing so, however, it seems right to ask whether a renewed understanding of Oettingen's theory means we can begin to put it to use. Does it offer us insights into the true mechanism of tonal music? Is the major-minor system fundamentally symmetrical? Is there ever a time where reading a harmony from the top down is appropriate?

David Lewin has explored a few convincing instances where a musical work seems to demand such a top-down reading. His examples involve foreground arpeggiations that start from the top. He cites the opening gesture played by the bassoon in Stravinsky's *Le Sacre du Printemps*. After the opening held C, the semiquaver sonority,

[43] As Oettingen rightly pointed out, even the cadences, which are in c^T and c^ς, have D as an axis; see *Harmoniesystem in dualer Entwickelung* (1866), p. 75.

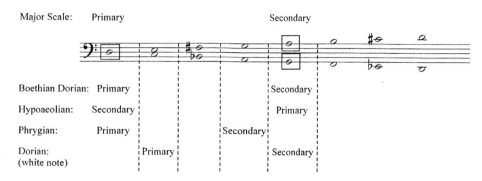

Example 7.8 Primary and secondary pitches in various modal readings of the phonic scale

B–G–E–B, is in his view a dual B minor triad: 'it does violence to the sense of the passage if one tries to hear an E root for the triad', he writes.[44] Similarly, he argues that the descending arpeggios in Brahms's Intermezzo, Op. 119 No. 1 are best interpreted as dual. Or, the kind of upside-down Alberti bass pattern (D–B–D–G) that opens the 'Alla Danza Tedesca' from Beethoven's String Quartet, Op. 130 is a dual D major sonority. For Lewin, then, duality is defined by the details of a composition *in toto*. In such situations, surface gesture is crucial to the analytical process, and the harmonies of such passages are considered dual because of direction they take. This is quite a different approach from Oettingen's, whose reading of a harmony depends on whether it is major or minor. For Lewin, reading from the top is not exclusively associated with the minor key – the 'Alla Danza Tedesca', for example, is major.

Oettingen did not demonstrate his theory by seeking out musical examples with descending arpeggios, with one telling exception: the opening motive of Beethoven's Fifth Symphony.[45] The manner in which he notated Beethoven's motive is significant: I mentioned earlier that, even after inventing the new clef, he continued to use conventional clefs when quoting musical works, the D-clef being reserved for demonstrating the theory of musical rudiments. To judge from Example 7.9, which uses the D-clef, some kind of theoretical point is surely being made. Technically, within Oettingen's theory it is immaterial that this descending motive belongs to a piece that is in a key whose constituent elements are also constructed in a descending, phonic order. But this is a powerful piece. This work has come to represent so much, and as far as Oettingen was concerned, it is as though Beethoven, through these two ambiguous notes, had made phonicity – the 'act' of descending – inextricably linked to the minor mode. It therefore warrants a D-clef. Oettingen wants us to know that the most famous motive in Western music needs his notation and, moreover, needs his system in order to grasp it.

While we might disagree with him on that point, Oettingen's theory – or rather its reception – can help us grasp something else. It is telling that the misreading of

[44] David Lewin, 'A Formal Theory of Generalized Tonal Functions', *Journal of Music Theory* 26 (1982), 43. The next three examples of duality also come from this article.
[45] Oettingen, 'Das duale System der Harmonie' (1902–6), 126.

SUZANNAH CLARK

Example 7.9   First motive from Ludwig van Beethoven, Symphony No. 5, from Oettingen,
'Das duale System der Harmonie', 126

Oettingen's phonic scale stems from an accidental (or persistent) application of the fundamental bass theory. Because the scale's tones were read according to tonic and not phonic principles, Oettingen's system was assumed not to be major-minor but rather major-phrygian. On this basis, these writers then concluded that Oettingen was not interested in following existing musical practice but rather in creating a new one to fit his new theory. In fact, Oettingen himself mentioned in the preface to his first treatise that he would be introducing very little that is new.[46] This admission was both true and ambitious: as far as Oettingen was concerned, he simply wanted to train musicians to rethink and rehear that which they already knew and heard. In other words, he wanted to keep musical practice as it was but offer us a new way of looking at it, a way he believed was the natural, symmetrical order of tonality.

The fact that, despite his warnings, his system was misinterpreted tells us something significant about ourselves: our way of understanding tonal music is so ingrained that it seems difficult to imagine it otherwise. We saw, for instance, that even Hauptmann was prepared to take his aural understanding as intuitive and correct, despite arguing that a dualistic theory was the natural theoretical condition of music. Oettingen's theoretical suggestions went much further, asking us to put our habits of reading and thinking aside and to question the degree to which Rameau's fundamental bass is natural for all aspects of the tonal system. Although dualism is not an accepted theory today, Oettingen's suggestions serve a profound purpose: they raise our awareness of how strongly we have absorbed a system of beliefs about how musical structure is ordered. Indeed, Oettingen alerts us to the fact that 'our' way of thinking might simply be 'second nature'. Of course, he attempted to persuade his readers that his way of construing the tonal system is *the* natural one, a customary pursuit of theorists until this century. But he might best serve to remind us not of what is natural or right in a music theory or in a musical practice but of what is habit.

---

[46] Although most immediately in the context of mentioning his theory of dissonance, which he suspected might provoke criticism, Oettingen makes a point that has implications for his theory as a whole: 'Ich bin davon überzeugt, dass viele sich dahin äussern werden, es läge hier nichts Neues vor', *Harmoniesystem in dualer Entwickelung* (1866), p. 6. See also note 10 above for Oettingen's assertion in the introduction to the 1866 treatise that the cadences and tonality he is dealing with are the 'normal' ones.

180

Part III

Constructions of identity

Chapter Eight

▬

The gendered eye: music analysis and the scientific outlook in German early Romantic music theory

IAN BIDDLE

INTRODUCTION: TEXTS AND THEIR READERS

In the prologue to his *Celestina*, published in Saragossa in 1507, Fernando de Rojas asked himself why the work had been understood, appreciated, and used in so many different ways since its first appearance in 1499 at Burgos. The question is simple: how can a text that is the same for everyone who reads it become an 'instrument of discord and battle between its readers, creating divergences between them, with each reader having an opinion depending on his own taste'?[1]

Roger Chartier's analytical trajectory draws us into a close analysis of some of the ways in which a history of reading might be constituted in the historically contingent activities that regulate and pattern reading practices: in the ways in which 'texts and the printed works that convey them organise the prescribed reading' and through the 'collection of actual readings tracked down in individual confessions or reconstructed on the level of communities of readers'.[2] This radically historical formulation insists on the conditionality of reading practices and on the fragmented and locally formed nature of such practices, and positions the reader between a theoretical 'freedom' to read, a 'secret' activity, if you will, and the constraints which the 'machinery' of the text is designed to affect.

This tantalising cultural-historical problem poses some interesting questions for historians of music theory: to what extent might the music-theoretical idiom itself represent a record of types of 'reading' and what is the nature of the 'text' in such readings? Such questions do not have simple answers since, as the New Historicism has taught us, 'texts' are not immutable receptacles of some ontological matter, but construed from the operations of often quite radically fluid reading practices.[3] The

---

[1] Roger Chartier, 'Texts, Printings, Readings', in *The New Cultural History*, ed. Lynn Hunt (Berkeley and Los Angeles: University of California Press, 1989), p. 154. [2] *Ibid.*, p. 158.

[3] Roger Chartier's work is seminal in this area. See in particular Roger Chartier (ed.), *The Culture of Print: Power and the Uses of Print in Early Modern Europe*, trans. Lydia G. Cochrane (Princeton: Princeton University Press, 1989); Chartier, *La correspondance: Les usages de la lettre au XIXe siècle* (Paris: Fayard, 1991); 'Text, Symbols and Frenchness', *Journal of Modern History* 57 (1985), 682–95; *Forms and Meanings:*

structural problem that attends a history of reading is thus centred on the relation of the reading subject to its object, on how that relation is legislated for and policed, and how the constitution of the text as an object of scrutiny competes with the contingency of that text – in short, on how cultural practices seek to maintain the ontological field of the text-object.

I propose here to scrutinise a crucial moment in the emergence of a new kind of reader and text-object, namely the period in German history that has been characterised as gripped by a *Lesewut[h]*, a rage for reading that consumed the middle classes from the second half of the eighteenth to the middle of the nineteenth century. Chartier has suggested that a new kind of reader, the so-called 'extensive' reader, emerged at this time,[4] but he nonetheless cautions against the all-too-easy juxtaposition of this new reader with the older 'intensive' reader – the reader faced only with a 'narrow and finite body of texts, which were read and reread, memorized and recited, heard and known by heart, transmitted from generation to generation':[5]

This view is open to discussion. There were, in fact, many 'extensive' readers during the period of the supposed 'intensive' reading . . . The inverse case is truer still: it was at the very moment of the 'reading revolution' that the most 'intensive' readings developed (with Rousseau, Goethe, and Richardson), readings in which the novel seized its readers to become a part of them and to govern them as the religious text had once done.[6]

I should like to suggest that, contrary to Chartier's caution, the extensive reader was an important cultural trope – an imagined reader that served as a useful cultural resource in the construction and maintenance of the identity of a group – what Hegel would term a *Stand* – that sought to exercise implacable cultural authority over reading practices at this time. The authority of these learned classes, or *Gelehrtenstand*, was sustained in part by the long-established, academy-mediated[7] practices of reading scholarly texts closely. Written by university professors for close scrutiny by students, these texts were based around a set of methodological problems and grounded on what was still largely an Aristotelian model of education.[8] The 'extensive' reader, whether

footnote 3 (*cont.*)

Texts, Performances and Audiences from Codex to Computer (Philadelphia: University of Pennsylvania Press, 1995); and *The Order of Books: Reader, Authors, and Libraries in Europe between the Fourteenth and Eighteenth Centuries*, trans. Lydia G. Cochrane (Stanford: Stanford University Press, 1994).

[4] Chartier, *Forms*, p. 17.

[5] Chartier's characterisation of the 'extensive' reader: 'The "extensive" reader, that of the *Lesewut* . . . is an altogether different reader – one who consumes numerous and diverse printed texts, reading them with rapidity and avidity and exercising a critical activity over them that spares no domain from methodological doubt.' *Ibid.* [6] *Ibid.*

[7] I use 'academy' here to denote not necessarily an institution as such, but in its more critical sense as applied to a practice that is sanctioned and sustained by some kind of recognised line of transmission such as master-to-pupil training. Clearly similar practices could also exist within institutions such as universities, but since musicology and analysis were not yet codified as university subjects, one has to re-think what might be meant by 'institution' and 'academy' in this context. See also Ernest Gellner, *Nations and Nationalism* (Oxford: Blackwell, 1983), p. 57.

[8] One such text is Friedrich W. J. Schelling's *Philosophie der Kunst* (1802–3) (Eßlingen: J. G. Cotta, 1859; rpt Darmstadt: Wissenschaftliche Buchgesellschaft, 1980).

truly distinguishable from the 'intensive' reader or not, served as a kind of identity-forming Other for the *Gelehrtenstand*.

The overt opposition that such figures as Goethe, Fichte and Schiller[9] provided in relation to the new 'narcotic' of extensive reading is part of a broader tendency to construct 'the popular' as the Other to the 'learned' discourses: the very identity of the *Gelehrtenstand* depended on this opposition. Of course, such oppositions are not unique to the nineteenth century, and historians recognise such forms of antagonism between 'high' and 'low' at many moments: Peter Burke recognises a process of bifurcation under way in 1500 (and certainly well established by 1800), while Jacques le Goff and Jean-Claude Schmitt discuss the seminal moment of the emergence of a 'lay culture' as early as the twelfth and thirteenth centuries respectively.[10] It seems, at any rate, that the recognition, maintenance and critique of a putative divide between 'popular' and 'learned' discourses has exercised many cultures in the past. It is thus my intention not to privilege the early nineteenth century over other such schisms, but to scrutinise the specificity of this divide in particular.

THE HISTORICITY OF THE GAZE

The logic of the divide between the *Gelehrtenstand* and its Other is founded, like many before, on an alteritous formulation – by which I mean an asymmetrical binary opposition in which the dominant element depends for its identity on a 'lesser', more fluid Other. In short, what we have already recognised as the structural problem of a history of reading, the relation of Subject and Object, comes into clear focus here: the construction of the learned 'I', the exemplary Subject of the *Gelehrtenstand*, contrasts itself, with all the cultural authority at its disposal, with its impoverished Other. What is particularly striking in the texts written by and for intensive readers at this time is the speculative attention they lavish on anything that seems to duplicate such alteritous formulations.

[9] Erich Schön, *Der Verlust der Sinnlichkeit oder die Verwandlung des Lesers: Mentalitätswandel um 1800* (Stuttgart: Klett-Cotta, 1987). For a useful overview of this process, see Daniel Leonhard Purdy, 'Reading to Consume: Fashionable Receptions of Literature in Germany, 1774–1816' (Ph.D. thesis, Cornell University, 1992), which challenges the traditional sociological view that fashionable reading was motivated by a desire to emulate higher class status. Instead, Purdy suggests that the *Lesewut* was fuelled initially by the eighteenth-century court semiotic in which 'luxury goods signified social status', to be very quickly superseded by a bourgeois semiotic system that 'read clothes and domestic decorations as signs of individual character and moral worth' (p. 205). Another useful account of this process can be found in Daren Ivan Hodson, 'The Institutionalisation of Literature in Eighteenth-Century France and Germany: The Functions of Reading in Rousseau, Novalis, Fichte and the *École Normale*' (Ph.D. thesis, University of Utah, 1995). See also Robert Darnton, 'Readers Respond to Rousseau: The Fabrication of Romantic Sensitivity', in *The Great Cat Massacre and Other Episodes in French Cultural History* (New York: Basic Books, 1984), pp. 215–56.

[10] Peter Burke, *Popular Culture in Early Modern Europe* (New York: Harper and Row, 1978); Jacques le Goff, 'Ecclesiastical Culture and Folklore in the Middle Ages: Saint Marcellus of Paris and the Dragon', in *Time, Work, and Culture in the Middle Ages*, trans. Arthur Goldhammer (Chicago: Chicago University Press, 1980), pp. 159–88; and Jean-Claude Schmitt, '"Religion populaire" et culture folklorique', *Annales: Economies, Sociétés, Civilisations* 28 (1976), 941–53.

I recognise here a certain intensification of the debates that rage around the nature of subjectivity, its agency in the natural world and the extent to which it can know itself without recourse to anything outside itself. Such debates resonate across many discourses. First, in the philosophical concerns of the *Naturphilosophen*, the growth and sustenance of the self is located in a speculative field of *Negativität*, which Hegel links to temporality and to music in particular.[11] Second, in the sciences, both speculative and empirical, one can discern what might be termed an 'intensification of scrutiny', where transitive activities (activities that require an object) become ever more intrusive, where scrutiny becomes ever more invasive and the object of scrutiny ever more distant, pacified, emptied out. Third, in other learned discourses, anxieties about the constitution of the object of scrutiny are transformed into quasi-scientific incursions into the objective realm. Indeed, Michel Foucault has characterised what might be termed the transitive descent into the object of scrutiny as a seminal re-orientation of the relation of the self to its environment.[12]

There is one image that captures this intensification of the 'learned' scrutiny – the image of the implacable gaze, exemplified in the very optic organ itself: the eye. Recent attention to the gaze has tended, with good reason, to concentrate on the act of looking itself, or on the obvious art forms in which the gaze is overtly engaged – film and the visual arts.[13] I want to suggest here that the gaze, as an act of power, can be engaged in ways that that are more covert, more figuratively grounded, and yet no less potent in their operation on the object of desire. In this sense, a history of reading might also, at certain moments, embrace a history of the gaze, a history of the surreptitious and secretive activities that surround the text-object and its users when mediated through sight or through figurative invocations of looking.

Before proceeding to an analysis of the mechanisms of learned scrutiny in the music-theoretical text, I want to propose, along Lacanian lines, a controversial formulation: that the gaze 'itself' is not a product of optics or of perception in a more general sense but that it resides *outside* the seeing subject. Lacan recognises this in Sartre's *Being and Nothingness*:

If you turn to Sartre's own text, you will see that, far from speaking of the emergence of this gaze as of something that concerns the organ of sight, he refers to the sound of rustling leaves, suddenly heard while out hunting, to a footstep heard in a corridor. And when are those sounds heard? At the moment when he has presented himself in the action of looking

[11] Georg W. F. Hegel, *Vorlesungen über die Ästhetik*, in *Theorie Werkausgabe*, vol. XV (Frankfurt am Main: Suhrkamp, 1970), p. 133: 'Dies Tilgen nicht nur der einen Raumdimension, sondern der totalen Räumlichkeit überhaupt, dies völlige Zurückziehen in die Subjektivität nach seiten des Inneren wie der Äußerung, vollbringt die zweite romantische Kunst – die Musik.'

[12] Michel Foucault, *The Order of Things: An Archaeology of the Human Science* (New York: Tavistock Publications, 1974), p. 239.

[13] Perhaps the seminal work in the role of the gaze in film is Laura Mulvey's 'Visual Pleasure and Narrative Cinema' first published in *Screen* in 1975, available in *The Sexual Subject: A Screen Reader in Sexuality* (London and New York: Routledge, 1992), pp. 22–34, and her follow-up: 'Afterthoughts on "Visual Pleasure and Narrative Cinema" inspired by *Duel in the Sun*', in *Visual and Other Pleasures* (London: Macmillan, 1989), pp. 29–39.

through a keyhole. A gaze surprises him in the function of a voyeur, disturbs him, overwhelms him and reduces him to a feeling of shame.[14]

Looking and being looked at can be constructed, as Lacan would have it, as a psycho-analytical function of identification or differentiation or, as Laura Mulvey would have it,[15] as the site of a particular kind of power relation between the bearer of the gaze and the Other made image. We can thus locate an analysis of the mechanisms that police and manipulate the gaze in early nineteenth-century German culture at the heart of a wider analysis showing how the authority of the learned scrutiny is consti-tuted. By recognising, for example, the relocation of the power relation of the gaze in, say, the field of poetic figuration, we open up the possibility of a structural analysis of the giving and receiving of transitive actions, of the constitution of the individual at various points between the exemplary subject and the wretched object and of the formation of a broader ideological field in which certain powerful social and cultural archetypes control the gaze to the detriment of others.

In early nineteenth-century thought, the 'eye' itself, that metonym of the gaze, is often a figuration of a kind of raw, destructive or unmediated subjectivity, surrepti-tiously linked to a fetishised (voyeuristic) scrutinising of an object of desire, or to the processes of objectification that invariably accompany a putatively rational and pur-posive observation; the eye is thus often linked to an *excessively empirical* self, an unfet-tered rational ego. Anyone familiar with Meyer H. Abrams's *The Mirror and the Lamp*[16] will also be familiar with the notion that pre-Romantic thought is best figured as *mimetic*, or as *binaristic*, and that the metaphors of 'looking' and 'mirroring' are often linked to the actions of a naïve unfettered ego, a Cartesian, mechanistic self or a less coherent antecedent of the exalted subject of the German Romantic ideology. This notion, best understood perhaps as modernist in orientation, figures North European Romanticism as a liberation from cultural atrophy, a loosening of paternal authority and a relocation of the self in a more fluid relation to its environment, an environ-ment which is often itself located within (or as) 'nature'. Yet Lacan would seem to condone such a view:

It is not for nothing that it was at the very period when the Cartesian meditation inaugurated in all its purity the function of the subject that the dimension of optics that I shall distinguish here by calling 'geometral' or 'flat' (as opposed to perspective) optics was developed.[17]

Lacan's remarks would seem to suggest, then, that the gaze is not an immutable process, but generated from and transformed by relatively finite historical contingen-cies of the order of what the *Annales* historians have called the *longue durée*.

What, then, characterises the historical specificity of the gaze in early nineteenth-century German culture? It is not so remarkable in itself that metaphorical recourse to 'looking' and other figurations of scrutiny are linked, as we have seen, to an

---

[14] Jacques Lacan, *The Four Fundamental Concepts of Psycho-Analysis*, ed. Jacques-Alain Miller, trans. Alan Sheridan (London and New York: Penguin, 1994), p. 84.   [15] Mulvey, 'Visual Pleasure', 25.
[16] Meyer H. Abrams, *The Mirror and the Lamp: Romantic Theory and the Critical Tradition* (Oxford: Oxford University Press, 1971).   [17] Lacan, *Concepts*, p. 85.

excessively empirical self. What is striking in this culture is the antagonism that this empirical self demonstrates towards what might be termed the 'ideal self': an antagonism that Schumann demonstrated quite clearly for Florestan's 'psychological' mode of criticism.[18] If, as Paul de Man has suggested, we figure the 'critical problem' of Romanticism as driven by the tension between the 'empirical self of the author and the self that appears as the speaking voice in the work',[19] then clearly an examination of the mechanisms of the text-object, of authorship as figured within and without the text-object, of readers and of the learned authority masquerading as a unified and universal subjectivity is crucial to an understanding of the 'web' of cultural processes at work in the birth of the modern music-theoretical idiom.

SEEING MUSIC

In attempting a location of the putative or speaking self in the music-theoretical text, we are confronted, first of all, by the distinctiveness of the music-theoretical idiom. This idiom allows its 'voice' (to use de Man's term again) to speak without denying or transcending the empirical self. Subjectivity is not merely a functional constituent of the text, not auctorial in its operation, but is crucial to the exposition of that text, as if it were turning the pages of the text itself. In other words, the music-theoretical text speaks with an authority that is dependent in particular upon a relatively clear and unproblematic location of the empirical-subjective voice within that text, as unmediated, unproblematic, pragmatic. Authors seem to take us through the process of their coming-to-be, the text acting as a kind of performative re-enactment of the author's journey of discovery.

Yet the very empirical self that is located within this textual process is the same self that was invariably constructed as the Other of the ideal Romantic self, as a mediocre, glib and reductive authority, imprisoned within the constraints of artificial *culture*. In general terms, we might be able to posit a general distinction between the empirical self of the music-theoretical text (ever more analytical, it seems) and the poetic self of certain forms of music criticism, exemplified perhaps most eloquently in the split that often occurs in Schumann's *noms de plume* (for example Florestan) or in the structural dualisms of hermeneutic criticism. A common trope in much German music criticism from this time is a sense of loss, of a fragmentation of a former organic wholeness into petty professional specialisation. What the poetic self felt so painfully as a loss was dealt with more covertly by the more empirical self of the music-theoretical

[18] See Robert Schumann's review of Berlioz's *Symphonie fantastique* in *Neue Zeitschrift der Musik* (1835): 1 (3 July), 1–2; 9 (31 July), 33–5; 10 (4 August), 37–8; 11 (7 August), 41–4; 12 (11 August), 45–8; 13 (14 August), 49–51. The first part (3 July) of the review is written by Schumann's 'poetic' incarnation Florestan. Schumann excised this section from the review for his *Gesammelte Schriften*. For more on this see my 'Policing Masculinity: Schumann, Berlioz and the Gendering of the Music-critical Idiom', *Journal of the Royal Musical Association* 124 (1999), 40–64.
[19] Paul de Man, *Romanticism and Contemporary Criticism: The Gauss Seminar and Other Papers*, ed. E. S. Burt, Kevin Newmark and Andrzej Warminski (Baltimore and London: Johns Hopkins University Press, 1993), p. 25.

idiom and was often the cause of much vitriol. This is particularly evident in Wackenroder:

> An eternally hostile chasm is entrenched between the feeling heart and the investigations of research, and the former is an independent, tightly sealed, divine entity, which cannot be unlocked and opened up by reason.[20]

Elsewhere, Wackenroder speaks of a 'mysterious merging' of properties,[21] a kind of idealised transcendence of the empirical ego that de Man recognises in the writings of Rousseau.[22] The unifying action implicit in this *rätselhaftes Verschmelzen* is thus deliberately anti-intellectual. There is no systematic or symmetrical unification of the two sides, but a violent incursion of the fictive 'I' of, for example, Hölderlin's *Friedensfeier* into the realm of the empirical 'I'. Wackenroder thereby attempts to transform the performative rigour of an academy-mediated idiom into a kind of idle chatter, an arbitrary making of signs:

> O, then I close my eyes to all the strife in the world – and withdraw quietly into the land of music, as into the *land of belief*, where all our doubts and our sufferings are lost in a resounding sea, – where we forget all the croaking of human beings, where no chattering of words and languages, no confusion of letters and monstrous hieroglyphics makes us dizzy but, instead, all the anxiety of our hearts is suddenly healed by the gentle touch.[23]

In doing so, he casts the empirical self out in a Rousseauesque quest for an original pre-cultural self, the self before Babel.

Cutting across the binary opposition of the empirical/ideal selves is the pairing of 'natural' or 'original' (i.e. pre-cultural) and cultural. The two pairings are not equivalents, nor do they map onto each other with any consistency. Their interaction is complex and fluid, figured differently in different localities or idioms. Wackenroder's figuration of the pairings is distinctly anti-analytical, in that the ideal self is under constant threat from the empirical self, reflected in the ideal self's quest for the pre-cultural, a yearning for a state of wholeness before having been cracked open by the contrivances of culture.

---

[20] 'Eine ewige feindselige Kluft ist zwischen dem fühlenden Herzen und den Untersuchungen des Forschens befestigt, und jenes ist ein selbständiges verschlossenes göttliches Wesen, das von der Vernunft nicht aufgeschlossen und gelöst werden kann.' Wackenroder, *Phantasien über die Kunst für Freunde der Kunst* (1799), rpt (Potsdam: Gustav Kiepenheuer, 1925), p. 186. Translation based on that by M. H. Schubert in Edward A. Lippman (ed.), *Musical Aesthetics: A Historical Reader*, vol. II: *The Nineteenth Century* (Stuyvesant, NY: Pendragon, 1988), p. 23.

[21] 'Keine andre [Kunst] vermag die Eigenschaften . . . auf eine so rätselhafte Weise zu verschmelzen.' Wackenroder, *Phantasien*, p. 183.

[22] Paul de Man, *Romanticism*, pp. 25–49.

[23] 'Oh, so schließ' ich mein Auge zu vor all dem Kriege der Welt – und ziehe mich still in das Land der Musik, als in das Land des Glaubens, zurück, wo alle unsre Zweifel und unsre Leiden sich in ein tönendes Meer verlieren – wo wir alles Gekrächze der Menschen vergessen, wo kein Wort- und Sprachengeschnatter, kein Gewirr von Buchstaben und monströser Hieroglyphenschrift uns schwindlig macht, sondern alle Angst unsres Herzens durch leise Berührung auf einmal geheilt wird.' Wackenroder, *Phantasien*, p. 165; Lippman, *Aesthetics*, p. 11.

MUSIC THEORY AND THE NATURAL SCIENCES

One way in which to understand attitudes to (and in) the analytical text is by examining how subjectivity is figured in other academy-mediated texts. The discourses that look to the empirical realm as their body of evidence are, of course, the discourses of the natural sciences and medicine. This is not to privilege such discourses over others, but to recognise that debates about the order and constitution of the empirical realm can often provide insights into the manner in which texts make claims to the truths of that realm and how they invoke its wisdoms in support of their own suppositions.

To speak simply of 'science' in early nineteenth-century German culture is, of course, problematic since *Wissenschaft* also embraces notions of scholarship and knowledge, a complexity borne out by Hegel's *Wissenschaft der Logik*.[24] Yet there *is* a body of texts in German concerned with physiognomy, anatomy, biology, physics and chemistry which might be termed *scientific* in orientation. What surprises about such texts is the extent to which they problematise the distinction between empirical analysis and speculation. At the edge of this body of texts lies the work of the *Naturphilosophen* for whom empirical observation is a supplement to the more pressing concerns of generalisation and speculation. Such works include Friedrich W. J. Schelling's *Erster Entwurf eines Systems der Naturphilosophie* (1799), the introduction to *Ideen zu einer Philosophie der Natur* (1797), *Über den wahren Begriff der Naturphilosophie und die richtige Art, ihre Probleme aufzulösen* (1801) and contemporary works by Hans Christian Oersted, Heinrich Steffens, Carl August Eschenmayer, Lorenz Oken, Gotthilf Schubert, Johann Wagner and others.[25]

For speculative biology and other hybrid sciences, the emergence of organicism as both a philosophical and an analytical metaphor is implicated in the demise of a view of science as encyclopaedic.[26] This view of science, driven largely by the instrumentalisation of the scientific discourse, came under threat from the speculative sciences as a result of the former's apparent inability to systematise the external world. K. F. von Kielmeyer, J. D. Brandis, J. F. Blumenbach and Franz von Baader all called for the supression of the encyclopaedic view in favour of a theoretically generated model of the world that would bring the ever-expanding scientific world within the limits of human cognition.[27] This drive for a deep-lying principle of order, for a

---

[24] Hegel, *Wissenschaft der Logik* (1812–16), rpt (Frankfurt am Main: Suhrkamp, 1970), p. 272.

[25] First editions of all of the Schelling works are: Eßlingen: J. G. Cotta, 1859; rpt Darmstadt: Wissenschaftliche Buchgesellschaft, 1980.

[26] See Joseph L. Esposito, *Schelling's Idealism and Philosophy of Nature* (Lewisburg: Bucknell University Press, 1977), pp. 125–59. Some of this part of my argument is based on my review of Ian Bent's two-volume *Music Analysis in the Nineteenth Century* (Cambridge: Cambridge University Press, 1994) for *Music and Letters* 79 (1998), 120–6.

[27] K. F. von Kielmeyer, 'Versuche über die sogenannte animalische Electrizität' [Experiments on so-called animal electricity], *Journal der Physik* 8 (1794); J. D. Brandis, *Versuch über die Lebenskraft* (Hanover: Hahn, 1795); J. F. Blumenbach, *Über den Bildungstrieb und Zeugungsgeschäfte* (Göttingen: Johann Christian Dieterich, 1781); and Franz von Baader, *Beiträge zur Elementar-Physiologie*, in *Sämmtliche Werke* (1797) (Leipzig: Hermann Bethmann, 1852).

circumscription of the world, can be usefully likened to the analytical drive to discover the structural essence, the *Bildungstrieb*, that internally orders the musical work.
Hence, the move from the loosely Cartesian encyclopaedic order of the world to a
compartmentalised, hierarchical order (from free-associative, visually apprehensible
nature to the ontological order of discrete yet structurally resonant parts in the post-
Cartesian universe) is implicated as much in the emergence of the *naturphilosophisch*
universe and the interpretative dualism as it is in the rise of the organic metaphor in
empirical biological science.

What the German speculative sciences suggest about constructions of subjectivity
is that they are distinctly fragile and contingent. If organicism thrives on the tension
between two levels of experience, the general and the particular, then subjectivity can
only be figured within that process as a kind of agent, a mediation of the levels, and
reflecting, as all good organic beings do, that schism within itself. The apparent
contradiction of the empirical and ideal selves can thus also be figured within the
scientific discourses as the conceptual contradictions of the fragmentary and whole,
the irrational and rational, the cyclical and linear, to name but a few. In the patterning
of such pairings, the empirical natural sciences sought in particular to 'still' the object
of scrutiny by controlling access to the mechanisms of scrutiny, by dictating who
could 'know' and who was constituted as an object-to-be-known.

Recent spectator theory holds that the bearer of the gaze is masculine and that the
image is feminine:

In a world ordered by sexual imbalance, pleasure in looking has been split between
active/male and passive/female. The determining male gaze projects its phantasy on to the
female figure which is styled accordingly. In their traditional exhibitionist role, women are
simultaneously looked at and displayed, with their appearance coded for strong visual and
erotic impact so that they can be said to connote *to-be-looked-at-ness*.[28]

To gender the gaze in this way is to recognise something profound about the way in
which transitive activities were invariably figured in Hollywood cinema. A similarly
hegemonic coding of the object of scrutiny of science is pervasive in the nineteenth
century. Woman, in particular, figured as an exemplary spectacle in the medical sciences and occupied a 'privileged' location as the body *par excellence*, beset by the vicissi-
tudes of womb vapours, hysteria, melancholia, narcissism and other 'infirmities'
which marked out an acceptable middle-class femininity from other more deviant
forms. Before we can proceed to an analysis of how gender is engaged in the music-
theoretical text, we must make some general observations about the nature of such
texts and how the gaze is constituted within them.

MUSIC ON DEAF EYES

The learned scrutiny is indebted to the empirical sciences for its construction of the
Subject/Object binarism. The authorial locus of the academy-trained learned self,

---

[28] Mulvey, 'Visual Pleasure', p. 27.

the 'intensive' reader who both fuelled and dismissed the populist *Lesewut*, is sustained in the music-theoretical idiom by a particularly close and constant attention to the nature of the object of scrutiny, by a turn, in short, to a kind of prototypically analytical activity. This object, the empirical corollary of the work, is formed through the creeping professionalisation of the music-theoretical idiom and an ever broader schism between the once unified pedagogical (compositional) and analytical projects. We must not, however, fall into the trap of characterising all that seems *analytical* as somehow positivist or 'scientific' in orientation. Few music theorists would ever have made such claims and even fewer would have understood the need to do so. Rather, the relationship between music-theoretical practices and the empirical sciences of the first half of the nineteenth century is much more fluid. Two points in particular demand our attention here: first, that the empirical sciences themselves were in a state of considerable methodological and epistemological flux, slowly unshackling themselves from the constraints of Leibnizian and Cartesian forms of speculation, only to encounter the unwieldy formulations of German *Naturphilosophie* – hence, to speak of the German empirical sciences as if they were a clearly characterised and finite set of practices is untenable; second, that although German music theory was undergoing a remarkable transformation, the final 'victory' of the analytical method over other more descriptive or critical activities was much later than is often made out. With these two points in mind, it becomes clear that the music-theoretical text is a wayward and rather hybrid beast.

The hybrid nature of such texts is easily demonstrable: one need only browse Ian Bent's two-volume *Music Analysis in the Nineteenth Century* to see how elucidation, speculation and description rub up against analytical procedures in an often bewildering profusion of approaches. There is also no point in denying that much of what passed for music theory was characterised by derivative and banal invocations of the latest intellectual vogues: sub-Hegel, pseudo-science and professional posturing – at its most banal, music theory could (and can) be tiresome. And yet, it is the very banality of some of these texts that opens up some interesting trajectories. Rather than dismiss what Wackenroder termed the 'chattering of words' and 'monstrous hieroglyphics' of the music-theoretical text as somehow sub-standard, I suggest that there is something fundamentally *readerly* to this hybridity, as if the wilful fluidity of approaches pointed beyond itself to some other text or texts.

This returns us to the tantalising prospect made at the outset of this chapter for music theory as a record of a kind of 'reading'. Whilst one cannot deny the acumen with which many theorists approached the musical work, one particularly deadly myth must be laid to rest: as an academy-mediated idiom, music theory does *not* spring first and foremost from an aural apprehension of the music. The act of making a music-theoretical text is a double process of both 'reading' the printed score and attempting to convince the reader that he or she is being made party to that reading. Two further notes of caution should be sounded before we can proceed along this trajectory. First, there is a considerable difference in the way 'listening' is constituted in nineteenth-century German culture and in our own – the music theorist's ability to construct (to 'hear') the work from the score was common practice, and the act of listening was always, figuratively speaking, 'in' the text. Second, domestic performances of well-known works were not uncommon, and piano reductions became readily available with the expansion of publishing and the drop in prices due to widespread pirating. This would seem to support the view that early nineteenth-century Germany sustained a broad range of cultures of listening and that attempts to characterise such cultures in terms of a singular experience are problematic. (Indeed, Schumann wrote his review of Berlioz's *Symphonie fantastique* having heard only Liszt's piano reduction, a fact that suggests that late twentieth-century scholarly notions of 'authenticity' or 'authentic listening' in scholarly apprehensions of the musical work are out of place in early nineteenth-century culture.) Despite this plurality of listening modes available to the music theorist, the production of a text is a laborious process that alienates, delays, distends and defers the subjective apprehension of the musical work. The theorist is thus constantly striving to capture the 'original' apprehension and doomed to fail in the quest for that 'immediate presence': in this very profound sense, the music-theoretical idiom engages the ear only figuratively.

Constituted in the very practices that the music-theoretical text purports to show is a highly transitive act linked more than just figuratively to the gaze. Clearly these texts posit a very specific kind of reading dependent not first and foremost on *listening*, but on *looking*. The eye, as our initial Lacanian formulation suggested, is little more than a pale metonym of the gaze itself. Since the subjective apprehension of the music is always deferred in such texts, the gaze has detached itself from the optics of perception and set itself free in search of an eternally deferred Other, the music itself, and attaches itself to neither the looking subject nor the 'image' of the music.

GENDERED LISTENING, GENDERED LOOKING

As Mulvey and Lacan have both shown, the gaze is linked intimately (and ultimately) to desire:

We can apprehend this privilege of the gaze in the function of desire, by pouring ourselves, as it were, along the veins through which the domain of vision has been integrated into the field of desire.[29]

The object of the gaze is thus the object of desire and the look passes from a simple relation of power to one of erotic potential. As we have seen, Mulvey has shown how this erotic potential is structured in the Hollywood epic to mark woman as the *to-be-seen* of the binarism and man as bearer of the gaze. We have also noted how this formulation finds a parallel in the late eighteenth- and early nineteenth-century medical construction of woman as the exemplary body and man as the exemplary mind. Endemic to a gaze grounded in this culture is the pleasure that looking at a woman gives a (heterosexual) male, a pleasure characterised usefully as a kind of

---

[29] Lacan, *Concepts*, p. 85.

scopophilia, an erotic pleasure in looking such that the look becomes almost as charged as the touch, the difference almost annihilated.

It would, of course, have been easier to engage questions of gender in music-theoretical texts by paying close attention to more overtly gendered quasi-narrative texts such as Schumann's review of the *Symphonie fantastique* or texts on opera such as Berlioz's review of Meyerbeer's *Les Huguenots*.[30] By concentrating on such texts, however, one privileges the overt over the covert, the externalised over the codified, the foreground over the background. Even in texts that are 'overt', furthermore, one cannot simply wade into the text looking for gender. It has to be located and grounded in the discourses that operate around the text and through which the text itself mediates constructions of gender. By concentrating on the structure of the gaze, however, one embraces the possibility of analysing the textual operations that hide, marginalise and objectify the feminine 'body' and of uncovering some of the ways in which misogynous assumptions on gender are incorporated in discourses apparently free of such concerns.

To return to the operations of the gaze, music analysis in its most 'elucidatory' mode, to use Bent's term, is usefully figured in terms of a kind of scrutiny premised on the notions that its object is somehow coquettish, wilfully complex and mischievously illusive. Moritz Hauptmann's analysis of Bach's *Art of Fugue*,[31] Simon Sechter's analysis of Mozart's 'Jupiter' Symphony,[32] Siegfried Wilhelm Dehn's analysis of Bach's *Well-tempered Clavier*[33] all construct a dramatic process of drawing back the veils of complexity to reveal the inner locus of the ontic core, through a range of interpretative trajectories. This process is perhaps more explicitly embraced in hermeneutic accounts such as Hoffmann's famous review of Beethoven's Fifth Symphony:

Beethoven's instrumental music unveils for us the realm of the almighty and the immeasurable. Here shining rays of light shoot through the darkness of night, and we become aware of giant shadows swaying back and forth, moving ever closer around us and destroying within us all feeling but the pain of infinite yearning, in which every desire, leaping up in sounds of exaltation, sinks back and disappears.[34]

The focused clarity of Gottfried Weber's analysis of a Mozart quartet stands in stark contrast, and yet tacitly engages the same model, that of a peeling away of veils to reveal an inner core:

[30] *Journal des débats* (10 November 1836), 1–2.
[31] Moritz Hauptmann, *Erläuterungen zu Joh. Sebastian Bachs KUNST DER FUGE . . . Beilage zum III. Bande der in obiger Verlags-Handlung erschienenen neuen Ausgabe von J. S. Bachs Werken* (Leipzig: C. F. Peters, 1841), pp. 3–14.
[32] Simon Sechter, 'Zergliederung des Finale aus Mozarts 4. Sinfonie in C', in Friedrich Wilhelm Marpurg, *Abhandlung von der Fuge, nach den Grundsätzen und Beispielen der besten in- und ausländischen Meister entworfen, von Friedrich Wilhelm Marpurg, neu bearbeitet, mit erläuternden Anmerkungen und Beispielen vermehrt von S. Sechter . . .*, ed. Simon Sechter, 2 vols. (Vienna: Anton Diabelli [1843]), vol. II, pp. 161–93.
[33] Siegfried Wilhelm Dehn, 'Dreistimmige Fuge aus dem "Wohltemperirten Clavier" von J. S. Bach', in *Analysen dreier Fugen aus Joh. Seb. Bach's 'wohltemperirtem Clavier' und einer Vocal-Doppelfuge A. M. Bononcini's* (Leipzig: C. F. Peters, 1858), pp. 1–7.   [34] Translation from Bent (ed.), *Analysis*, vol. II, p. 145.

The sole task that I have set myself here is to carry out just such an enquiry, to produce just such an analysis . . .

I believe that I can best carry out the promised analysis of the passage in question if first, in preparation, I:

1 examine it from the point of view of its underlying chord progression or tonal scheme; then
2 consider the notes foreign to chords, otherwise known as passing notes, that occur in the passage, and then
3 a few so-called cross-relations that are lurking there; as well as
4 some parallel progressions between voices that are worthy of note; but finally examine the entire passage once again, bringing all the above points into conjunction with one another.[35]

Even later, Hauptmann is able to invoke an interiority, despite his positivist pretensions:

What it is, on the one hand, that enables a work of art to communicate with us as a living source deep within; or what it is that empowers the often recalcitrant raw materials, under such irksome constraints as these, to take shape in the master's hand as free and profoundly inspired forms, and that reveals its creator to us, the object equally of our admiration and our astonishment, – all of this can be understood and appreciated through kindred feeling.[36]

In Hoffmann and Hauptmann, the 'poetic' tone, often figured as an 'aside' or throwaway encomium, is the locus of a shift in conceptions of what the analytical project can be. Such encomia are clearly integrated into the text in Hoffmann, whereas they reside at the fringes of Hauptmann's analytical argument (and are already largely absent from Weber's terse analysis). It is, indeed, this purification or filtering out of the idealising subjectivity that marks the ascendancy of the much later positivist outlook.

By recourse to a more overtly rigorous and 'scientific' idiom, music theory attempted over and over in the latter half of the nineteenth century to validate itself according to more clearly 'scientific' models that cast out the speculative biology of the early nineteenth century in favour of more rigorously empirical methodologies. Hence, the gaze intensifies with all the fecundity of the camera, constructing a view of the human anatomy based on fidelity to the original, premised on the belief that external reality has independent existence that can be captured in the act of looking and recounting through the visual image. As nature unveils itself to the gaze of positivist scrutiny in the statue by Louis Ernest Barras, *La Nature se dévoilant devant la Science*, so feminine music lays bare its internal organs to the scrutiny of the analyst. What resounds most clearly in the transition from speculative to positivist music theory is the transformation of figurations of musical material as natural, to a kind of frozen existential time, hung in the concert hall like a great delicate net.

Authority and subjectivity in the positivist analytical text centre around an empirical self that is exemplary. The gaze of the positivist music analysis is gendered –

---

[35] Gottfried Weber, 'Ueber eine besonders merkwürdige Stelle in einem Mozart'schen Violinquartett aus C', in *Versuch einer geordneten Theorie der Tonsetzkunst zum Selbstunterricht*, 4 vols. (Mainz: Schott, 1830–2), vol. III, pp. 196–226. Translation from Bent (ed.), *Analysis*, vol. I, p. 163.
[36] Moritz Hauptmann, *Erläuterungen*, p. 15; translation from Bent (ed.), *Analysis*, vol. I, p. 76.

invariably – in terms of the more readily masculine side of the binary pairs: rational, clear, incisive, penetrative, unveiling. Within this cultural-historical configuration, the gaze is always owned by men. Gender occupies an exemplary position within the logic of alterity since its dualism always seemed to be grounded in a pre-ordained biology, in 'nature' itself. The putatively 'natural' dualism, the differences 'given' in nature thus constituted a useful, apparently empirical, model for the other asymmetrical binarisms of alterity. In the music-theoretical idiom, the gendered gaze designated the academy-mediated authority of the analyst/theorist as invariably masculine since gender itself is often held up in the scientific/medical discourses as *the* binarism *par excellence*. It is, so to speak, the ultimate duality on which the construction of the analytical/empirical 'I' rests.

The nineteenth century frames a remarkable transformation of music theory from a kind of desirous 'reading' to an activity closer to an exploratory invasion of the musical 'body'. If the desire located in the deferral of the musical 'object' is linked to the gaze, then the shift from 'reading' to 'analysis' is thus a shift from the gaze as yearning or questing to a fetishistic, stifling, scopophilic gaze that reduces the object of scrutiny to a mere captive image. It is of little surprise that the polemicists of analysis and a thoroughly professionalised *Musikwissenschaft* should emerge at the very moment that the first audiences could gaze from the darkened auditorium on the first moving images taken by camera.

Chapter Nine

—

On the primitives of music theory: the savage and subconscious as sources of analytical authority

PETER A. HOYT

The writings of the Age of Reason often abandon the realm of reason altogether, turning instead to unsettling depictions of savages inhabiting distant lands, wild creatures that only approximate human form, and feral children suckled by bears or wolves. These passages may appear quite imaginative, as when a 1498 report portrays the residents of the New World as 'blue in colour and with square heads',[1] but such accounts also suggest the extent to which the paradigms held by the European explorers impinged upon their powers of observation. Within the Aristotelian, Thomist, and Neoplatonic traditions of the Renaissance, a specifically human nature could only be conceptualised negatively: the Great Chain of Being simply placed mankind in the space above the beasts and below the angels.[2] This position was surprisingly precarious, allowing for an infinite number of minute gradations between man and the quadrupeds. Consequently, anything serving to obscure the boundaries between categories was a source of great consternation and confusion: the barking of dogs, for example, concerned the Medieval semioticians because it suggested a type of language, and language was a characteristic by which these scholars attempted to distinguish themselves from the lower orders.[3] The first European explorers in the

---

[1] This description appeared in John of Holywood's *Sphera mundi*, quoted here from Lewis Hanke, *Aristotle and the American Indians: A Study in Race Prejudice in the Modern World* (Chicago: Henry Regnery Co., 1959), p. 4.

[2] Hayden White, 'The Noble Savage Theme as Fetish', in *Tropics of Discourse: Essays in Cultural Criticism* (Baltimore: Johns Hopkins, 1978), p. 186.

[3] See Umberto Eco, Roberto Lambertini, Costantino Marmo and Andrea Tabarroni, 'On Animal Language in the Medieval Classification of Signs', in *On the Medieval Theory of Signs*, ed. Umberto Eco and Costantino Marmo (Amsterdam: John Benjamins, 1989), pp. 3–41. Numerous writings testify to the instability of man's nature. John Amos Comenius, for example, stated that 'since it is to be desired that no man should degenerate into not being a man, it is therefore to be desired that no man should remain without education; for through the force of human nature itself it is very easy for those who are devoid of education to degenerate so' (Jean Piaget, ed., *Johann Amos Comenius, 1592–1670: Selections*, trans. Iris Urwin (Paris: Unesco, 1957), p. 102). On the other hand, it was equally possible for the lower orders to ascend. La Mettrie, publishing in 1747, wrote that 'the similarity of the ape's structure and functions is such that I hardly doubt at all that if this animal were perfectly trained, we would succeed in teaching him to utter sounds and consequently to learn a language. Then he would no longer be a wild man, nor an imperfect man, but a perfect man, a little man of the town, with as much substance or muscle for thinking and taking advantage of his education as we have.' This belief is

Caribbean were therefore prepared to be profoundly disturbed by any commonalities between themselves and the unclothed natives. Given the desire to minimise the human attributes of the savage, it was perhaps inevitable that the heads of the Americans would assume a square, bluish form. Even those Europeans who were capable of seeing human qualities in the natives found them a cause for anxiety, for the savage challenged basic presumptions concerning the order of God's creation.

The extent of this anxiety can be gauged by the manner in which the discoveries of 1492 were quickly followed by significant reformulations of man's position in the universe. These alternative visions included Copernicus's heliocentric theories, which began to circulate among astronomers in approximately 1515, Thomas More's *Utopia*, which was published in 1516, and Martin Luther's challenge to the ecclesiastical hierarchy, which was posted on the church door in Wittenberg in 1517.[4] Europe's confrontation with the savage also had profound implications for the self-understanding of the individual, and by the early sixteenth century the existence of the liminal man had to be incorporated implicitly into the definition of human nature. At the same time, the individual increasingly appeared as the starting point for philosophical inquiry; Descartes's famous 'I think, therefore I am' from the *Discourse on Method* of 1637 provides only the most famous instance of this tendency. Consequently, as human nature became central to the Enlightenment's intellectual standpoint, the savage entered surreptitiously into the axioms upon which further speculation was built. The primitives of distant lands thus became the primitives of Europe's theories, including those about music.

In the process of redefining human nature, the actual characteristics of the non-European were almost irrelevant. The facts gathered by travellers were shaped by the paradigms they carried with them, and the savage inevitably conformed to the categories these preconceptions made available. Columbus's expectations, for example, were informed by his knowledge of Homer's *Odyssey*. Having read about Cyclopes and Amazons, his exchanges with Indians inevitably confirmed the existence of one-eyed cannibals (living on the north coast of Cuba) and of a civilisation consisting exclusively of women (on the island of Martino). Similarly, Columbus was told of men with the noses of dogs, comparable to those described in Sir John Mandeville's fourteenth-century collection of travel narratives, with which he was also familiar.[5]

footnote 3 (*cont.*)

based on the presumption that 'from animals to man there is no abrupt transition, as true philosophers will agree' (Julien Offray de la Mettrie, *Machine Man and Other Writings*, trans. Ann Thomson (Cambridge: Cambridge University Press, 1996), pp. 12–13).

[4] The relationship between the voyages of discovery and Europe's reorganisation is discussed in Michel-Rolph Trouillot, 'Anthropology and the Savage Slot: The Poetics and Politics of Otherness', in *Recapturing Anthropology*, ed. Richard G. Fox (Santa Fe: School of American Research Press, 1991), pp. 17–44. The date for the spread of Copernicus's ideas is taken from Thomas S. Kuhn, *The Copernican Revolution: Planetary Astronomy in the Development of Western Thought* (Cambridge, Mass.: Harvard University Press, 1957), p. 185.

[5] Stanley L. Robe, 'Wild Men and Spain's Brave New World', in *The Wild Man Within: An Image in Western Thought from the Renaissance to Romanticism*, ed. Edward Dudley and Maximillian E. Novak (Pittsburgh: University of Pittsburgh Press, 1972), pp. 42–4.

As accounts gradually accumulated, European biologists would be forced to account for an almost infinite variety of human forms. Thus, in 1735, Linnaeus grouped the orang-utan together with 'the *tailed man*, of whom modern travellers relate so much'.[6] Other reports led him to create a distinct category for the *Homo ferus*, to which he assigned the various 'four-footed, mute, and hairy' juveniles who were periodically discovered living wild in Europe's fields and forests.[7] Linnaeus and other writers constantly cite the reports of travellers as authority for their accounts, but of all the stories brought back from abroad, Europe allowed itself to retain only what was convenient. The colonisers saw what they needed to see: the Spanish, who needed labour, found people who fitted Aristotle's description of the 'natural slave', whereas French Jesuit missionaries, as if to comment upon the morals of the court in Versailles, postulated that the Canadian Indians could not be descendants of Adam and Eve, and therefore found them to be free of the stain of Original Sin.[8] Over and over again, the savage served as a blank slate upon which the West inscribed both uneasy and optimistic visions of its own potential.

Within the European tradition, therefore, the savage served simultaneously as a locus for fantasy and as a component of fundamental presumptions. Primitive man was both an absolute fabrication and part of the bedrock of truth upon which the West built its self-image. One might expect there to be a profound conflict between these arbitrary and foundational aspects, but this combination is so familiar that any tension is easily overlooked. After all, these seemingly incongruous qualities mirror those of language, which is also arbitrary (in that the relationship between a word and what it signifies is entirely conventional) and yet also foundational (in that language influences the forms that thought may assume). And so it was not at all difficult to incorporate a completely ungrounded concept of the savage at the centre of the West's presumptions concerning human nature; it required no more effort than using language.

The nature of language entails that a speaker partakes in the traditions and values of a social group: the use of a conventional medium implies an adherence – in however limited a fashion – to the group's conventions. This participation may be a source of anxiety on the part of the individual, and it may require that certain private connotations be concealed within the subconscious. These repressed associations, however, may resurface in the guise of certain irregularities in speech, such as slips of the tongue. In a somewhat similar manner, the suppressed figure of the savage may re-emerge when foundational presumptions are at issue, and therefore a cause for anxiety. An example of such an intrusion appears in the opening pages of Antoine Reicha's 1814 *Traité de mélodie*, in which the savage is invoked as a means of conferring authority upon the analytical perspective presented in the text.

[6] John G. Burke, 'The Wild Man's Pedigree: Scientific Method and Racial Anthropology', in *The Wild Man Within*, p. 266.

[7] George Humphrey, introduction to Jean-Marc Gaspard, *The Wild Boy of Aveyron*, trans. George and Muriel Humphrey (New York: Meredith, 1962), p. ix.

[8] See Hanke, *Aristotle and the American Indians*, pp. 12–27; Geoffrey Symcox, 'The Wild Man's Return: The Enclosed Vision of Rousseau's *Discourses*', in *The Wild Man Within*, pp. 226–9.

Example 9.1   Reicha's Example *A* from *Traité de mélodie*

Antoine Reicha (1770–1839) was born in Prague and trained in Bonn, where he was a musical colleague of the young Ludwig van Beethoven. Reicha later resided in Vienna, where he was on close terms with the aging Joseph Haydn, before he settled permanently in Paris in 1808. In France, he began teaching music theory and composition privately, and his students eventually included musicians who were already professors at the Paris Conservatoire (including Baillot, Habeneck and Rode). Despite this personal acquaintance with the faculty, it was not until 1818 that Reicha was himself appointed to the institution. His students at the Conservatoire included Berlioz, César Franck, Charles Gounod, George Onslow and Schumann's close friend Ludwig Schunke. Franz Liszt, who as a foreigner was denied admission to the school, studied privately. Despite his involvement with the young generation of Romantics, and despite his openness to new approaches (to which Berlioz referred), Reicha's aesthetic was shaped primarily by the music of the late eighteenth century. His textbooks often cite the works of Mozart and Haydn, whereas Beethoven goes virtually unrepresented.

The beginning of the *Traité de mélodie* reveals a Classical perspective through its emphasis upon symmetrical phrase structure:

Experience teaches us that we feel a certain pleasure when we hear a gesture [*mouvement*] that proceeds in a symmetrical and well-cadenced manner; a simple drum, making a rhythmic gesture in the following manner, would be sufficient to fix our attention for a moment.[9]

Reicha then refers the reader to his first musical example (his Example *A*) which is reproduced in Example 9.1. This presents a series of similar rhythmic patterns, divided into four groups. The first and third divisions are identical, whereas the second division differs from these two others only in its ending. The fourth group ends in the same way as the second, but also introduces a new semiquaver figure where all preceding divisions had four quavers. In explaining why this rhythm manages to be interesting, Reicha cites the elements that create symmetry, noting that each segment is a two-bar unit, that points of repose (or cadences) separate each division, and that these points are evenly spaced, so that weak cadences are found in bars two and six, while strong cadences appear in the fourth and eighth bars. 'In short', says Reicha, here 'one observes a regular plan, and it is this alone that captures our attention.'[10]

For the sake of contrast, Reicha offers Example *B* (reproduced here as Example 9.2), which consists of an undifferentiated series of crotchets that (as indicated by the 'et cetera' marked at the end of the example) continues beyond the notated rhythm. Reicha states that this series has 'neither symmetry, nor plan, produces only monotony, and bores and fatigues after the third bar'.[11]

[9] Reicha, *Traité de mélodie*, 2nd edn (Paris: A. Farrenc, 1832), pp. 8–9.   [10] *Ibid.*, p. 9.   [11] *Ibid.*

Example 9.2   Reicha's Example *B* from *Traité de mélodie*

Example 9.3   Reicha's Example *C*, adapting Joseph Haydn, Symphony No. 53

Reicha goes on to say that the appeal of the first rhythmic pattern, which he calls a *dessin*, can be heightened by the proper choice of tones to accompany the rhythm. As a demonstration of such a compositional procedure, he layers pitches over his Example *A* to produce a version of the opening of one of Haydn's most charming melodies, the Andante to Symphony No. 53, given in Example *C* (see Example 9.3). This symphony, which was extremely popular in Paris, is known as *L'Impériale*, a nickname that seems somewhat ironic in light of the imperialistic aspect of Reicha's subsequent remarks.[12] Haydn's melody departs from Reicha's symmetrical drum pattern only in the final two bars, where Haydn's theme actually seems *more* symmetrical than Reicha's example, in that it does not have the isolated semiquaver figure found in division four of Example *A*. Haydn's melody also differs from Reicha's example in the final bar, as it also uses the 'weak' cadence found in the first and third divisions. Reicha does not discuss these minor differences. Rather, he explains that 'all symmetrical movement provides a type of regular melody; it is only a question of choosing the proper sounds to express this motion, and to make the end of each phrase distinctly felt by means of sufficient repose'. He proposes that as an exercise students create melodies on the basis of symmetrical rhythmic patterns such as found in his first example. By changing the notes, Reicha says, one may create an infinite variety of melodies.[13]

The generation of music from pre-existing rhythmic structures is striking, particularly in light of the modern tendency to see the tonal composition as an immense elaboration of certain fundamental melodic and harmonic progressions. This perspective is central, of course, to Schenker's seminal theory of the *Ursatz*, which typically addresses rhythmic values only at the most immediate layers of structure.[14] It is also a component of other views, as evident in Charles Rosen's statement that

[12] Further irony may be found in the use of Haydn's melody – in considerably altered form – as the basis for several militaristic hymns (including 'Brightly Gleams Our Banner' and the first setting of 'Onward Christian Soldiers') during the Victorian period. For a discussion of some adaptations of Haydn's melody in the late eighteenth and early nineteenth centuries, see Gretchen A. Wheelock, 'Marriage à la Mode: Haydn's Instrumental Works "Englished" for Voice and Piano', *Journal of Musicology* 8 (1990), 389–94.   [13] Reicha, *Traité de mélodie*, p. 9.

[14] This is not to say, of course, that a Schenkerian approach cannot address rhythmic issues in a dynamic and enlightening manner. See the essays collected under the heading 'Rhythm and Linear Analysis' in Carl Schachter, *Unfoldings: Essays in Schenkerian Theory and Analysis*, ed. Joseph N. Straus (New York: Oxford University Press, 1999).

Example 9.4   Reicha's version of Haydn's melody compared with the original

classical sonata form consists of 'an immense melody, an expanded classical phrase'.[15] Given the modern emphasis on such approaches, Reicha's use of symmetrical patterns to generate a melody is certainly noteworthy.

It is also significant that Reicha's Example *C* as well as the complete version of the melody given in his Example *H* both depart from the original shape of Haydn's theme. As can be seen in Example 9.4, Haydn consistently uses a dotted rhythm as an opening gesture of each division, whereas Reicha transforms this gesture into two even semiquavers. Reicha also changes several notes without comment, including those in the upbeat to the ninth bar. Most arresting, however, are Reicha's alterations to the climactic passage in the fourteenth bar. In Haydn's symphony, this bar introduces an entirely new rhythmic gesture, in which a dotted quaver moves through a semiquaver to a high C♯. This new figure is just one feature that draws attention to this prominent moment in the melody: the C♯ is by far the highest note so far encountered, and the passage presents the only time the two-bar figure ends with an upward leap. All previous leaps had descended.

Although Reicha's changes might seem minor, they could not be incorporated into Haydn's symphony without significant damage to the large-scale contrasts that distinguish this movement. This Andante is cast in the Haydnesque theme-and-variations design that Elaine Sisman has called 'alternating variations'.[16] The movement presents two themes: the first – the one Reicha invokes – is in A major and begins with a dotted rhythm that prepares for the use of short rhythmic values in the accompaniment. The second theme (given in Example 9.5) is clearly related in some aspects of melodic contour, but it employs the parallel minor and presents a flowing accompanimental figure that contrasts with the detached figures in the opening theme.

Because Reicha's alteration of the initial upbeat figure eliminates this source of contrast, it seems obvious that he is not concerned with the large-scale structural

[15] Charles Rosen, *The Classical Style: Haydn, Mozart, Beethoven* (New York: Norton, 1972), p. 87.

[16] Elaine R. Sisman, *Haydn and the Classical Variation* (Cambridge, Mass.: Harvard University Press, 1993), pp. 159–60.

Example 9.5   Joseph Haydn, Symphony No. 53, Andante, second theme

implications of Haydn's rhythms. Instead, the changes seem designed to make Haydn's theme more singable and thus more 'melodic' in the eighteenth-century sense of giving priority to *vocal* melody.[17] The pitch alterations certainly fall into this category: the revision of bar 9 creates a much more manageable melodic contour, just as the elimination of the high C♯ keeps the melody within the span of an eleventh, which is certainly more comfortable than the original range of slightly less than two octaves. Moreover, the recomposition of bar 14 eliminates a complexity that characterises the original orchestral setting: in Haydn's version, the semiquaver A♮ sounds against G♯ and B♮ in the inner parts, compounding the challenges this line poses to a singer.[18] That Reicha felt the need to alter the original theme may reflect the common contemporaneous criticism of Haydn, in which it was often asserted that his music was instrumental – not vocal – in nature.[19]

But Reicha's changes in bar 14 also happen to serve his theoretical position. As noted earlier, he is advancing a perspective in which melody is spun out of symmetrical patterns. In its original form, Haydn's theme may actually suggest the opposite: the prominence given to bar 14 suggests that the psychological effect of this melody is achieved by *departing* from symmetry – that the opening series of balanced units merely serves to create expectations that can later be exploited by introducing an irregularity. Such is the plan of the first part of the famous theme from the Andante of Haydn's *Surprise* Symphony, which also sets up a regular pattern of rhythmic units, only to depart memorably from the initial model when the opening phrases are repeated. From this perspective, the symmetrical patterns that are so important to Reicha merely provide a background against which asymmetrical moments can emerge in bold relief. Indeed, Reicha's own drum pattern in Example *A* suggests a sensitivity to the power of asymmetry, in that the anomalous semiquaver group in division four helps create a sense of closure.

Although such asymmetries might simply reflect the common eighteenth-century desire to balance unity with variety, it is possible to interpret Haydn's original theme as seriously undercutting the point Reicha wishes to make. The modifications of bar 14 in Example *H* of the *Traité de mélodie* seem designed to eliminate such possibly contradictory matters from consideration.

[17] See Gretchen A. Wheelock, *Haydn's Ingenious Jesting with Art: Contexts of Musical Wit and Humor* (New York: Schirmer, 1992), p. 41, and John Neubauer, *The Emancipation of Music from Language: Departure from Mimesis in Eighteenth-Century Aesthetics* (New Haven: Yale University Press, 1986), pp. 64–70.

[18] James Webster refers to the underlying harmony here as 'a highly dissonant triple suspension–resolution into the I⁶ chord'. See his 'Haydn's Symphonies Between *Sturm und Drang* and "Classical Style": Art and Entertainment', in *Haydn Studies*, ed. W. Dean Sutcliffe (Cambridge: Cambridge University Press, 1998), p. 235.

[19] See, for example, the criticism in *Zeitung für die elegante Welt* for 22 December 1801 (No. 153), cited in H. C. Robbins Landon, *Haydn: Chronicle and Works*, 5 vols. (Bloomington: Indiana University Press, 1976–80), vol. IV, p. 600.

The need for such changes also illustrates another problematic aspect of Reicha's position: there are very few distinguished melodies that actually exemplify the type of symmetrical construction that the theorist portrays as foundational.[20] Reicha therefore did not have many options in choosing a theme to convey his central ideas, and yet he obviously needed some piece of music – preferably a well-known work – to exemplify the basic conditions of his theory. This need may have led to Reicha's alterations of Haydn's melody.

The paucity of works that actually conform to the elemental type of uniformity exemplified in Reicha's Example *A* requires that he both exaggerate the number of such passages and – ultimately – downplay the significance of strict regularity within the symmetrical units. Later in the *Traité de mélodie*, Reicha states that

Only rarely in a period [*période*] is there a phrase [*membre*] that is not composed of two rhythmic figures [*dessins*], whether similar or not. Sometimes a single figure dominates the entire period, as we have seen above in the period of Haydn (see Example *H*), where the following figure [Reicha here refers to the two bars that begin Haydn's theme] is repeated eight times in succession, that is, two times in each member of the period. Frequently a single figure may dominate in a period, as in the example cited; at other times there are two figures that alternate in the period; frequently the same figure is repeated with some modifications; at other times all the figures are different. In short, in this there is a great variety between periods and their members. But phrase length [*rhythme*] is a completely different thing: it is not susceptible to many changes.[21]

[20] A preliminary survey of the opening material in movements of Haydn's symphonies reveals that a large number of the composer's themes (particularly in the later works) begin with a series of repeated rhythmic units in the manner of Symphony No. 53/ii. The vast majority of these, however, depart from symmetrical formations near the conclusion of the theme. For example, Symphonies Nos. 87/ii, 99/i (after the slow introduction) and 99/iv abandon such patterns in the seventh bar. Themes in rounded binary form, such as found in Symphony No. 88/iv, often move away from a regular rhythmic structure in the central section. At times, Haydn uses the gesture that disturbs the equilibrium as the basis for further developments; see, for example, Symphony No. 85/ii, where the figure of bar 19 becomes very prominent at the close of the movement and also serves in the foreshortening of the second variation. Symphony No. 92/iv, on the other hand, has a theme that almost conforms perfectly to Reicha's account (bars 8 and 16 depart only slightly from the established rhythmic pattern). As the movement unfolds, however, the composer introduces asymmetry into subsequent versions of the theme (as in bars 98–105, 114–21, and 299–312); the dramatic silence introduced into bars 120–1 may therefore be seen as a response to the particular constitution of the theme, rather than an example of Haydn's general penchant for 'comic fooling'. When a theme actually does exhibit the type of regularity described by Reicha, Haydn often handles it with particular care. The antecedent and consequent phrases of the theme in Symphony No. 55/ii provide a wonderful example of Reicha's premises, but Haydn separates these phrases (bars 1–8 and 17–24) with written-out varied reprises (bars 9–16 and 25–32) that introduce variety in the form of new figurations.

Some of Haydn's most extraordinary passages stem from the technique of following a series of symmetrical rhythmic units with material that diverges from the established pattern. The remarkable opening theme to the first movement of the String Quartet in E♭ Major, Op. 76 No. 6, contains an initial eight-bar unit that is answered by a phrase extended to a length of twenty-eight bars.

[21] Reicha, *Traité de mélodie*, pp. 12–13. For a recent discussion of Reicha's terminology, see Nancy Kovaleff Baker, 'An *Ars Poetica* for Music: Reicha's System of Syntax and Structure', in *Musical Humanism and its Legacy: Essays in Honor of Claude V. Palisca*, ed. Nancy Kovaleff Baker and Barbara Russano Hanning (Stuyvesant, NY: Pendragon Press, 1992), pp. 419–49.

Reicha's here progresses from practices that appear 'rarely' (*rarement*), those found 'sometimes' (*quelquefois*), and those occurring 'frequently' (*souvent*) until he arrives at a consideration that is portrayed as almost invariable. In this progression, Reicha quietly increases the presence of the procedures exemplified in his version of Haydn's theme: the use of a single figure is initially portrayed as only an occasional practice, but Reicha immediately amplifies its significance by citing its 'frequent' use. He then moves to a level that subsumes altogether the level of structure he has been examining: the *rhythme* is introduced as a unit whose length is absolutely determined by its relationship with the length of its accompanying unit. This need for a balanced presentation of phrase lengths, according to Reicha, 'does not permit (like the *dessin*) an arbitrary treatment'.[22] The content of the *rhythme* (the number of bars in the unit) is seen to be limited by its complementary *rhythme*, whereas the content of the *dessin* is entirely unrestricted. Following Reicha's use of the *dessin* as the starting point for his account of melody, it is quite striking to find that its internal constitution may be treated arbitrarily.

All this serves to reinforce a difficulty that arises when Reicha first compares the two types of drum patterns, for it is not at all clear why the symmetrical pattern of Example *A* should be preferred to the additive pattern found in Example *B*. That is, there seems little reason not to regard Reicha's fundamental presumptions – like the contents of his basic units – as arising arbitrarily.

It is therefore imperative that Reicha find some way to justify his position, and he provides grounds for his views in a footnote to the passage cited above in which the two drum patterns are compared. To support his advocacy of symmetrical organisation, he asserts that the rhythmic gesture of Example *A* 'would already be music to a savage people, as voyagers assure us'.[23] According to Reicha's unnamed travellers, it seems, such a pattern is itself a type of melody, just as he maintains in his next paragraphs, where he says that 'all symmetrical motion presents a species of regular melody'.[24] The strategy behind invoking these savages seems straightforward: by asserting that symmetry is a basic condition for even the music of savages, Reicha elevates his personal preference to the status of a universal principle.

Reicha's footnote seems designed to answer questions concerning the importance of symmetry, but there is nothing self-evident about his appeal: after all, why should the preferences of the savage serve as authority for a theoretical position advanced in nineteenth-century Paris? Such primitives could just as easily be eliminated from consideration, as in discussion of national styles in Johann Joachim Quantz's 1752 *Versuch*. There it is stated that each nation has something in its music that is more pleasing to it than to others, 'except among barbarians'.[25] Quantz's point would have been made just as well by reversing it – by saying that '*Even* barbarians find something in their music that they prefer to other styles.' But Quantz – that central figure in

---

[22] Reicha, *Traité de mélodie*, p. 13.   [23] *Ibid.*, p. 9.   [24] *Ibid.*
[25] Johann Joachim Quantz, *On Playing the Flute*, trans. Edward R. Reilly, 2nd edn (New York: Schirmer, 1985), p. 320.

Frederick the Great's expansionist Prussia – simply asserts that not even barbarians could prefer their own music. Here the primitive music of savages represents a type of negative space, a vacuum that could be filled, one presumes, by some European style in favour at Frederick's court.

Reicha's invocation of the savage, on the other hand, seeks to establish symmetry as a component of all music, and he thereby attempts to imply its natural and universal qualities. Although appeals to the natural became common after Rousseau, this footnote may clearly be seen as an example of the tendency of civilisation's Other to resurface in European discourse during the articulation or re-evaluation of organising principles. The opening pages of a treatise, of course, must establish foundational premises in an authoritative manner. This process poses particular difficulties for Reicha because his basic presumptions concerning symmetry are only weakly supported by the musical example he has chosen. Reicha's invocation of the savage seems to stem precisely from the type of anxiety that accompanies the assertion of premises that are – at bottom – arbitrary.

This anxiety may stem, in part, from Reicha's confrontation with a prior theoretical orientation. An examination of earlier writings suggests that his remarks belong to a tradition that he is trying to both subsume and subvert. There are, for example, strong parallels between the *Traité* and the article on 'Musik' in Johann Georg Sulzer's *Allgemeine Theorie der schönen Künste*, which appeared in the early 1770s. Sulzer, however, traces the origins of music to a rhythmic pattern more like Example *B* than Haydn's Symphony No. 53:

We find enjoyable any measured movement proceeding in regular beats such as walking: such rhythmic regularity sustains our attention in tasks that would otherwise be wearisome. This is known or felt by the least reflective of men . . .

This measured motion can be easily joined to a series of musical sounds, since musical sounds themselves always imply an idea of movement . . . On the basis of these observations, one should not be surprised to find that the most primitive of peoples have discovered music, and taken at least a few steps toward its perfection.[26]

From this, Sulzer concludes that music is 'an art that is rooted in the nature of man' with 'immutable principles'. He contrasts this view with the 'prejudice widely held in music (but also in other arts) against universal principles'.[27] This prejudice against universals is based on the type of national preferences mentioned by Quantz: Sulzer characterises this view as asserting that 'the Chinese have no ear for European music, while Europeans cannot bear to hear Chinese music. The conclusion, then, is that this art has no general principles grounded in human nature.'[28] Sulzer thus places the exotic Other at the centre of a debate over universal principles.

To argue for the existence of such universals, he notes that music must arouse emotions, which requires sustaining sound in a manner so that it does not lose energy.

---

[26] Cited in Nancy Kovaleff Baker and Thomas Christensen (eds.), *Aesthetics and the Art of Musical Composition in the German Enlightenment: Selected Writings of Johann Georg Sulzer and Heinrich Christoph Koch* (Cambridge: Cambridge University Press, 1995), p. 82.   [27] *Ibid.*, pp. 82–3.   [28] *Ibid.*, p. 83.

This would allow the attention of the listener to wander. In sustaining sound, metre becomes essential:

All people with any degree of sensitivity feel this, whether they be Siberians, Indians, Iroquois, or the refined Greeks. Whenever there is meter and rhythm, there is order and rule. This is the first principle [of music] obeyed by all people.[29]

Sulzer notes the almost infinite variety of metre and that this variety is reflected in the many kinds of dance melodies. However, 'Only general rules of order and regularity remain the same everywhere.'[30]

So far, all this corresponds with Reicha's account, including the emphasis on rhythmic regularity as a generating principle. Sulzer, however, goes on to note that 'more primitive folk desire less variety and not such determined symmetry in their music as do people who have a more cultured sensibility for beauty'. Nevertheless, according to Sulzer, 'differences in taste here – as in other arts – do not demonstrate the absence of any firm basis of human nature'.[31] The universal rules of order, then, operate at a level *deeper* than the symmetry Reicha regards as fundamental. But Reicha's subsequent perspective requires an absolute differentiation between the symmetrical and the sequential, and so his account must find a means of superseding Sulzer's.

When Sulzer traces the origins of music to a rhythmic pattern more like Example *B* than Haydn's Symphony No. 53, he participates in a tradition that has more distant, and even more authoritative, antecedents. Rameau, in the 1722 *Traité de l'harmonie* stated that 'meter comes naturally to every one: it forces us, as if against our will, to follow its movement and we cannot claim to be insensitive to it under ordinary circumstances'.[32] Rameau goes on to observe:

Furthermore, since meter depends upon an equal series of movements, we may reduce it to two beats, as the space of time placed between the first and the second movements continues naturally with regularity. The truth of this may be seen by our experience with all natural movements, such as walking, clapping our hands, or shaking our head several times. All our movements will certainly be equal to the first two movements, unless we expressly alter them, exercising our will against nature.[33]

Walking, clapping, and the shaking of heads are all examples of additive organisation, and they are certainly better represented conceptually by Reicha's Example *B* than by Haydn's Andante. Moreover, Reicha's basically empirical approach, with its emphasis upon 'experience' (as seen in his statement quoted above, that 'Experience teaches us that we feel a certain pleasure' in symmetrical, well-cadenced motions) is in direct conflict with the orientation Rameau advances in the first paragraph of his Preface. As the opening gesture of his text, Rameau notes how 'we neglect today all the advantages to be derived from the use of reason in favour of purely practical experience',

---

[29] *Ibid.*   [30] *Ibid.*   [31] *Ibid.*

[32] Jean-Philippe Rameau, *Treatise on Harmony*, trans. Philip Gossett (New York: Dover, 1971), p. 164.

[33] *Ibid.*, p. 165. As Philip Gossett observes in his notes to this passage, Rameau suppressed the final clause quoted here in the Supplement he appended to his text.

and he complains that 'one might say that reason has lost its rights, while experience has acquired a certain authority'.[34] And so Reicha's use of experience as a basis for authority represents in many ways a challenge to the rationalistic emphasis of his great predecessor.

Reicha has, however, also implicitly challenged a luminary even more central to the French intellectual tradition, for Rameau drew upon René Descartes as authority for the view that 'meter comes naturally to everyone', even animals, who 'might be taught to dance metrically, if they were so trained or if they became accustomed to it over a long period of time. All that is needed for this is effort and natural movement.'[35] Descartes's *Compendium Musicae*, which was written in 1618 but not published until after his death in 1650, emphasises the physical impact of sound, which 'strikes all bodies on all sides, and which therefore has a great impact on our spirits, and thus rouses us to motion'. It follows, Descartes reasons, that animals can be taught to dance, as the physical stimulus itself achieves this reaction.[36]

At this point, Descartes defers a detailed investigation of the movements of the soul. (This of course will appear in his later writings on the passions.) He finds, however, that he cannot resist saying that

time in music has such power that it alone can be pleasurable by itself; such is the case with the military drum, where we have nothing [to perceive] but the beat; in this case I am of the opinion that here the meter can be composed not only of two or three units but perhaps even of five, seven, or more. For with such an instrument the ear has nothing to occupy its attention except the time; therefore, there can be more variety in time in order to hold the attention.[37]

René Descartes, it appears, could listen quite happily to rhythmic patterns that Reicha would consider annoying and boring after a few bars. It is now possible to posit further reasons why Reicha might have experienced the type of internalised crisis of authority described earlier. All these passages quoted above present foundational presumptions: Descartes and Rameau assert the universal mechanical effect of sound, Sulzer modifies this to propose a universal aesthetic desire for regularity, and finally Reicha, rejecting aspects of this authoritative theoretical tradition, attempts to limit the desire for regularity to a universal pleasure in symmetry.

In 1814, of course, Reicha's classical orientation already represented an embattled aesthetic; Beethoven's works, for example, had already begun to explore modes of organisation very different from the symmetrical phrasing often found in Haydn and Mozart. The confrontation with new artistic principles would in itself be disconcerting, as the conflict makes palpable the arbitrariness of Reicha's beliefs. Moreover, Reicha has chosen a difficult starting point, as revealed by the numerous modifications to Haydn's Symphony No. 53. Compounding the situation is Reicha's implicit rejection of a distinguished theoretical tradition dating back to Descartes. The appearance of the savage in the *Traité de mélodie* appears to stem from an under-

---

[34] *Ibid.*, p. xxxiii.   [35] *Ibid.*, p. 164.
[36] René Descartes, *Compendium of Music*, trans. Walter Robert, notes by Charles Kent (n.p.: American Institute of Musicology, 1961), p. 15.   [37] Descartes, *Compendium*, p. 15.

standable concern for the authoritative assertion of foundational principles. As in many passages in European writings, an arbitrary concept of liminal man emerges to validate the central tenets of a theoretical perspective.

Moreover, Reicha's anxiety seems absolutely justified, because one of the dangers attending the West's encounter with the primitive was the possibility – if not inevitability – that one could stumble on the Scale of Being and become more like the barbaric Other. This danger may provide insights into one of the most inexplicable, yet one of the most consistent, rhythmic modifications Reicha imposes on Haydn's melody. Given Reicha's own theories, it is not at all clear why he replaces the dotted semiquaver and a demisemiquaver with two even semiquavers. This modification, after all, does nothing to make the passage more symmetrical, and it therefore seems entirely unnecessary.

But because he will attempt to justify his perspective by invoking the musical practices of savage people, Reicha must make the rhythm of Example *A* conform to what his nineteenth-century European readership could believe about the rhythmic practices of primitive man. Given such a readership, Haydn's dotted rhythms might have seemed too intricate to be plausibly attributed to non-Europeans. It may therefore have seemed necessary to make Haydn's music less complex – which is to say, more primitive. And so Reicha's modifications represent Haydn in a manner that imposes primitiveness upon him. In order to use the barbarian as a source of authority, Reicha must make Haydn resemble the savages that populate his own imagination.

The irony of all this, of course, is that Reicha's imagination is limited – far too limited – by the relatively homogeneous rhythmic practices of late eighteenth-century European art music. Many non-Western cultures employ rhythmic patterns of far greater complexity and subtlety than anything found in the Andante of *L'Impériale*. And so, once again, a completely fictitious concept of the savage becomes inscribed in the foundational presumptions of Western thought. This fiction has enormous consequences, for Reicha lived at the time when music was beginning to be hailed as a universal language.

This view can be found in a number of German writers at the end of the eighteenth century, and the assertion is repeated in the final footnote in Reicha's text: 'Not only is music a language in itself without recourse to words, but it is also a universal language, superior to all others that are only conventional, and that cannot be understood without having been learned.'[38]

The savages that Reicha imagined, however, acted to limit what could plausibly be seen as universal, and therefore he had to eliminate some intricacies from Haydn's theme. The need for such alterations suggests that the theorist saw a gulf opening between contemporaneous musical practice and the understanding that might be expected of the average listener. This gulf would come to be regarded as a commonplace; it appears in the nineteenth century's tendency to characterise the composer as an isolated individual who struggled against the incomprehension of the general

---

[38] Reicha, *Traité de mélodie*, p. 105.

audience. This sense of isolation has perhaps only deepened in the twentieth century, particularly among creative artists whose music exhibits a high degree of technical complexity. By envisioning music as a universal language, and by using an artificial standard of the savage as an authority for the basic presumptions of that language, writers such as Reicha introduced a perspective that would transform the composer – like the primitives of the European imagination – into a figure on the margins of society.

In light of the dangers of using barbarians as a source of authority for an aesthetic perspective, it seems necessary to inquire – at least briefly – into the location of the primitive in modern music theory. It appears that something has happened to the savages, to the wild creatures, and to the feral children that once haunted the pages of scholarly discourse. Ethnomusicology – which might seem a place to look for such characterisations – is now highly reluctant to portray its subjects as primitive, nor is this discipline inclined to use its detailed research as a basis for sweeping generalisations concerning universals of human behaviour. Moreover, one of the savage's most necessary attributes was physical and psychological inaccessibility – an absolute remoteness – that allowed the West free play for its fantasies. Ethnomusicology, as now constituted, struggles continuously against this very sense of distance.[39]

It may be that the savage, no longer available in the world outside, has been repositioned. For music theory, the functions provided by the primitive Other now seem to have been internalised, and it is now the subconscious that serves as a slate upon which to map both our fantasies and our foundational presumptions. Such a usage can be seen in a passage written by Kenneth Levy, a prominent scholar whose excellent introductory textbook *Music: A Listener's Introduction* was used for many years in American universities. The following excerpt is taken from a discussion of sonata form – certainly an important concept in current thought on music – and emphasises the importance of the beginning of the recapitulation in sonata form:

The chief event in any sonata-allegro movement comes as the development ends and the recapitulation begins. At this point the developmental fragmentations and tonal peregrinations are at an end and the opening theme and opening key reappear, coordinated as they were at the beginning of the exposition . . . The development can reach out to keys that have only a slight relation to the home key. Yet even at the farthest point in the tonal journey, the organizing force of the home key is felt in the background of our memory. Each key that is visited is linked subconsciously to the reference of the home key.[40]

This passage reflects the influence of Levy's colleague at Princeton University, Edward T. Cone, whose codification of the so-called 'sonata principle' is a touchstone of current thought on the design.

Cone maintains that, in sonata form, important material presented in a key other

---

[39] Ethnographic work of the past few decades often casts the anthropologist in the role of the isolated outsider, thus projecting an order that reverses the presumptions of the past.

[40] Kenneth Levy, *Music: A Listener's Introduction* (New York: Harper and Row, 1983), p. 163.

than the tonic 'must either be re-stated in the tonic, or brought into a closer relation with the tonic, before the movement ends'.[41] This principle leads to a metaphor, in which non-tonic material is regarded as a dissonance that must be resolved by its restatement in the home key. This is now often presented as a governing principle of the sonata designs of such composers as Haydn, Mozart, and Beethoven. The large-scale manipulation of tension and release, of course, would go undetected if our subconscious could not recognise the moments of tonal resolution represented by the beginning of the recapitulation and the transposition of initially dissonant material into the tonic. As seen in Levy's brief discussion, it is a foundational presumption of twentieth-century sonata theory that the subconscious is able to perform these functions.

The problem, of course, is that the subconscious appears to do nothing of the sort. This foundational experience, so vividly heard by those who hold the necessary paradigms, is as fantastic and arbitrary as the perception of those Americans with square blue heads. Nicholas Cook published in 1987 the results of a series of experiments, in which he demonstrated that listeners expressed no significant statistical preference for musical works that end in the home key over works subtly modified so as to end outside the tonic.[42] Cook's subjects did not exhibit a sense of discomfort at the absence of tonal resolution, despite the importance of some desire for resolution in modern notions of the workings of sonata form. Cook's research suggests that there is no subconscious process such as that described by Levy.

But perhaps we should not expect listeners to remember or recognise the tonic key: the writings of eighteenth-century theorists exhibit a significant number of passages in which young composers are explicitly advised to return to the tonic *soon after the central repeat signs*, precisely so that the audience will not forget the location of the tonic. Such accounts range from Christian Ziegler's general discussion of tonal form in 1739, Joseph Riepel's writings of 1755, and Carlo Gervasoni's description of sonata form in 1800.[43] These authors are not alone in their advocacy of such tonal returns, for such theorists as Löhlein, Koch, Galeazzi and Reicha all mention the practice, or cite works with such returns as exemplars of sonata form.[44] If we accept

---

[41] Edward T. Cone, *Musical Form and Musical Performance* (New York: Norton, 1968), p. 77.

[42] Nicholas Cook, 'The Perception of Large-Scale Tonal Closure', *Music Perception* 5 (1987), 197–205.

[43] For a discussion of Christian Gottlieb Ziegler's *Anleitung zur musikalischen Composition* (manuscript in the Drexel collection of the New York Public Library), see Fred Ritzel, *Die Entwicklung der 'Sonatenform' in musiktheoretischen Schrifttum des 18. und 19. Jahrhunderts*, 2nd edn (Wiesbaden: Breitkopf und Härtel, 1969), p. 56; Joseph Riepel, *Grundregeln zur Tonordnung insgemein* (Ulm: Christian Ulrich Wagner, 1755), p. 67; and Carlo Gervasoni, *Scuola della Musica* (Piacenza: N. Orcesi, 1800), p. 467.

[44] Georg Simon Löhlein, *Clavier-Schule* (Leipzig and Züllichau: Waisenhaus und Frommanische Buchhandlung, 1765), p. 181; Heinrich Christoph Koch, *Versuch einer Anleitung zur Composition*, 3 vols. (Leipzig: A. F. Böhme, 1793; rpt Hildesheim: Georg Olms, 1969), vol. III, pp. 307–11; Bathia Churgin, 'Francesco Galeazzi's Description (1796) of Sonata Form', *Journal of the American Musicological Society* 21 (1968), 198 (noting the articulation of the tonic in bar 32); and the analyses in Reicha, *Traité de mélodie*, pp. 43–50, as well as the discussions of the Woodwind Quintet in F minor in Antoine Reicha, *Traité de haute composition musicale* (1826), vol. II, pp. 290–2, and second part of the *grande coupe binaire* in general (pp. 298–300).

these contemporaneous explanations for these passages, it is clear that during the eighteenth century, nobody was expected to feel 'the organizing force of the home key' in the background of their memory, nor would it be held that 'each key that is visited is linked subconsciously to the reference of the home key'. The writers of the past recognised the possibility of a type of tonal amnesia that modern theorists have presumed to be impossible.

This returns us to the important question, briefly mentioned above in connection to Reicha's discussion of rhythmic patterns, concerning the forces that generate a musical work. Modern music theory has come to regard the tonal composition as the expansion of a fundamental progression similar to a cadential formula. This model requires the participation of the subconscious, particularly in the ability to recognise the return of important tonal areas. But there is no evidence that the subconscious actually performs this way or that eighteenth-century composers *expected* it to perform this way. It seems that the subconscious – like the savage before it – serves as an area for the inscription of both our foundational presumptions and our fantasies.

The appeal to the subconscious is so fundamental to the authority of modern analytical discourse that there may be no way to eliminate it from our interpretations. The belief that the mind harbours hidden workings has now been incorporated into twentieth-century concepts of human nature, just as the existence of savages entered into the self-understanding of the Early Modern period. Within such circumstances, what become significant are the moments when it is necessary for an author to invoke the subconscious during the assertion of a theoretical position. If the re-emergence of the primitive in Enlightenment theory is a sign of some form of anxiety, what sort of crisis is represented by modern appeals to the subconscious? Recent analytical writings suggest that such anxiety is often associated with interpretative procedures that reveal structures that could not have arisen consciously during composition or could not have been expected to be heard in performance. At such points, we now call upon the subconscious to lend authority to perspectives that may be no less arbitrary – but also no less fundamental to our basic presumptions – than past constructions of the savage in the state of nature.

Bibliography

Abbate, Carolyn, *Unsung Voices: Opera and Musical Narrative in the Nineteenth Century*, Princeton: Princeton University Press, 1991.

Abrams, Meyer H., *The Mirror and the Lamp: Romantic Theory and the Critical Tradition*, Oxford: Oxford University Press, 1971.

Adler, Guido (ed.), *Handbuch der Musikgeschichte*, Frankfurt am Main: Frankfurter Verlagsanstalt, 1924.

Adorno, Theodor W., *Philosophie der neuen Musik*, Frankfurt am Main: Suhrkamp, 1949; trans. Anne G. Mitchell and Wesley V. Blomster as *Philosophy of Modern Music*, London: Sheed and Ward, 1987.

 Versuch über Wagner (1952); trans. Rodney Livingstone as *In Search of Wagner*, London: Verso, 1991.

 Aesthetic Theory, trans. Robert Hullot-Kentor, London: Athlone Press, 1995.

 Beethoven: Philosophie der Musik, Frankfurt am Main: Suhrkamp, 1993; trans. Edmund Jephcott as *Beethoven: The Philosophy of Music*, Cambridge: Polity Press, 1998.

Adorno, Theodor W. and Horkheimer, Max, *Dialectic of Enlightenment*, trans. John Cumming, London: Verso, 1979.

Albanese, Denise, *New Science, New World*, Durham, NC and London: Duke University Press, 1996.

Ammann, Peter J., 'The Musical Theory and Philosophy of Robert Fludd', *Journal of the Warburg and Courtauld Institutes* 30 (1967), 198–227.

Anon., *The Praise of Musicke*, Oxford: Joseph Barnes, 1586.

Aristotle, *The Complete Works of Aristotle: The Revised Oxford Translation*, 2 vols., ed. Jonathan Barnes, Bollingen Series LXXI.2, Princeton: Princeton University Press, 1984.

Ashworth, William B., 'Catholicism and Early Modern Science', in *God and Nature: Essays on the Encounters Between Christianity and Science*, ed. David C. Lindberg and Ronald L. Numbers, Berkeley and Los Angeles: University of California Press, 1986, pp. 136–66.

 'Natural History and the Emblematic World View', in *Reappraisals of the Scientific Revolution*, ed. David C. Lindberg and Robert S. Westman, Cambridge: Cambridge University Press, 1990, pp. 303–32.

Atcherson, W. T., 'Symposium on Seventeenth-Century Music Theory – England', *Journal of Music Theory* 16 (1972), 6–15.

Atran, Scott, *Cognitive Foundations of Natural History: Toward an Anthropology of Science*, Cambridge: Cambridge University Press, 1990.

Bibliography

Austern, Linda Phyllis, 'Nature, Culture, Myth and the Musician in Early Modern England', *Journal of the American Musicological Society* 51 (1998), 1–49.

'The Siren, the Muse and the God of Love: Music in Seventeenth-Century English Emblem Books', *The Journal of Musicological Research* 18 (1999), 95–138.

'Musical Treatments for Lovesickness: The Early Modern Heritage', in *A History of Music Therapies from Antiquity*, ed. Peregrine Horden, Aldershot: Ashgate Publishing, 2000, pp. 213–45.

'"My Mother Musicke": Music and Early Modern Fantasies of Embodiment', in *Mothers and Others: Caregiver Figures in Early Modern Europe*, ed. Naomi Miller and Naomi Yavneh, Aldershot: Ashgate Publishing, 2000, pp. 239–81.

Baader, Franz von, *Beiträge zur Elementar-Physiologie*, in *Sämmtliche Werke* (1797), Leipzig: Hermann Bethmann, 1852.

Bacon, Francis, *The Twoo Bookes Of the Proficiencie and Advancement of Learning*, London: Henrie Tomes, 1605.

Sylva Sylvarum or a Naturall History, 2nd edn, London: W. Lee, 1629.

The Essays, Newly Enlarged, London: John Haviland, 1632.

Baker, Nancy Kovaleff, 'An *Ars Poetica* for Music: Reicha's System of Syntax and Structure', in *Musical Humanism and its Legacy: Essays in Honor of Claude V. Palisca*, ed. Nancy Kovaleff Baker and Barbara Russano Hanning, Stuyvesant, NY: Pendragon Press, 1992, pp. 419–49.

Baker, Nancy Kovaleff and Christensen, Thomas (eds.), *Aesthetics and the Art of Musical Composition in the German Enlightenment: Selected Writings of Johann Georg Sulzer and Heinrich Christoph Koch*, Cambridge: Cambridge University Press, 1995.

Barnes, Jonathan (ed.), *The Complete Works of Aristotle: The Revised Oxford Translation* (Princeton: Princeton University Press, 1984).

Batteux, Charles, *Les Beaux-Arts réduits à un même principe*, Paris: Durand, 1746; critical edn, Jean-Rémy Mantion, Paris: Aux Amateurs des Livres, 1989.

Bekker, Paul, *Beethoven*, Berlin: Schuster und Loeffler, 1912.

'Wohin treiben wir?', in *Kritische Zeitbilder*, Berlin: Schuster und Loeffler, 1921, pp. 247–59.

Bellermann, Heinrich, *Der Contrapunct*, Berlin: Julius Springer, 1862.

Bennett, Tony, *The Birth of the Museum: History, Theory, Politics*, London and New York: Routledge, 1995.

Bent, Ian (ed.), *Music Analysis in the Nineteenth Century*, 2 vols., Cambridge: Cambridge University Press, 1994.

Berlioz, Hector, review of Meyerbeer's *Les Huguenots*, in *Journal des débats* (10 November 1836), 1–2.

Bernstein, David W., 'Symmetry and Symmetrical Inversion in Turn-of-the-Century Theory and Practice', in *Music Theory and the Exploration of the Past*, ed. Christopher Hatch and David W. Bernstein, Chicago: University of Chicago Press, 1993, pp. 377–407.

Bevin, Elway, *A Briefe and Short Instruction of the Art of Musicke*, London: R. Young, 1631.

Bianconi, Lorenzo, *Music in the Seventeenth Century*, trans. David Bryant, Cambridge: Cambridge University Press, 1987.

Biddle, Ian, review of Ian Bent (ed.), *Music Analysis in the Nineteenth Century*, in *Music and Letters* 79 (1998), 120–6.

'Policing Masculinity: Schumann, Berlioz and the Gendering of the Music-critical Idiom', *Journal of the Royal Musical Association* 124 (1999), 40–64.

B[lount], T[homas], *Glossographia: Or a Dictionary Interpreting All Such Hard Words . . . As Are Now Used in Our Refined English Tongue*, London: Tho[mas] Newcomb for Humphrey Moseley, 1656.

Blasius, Leslie D., 'The Mechanics of Sensation and the Romantic Construction of Musical Experience', in *Music Theory in the Age of Romanticism*, ed. Ian Bent, Cambridge: Cambridge University Press, 1996, pp. 3–24.

    Schenker's Argument and the Claims of Music Theory, Cambridge: Cambridge University Press, 1997.

Blondel, Eric, *Nietzsche, le corps et la culture* (1986), trans. Seán Hand as *Nietzsche: The Body and Culture*, Stanford: Stanford University Press, 1991.

Blumenbach, Johann Friedrich, *Über den Bildungstrieb und Zeugungsgeschäfte*, Göttingen: Johann Christian Dieterich, 1781.

Boethius, Anicius Manlius Severinus, *De institutione musica*, trans. Calvin M. Bower as *Fundamentals of Music*, New Haven: Yale University Press, 1989.

Bonds, Mark Evan, *Wordless Rhetoric: Musical Form and the Metaphor of the Oration*, Cambridge, Mass. and London: Harvard University Press, 1991.

Bono, James J., *The Word of God and the Languages of Man: Interpreting Nature in Early Modern Science and Medicine*, vol. I: *Ficino to Descartes*, Madison: University of Wisconsin Press, 1995.

Bordo, Susan, 'The Cartesian Masculinization of Thought', in *Sex and Scientific Inquiry*, ed. Sandra Harding and Jean F. O'Barr, Chicago and London: University of Chicago Press, 1987, pp. 247–64.

Borgmann, Albert, 'The Nature of Reality and the Reality of Nature', in *Reinventing Nature? Responses to Postmodern Deconstruction*, ed. Michael E. Soulé and Gary Lease, Washington, DC and Covelo, Calif.: Island Press, 1995, pp. 31–46.

Brady, Nicholas, *Church-Musick Vindicated*, London: Joseph Wilde, 1697.

Brandis, Joachim Dietrich, *Versuch über die Lebenskraft*, Hanover: Hahn, 1795.

Brennecke, Ernest, Jr., 'Dryden's Odes and Draghi's Music', *Proceedings of the Modern Language Association* 49 (1934), 1–36.

Briscoe, Roger, 'Rameau's "Démonstration du principe de l'harmonie" and "Nouvelles réflexions": An Annotated Translation', Ph.D. thesis, Indiana University, 1975.

Brody, Martin, '"Music for the Masses": Milton Babbitt's Cold War Music Theory', *Musical Quarterly* 77 (1993), 161–92.

Bullokar, John, *An English Expositor: Teaching the Interpretation of the Hardest Words Used in Our Language*, London: John Leggatt, 1616.

Bülow, Gottfried von (ed. and trans.), 'Diary of the Journey of Philip Julius, Duke of Stettin-Pomerania, Through England in the Year 1602', *Transactions of the Royal Historical Society*, new series 6 (1892), 1–67.

Burke, John G., 'The Wild Man's Pedigree: Scientific Method and Racial Anthropology', in *The Wild Man Within: An Image in Western Thought from the Renaissance to Romanticism*, ed. Edward Dudley and Maximillian E. Novak, Pittsburgh: University of Pittsburgh Press, 1972, pp. 259–80.

Burke, Peter, *Popular Culture in Early Modern Europe*, New York: Harper and Row, 1978.

    'Fables of the Bees: A Case-Study of Views of Nature and Society', in *Nature and Society in Historical Context*, ed. Mikuláš Teich, Roy Porter and Bo Gustafsson, Cambridge: Cambridge University Press, 1997, pp. 112–23.

Burnett, Charles, Fend, Michael and Gouk, Penelope (eds.), *The Second Sense: Studies in Hearing*

Bibliography

and Musical Judgment from Antiquity to the Seventeenth Century, London: Warburg Institute, 1991.

Burnham, Scott, 'Criticism, Faith, and the *Idee*: A. B. Marx's Early Reception of Beethoven', *19th-Century Music* 13 (1990), 183–92.

Beethoven Hero, Princeton: Princeton University Press, 1995.

'How Music Matters: Poetic Content Revisited', in *Rethinking Music*, ed. Nicholas Cook and Mark Everist, Oxford: Oxford University Press, 1999, pp. 193–216.

Busoni, Ferruccio, *Sketch to a New Esthetics of Music*, in *Three Classics in the Aesthetics of Music*, trans. Th. Baker, New York: Dover, 1962.

Butler, Charles, *The Feminine Monarchie or the History of Bees*, London: John Haviland for Roger Jackson, 1623.

The Principles of Musik, in Singing and Setting, London: John Haviland, 1636.

Campion, Thomas, *The Art of Descant: Or, Composing of Musick in Parts*, annotated by Chr[isto-pher] Simpson, London: John Playford, 1674.

Carpenter, Nan Cooke, 'Charles Butler and the Bees' Madrigal', *Notes and Queries* n.s. 2 (1955), 103–6.

Case, John, *Apologia musices tam vocalis quam instrumentalis et mixtae*, Oxford: Joseph Barnes, 1588.

Céard, Jean, *La Nature et les prodiges: l'insolite au XVIe siècle, en France*, Geneva: Librairie Droz, 1977.

Chandler, Glenn, 'Rameau's "Nouveau système de musique théorique": An Annotated Translation with Commentary', Ph.D. thesis, Indiana University, 1975.

Chartier, Roger, 'Text, Symbols and Frenchness', *Journal of Modern History* 57 (1985), 682–95.

'Texts, Printings, Readings', in *The New Cultural History*, ed. Lynn Hunt, Berkeley and Los Angeles: University of California Press, 1989, pp. 154–75.

La correspondance: Les usages de la lettre au XIXe siècle, Paris: Fayard, 1991.

The Order of Books: Reader, Authors, and Libraries in Europe between the Fourteenth and Eighteenth Centuries, trans. Lydia G. Cochrane, Stanford: Stanford University Press, 1994.

Forms and Meanings: Texts, Performances, and Audiences from Codex to Computer, Philadelphia: University of Pennsylvania Press, 1995.

Chartier, Roger (ed.), *The Culture of Print: Power and the Uses of Print in Early Modern Europe*, trans. Lydia G. Cochrane, Princeton: Princeton University Press, 1989.

Cherlin, Michael, 'Hauptmann and Schenker: Two Adaptations of Hegelian Dialectics', *Theory and Practice* 13 (1988), 117–31.

Chomsky, Noam, *Aspects of the Theory of Syntax*, Cambridge, Mass.: MIT Press, 1965.

Rules and Representations, Cambridge, Mass.: Blackwell, 1980.

Knowledge of Language: Its Nature, Origin, and Use, New York: Praeger, 1986.

Christensen, Thomas, 'The *Règle de l'octave* in Thorough-Bass Theory and Practice', *Acta musicologica* 64 (1992), 91–117.

Rameau and Musical Thought in the Enlightenment, Cambridge: Cambridge University Press, 1993.

'*Sensus, Ratio*, and *Phthongos*: Mattheson's Theory of Tone Perception', in *Musical Transformation and Musical Intuition: Eleven Essays in Honor of David Lewin*, ed. Raphael Atlas and Michael Cherlin, Dedham, Mass.: Ovenbird Press, 1994, pp. 1–22.

Chua, Daniel K. L., *Absolute Music and the Construction of Meaning*, Cambridge: Cambridge University Press, 1999.

Churgin, Bathia, 'Francesco Galeazzi's Description (1796) of Sonata Form', *Journal of the American Musicological Society* 21 (1968), 181–99.

Cohen, Bernard, *Revolution in Science*, Cambridge, Mass.: Harvard University Press, 1985.

Cohen, H. F., *Quantifying Music: The Science of Music at the First Stage of the Scientific Revolution, 1580–1650*, Dordrecht, Boston and Lancaster: D. Reidel Publishing Company, 1984.

Cone, Edward T., *Musical Form and Musical Performance*, New York: Norton, 1968.

Connolly, Thomas, *Mourning into Joy: Music, Raphael, and St. Cecilia*, New Haven and London: Yale University Press, 1994.

Cook, Harold J., 'The New Philosophy and Medicine in Seventeenth-Century England', in *Reappraisals of the Scientific Revolution*, ed. David C. Lindberg and Robert S. Westman, Cambridge: Cambridge University Press, 1990, pp. 397–436.

Cook, Nicholas, 'The Perception of Large-Scale Tonal Closure', *Music Perception* 5 (1987), 197–205.

Cook, Vivian J. and Newson, Mark, *Chomsky's Universal Grammar: An Introduction*, 2nd edn, Cambridge, Mass.: Blackwell, 1996.

Cooper, Barry, 'Englische Musiktheorie im 17. und 18. Jahrhundert', in *Entstehung nationaler Traditionen: Frankreich [und] England*, ed. Barry Cooper and Wilhelm Seidel, in *Geschichte der Musiktheorie*, vol. IX, Darmstadt: Wissenschaftliche Buchgesellschaft, 1986, pp. 141–314.

Cottingham, John, *Descartes*, Oxford: Blackwell, 1986.

Crystal, David, *A Dictionary of Linguistics and Phonetics*, 3rd edn, Cambridge, Mass.: Blackwell, 1991.

d'Indy, Vincent, *Cours de composition musicale*, 3 vols., 3rd edn, Paris: A. Durand, 1912.

Dahlhaus, Carl, '"Von zwei Kulturen der Musik": Die Schlußfuge aus Beethovens Cellosonate op. 102, 2', *Die Musikforschung* 31 (1978), 397–405.

    'Zur Formidee in Beethovens d-moll-Sonate op. 31, 2', *Die Musikforschung* 33 (1980), 310–12.

    Die Musiktheorie im 18. und 19. Jahrhundert: Erster Teil, Grundzüge einer Systematik, Darmstadt: Wissenschaftliche Buchgesellschaft, 1984.

    Die Musiktheorie im 18. und 19. Jahrhundert: Zweiter Teil, Deutschland, ed. Ruth E. Müller, Darmstadt: Wissenschaftliche Buchgesellschaft, 1989.

    Ludwig van Beethoven: Approaches to his Music, trans. Mary Whittall, Oxford: Clarendon Press, 1991.

Darnton, Robert, 'Readers Respond to Rousseau: The Fabrication of Romantic Sensitivity', in *The Great Cat Massacre and Other Episodes in French Cultural History*, New York: Basic Books, 1984, pp. 215–56.

Darwin, Charles, *The Descent of Man and Selection in Relation to Sex*, intro. John Tyler Bonner and Robert M. May, 2 vols. in 1, Princeton: Princeton University Press, 1981.

Daston, Lorraine, and Park, Katharine, *Wonders and the Order of Nature 1150–1750*, New York: Zone Books, 1998.

Davies, Catherine Glyn, *Conscience as Consciousness: The Idea of Self-Awareness in French Philosophical Writing from Descartes to Diderot*, Studies on Voltaire and the Eighteenth Century, No. 272, Oxford: The Voltaire Foundation, 1990.

Day, John, *Days Descant on Davids Psalmes*, Oxford: John Lichfield and James Short, 1610.

de Certeau, Michel, *The Writing of History*, trans. Tom Conley, New York: Columbia University Press, 1988.

de Man, Paul, *Romanticism and Contemporary Criticism: The Gauss Seminar and Other Papers*, ed. E. S.

Burt, Kevin Newmark and Andrzej Warminski, Baltimore and London: Johns Hopkins University Press, 1993.

Deason, Gary B., 'Reformation Theology and the Mechanistic Conception of Nature', in *God and Nature: Historical Essays on the Encounter Between Christianity and Science*, ed. David C. Lindberg and Ronald L. Numbers, Berkeley and Los Angeles: University of California Press, 1986, pp. 167–91.

Dehn, Siegfried Wilhelm, 'Dreistimmige Fuge aus dem "Wohltemperirten Clavier" von J. S. Bach', *Analysen dreier Fugen aus Joh. Seb. Bach's 'wohltemperirtem Clavier' und einer Vocal-Doppelfuge A. M. Bononcini's*, Leipzig: C. F. Peters, 1858, pp. 1–7.

Della Porta, Giovanni Battista [John Baptista Porta], *Natural Magick in Twenty Books*, London: Thomas Young and Samuel Speed, 1658.

Derrida, Jacques, *Of Grammatology*, trans. Gayatri C. Spivak, corrected edn, Baltimore and London: Johns Hopkins University Press, 1998.

Descartes, René [Renatus Cartesius], *Compendium of Music*, London: Thomas Harper for Humphrey Moseley, 1653.

Compendium of Music, trans. Walter Robert, notes by Charles Kent, n.p.: American Institute of Musicology, 1961.

Œuvres de Descartes, ed. Charles Adam and Paul Tannery, rev. edn, Paris: Vrin/C.N.R.S., 1964–76.

The Philosophical Writings of Descartes, trans. John Cottingham, Robert Stoothoff and Dugald Murdoch, 3 vols., Cambridge: Cambridge University Press, 1984–91.

Leitfaden der Musik, trans. and ed. Johannes Brockt, 2nd edn, Darmstadt: Wissenschaftliche Buchgesellschaft, 1992.

Diderot, Denis and d'Alembert, Jean le Rond (eds.), *Encyclopédie ou Dictionnaire raisonné des sciences, des arts, et des métiers*, 35 vols., Paris: Briasson, David, Le Breton, Durand, 1751–80; rpt Stuttgart-Bad Cannstatt: Friedrich Frommann, 1988.

Drake, Stillman, *Galileo at Work. His Scientific Biography*, Chicago: University of Chicago Press, 1970.

'Renaissance Music and Experimental Science', *Journal of the History of Ideas* 31 (1970), 483–500.

Dreier, Franz Adrian, 'The *Kunstkammer* of Hessian Landgraves in Kassel', in *The Origins of Museums: The Cabinet of Curiosities in Sixteenth- and Seventeenth-Century Europe*, ed. Oliver Impey and Arthur MacGregor, Oxford: Clarendon Press, 1985.

Dreyfus, Hubert L. and Rabinow, Paul, *Michel Foucault: Beyond Structuralism and Hermeneutics*, Brighton: Harvester, 1982.

Dubiel, Joseph, '"When You are a Beethoven": Kinds of Rules in Schenker's "Counterpoint"', *Journal of Music Theory* 34 (1990), 291–340.

Dubois, Page, 'Subjected Bodies, Science and the State: Francis Bacon, Torturer', in *Body Politics: Disease, Desire and the Family*, ed. Michael Ryan and Avery Gordon, Boulder, San Francisco and Oxford: Westview Press, 1994.

Duchez, Marie-Elisabeth, 'Valeur épistémologique de la théorie de la basse fondamentale de Jean-Philippe Rameau: connaissance scientifique et représentation de la musique', *Studies on Voltaire and the Eighteenth Century* 254 (1986), 91–130.

Dudley, Edward and Novak, Maximillian E. (eds.), *The Wild Man Within: An Image in Western Thought from the Renaissance to Romanticism*, Pittsburgh: University of Pittsburgh Press, 1972.

Bibliography

Dyson, Kenneth, *The State Tradition in Western Europe*, Oxford: Martin Robertson, 1980.

Eamon, William, *Science and the Secrets of Nature: Books of Secrets in Medieval and Early Modern Culture*, Princeton: Princeton University Press, 1994.

Eco, Umberto, Lambertini, Roberto, Marmo, Costantino and Tabarroni, Andrea, 'On Animal Language in the Medieval Classification of Signs', in *On the Medieval Theory of Signs*, ed. Umberto Eco and Costantino Marmo, Amsterdam: John Benjamins, 1989, pp. 3–41.

Eggebrecht, Hans Heinrich, 'Musikalisches and Musiktheoretisches Denken', in *Geschichte der Musiktheorie*, vol. I, ed. Frieder Zaminer, Darmstadt: Wissenschaftliche Buchgesellschaft, 1985.

Eliot, T. S., *What is a Classic?* London: Faber and Faber, 1945.

Esposito, Joseph L., *Schelling's Idealism and Philosophy of Nature*, Lewisburg: Bucknell University Press, 1977.

Fattori, Marta (ed.), *Francis Bacon: Terminologia e fortuna nel XVII secolo*, Rome: Edizioni dell'Ateneo, 1984.

Fend, Michael, 'The Changing Function of *Senso* and *Ragione* in Italian Music Theory of the Late Sixteenth Century', in *The Second Sense: Studies in Hearing and Musical Judgment from Antiquity to the Seventeenth Century*, ed. Charles Burnett, Michael Fend and Penelope Gouk, London: Warburg Institute, 1991, pp. 199–221.

Fletcher, John, 'Poetry, Gender, and Primal Fantasy', in *Formations of Fantasy*, ed. Victor Burgin, James Donald and Cora Kaplan, London and New York: Routledge, 1986, pp. 109–41.

Fludd, Robert [Robertus Fluctibus], *Utriusque Cosmi Majoris scilicet et Minoris Metaphysica, Physica atque Technica Historia*, Oppenheim: Johann-Theodore de Bry, 1617.

Fortlage, Karl, *Das musikalische System der Griechen in seiner Urgestalt*, Leipzig, 1847.

Foucault, Michel, *The Order of Things: An Archaeology of the Human Sciences*, New York: Random House, 1973; *The Order of Things: An Archaeology of the Human Sciences*, London: Tavistock/Routledge, 1974.
   The History of Sexuality, vol. I, trans. Robert Hurley, Harmondsworth: Penguin, 1978.
   Discipline and Punish, trans. Alan Sheridan, Harmondsworth: Penguin, 1979.

Galilei, Vincenzo, *Dialogo della musica antica e della moderna* (1581), in *Source Readings in Music History*, ed. Oliver Strunk, New York: Norton, 1950, pp. 302–22.

Gaspard, Jean-Marc, *The Wild Boy of Aveyron*, trans. George and Muriel Humphrey, New York: Meredith, 1962.

Gebhard, Wolfgang, *Der Zusammenhang der Dinge: Weltgleichnis und Naturverklärung im Totalitätsbewußtsein des 19. Jahrhunderts*, Hermaea Germanistische Forschungen, Neue Folge, ed. Hans Fromm and Hans-Jürgen Mähl, vol. XLVII, Tübingen: Max Niemeyer, 1984.

Gellner, Ernest, *Nations and Nationalism*, Oxford: Blackwell, 1983.

Gerbi, Antonello, *Nature in the New World: From Christopher Columbus to Gonzalo Fernandez de Oviedo*, trans. Jeremy Moyle, Pittsburgh: University of Pittsburgh Press, 1985.

Gervasoni, Carlo, *Scuola della Musica*, Piacenca: N. Orcesi, 1800.

Gifford, Humfrey, *A Posie of Gillonflowers*, London: John Perin, 1580.

Godwin, Joscelyn, 'Instruments in Robert Fludd's *Utriusque Cosmi . . . Historia*', *Galpin Society Journal* 26 (1973), 2–14.
   'Robert Fludd on the Lute and Pandora', *Lute Society Journal* 15 (1973), 11–19.

Goehr, Lydia, *The Imaginary Museum of Musical Works: An Essay in the Philosophy of Music*, Oxford: Oxford University Press, 1992.

Bibliography

Goethe, Johann Wolfgang von, 'Über Laokoon', in *Werke (Hamburger Ausgabe)*, vol. XII: *Schriften zur Kunst und Literatur, Maximen und Reflexionen*, 12th edn, Munich: C. H. Beck, 1994.

Gouk, Penelope M., 'The Role of Acoustics and Music Theory in the Scientific Work of Robert Hook', *Annals of Science* 37 (1980), 573–605.

'Music in Francis Bacon's Natural Philosophy', in *Francis Bacon: Terminologia e fortuna nel XVII secolo*, ed. Marta Fattori, Rome: Edizioni dell'Ateneo, 1984, pp. 139–54.

'Horological, Mathematical and Musical Instruments. Science and Music at the Court of Charles I', in *The Late King's Goods: Collections, Possessions and Patronage of Charles I in the Light of Commonwealth Sale Inventories*, ed. Arthur MacGregor, London and Oxford: Alistair McAlpine in Association with Oxford University Press, 1989, pp. 387–402.

'Speculative and Practical Music in Seventeenth-Century England: Oxford University as a Case Study', in *Atti del XIV congresso della società internazionale di musicologia: trasmissione e recezione delle forme di cultura, 1987*, ed. Angelo Pompilio, Lorenzo Bianconi and F. Alberto Gallo, Turin: E. D. T. edizioni di Torino, 1990, pp. 199–205.

'Some English Theories of Hearing in the Seventeenth Century: Before and After Descartes', in *The Second Sense: Studies in Hearing and Musical Judgment from Antiquity to the Seventeenth Century*, ed. Charles Burnett, Michael Fend and Penelope Gouk, London: Warburg Institute, 1991, pp. 95–114.

'Performance Practice: Music, Medicine and Natural Philosophy in Interregnum Oxford', *British Journal of the History of Science* 29 (1996), 257–88.

Grabner, David M., 'Resolute Biocentrism: The Dilemma of Wilderness in National Parks', in *Reinventing Nature? Responses to Postmodern Deconstruction*, Washington, DC and Covelo, Calif.: Island Press, 1995.

Grant, Cecil Powell, 'The Real Relationship Between Kirnberger's and Rameau's Concept of the Fundamental Bass', *Journal of Music Theory* 21 (1977), 324–38.

Green, Burdette L., 'The Harmonic Series from Mersenne to Rameau: An Historical Study of Circumstances Leading to Its Recognition and Application to Music', Ph.D. thesis, The Ohio State University, 1969.

Guidobaldi, Nicoletta, 'Images of Music in Cesare Ripa's *Iconologia*', *Imago Musicae* 7 (1990), 41–68.

Halm, August, *Von zwei Kulturen der Musik*, ed. Gustav Wyneken, 3rd edn, Stuttgart: Ernst Klett, 1947.

Bruckner, 2nd edn, Munich: Georg Müller, 1923; rpt Hildesheim: Georg Olms, 1978.

Von Form und Sinn der Musik: Gesammelte Aufsätze zur Musik, ed. Siegfried Schmalzriedt, Wiesbaden: Breitkopf und Härtel, 1978.

Hanke, Lewis, *Aristotle and the American Indians: A Study in Race Prejudice in the Modern World*, Chicago: Henry Regnery Co., 1959.

Hankins, Thomas L. and Silverman, Robert J., *Instruments and Imagination*, Princeton: Princeton University Press, 1995.

Haraway, Donna J., *Primate Visions: Gender, Race, and Nature in the World of Modern Science*, New York: Routledge, 1989.

Simians, Cyborgs, and Women: The Reinvention of Nature, New York: Routledge, 1991.

Harding, Sandra and O'Barr, Jean F. (eds.), *Sex and Scientific Inquiry*, Chicago and London: University of Chicago Press, 1987.

Harris, Ellen, *Handel and the Pastoral Tradition*, London: Oxford University Press, 1980.

Harris, John, 'Oh Happy Oxnead', *Country Life* 88 (5 June 1986), 1630–2.

Harrison, Daniel, *Harmonic Function in Chromatic Music: A Renewed Dualist Theory and an Account of Its Precedents*, Chicago: University of Chicago Press, 1994.

Hatfield, Gary, 'Descartes' Physiology and its Relation to his Psychology', in *The Cambridge Companion to Descartes*, ed. John Cottingham, Cambridge and New York: Cambridge University Press, 1992, pp. 335–70.

Hauptmann, Moritz, *Erläuterungen zu Joh. Sebastian Bachs KUNST DER FUGE . . . Beilage zum III. Bande der in obiger Verlags-Handlung erschienenen neuen Ausgabe von J. S. Bachs Werken*, Leipzig: C. F. Peters, 1841.

    The Nature of Harmony and Metre, trans. William Edward Heathcote, London: Swan Sonnenschein, 1888; rpt New York: Da Capo Press, 1989.

Hayes, Deborah, 'Rameau's Theory of Harmonic Generation: An Annotated Translation and Commentary of *Génération harmonique* by Jean-Philippe Rameau', Ph.D. thesis, Stanford University, 1968.

Hayes, Gerald R., 'Charles Butler and the Music of the Bees', *The Music Times* 66 (1 June 1925), 512–15.

Head, Matthew, 'Birdsong and the Origins of Music', *Journal of the Royal Musical Association* 122 (1997), 1–23.

Heath, Robert, *Clarastella*, London: Humph[rey] Moseley, 1650.

Hegel, Georg W. F., *Enzyklopädie: III. Philosophie des Geistes*, ed. Hermann Glockner, *Jubiläumsausgabe*, vol. X, 4th edn, Stuttgart-Bad Cannstadt: Friedrich Frommann, 1964.

    Grundlinien der Philosophie des Rechts, Stuttgart: Reclam, 1970; trans. H. B. Nisbet as *Elements of the Philosophy of Right*, Cambridge: Cambridge University Press, 1991.

    Vorlesungen über die Ästhetik, in *Theorie Werkausgabe*, vol. XV, Frankfurt am Main: Suhrkamp, 1970.

    Wissenschaft der Logik (1812–16); rpt Frankfurt am Main: Suhrkamp, 1970.

    Vorlesungen über die Philosophie der Geschichte, in *Theorie Werkausgabe*, vol. XII, 4th edn, Frankfurt am Main: Suhrkamp, 1994.

Helmholtz, Hermann von, *On the Sensations of Tone*, trans. Alexander J. Ellis; rpt New York: Dover, 1954.

Hine, William L., 'Marin Mersenne: Renaissance Naturalism and Renaissance Magic', in *Occult and Scientific Mentalities in the Renaissance*, ed. Brian Vickers, Cambridge: Cambridge University Press, 1984, pp. 165–76.

Hirst, R. J., 'Perception' and 'Sensa', in *The Encyclopedia of Philosophy*, ed. Paul Edwards, New York: Macmillan, 1967, vol. VI, pp. 79–87; vol. VII, pp. 407–15.

Hobbes, Thomas, *Humane Nature: or, the Fundamental Elements of Policie*, London: T. Newcomb for Fra[ncis] Bowman, 1650.

    Elements of Philosophy, London: R. and W. Leybourn for Andrew Crooke, 1656.

Hodgen, Margaret T., *Early Anthropology in the Sixteenth and Seventeenth Centuries*, Philadelphia: University of Pennsylvania Press, 1964.

Hodson, Daren Ivan, 'The Institutionalisation of Literature in Eighteenth-Century France and Germany: The Functions of Reading in Rousseau, Novalis, Fichte and the *Ecole Normale*', Ph.D. thesis, University of Utah, 1995.

Hoffmann, E. T. A., review of Beethoven's Fifth Symphony, in *Allgemeine musikalische Zeitung* 12/40–1 (1810), 630–42, 652–9.

Holder, William, *A Treatise of the Natural Grounds and Principles of Harmony*, London: J. Heptinstall for J. Carr, B. Aylmer and L. Meredith, 1694.

Bibliography

Hollander, John, *The Untuning of the Sky: Ideas of Music in English Poetry 1500–1700*, Princeton: Princeton University Press, 1961.

Holman, Peter, *Henry Purcell*, Oxford: Oxford University Press, 1995.

Hooper-Greenhill, Eilean, *Museums and the Shaping of Knowledge*, London and New York: Routledge, 1992; rpt edn, 1995.

Hoyt, Peter A., 'The Concept of *développement* in the Early Nineteenth Century', in *Music Theory in the Age of Romanticism*, ed. Ian Bent, Cambridge: Cambridge University Press, 1996, pp. 141–62.

'Haydn's New Incoherence', *Music Theory Spectrum* 19 (1997), 264–84.

Hunter, Michael, *Science and Society in Restoration England*, Cambridge: Cambridge University Press, 1981.

Husk, William Henry, *An Account of the Musical Celebrations on St. Cecilia's Day*, London: Bell and Daldy, 1857.

Hyer, Brian, '"Sighing Branches": Prosopopoeia in Rameau's *Pygmalion*', *Music Analysis* 13 (1984), 7–50.

'Reimag(in)ing Riemann', *Journal of Music Theory* 39 (1995), 101–38.

'Before Rameau and After', *Music Analysis* 15 (1996), 75–100.

Jorgenson, Dale, 'A Résumé of Harmonic Dualism', *Music and Letters* 44 (1963), 31–42.

Kant, Immanuel, *Kritik der Urteilskraft*, ed. Wilhelm Weischedel, Frankfurt am Main: Suhrkamp, 1968.

Kassler, Jamie C., *Inner Music: Hobbes, Hooke and North on Internal Character*, Madison and Teaneck: Fairleigh Dickinson University Press, 1995.

Kassler, J. C. and Oldroyd, D. R., 'Robert Hook's Trinity College "Musick Scripts", His Music Theory and the Role of Music in His Cosmology', *Annals of Science* 40 (1983), 559–95.

Katz, Ruth, *The Powers of Music: Aesthetic Theory and the Invention of Opera*, New Brunswick: Transaction Publishers, 1994.

Kauffman, Thomas DaCosta, *The Mastery of Nature: Aspects of Art, Science and Humanism in the Renaissance*, Princeton: Princeton University Press, 1993.

Keiler, Allan R., 'Bernstein's *The Unanswered Question* and the Problem of Musical Competence', *The Musical Quarterly* 64 (1978), 195–222.

'Music as Metalanguage: Rameau's Fundamental Bass', in *Music Theory: Special Topics*, ed. Richmond Browne, New York: Academic Press, 1981, pp. 83–100.

Keller, Evelyn Fox and Longino, Helen (eds.), *Feminism in Science*, Oxford and New York: Oxford University Press, 1996.

Kenseth, Joy (ed.), *The Age of the Marvelous*, Hanover, NH: Hood Museum of Art, Dartmouth College, 1991.

Kielmeyer, Karl Friedrich von, 'Versuche über die sogenannte animalische Electrizität', *Journal der Physik* 8 (1794), 64–76.

Kircher, Athanasius, *Musurgia universalis*, 2 vols., Rome: Francesco Corbelletti (vol. I) and Ludovico Grignani (vol. II), 1650.

Koch, Heinrich Christoph, *Versuch einer Anleitung zur Composition*, vol. III, Leipzig: A. F. Böhme, 1793; rpt Hildesheim: Georg Olms, 1969.

Koyré, Alexandre, *Metaphysics and Measurement: Essays in Scientific Revolution*, London: Chapman and Hall, 1968.

Kramer, Richard, '*Gradus ad Parnassum*: Beethoven, Schubert, and the Romance of Counterpoint', *19th-Century Music* 11 (1987), 107–20.

Kuberski, Philip, *The Persistence of Memory: Organism, Myth, Text*, Berkeley and Los Angeles: University of California Press, 1992.

Kuhn, Thomas S., *The Copernican Revolution: Planetary Astronomy in the Development of Western Thought*, Cambridge, Mass.: Harvard University Press, 1957.

The Structure of Scientific Revolutions, Chicago: University of Chicago Press, 1970.

Kurth, Ernst, *Bruckner*, 2 vols., Berlin, 1925; rpt Hildesheim: Georg Olms, 1971.

Lacan, Jacques, *The Four Fundamental Concepts of Psycho-Analysis*, ed. Jacques-Alain Miller, trans. Alan Sheridan, London and New York: Penguin, 1994.

Lakeland, Paul, *The Politics of Salvation: The Hegelian Idea of the State*, Albany, NY: State University of New York Press, 1984.

Langbehn, Julius (pseud.: *Ein Deutscher*), *Rembrandt als Erzieher*, Leipzig: C. L. Hirschfeld, 1890.

Lawrence, Robert E., 'Science, Lute Tablature, and Universal Languages: Thomas Salmon's *Essay to the Advancement of Musick* (1672)', *Journal of the Lute Society of America* 26–7 (1993–4), 53–69.

le Goff, Jacques, 'Ecclesiastical Culture and Folklore in the Middle Ages: Saint Marcellus of Paris and the Dragon', in *Time, Work, and Culture in the Middle Ages*, trans. Arthur Goldhammer, Chicago: University of Chicago Press, 1980, pp. 159–88.

Leary, John O., *Francis Bacon and the Politics of Science*, Ames: Iowa State University Press, 1994.

Leppert, Richard, 'Music, Representation, and Social Order in Early-Modern Europe', *Cultural Critique* 4 (1989), 25–54.

Levy, Janet, 'Covert and Casual Values in Recent Writings About Music', *Journal of Musicology* 5 (1987), 7–11.

Levy, Kenneth, *Music: A Listener's Introduction*, New York: Harper and Row, 1983.

Lewin, David, 'A Formal Theory of Generalized Tonal Functions', *Journal of Music Theory* 26 (1982), 23–100.

'Amfortas's Prayer to Titurel and the Role of D in *Parsifal*: The Tonal Spaces of the Drama and the Enharmonic C♭/B', *19th-Century Music* 7 (1984), 336–49.

Lindberg, David C. and Numbers, Ronald L. (eds.), *God and Nature: Historical Essays on the Encounter Between Christianity and Science*, Berkeley and Los Angles: University of California Press, 1986.

Lindberg, David C. and Westman, Robert S. (eds.), *Reappraisals of the Scientific Revolution*, Cambridge: Cambridge University Press, 1990.

Lippman, Edward A. (ed.), *Musical Aesthetics: A Historical Reader*, 4 vols., Stuyvesant, NY: Pendragon, 1986–90.

Lloyd, Genevieve, 'Reason, Science, and the Domination of Matter', in *Feminism in Science*, ed. Evelyn Fox Keller and Helen Longino, Oxford: Oxford University Press, 1996, pp. 41–53.

Locke, Matthew, *The Present Practice of Musick Vindicated Against the Exceptions and New Way of Attaining Musick*, London: N. Brooke and J. Playford, 1673.

Löhlein, Georg Simon, *Clavier-Schule*, Leipzig and Züllichau: Waisenhaus und Frommanische Buchhandlung, 1765.

Lovejoy, Arthur O., *The Great Chain of Being*, Cambridge, Mass.: Harvard University Press, 1936.

Luckett, Richard, 'St. Cecilia and Music', *Proceedings of the Royal Musical Association* 99 (1972–3), 15–30.

Lucks, Henry A., 'Natura Naturans/Natura Naturata', *The New Scholasticism* 12 (1935), 1–24.

Bibliography

Mace, Tho[mas], *Musicks Monument: Or, a Remembrancer Of the Best Practical Musick*, London: T. Ratcliffe and N. Thompson for Thomas Mace and John Carr, 1976.

MacGregor, Arthur, 'Collectors and Collections of Rarities in the Sixteenth and Seventeenth Centuries', in *Tradescant's Rarities: Essays on the Foundation of the Ashmolean Museum 1683*, ed. MacGregor, Oxford: Clarendon Press, 1983.

MacGregor, Arthur (ed.), *The Late King's Goods: Collections, Possessions and Patronage of Charles I in the Light of Commonwealth Sale Inventories*, London and Oxford: Alistair McAlpine in Association with Oxford University Press, 1989.

MacIntyre, Alasdair, *After Virtue*, London: Duckworth, 1981.

Maconie, Robin, *The Concept of Music*, Oxford: Clarendon Press, 1990.

Markham, G[ervase], *Country Contentments. Or, the Husbandmans Recreations*, 11th edn, London: George Sawbridge, 1675.

Marx, Adolf B., *Die Lehre von der musikalischen Komposition, praktisch-theoretisch*, 4 vols., 2nd edn, Leipzig: Breitkopf und Härtel, 1848.

Marx, A. B., *Die Lehre von der musikalischen Composition*, vol. I, Leipzig: Breitkopf und Härtel, 1863.

Mayrberger, Karl, 'Die Harmonik Richard Wagner's an den Leitmotiven aus *Tristan und Isolde* erläutert' (1881); trans. Ian Bent as 'The Harmonic Style of Richard Wagner, Elucidated with Respect to the Leitmotifs of *Tristan and Isolde*', in *Music Analysis in the Nineteenth Century*, ed. Ian Bent, Cambridge: Cambridge University Press, 1994, vol. I, pp. 226–52.

McCune, Mark P., 'Oettingen', in *The New Grove Dictionary of Music and Musicians*, ed. Stanley Sadie, London: Macmillan, 1980.

'Moritz Hauptmann: *Ein Haupt Mann* in Nineteenth Century Music Theory', *Indiana Theory Review* 7 (1986), 1–28.

McGeary, Thomas, 'Harpsichord Decoration – A Reflection of Renaissance Ideas About Music', *Explorations in Renaissance Culture* 6 (1980), 1–27.

Menzhausen, Joachim, 'Elector Augustus's *Kunstkammer*: An Analysis of the Inventory of 1587', in *The Origins of Museums: The Cabinet of Curiosities in Sixteenth- and Seventeenth-Century Europe*, ed. Oliver Impey and Arthur MacGregor, Oxford: Clarendon Press, 1985.

Merchant, Carolyn, *The Death of Nature: Women, Ecology, and the Scientific Revolution*, San Francisco: Harper and Row, 1980.

Mettrie, Julien Offrai de la, *Machine Man and Other Writings*, trans. Ann Thomson, Cambridge: Cambridge University Press, 1996.

Meyer, Leonard B., 'Exploiting Limits: Creation, Archetypes, and Style Change', *Daedalus* 109/2 (1980), 177–205.

Mickelsen, William Cooper, *Hugo Riemann's Theory of Harmony, with a Translation of Riemann's 'History of Music Theory', Book 3*, Lincoln, Nebraska: Nebraska University Press, 1977.

Mirollo, James V., *The Poet of the Marvelous: Giambattista Marino*, New York and London: Columbia University Press, 1963.

'The Aesthetics of the Marvelous: The Wondrous Work of Art in a Wondrous World', in *The Age of the Marvelous*, ed. Joy Kenseth, Hanover, NH: Hood Museum of Art, Dartmouth College, 1991, pp. 60–79.

Moore, Andrew W., *Dutch and Flemish Painting in Norfolk: A History of Taste and Influence, Fashion and Collecting*, London: Her Majesty's Stationery Office, 1988.

Moreno, Jairo, 'The Complicity of the Imaginary: Rameau's Implied Dissonances', unpublished paper presented at the 21st Meeting of the Society of Music Theory at Chapel Hill, NC, December 1998.

Bibliography

Morley, Thomas, *A Plain and Easie Introduction to Practicall Musicke*, London: Peter Short, 1597.

Mullaney, Steven, *The Place of the Stage: License, Play and Power in Renaissance England*, Chicago and London: University of Chicago Press, 1988.

Mulvey, Laura, 'Afterthoughts on "Visual Pleasure and Narrative Cinema" inspired by *Duel in the Sun*', in *Visual and Other Pleasures*, London: Macmillan, 1989, pp. 29–39.

'Visual Pleasure and Narrative Cinema', in *The Sexual Subject: A Screen Reader in Sexuality*, London and New York: Routledge, 1992, pp. 22–34.

Neff, Severine, 'Schoenberg and Goethe: Organicism and Analysis', in *Music Theory and the Exploration of the Past*, ed. Christopher Hatch and David W. Bernstein, Chicago: University of Chicago Press, 1993, pp. 409–33.

Nettesheim, Henry Cornelius Agrippa von, *Three Books of Occult Philosophy*, trans. J. F., London: R. W. for Gregory Moule, 1657.

Neubauer, John, *The Emancipation of Music from Language: Departure from Mimesis in Eighteenth-Century Aesthetics*, New Haven: Yale University Press, 1986.

Newbigin, Lesslie, *Foolishness to the Greeks: The Gospel and Western Culture*, London: SPCK, 1986.

Newcomb, Anthony, 'Schumann and Late Eighteenth-Century Narrative Strategies', *19th-Century Music* 11 (1987), 164–75.

Nietzsche, Friedrich, *Nietzsche contra Wagner: Aktenstücke eines Psychologen*, Leipzig: Naumann, 1895.

Nachgelassene Werke: Der Wille zur Macht: Versuch einer Umwerthung aller Werthe, trans. Walter Kaufmann and R. J. Hollingdale as *The Will to Power*, New York: Vintage Books, 1968.

Zur Genealogie der Moral (1887), trans. Walter Kaufmann as 'On the Genealogy of Morals', in *Basic Writings of Nietzsche*, New York: The Modern Library, 1992, pp. 449–599.

Der Fall Wagner (1888), trans. Walter Kaufmann as 'The Case of Wagner', in *Basic Writings of Nietzsche*, New York: The Modern Library, 1992, pp. 609–48.

Nordau, Max, *Degeneration*, London: Heinemann, 1913.

O'Brien, Grant, *Ruckers: A Harpsichord and Virginal Building Tradition*, Cambridge: Cambridge University Press, 1990.

Oettingen, Arthur von, *Harmoniesystem in dualer Entwickelung: Studien zur Theorie der Musik*, Dorpat and Leipzig: W. Glaser, 1866.

'Das duale System der Harmonie', *Annalen der Naturphilosophie* 1–5 (1902–6), 1: 62–75, 2: 375–403, 3: 241–69, 4: 116–36, 301–38; 5: 449–503.

Das duale Harmoniesystem, Leipzig: Linnemann, 1913.

Palisca, Claude V., 'Vincenzo Galilei's Counterpoint Treatise: A Code for the *Seconda Prattica*', *Journal of the American Musicological Society*, 9 (1956), 81–96.

'The Alterati of Florence, Pioneers in the Theory of Dramatic Music', in *New Looks at Italian Opera: Essays in Honor of Donald J. Grout*, ed. W. W. Austin (Ithaca: Cornell University Press, 1968), pp. 9–38.

Baroque Music, Englewood Cliffs, NJ: Prentice Hall, 1981.

Palisca, Claude V. (ed.), *The Florentine Camerata: Documentary Studies and Translations*, New Haven: Yale University Press, 1989.

Pastille, William, 'Music and Morphology: Goethe's Influence on Schenker's Thought', in *Schenker Studies*, ed. Hedi Siegel, Cambridge: Cambridge University Press, 1990, p. 29–44.

Paul, Charles, 'Rameau's Musical Theories and the Age of Reason', Ph.D. thesis, University of California, Berkeley, 1966.

'Jean-Philippe Rameau (1683–1764): The Musician as *Philosophe*', *Proceedings of the American Philosophical Society* 114 (1970), 140–54.

Bibliography

Piaget, Jean, ed., *Johann Amos Comenius, 1592–1670: Selections*, trans. Iris Urwin, Paris: Unesco, 1957.

Pick, Daniel, *Faces of Degeneration: A European Disorder, c.1848–c.1918*, Cambridge: Cambridge University Press, 1989.

Pirrotta, Nino, 'Early Opera and Aria', in *New Looks at Italian Opera: Essays in Honor of Donald J. Grout*, ed. W. W. Austin, Ithaca: Cornell University Press, 1968, pp. 72–89.

Platt, Hugh, *The Jewel House of Art and Nature*, London: Elizabeth Alsop, 1653.

Playford, John, *An Introduction to the Skill of Musick*, London: W. Godbid for J. Playford, 1674.

Pliny [C. Plinius, Secundus], *The Historie of the World. Commonly called, The Natural Historie*, London: Adam Islip, 1601.

Polanyi, Michael, *Personal Knowledge: Towards a Post-Critical Philosophy*, Chicago: University of Chicago Press, 1958.

Pomian, Krzystof, *Collectors and Curiosities: Paris and Venice, 1500–1800*, trans. Elizabeth Wiles-Portier, Cambridge: Polity Press, 1990.

Pomme de Mirimonde, Albert, 'La Musique dans les allégories de l'Amour II – Eros', *Gazette des beaux-arts* 69 (1967), 319–46.

Powell, Joseph M., *Mirrors of the New World: Images and Image-makers in the Settlement Process*, Folkestone: Dawson, 1977.

Powers, Harold S., 'Mode', *The New Grove Dictionary of Music and Musicians*, ed. Stanley Sadie, London: Macmillan, 1980.

Pruett, James, 'Charles Butler – Musician, Grammarian, Apiarist', *The Musical Quarterly* 49 (1963), 498–511.

Ptolemy, *Harmonics*, in *Greek Musical Writings*, vol. II: *Harmonic and Acoustic Theory*, trans. Andrew Barker, Cambridge: Cambridge University Press, 1989.

Purdy, Daniel Leonhard, 'Reading to Consume: Fashionable Receptions of Literature in Germany, 1774–1816', Ph.D. thesis, Cornell University, 1992.

Quantz, Johann Joachim, *On Playing the Flute*, trans. Edward R. Reilly, 2nd edn, New York: Schirmer, 1985.

Radford, Andrew, *Syntax: A Minimalist Introduction*, Cambridge: Cambridge University Press, 1997.

Radkau, Joachim, 'The Wordy Worship of Nature and the Tacit Feeling for Nature in the History of German Forestry', in *Nature and Society in Historical Context*, ed. Mikuláš Teich, Roy Porter and Bo Gustafsson, Cambridge: Cambridge University Press, 1997.

Rameau, Jean-Philippe, *Traité de l'harmonie réduite à ses principes naturels*, Paris: Ballard, 1722, in *CTW*, vol. I. *Treatise on Harmony*, trans. Philip Gossett, New York: Dover, 1971.

    Nouveau système de musique théorique et pratique, Paris: Ballard, 1726, in *CTW*, vol. II. Trans. Chandler (1975).

    Génération harmonique ou traité de musique théorique et pratique, Paris: Prault fils, 1737, in *CTW*, vol. III. Trans. Hayes (1974).

    Démonstration du principe de l'harmonie servant de base à tout l'art musical théorique et pratique, Paris: Durand, 1750, in *CTW*, vol. III. Trans. Briscoe (1975).

    Observations sur notre instinct pour la musique et sur son principe, Paris: Prault fils, 1754, in *CTW*, vol. III.

    Complete Theoretical Writings, ed. Erwin Jacobi, 6 vols., Rome: American Institute of Musicology, 1967–72. (Cited as *CTW*)

Ramos de Pareia, Bartolomeo, *Musica Practica* (1482), ed. Johannes Wolf, Leipzig: s.n., 1901.

Rasch, Rudolf (ed.), *Joseph Sauveur: Collected Writings on Musical Acoustics (Paris 1700–1713)*, Utrecht: Diapason Press, 1984.

Ratner, Leonard, 'Harmonic Aspects of Classic Form', *Journal of the American Musicological Society* 2 (1949), 159–68.

Classic Music: Expression, Form, and Style, New York: Schirmer Books, 1980.

Ravenscroft, Thomas, *A Briefe Discourse Of the true (but neglected) use of Charac'tring the Degrees*, London: Edw[ard] Allde for Tho[mas] Adams, 1614.

Reicha, Antoine, *Traité de Mélodie*, 2nd edn, Paris: 1832.

Repton, John Adey, 'Inventory of Ornamental Plate, &c. Formerly at Oxnead Hall', *The Gentleman's Magazine* (1844), 23–4 and 150–3.

Riemann, Hugo (pseud. Hugibert Ries), 'Musikalische Logik: Ein Beitrag zur Musiktheorie', *Neue Zeitschrift für Musik* 68/28–9, 36–8 (1872), 279–82, 287–8, 353–5, 363–4, 373–4.

Musikalische Logik: Hauptzüge der physiologischen und psychologischen Begründung unseres Musiksystems, Leipzig: C. F. Kahnt, 1874.

Die Hülfsmittel der Modulation, Kassel: Luckhardt'sche Verlagsbuchhandlung, 1875.

'Die objective Existenz der Untertöne in der Schallwelle', *Allgemeine deutsche Musikzeitung* 2/25–6 (1875), 205–6, 213–15.

Musikalische Syntaxis: Grundzüge der harmonischen Satzbildungslehre, Leipzig: Breitkopf und Härtel, 1877.

Skizze einer neuen Methode der Harmonielehre, Leipzig: Breitkopf und Härtel, 1880.

'Die Natur der Harmonik', *Sammlung musikalischer Vorträge* 4 (1882), 157–90.

Neue Schule der Melodik, Hamburg: Karl Grädener and J. F. Richter, 1883.

Musikalische Dynamik und Agogik: Lehrbuch der musikalischen Phrasierung, Hamburg: Rahter, 1884.

Systematische Modulationslehre als Grundlage der musikalischen Formenlehre, Hamburg: J. F. Richter, 1887.

Lehrbuch des einfachen, doppelten und imitierenden Kontrapunkts, Leipzig: Breitkopf und Härtel, 1888.

Wie hören wir Musik? Drei Vorträge, Leipzig: Max Hesse, 1888.

Große Kompositionslehre, 3 vols., Berlin and Stuttgart: W. Spemann, 1902–13.

'Degeneration und Regeneration in der Musik', *Max Hesses deutscher Musiker-Kalender* 23 (1908), 136–41; reprinted in *'Die Konfusion in der Musik': Felix Draesekes Kampfschrift von 1906 und ihre Folgen*, ed. Susanne Shigihara, Bonn: G. Schröder, 1990.

Riemann, Hugo, 'Ideen zu einer "Lehre von den Tonvorstellungen"' (1914/15), trans. Robert W. Wason and Elizabeth West Marvin as 'Riemann's "Ideen zu einer 'Lehre von den Tonvorstellungen'": an Annotated Translation', *Journal of Music Theory* 36 (1992), 69–117.

Riepel, Joseph, *Grundregeln zur Tonordnung insgemein*, Ulm: Christian Ulrich Wagner, 1755.

Ripa, Cesare, *Della Novissima Iconologia*, [Padua: Tozzi, 1624].

Iconologia: Or, Moral Emblems, London: Benj[amin] Motte, 1709.

Ritzel, Fred, *Die Entwicklung der 'Sonatenform' in musiktheoretischen Schrifttum des 18. und 19. Jahrhunderts*, 2nd edn, Wiesbaden: Breitkopf und Härtel, 1969.

Robbins Landon, H. C., *Haydn: Chronicle and Works*, 5 vols., Bloomington: Indiana University Press, 1976–80.

Robe, Stanley L., 'Wild Men and Spain's Brave New World', in *The Wild Man Within: An Image in Western Thought from the Renaissance to Romanticism*, ed. Edward Dudley and Maximillian E. Novak, Pittsburgh: University of Pittsburgh Press, 1972, pp. 39–54.

Robinson, Thomas, *The Schoole of Musicke: Wherin is Taught the Perfect Method of True Fingering of the Lute, Pandora, Orpharion, and Viol da Gamba*, London: Tho[mas] Este for Simon Waterson, 1603.

Robinson, Timothy A., *Aristotle in Outline*, Indianapolis and Cambridge, Mass.: Hackett, 1995.

Rodis-Lewis, Geneviève, *Le problème de l'inconscient et le cartésianisme*. Paris: Presses Universitaires de France, 1950.

Rogerson, Brewster, 'The Art of Painting the Passions', *Journal of the History of Ideas* 14 (1953), 68–94.

Rosen, Charles, *The Classical Style: Haydn, Mozart, Beethoven*, New York: Norton, 1972.
Sonata Forms, rev. edn, New York: W.W. Norton, 1988.

Rossi, Paolo, *Bacon: From Magic to Science*, trans. Sacha Rabinovitch, Chicago: University of Chicago Press, 1968.

Rothfarb, Lee A., *Ernst Kurth: Selected Writings*, Cambridge: Cambridge University Press, 1991.
'The "New Education" and Music Theory, 1900–1925', in *Music Theory and the Exploration of the Past*, ed. Christopher Hatch and David W. Bernstein, Chicago: Chicago University Press, 1993, pp. 449–72.
'Beethoven's Formal Dynamics: August Halm's Phenomenological Perspective', in *Beethoven Forum IV*, ed. James Webster and Lewis Lockwood, Lincoln: University of Nebraska Press, 1995, pp. 65–84.
'Music Analysis, Cultural Morality and Sociology in the Writings of August Halm', *Indiana Theory Review* 16/1–2 (1995), 171–96.

Rousseau, *Discours sur l'origine et les fondements de l'inégalité parmi les hommes* (1755), in *Œuvres complètes*, ed. B. Gagnebin and M. Raymond, Paris: Pléiade, 1959–95, vol. III, pp. 111–94.
Essai sur l'origine des langues (1764), trans. John H. Moran and Alexander Gode as *The Origin of Language*, New York: Frederick Ungar, 1966.
Essai sur l'origine des langues (1764), ed. and trans. Victor Gourevitch as *The First and Second Discourses together with the replies to Critics and Essay on the Origin of Languages*, New York: Harper and Row, 1986.

Ruff, Lillian M., 'The Social Significance of the Seventeenth-Century English Music Theory Treatises', *The Consort* 26 (1970), 412–22.

Rummenhöller, Peter, *Moritz Hauptmann als Theoretiker: Eine Studie zum erkenntniskritischen Theoriebegriff in der Musik*, Wiesbaden: Breitkopf und Härtel, 1963.
Musiktheoretisches Denken im 19. Jahrhundert: Versuch einer Interpretation erkenntnistheoretischer Zeugnisse in der Musiktheorie, Studien zur Musikgeschichte des 19. Jahrhunderts, vol. XII, Regensburg: Gustav Bosse Verlag, 1967.

Ryan, Michael and Gordon, Avery (eds.), *Body Politics: Disease, Desire and the Family*, Boulder, San Francisco and Oxford: Westview Press, 1994.

Salmon, Thomas, *An Essay To the Advancement of Musick*, London: J. Macock, 1672.

Sauveur, Joseph, 'Rapport des sons des cordes d'instrumens de musique, aux fleches des cordes: et nouvelle détermination des sons fixes', *Mémoires de l'Académie Royale des Sciences, Année 1713*, 2nd edn, Paris, 1739, pp. 324–50. Ed. in Rasch (1984).
'Système général des intervalles des sons, & son application à tous les systèmes & à tous les instrumens de musique', *Mémoires de l'Académie Royale des Sciences, Année 1701*, 2nd edn, Paris, 1743, pp. 299–366. Ed. in Rasch (1984).
'Application des sons harmoniques à la composition des jeux d'orgues', *Mémoires de l'Académie Royale des Sciences, Année 1702*, 2nd edn, Paris, 1743, pp. 308–28. Ed. in Rasch (1984).

228

Schachter, Carl, *Unfoldings: Essays in Schenkerian Theory and Analysis*, ed. Joseph N. Straus, New York: Oxford University Press, 1999.

Schaer, Roland, *L'Invention des musées*, Paris: Gallimard, 1993.

Schelling, Friedrich W. J., *Philosophie der Kunst* [1802–3], Eßlingen: J. G. Cotta, 1859; rpt Darmstadt: Wissenschaftliche Buchgesellschaft, 1980.

Werke, Eßlingen: J. G. Cotta, 1859; rpt Darmstadt: Wissenschaftliche Buchgesellschaft, 1980.

Schenker, Heinrich, *Neue musikalische Theorien und Phantasien*, vol. I: *Harmonielehre* (Vienna: Universal Edition, 1906), trans. Elisabeth Mann Borghese as *Harmony*, Chicago: University of Chicago Press, 1954.

New Musical Theories and Fantasies, vol. III: *Free Composition*, trans. and ed. Ernst Oster, New York: Longman, 1979.

Die letzten fünf Sonaten Beethovens, 4 vols., Vienna: Universal Edition, 1913, 1914, 1915, 1920.

Schiebinger, Londa, *Nature's Body: Gender and the Making of Modern Science*, Boston: Beacon Press, 1993.

Schindler, Anton F., *Beethoven As I Knew Him*, ed. Donald W. MacArdle, trans. Constance S. Jolly, London: Faber and Faber, 1956.

Schleuning, Peter, *Die Sprache der Natur: Natur in der Musik des 18. Jahrhunderts*, Stuttgart: Metzler, 1998.

Schmalfeldt, Janet, 'Form as the Process of Becoming: The Beethovenian-Hegelian Tradition and the "Tempest" Sonata', in *Beethoven Forum V*, ed. James Webster and Lewis Lockwood, Lincoln: University of Nebraska Press, 1996, pp. 37–71.

Schmaltz, Tad M., *Malebranche's Theory of the Soul: A Cartesian Interpretation*, New York and Oxford: Oxford University Press, 1996.

Schmitt, Jean-Claude, '"Religion populaire" et culture folklorique', *Annales: Economies, Sociétés, Civilisations* 28 (1976), 941–53.

Schmitz, Arnold, *Beethovens zwei Principe*, Bonn and Berlin: Ferdinand Dümmler, 1923.

Schneider, Herbert, *Jean-Philippe Rameaus letzter Musiktraktat 'Vérités également ignorées et intéressantes tirées du sein de la Nature' (1764): kritische Ausgabe mit Kommentar*, Beihefte zum Archiv für Musikwissenschaft, vol. XXV, Wiesbaden and Stuttgart: Franz Steiner, 1986.

'Rameaus musiktheoretisches Vermächtnis', *Musiktheorie* 1/2 (1986), 153–61.

Schoenberg, Arnold, *Harmonielehre* (1911), trans. Roy Carter as *Theory of Harmony*, Berkeley: University of California Press, 1978.

Theory of Harmony, trans. Roy E. Carter, London: Faber and Faber, 1978.

Schön, Erich, *Der Verlust der Sinnlichkeit oder die Verwandlung des Lesers: Mentalitätswandel um 1800*, Stuttgart: Klett-Cotta, 1987.

Schott, Howard, *Catalogue of Musical Instruments in the Victoria and Albert Museum, Part I: Keyboard Instruments*, London: Victoria and Albert Museum, 1998.

Schumann, Robert, review of Berlioz's *Symphonie fantastique*, *Neue Zeitschrift der Musik* 3 (1835): 1 (3 July), 1–2; 9 (31 July), 33–5; 10 (4 August), 37–8; 11 (7 August), 41–4; 12 (11 August), 45–8; 13 (14 August), 49–51.

Sechter, Simon, 'Zergliederung des Finale aus Mozarts 4. Sinfonie in C', in *Abhandlung von der Fuge, nach den Grundsätzen und Beispielen der besten in- und ausländischen Meister entworfen, von Friedrich Wilhelm Marpurg, neu bearbeitet, mit erläuternden Anmerkungen und Beispielen vermehrt von S. Sechter . . .*, vol. II, Vienna: Anton Diabelli, [1843], pp. 161–93.

Seelig, Lorenz, 'The Munich *Kunstkammer*', in *The Origins of Museums: The Cabinet of Curiosities in*

Sixteenth- and Seventeenth-Century Europe, ed. Oliver Impey and Arthur MacGregor, Oxford: Clarendon Press, 1985, pp. 76–89.

Shapiro, Barbara J., *Probability and Certainty in Seventeenth-Century England: A Study of the Relationships Between Natural Science, Religion, History, Law, and Literature*, Princeton: Princeton University Press, 1983.

Shirlaw, Matthew, *The Theory of Harmony: An Inquiry into the Natural Principles of Harmony, with an Examination of the Chief Systems of Harmony from Rameau to the Present Day*, London: Novello, 1917.

Simpson, Christopher, *A Compendium of Practical Music Reprinted from the Second Edition of 1667*, ed. Phillip Lord, Oxford: Blackwell, 1970.

Sisman, Elaine R., *Haydn and the Classical Variation*, Cambridge, Mass.: Harvard University Press, 1993.

Snarrenberg, Robert, *Schenker's Interpretive Practice*, Cambridge: Cambridge University Press, 1997.

Solie, Ruth A., 'The Living Work: Organicism and Music Analysis', *19th-Century Music* 3 (1980), 147–56.

Soper, Kate, *What is Nature?* Oxford: Blackwell, 1995.

Spengler, Oswald, *Decline of the West*, trans. Charles Francis Atkinson, London: George Allen and Unwin, 1926.

Spiller, Michael R. G., *'Concerning Natural Experimental Philosophie': Meric Casaubon and the Royal Society*, The Hague, Boston and London: Martinus Nijhoff, 1980.

Spink, Ian, 'Purcell's Odes: Propaganda and Panegyric', in *Purcell Studies*, ed. Curtis Price, Cambridge: Cambridge University Press, 1995, pp. 145–71.

Spratt, Tho[mas], *The History of the Royal-Society of London, for the Improving of Natural Knowledge*, London: T. R. for J. Martyn, 1667.

Stewart, Susan, *On Longing: Narratives of the Miniature, the Gigantic, the Souvenir, the Collection*, Baltimore and London: Johns Hopkins University Press, 1984.

Stumpf, Carl, *Beiträge zur Akustik und Musikwissenschaft*, Leipzig: Johann Ambrosius Barth, 1898.

Symcox, Geoffrey, 'The Wild Man's Return: The Enclosed Vision of Rousseau's *Discourses*', in *The Wild Man Within: An Image in Western Thought from the Renaissance to Romanticism*, ed. Edward Dudley and Maximillian E. Novak, Pittsburgh: University of Pittsburgh Press, 1972, pp. 223–49.

Taylor, Francis Henry, *The Taste of Angels: A History of Art Collecting from Rameses to Napoleon*, Boston: Little, Brown and Company, 1948.

Thaler, Lotte, *Organische Form in der Musiktheorie des 19. und beginnenden 20. Jahrhunderts*, Berliner musikwissenschaftliche Arbeiten, vol. XXV, ed. Carl Dahlhaus and Rudolf Stephan, Munich and Salzburg: Katzbichler, 1984.

Thomas, Downing A., *Music and the Origins of Language*, Cambridge: Cambridge University Press, 1995.

Thomas, Keith, *Man and the Natural World: Changing Attitudes in England 1500–1800*, London: Allen Lane, 1983.

Tomlinson, Gary, *Music in Renaissance Magic: Toward a Historiography of Others*, London and Chicago: University of Chicago Press, 1993.

Toulmin, Stephen, *The Return to Cosmology: Postmodern Science and the Theology of Nature*, Berkeley and Los Angeles: University of California Press, 1982.

Tovey, Donald F., *Essays in Musical Analysis: Symphonies and other Orchestral Works*, Oxford: Oxford University Press, 1989.

Trouillot, Michel-Rolph, 'Anthropology and the Savage Slot: the Poetics and Politics of Otherness', in *Recapturing Anthropology*, ed. Richard G. Fox, Santa Fe: School of American Research Press, 1991, pp. 17–44.

Verba, Cynthia, 'The Development of Rameau's Thoughts on Modulation and Chromaticism', *Journal of the American Musicological Society* 26 (1973), 69–97.

'Rameau's Views on Modulation and Their Background in French Theory', *Journal of the American Musicological Society* 31 (1978), 467–79.

Vergil, *Aeneid*, Book VI, in *P. Vergili Maronis Opera*, ed. R. A. B. Mynors, Oxford: Oxford University Press, 1969, rpt with corr. 1972.

Vickers, Brian, 'Analogy Versus Identity: The Rejection of Occult Symbolism, 1580–1680', in *Occult and Scientific Mentalities in the Renaissance*, ed. Brian Vickers, Cambridge: Cambridge University Press, 1984, pp. 95–164.

Vogel, Martin, 'Arthur v. Oettingen und der harmonische Dualismus', in *Beiträge zur Musiktheorie des 19. Jahrhunderts*, ed. Martin Vogel, Studien zur Musikgeschichte des 19. Jahrhunderts, vol. IV (Regensburg: Gustav Bosse Verlag, 1966), pp. 103–32.

W[alkington], T[homas], *The Opticke Glasse of Humors*, [London:] J. D. for L. B., 1639.

Wackenroder, Wilhelm H., *Phantasien über die Kunst für Freunde der Kunst* (1799), rpt Potsdam: Gustav Kiepenheuer, 1925.

Wagner, Richard, *Oper und Drama* (1851), trans. William Ashton Ellis as *Opera and Drama*, Lincoln: University of Nebraska Press, 1995.

'Bericht an Seine Majestät den König Ludwig II von Bayern über eine in München zu errichtende deutsche Musikschule' (1865), trans. William Ashton Ellis as 'A Music-School for Munich', in *Richard Wagner's Prose Works*, ed. Albert Goldman, vol. IV, New York: Broude Brothers, 1966, pp. 171–224.

Walker, Daniel P., *Studies in Musical Science in the Late Renaissance*, London: The Warburg Institute, 1978; Leiden: E. J. Brill, 1978.

Weber, Gottfried, 'Ueber eine besonders merkwürdige Stelle in einem Mozart'schen Violinquartett aus C', in *Versuch einer geordneten Theorie der Tonsetzkunst zum Selbstunterricht*, vol. III, Mainz: Schott, 1830–2, pp. 196–226.

Weber, Max, 'Science as Vocation' (1917), in *From Max Weber*, ed. H. H. Mills and C. Wright Mills, New York: Oxford University Press, 1946, pp. 129–56.

Methodology of the Social Sciences, ed. E. A. Shils and H. A. Finch, New York: The Free Press, 1949.

The Rational and Social Foundations of Music, trans. Don Martindale, Johannes Riedel and Gertrude Neuwirth, Carbondale and Edwardsville: Southern Illinois University Press, 1958.

The Protestant Ethic and the Spirit of Capitalism, trans. Talcott Parsons, London: George Allen and Unwin, 1976.

Webster, James, 'Sonata Form', in *The New Grove Dictionary of Music and Musicians*, ed. Stanley Sadie, London: Macmillan, 1980.

Haydn's 'Farewell' Symphony and the Idea of Classical Style, Cambridge: Cambridge University Press, 1991.

'Haydn's Symphonies Between *Sturm und Drang* and "Classical Style": Art and Entertainment', in *Haydn Studies*, ed. W. Dean Sutcliffe, Cambridge: Cambridge University Press, 1998, pp. 218–46.

Bibliography

Weelkes, Thomas, *Madrigals of 5. and 6. Parts, Apt for the Viols and Voices*, London: Thomas Este for Thomas Morley, 1600.

Weinrich, Harald, 'Semantik der kühnen Metapher', in *Theorie der Metapher*, ed. Anselm Haverkamp, 2nd edn, Darmstadt: Wissenschaftliche Buchgesellschaft, 1996, pp. 316–39.

Wenley, Robert, 'Robert Paston and *The Yarmouth Collection*', *Norfolk Archaeology* 41 (1991), 113–44.

Westerby, Herbert, 'The Dual Theory of Harmony', *Proceedings of the Musical Association* 29 (1902–3), 21–72.

Westphal, Kenneth, 'The Basic Context and Structure of Hegel's *Philosophy of Right*', in *The Cambridge Companion to Hegel*, ed. Frederick C. Beiser, Cambridge: Cambridge University Press, 1993, pp. 234–69.

Wheelock, Gretchen A., 'Marriage à la Mode: Haydn's Instrumental Works "Englished" for Voice and Piano', *Journal of Musicology* 8 (1990), 357–97.

  Haydn's Ingenious Jesting with Art: Contexts of Musical Wit and Humor, New York: Schirmer, 1992.

White, Hayden, *Tropics of Discourse: Essays in Cultural Criticism*, Baltimore: Johns Hopkins, 1978.

Whitney, Charles, *Francis Bacon and Modernity*, New Haven and London: Yale University Press, 1986.

Williams, Raymond, *Problems in Materialism and Culture*, London and New York: Verso, 1980.

Winternitz, Emanuel, *Musical Instruments and Their Symbolism in Western Art*, London: Faber and Faber, 1967.

Wood, Bruce, 'Purcell's Odes: A Reappraisal', *The Purcell Companion*, ed. Michael Burden, Portland: Amadeus Press, 1995.

Young, Julian, *Nietzsche's Philosophy of Art*, Cambridge: Cambridge University Press, 1992.

Index

233

Index

composition 47, 58, 81, 100–2, 104, 107, 212
Cone, Edward T. 210
conscience 95, 104–6
consonance 7, 27, 50, 69, 97, 164
control 20–1, 25, 28, 40, 42, 44, 47, 49, 57, 73
Cook, Nicholas 211
Copernicus, Nicolaus 198
Corelli, Arcangelo 81
corps sonore 9, 69, 71, 74–5, 77–8, 81, 86–91, 101
correspondences *see* resemblances
cosmology 28, 30, 152, 158–60
cosmos 18, 20–3, 28–9, 45, 47
counterpoint 27, 29, 101, 105–6, 170
Cowley, Abraham 35
craftsmanship 41–2, 52, 60
creation 12, 22, 31, 45, 63, 78, 164
creator 31, 38, 47
    see also composer, God
creativity 12, 35, 46, 58, 103, 144, 152
criticism, music 188
culture, aspects of 4, 8, 51, 95, 107, 142, 160, 184–5, 187–9

Dahlhaus, Carl 8, 148
dance 207–8
Darwin, Charles 3–5
de Man, Paul 189–90
death 1, 9, 63, 140, 156
    'dead' science 9
debt 152–3
decadence 96
degeneration 7
Dehn, Siegfried Wilhelm 194
Deleuze, Gilles 93 n. 1
Derrida, Jacques 28, 93 n. 1
Descartes, René 1–2, 6, 31, 58, 74, 79, 83–7, 187, 191–2, 198, 208
desire 8, 13, 25, 29, 52, 59, 95, 159, 186–7, 193–4, 196, 208, 211
dialectics 28, 29, 158–9, 161–2, 166
diatonicism 6, 77
Dilthey, Wilhelm 104 n. 20
discipline 13, 18, 30–1, 38, 44, 47, 51, 94, 96, 100–2, 105–7
disenchantment 6, 8, 18, 20–3, 25–9, 51, 67
disorder 40
dissonance 29, 50
divine, the 30–1, 44–6, 49, 58, 60, 63, 189
    angels 63, 67, 197
    command 49
    enchanted cosmos of divine essences 18, 20
    language 42, 49
    music as divine force 6, 39
    nature as divine force 90
    plan 38
    presence 28
dominant 111–12, 118, 121, 136, 140, 162, 168, 171–2
Drake, Stillman 23
dualism, harmonic 7, 161–4, 175, 177–80
Dubiel, Joseph 106
Duchez, Marie-Elisabeth 68, 71, 76

ear 18, 21, 23, 25, 27, 30, 60, 106, 162, 193
    as agency 71–2, 74–9, 82, 86–8, 90–1
    and correctness of theory 82, 162
    physiology and function of 8
    see also hearing, hearer, listener
early modern period 33, 42, 44, 59, 212
earth 22, 46–7, 49, 55, 58
economy 11, 52, 104, 153
eco-system 25
Eden 20, 25–6, 29
education 160, 167, 184
    popular/learned discourse 184–5
ego 28, 187
Eliot, T. S. 138
emblematics 41, 49
emblems 31, 33, 55, 61, 63
emotions 28
Empedocles 26
empiricism 2, 18, 23, 25–6, 29, 35 n. 12, 44, 49, 51, 74, 89–91, 98–100, 102–6, 190–2, 195–6, 207
    British Empiricists 82 n. 37
    empirical musicology 94, 97
    empirical self 187–9
encyclopaedia 190, 191
    Encyclopédie 90
engineering 44, 47
England 9, 30–1, 33, 38–9, 44, 49, 57–60
enharmonicism 6, 24
Enlightenment 20, 33, 82 n. 37, 198, 212
episteme 22, 35, 59, 80, 107
epistemology 1, 8, 17, 31, 41, 67, 91, 96–7, 99–100, 103, 105–6, 192
eroticism 35, 41, 193–4
eschatology 152
Eschenmeyer, Carl August 190
ethnography 57
ethnomusicology 210
evolution 12, 143
Euler, Leonhard 161
Europe 4–5, 31, 51, 53, 197–9, 206, 209–10
Euterpe 55
exoticism 5, 40, 42, 51–3, 206
experience, sensory 25, 49, 51–2, 78–82, 87–8, 93, 112–13, 191, 207–8
experimentation 6, 18, 23–4, 32, 35, 50, 78, 90
exploitation 11
eye 45, 186–7, 189, 193

fable 26, 52–3
    the fabulous 5
fact 38, 51, 93
    music as acoustical fact 18–19, 23, 25
    vs. value 18, 20, 23, 29
    without meaning 20
fantasy 47
fate 20
    of music 21
feeling 75, 79, 81–3, 88–90
feminism 6
    see also body, female
Fichte, Johann Gottlieb 185
Ficino, Marsilio 22, 26, 47

Index

Index

Index

Printed in the United States
46817LVS00001B/243-250